ENCYCLOPEDIA OF

LIBRARY AND

INFORMATION SCIENCE

VOLUME 64

ENCYCLOPEDIA OF

LIBRARY AND

INFORMATION SCIENCE

Executive Editor

ALLEN KENT

SCHOOL OF INFORMATION SCIENCES
UNIVERSITY OF PITTSBURGH
PITTSBURGH, PENNSYLVANIA

Administrative Editor

CAROLYN M. HALL

ARLINGTON, TEXAS

VOLUME 64

SUPPLEMENT 27

MARCEL DEKKER, INC.   NEW YORK · BASEL

HEADQUARTERS
Marcel Dekker, Inc.
270 Madison Avenue, New York, New York 10016
tel: 212-696-9000; fax: 212-685-4540

EASTERN HEMISPHERE DISTRIBUTION
Marcel Dekker AG
Hutgasse 4, Postfach 812, CH-4001 Basel, Switzerland
tel: 41-61-261-8482; fax: 41-61-261-8896

WORLD WIDE WEB
http://www.dekker.com

LIBRARY OF CONGRESS CATALOG CARD NUMBER 68-31232

ISBN 0-8247-2064-4

Current Printing (last digit):
10 9 8 7 6 5 4 3 2 1

PRINTED IN THE UNITED STATES OF AMERICA

CONTENTS OF VOLUME 64

CONTRIBUTORS TO VOLUME 64

STEPHANIE C. ARDITO, President, Ardito Information & Research, Inc., Wilmington, Delaware: *Electronic Copyright*

EKKEHARD BAISCH, Software Quality Manager, Alcatel, Stuttgart, Germany: *Knowledge-Based Classification Techniques for Software Quality Management*

AMELIA A. BALDWIN, Associate Professor, School of Accounting, Florida International University, Miami, Florida: *Strategy and Impacts of Expert Systems for Bank Lending*

HAL BERGHEL, Professor of Computer Science and Computer Engineering, University of Arkansas, Fayetteville, Arkansas: *The Client Side of the World Wide Web*

KO BESUIJEN, Ergonomics Department, University of Twente, Enschede, The Netherlands: *Visual Display Quality*

JAMES BOWEN, Vice President, CompEngServ Limited, Ottawa, Ontario, Canada: *Conducting Research on the Internet*

CHRISTOF EBERT, Software Process Manager, Alcatel, Antwerp, Belgium: *Knowledge-Based Classification Techniques for Software Quality Management*

LEO EGGHE, Chief Librarian, Limburgs Universitaire Centrum and Professor, Universitaire Instelling Antwerpen, Antwerp, Belgium: *Sensitivity Aspects of Inequality Measures*

SUSAN FELDMAN, DataSearch, Ithaca, New York: *Search Engines*

RICHARD FOX, Associate Professor, Department of Computer Science, The University of Texas-Pan American, Edinburg, Texas: *An Algorithm for Abductive Inference in Artificial Intelligence; A Generic Task Strategy for Solving Routine Decision-Making Problems*

ALAN GILCHRIST, Consultant, Director, CURA Consortium, Brighton, England: *Library and Information Consultancy in the United Kingdom*

ANNE GOULDING, Reader in Information Services Management, Department of Information and Library Studies, Loughborough University, Loughborough, England: *Flexible Working in U.K. Library and Information Services*

JULIE HARTIGAN, Technical Sales Manager, Federal Division, Autonomy, Inc., San Francisco, California: *An Algorithm for Abductive Inference in Artificial Intelligence*

KIM M. HOLLEY, Department of Government and Politics, University of Maryland, College Park, Maryland: *The Use of Decision Support Systems in Crisis Negotiation*

LAURA TOWNSEND KANE, Head of Cataloging & Acquisitions, School of Medicine Library, University of South Carolina, Columbia, South Carolina: *Access Versus Ownership*

EVELYN KERSLAKE, Researcher, Department of Information and Library Studies, Loughborough University, Loughborough, England: *Flexible Working in U.K. Library and Information Services*

SARIT KRAUS, Associate Professor, Department of Mathematics and Computer Science, Bar Ilan University, Ramat Gan, Israel: *The Use of Decision Support Systems in Crisis Negotiation*

CONROY MALLEN, Research Fellow, Computer Based Learning Unit, Leeds University, Leeds, England: *Using Design to Provide Intelligent Help in Information Processing Systems*

BRUCE P. MONTGOMERY, Associate Professor and Curator/Head of Archives, University of Colorado at Boulder, Boulder, Colorado: *Collecting Human Rights Evidence: A Model for Archival Collection Development*

ALAN SANGSTER, Professor of Accounting, Open University Business School, Walton Hall, Milton Keynes, England: *Strategy and Impacts of Expert Systems for Bank Lending*

HENK G. SOL, Professor, Faculty of Technology, Policy and Management, Delft University of Technology, Delft, The Netherlands: *The Design of Document Information Systems*

GERD P. J. SPENKELINK, Ergonomics Department, University of Twente, Enschede, The Netherlands: *Visual Display Quality*

THOMPSON SIAN HIN TEO, Senior Lecturer, Department of Decision Sciences, Faculty of Business Administration, National University of Singapore, Singapore: *Integrating Business and Information Systems Planning*

KEES VAN DER MEER, Associate Professor, Faculty of Information Technology and Systems, Delft University of Technology, Delft, The Netherlands and Specialised Studies Unit on Information and Library Science, Antwerp University, Antwerp, Belgium: *The Design of Document Information Systems*

W. JOHN WILBUR, Senior Scientist, National Center for Biotechnology Information, National Library of Medicine, Bethesda, Maryland: *Human Subjectivity and Performance Limits in Document Retrieval*

JONATHAN WILKENFELD, Professor and Chair, Department of Government and Politics, University of Maryland, College Park, Maryland: *The Use of Decision Support Systems in Crisis Negotiation*

CONSTANTIN ZOPOUNIDIS, Professor of Financial Management, Department of Production Engineering and Management, Technical University of Crete, Chania, Greece: *The Use of Knowledge-Based Decision Support Systems in Financial Modeling*

ENCYCLOPEDIA OF

LIBRARY AND

INFORMATION SCIENCE

VOLUME 64

ACCESS VERSUS OWNERSHIP

Introduction

For 2500 years the basic principles of libraries and librarianship have been deeply rooted in the common mind of the scholarly world. Some of these principles include the concept of libraries as warehouses of information and librarians as collectors of information. The perceived success of a library has always been dependent upon its size; the bigger a library's collection the greater its success. In the last two decades of the twentieth century—a span of time indicated by a mere speck on the time line of library history—a series of technological advancements precipitated a dramatic upheaval comparable to that which occurred after the invention of the printing press in the fifteenth century. These breakthroughs in technology included the development of the computer and, ultimately, the advent of the Internet. From the chaos of discovery emerged a phrase that continues to incite furor and heated debate in the academic world. The phrase is "access versus ownership."

Origins of the Principles of Ownership

In the seventh century B.C. there existed a library in Assyria Nineveh that was as comprehensive and well arranged as any equivalent national library of modern times. The ruler of Nineveh, Ashurbanipal, created a storehouse of some tens of thousands of clay tablets containing religious, historical, geographical, legal, and scientific knowledge from all parts of the known world (*1*). Three centuries later, in the Egyptian city of Alexandria, a library generally known as the greatest library in antiquity emerged. Like Ashurbanipal in Nineveh, the founders of the Alexandrian library deliberately set out to create a universal storehouse of knowledge. So successful were they that the Alexandrian library, also called the "museum," eventually housed hundreds of thousands of papyrus rolls, almost all of the extant literature of ancient times (*2*).

From these two libraries of antiquity came the birth of the principle that the primary purpose of a library should be the storage of knowledge. In those times, as in modern times, a large, renowned library was an indicator of a wealthy, educated, and powerful society. Egypt's rulers were so eager to enrich their library in Alexandria that "they

1

employed highhanded methods for that purpose" (2). King Ptolemaios III Evergetes, who ruled from 247–222 B.C., ordered that all travelers reaching Alexandria should surrender their books. Copies were made of these books on cheap papyrus, which were then given to the original owners. The originals, however, were kept permanently in the library. The Alexandrian library grew so quickly that by the middle of the third century it was necessary to create a secondary library, to which 42,800 papyrus rolls were transferred (2).

"Bigger is better" might easily have been inscribed in neat hieroglyphics upon ancient Egyptian edifices. It is a motto that has been the foundation of libraries throughout the centuries and into modern times. The Library of Congress, established in 1800, contains virtually all of man's recorded knowledge and is easily the most renowned library of our time. In a treatise on the history of books and libraries, John P. Feather calls the book a "cultural symbol" (3). The affluence and influence of a culture can be evaluated in part by the size and scope of its libraries. Even the size of private libraries is a social indication of wealth and education; "Even today books in the home are a far more potent status symbol than phonograph records or videotapes" (3). Private libraries in the ancient Roman Empire were eventually so common that they were considered "as necessary an ornament of a house as a bathroom...books were bought by the rich for show, and were numbered by the thousands, even though their owners never read them" (1).

If libraries have been known throughout history as storehouses of knowledge, then it is logical that librarians have long been viewed as "collectors" of knowledge. The role of the librarian as collector of books and information has been a standard throughout history. In a work that is generally accepted as one of the first modern treatises on the role of the librarian, published in 1650, librarians are referred to as "Librarie-Keepers" (1). In recent times, the "role of librarian as the 'keeper of books' dates back to the early 1800s when libraries' basic form of acquisition and collection development was accomplished through gifts" (4). Early university libraries in the United States were not designed for student use and were only open a few hours per week: "in 1850 the libraries at Amherst and Trinity were open once a week from 1:00 p.m. to 3:00 p.m.; at Princeton, one hour twice a week; at the University of Missouri, one hour every two weeks. At the University of Alabama books were received at the door without admitting patrons" (5). Early academic libraries were, in effect, museums of rare books run by specialized collectors of information.

These two significant principles—the library as a storehouse of knowledge and the librarian as a keeper of knowledge—were reinforced by the invention of the printing press in the fifteenth century. Printing began in Europe when Johannes Gutenberg in Mainz, Germany, began using movable type. By the year 1462, there were already fifty-one printers in Germany alone, and in Italy there were more than seventy-three printers by the end of the fifteenth century. While books had previously been relatively scarce due to the painstaking copying process, now they could be printed and distributed by the thousands. By the middle of the sixteenth century the average print run of books exceeded 1000 copies, and in that century alone it is estimated that more than 100,000 different books were printed in Europe. This means a total of 100 million books was available by the end of the 1500s! The printing industry continued to escalate rapidly. In the nineteenth century, inventions such as the steam press made

TABLE 1

The Principles of Librarianship

1.	Libraries are created by society.
2.	Libraries are conserved by society.
3.	Libraries are for the storage and dissemination of knowledge.★
4.	Libraries are centers of power.
5.	Libraries are for all.
6.	Libraries must grow.★
7.	A national library should contain all national literature, with some representation of other national literatures.
8.	Every book is of use.
9.	A librarian must be a person of education.
10.	A librarian is an educator.
11.	A librarian's role can only be an important one if it is fully integrated into the prevailing social and political system.
12.	A librarian needs training and/or apprenticeship.
13.	It is a librarian's duty to increase the stock of his library.★
14.	A library must be arranged in some kind of order, and a list of its contents provided.
15.	Since libraries are storehouses of knowledge, they should be arranged according to subject.★
16.	Practical convenience should dictate how subjects are to be grouped in a library.
17.	A library must have a subject catalogue.

Source: Adapted from Ref. *1*.

the printing of books even more prolific. In the mid-1800s *Uncle Tom's Cabin* sold a million and a half copies in one year. Understandably, this created a snowball effect upon society. "The multiplicity of books... increased literacy, promoted more widely a taste for library culture, and opened wide the doors of learning. This in its turn led to more books being written, and so even more books being printed" (*1*).

Table 1 outlines seventeen principles that have been the foundation of librarianship since the existence of the libraries of Nineveh and Alexandria 2500 years ago. Many of the principles listed, particularly the ones marked with stars, are based on the idea of libraries as "storehouses" and librarians as "storekeepers." The list is adapted from a book published in 1977. It was not long after that date that the basic principles of ownership began to crumble, threatening the once-solid foundation of librarianship.

The Shift Toward Access

Public access to libraries and the materials housed in libraries is most definitely not a new concept. The Alexandrian library was initially formed for the use of scholars, but was later made available for free public access. In ancient Greece libraries were common, and any Greek citizen could use the libraries' resources. In ancient Rome, the first emperor, Augustus, built two public libraries which were at the service of all citizens who could read. By 350 A.D. there were some twenty-eight public libraries in Rome (*2*).

The form of "access" that began to cause such furor among the library community

TABLE 2

Access Versus Ownership: A Comparison

Traditional model (ownership)	Contemporary model (access)
The library as a warehouse of information	The library as a gateway to information
The librarian as a collector of information	The librarian as a gatekeeper to information
Bigger is better (emphasis on the size of a collection)	Availability is key (emphasis on the availability and delivery of information)
The library as a "stand-alone" entity (with multiple comprehensive collections)	The library as a link in a network of shared resources

during the past two decades refers to access to materials *not physically housed in the library*. This is not, however, such a new concept. Interlibrary loan, which is one method of accessing materials not physically housed in the library, was begun as early as 1901 (*6*). The effectiveness of interlibrary loan has never been questioned because it is successful *as a supplement to ownership*. It is when access is considered an *alternative to ownership* that the controversy begins.

Table 2 illustrates the philosophical differences basic to the access versus ownership debate. The traditional model, as discussed above, is based on ownership. The library is viewed as a warehouse of information, librarians are the collectors of information, and those libraries with multiple comprehensive collections are considered the most successful. The contemporary model is based on access to information rather than ownership of information. No longer is the library a warehouse of information, but rather a gateway to information. Availability is now the key to success. The librarian is not a collector, but rather a gatekeeper to information. The library, as opposed to a "stand-alone" entity with multiple comprehensive collections, is now a link in a network of shared resources.

How, we might ask, was this revolutionary library model conceived? What are the reasons for this shift toward access rather than ownership? Harloe and Budd states, "economic forces and technological advances have combined together to create a new environment, one where access to collective scholarly resources...supersedes the historic quest for the great comprehensive collection" (*7*). What were these technological advances and economic forces that caused such upheaval in library philosophy?

ADVANCES IN TECHNOLOGY

"Successful technological innovation is more than merely a demonstration of the inherent cleverness of inventors. It is a response to social, economic, and political demand" (*3*). This statement can be applied to all technological advancements throughout history. The printing press was a technological innovation driven by social, economic, and political demands. Likewise, technology in our own time continues to be driven by the same forces. The first library school in the United States, the School of Library Economy at Columbia College which opened in January 1887, emphasized technology in its curriculum (*5*). It is remarkable that even then the founders of this first library school were aware that advancements in technology would push librarianship through the twentieth century.

The year 1949 has been cited as the beginning of interest in the use of computers as tools for research in the humanities. That was the year in which the computer was used to create the first electronic index, the *Index Thomisticus*, which anthologized the works of Saint Thomas Aquinas (*4*). Since then the use of the computer in libraries has escalated at an astonishing rate. It wasn't until the 1980s, however, that technological advancements began to change the traditional shape of libraries.

The implementation of electronic bibliographic access was inaugurated in the 1980s when libraries first began to replace cards catalogs with online catalogs (*8*). This process, facilitated by the rise of bibliographic utilities such as OCLC and RLIN, gave electronic bibliographic access to records for monographs and the occasional serial. In the late 1980s, bibliographic access to journal literature was established when some libraries began to mount abstracting and indexing databases onto their local systems. It wasn't long before these abstracting and indexing databases virtually replaced print indexes as "the tool of choice among patrons of academic libraries" (*8*).

Crawford puts it well when he states that the 1980s were "remarkable times for academic libraries and technology. Those were growth years, when everything seemed possible and everything desirable seemed almost inevitable" (*9*). Caught up in the excitement of electronic access and technology, many academics, later called "futurists," began to prophesy the death of print altogether. Perryman writes:

> Many doomsters in the field appeared to assume that the advent of electronic access to information sources would sound the death knell for traditional print media as a viable source of current information. As an extension of this thinking, it seemed only a matter of time before libraries would become museums where books, journals, and other print formats would be venerated and preserved more for their archival or artifactual import, than for the knowledge, information, and data which they conveyed. Those in need of the most up-to-date information would simply tap into their electronic resource, without ever needing to visit their local library facility (*10*).

The contemporary "access model" library began to take precedence over the traditional "ownership model." The controversy had begun. Futurists began to extol the virtues of electronic access and the "virtual library" of the new millennium. Traditionalists began to fret that this "paradigm shift," as it has often been called, would lead to the demise of the library and librarianship.

The advent of the Internet further heightened the development of the electronic format and the access versus ownership debate. The year 1993 marks the introduction of the first graphical World Wide Web browser (*11*). Before then (since 1981), the Internet had primarily been used for listserv and gopher activity. After 1993, however, access to the Internet in public and academic libraries became a priority. According to "The 1997 National Survey of U.S. Public Libraries and the Internet," nearly three-fifths of the nation's public library systems offer some type of Internet access. It was predicted that in 1997 public libraries would spend an estimated $280 million on Internet access alone. Additionally, nearly 10 percent of all public libraries have their own Web sites (*12*).

It might be interesting to correlate the advent of the Internet with the invention of the printing press. Both were revolutionary technological advances. Both have caused major social and cultural reformations. Just as the printing press increased literacy and promoted literary culture, the Internet has elevated computer literacy and heightened interest in technology. There is a major disparity between the two inventions, however. The printing press produced books that were sold, distributed, and neatly organized within personal and public libraries. The Internet, on the other hand, could be perceived as a printing press gone haywire. Information is being spewed out from every imaginable direction, and wherever it happens to land is where it stays. Organization and standardization are seriously lacking. Information seekers are expected to sift through tens of millions of Web pages on the Internet to find what they are looking for, much like the process one would go through to find a specific book in the rubble of the Library of Congress after it survived a hurricane. Coyle calls the Internet an "undifferentiated mass of documents and information" (*13*). In the access versus ownership debate, the Internet is the source of considerable turbulence.

Technological developments have done much to change the way libraries operate. Not only must library users know how to read, they now must be able to type, to use a mouse, to interpret computer menus, to understand types of user interfaces, and to search various databases (*14*). Whereas in the past only one person could use a book or a journal at a time, now multiple users are able to use electronic books and journals simultaneously, but it was not technological advancement alone that led to the shift from ownership to access. Economic factors were contributors as well.

INCREASED SCHOLARLY PRODUCTION

In the past two decades the number of scholarly journals being produced has increased dramatically. In part, this increase "reflects the growing specialization of research fields, questions, and methods" (*15*). Much of the almost mind-boggling growth, however, can be attributed to the complex "publish or perish" system of tenure within the academic community. In a recent statement released by the International Coalition of Library Consortia, the scholarly publication system in place today was labeled "dysfunctional" (*16*). University and college professors are being rewarded with tenure based largely on the number of articles they have published. Some claim that emphasis in the tenure process is placed on the quantity of articles produced rather than the quality (*15*). More specialized journals are emerging to contain the swelling number of articles being produced, but since they are increasingly specialized they are of interest to fewer and fewer people. The circulation of these highly specialized journals is minimal. Such a small demand for these new journals leads to higher prices, which is the next economic factor contributing to the emphasis on access rather than ownership within libraries.

RISING JOURNAL PRICES AND STATIC BUDGETS

While library budgets have remained essentially static during the past two decades, the cost of journal subscriptions has skyrocketed. To compensate for the yearly increase in journal costs, libraries have had to drastically cut back their total number of subscriptions. Figure 1 illustrates this phenomenon. It is clear that from 1993 to 1997

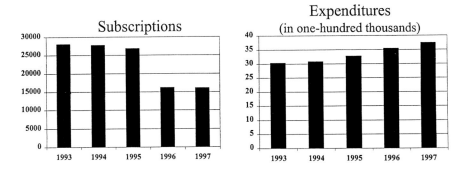

FIGURE 1. *Serial subscriptions vs. serial expenditures in ARL libraries: average per library (1993–1997). Data from Ref. 17.*

the average number of serial subscriptions per institution in the Association of Research Libraries dropped considerably, yet the average expenditures for those fewer serial titles steadily increased. In fact, in the ten-year period from 1986 to 1996, serial expenditures in ARL libraries increased 124 percent, while the number of serials purchased dropped 7 percent (*17*). The actual cost of scholarly journals increased 148 percent, "more than three times the rate of inflation" (*15*).

It has been clear for years that libraries are no longer capable of purchasing all of the sources that would satisfy the information needs of their patrons: "A gap has emerged between the range of titles libraries would like to hold and what they can afford to hold" (*18*). While academic institutions continue to encourage scholarly output, libraries are expected to carry the journals that contain results of this scholarly output. Those same institutions, however, have failed to provide adequate funds to do so. There is a "permanent imbalance between the funds accorded to research libraries and the volume of scholarly output these libraries are expected to purchase and manage" (*15*).

THE FACTORS COMBINED

Technological innovations in the 1980s and 1990s planted the seed of the access-based library within the mind of the library community. Perhaps, had economic problems not become factors, the access-based library would have evolved in due time with minimal controversy, however, the issue of access as an alternative to ownership was forced upon libraries when the information needed by library patrons was no longer affordable. Insufficient budgets and increasing journal costs led librarians to conclude that they could no longer maintain multiple comprehensive collections. Librarians were compelled to pursue alternative methods of fulfilling the information needs of their patrons, hence, the contemporary library model based on access to information rather than ownership of information began essentially as a "survival mechanism" (*19*).

Forms of Access

In the modern library, which relies heavily upon access, "the discussion of what constitutes a 'collection' becomes somewhat metaphysical" (*20*). From the traditional point of view, a collection consists of physical items that have been purchased. In the contemporary library model, however, the collection consists of that universe of information that can be accessed upon demand. Intner defines accessed materials as (1) interlibrary loan materials owned by other libraries, (2) computer databases located at remote sites and not under the library's control, and (3) materials whose ownership is shared among a group of partners (*21*). In the quest to locate information that is not actually housed within a library's four walls, librarians have been faced with a number of access choices. We will examine in detail some of the major forms of access, including interlibrary loan, commercial document delivery, computerized indexes and abstracts, and electronic journals and monographs.

INTERLIBRARY LOAN AND COMMERCIAL DOCUMENT DELIVERY

Document delivery is defined as the purchase of photocopies, usually of journal articles, from either libraries or commercial document delivery suppliers (*4*). One form of document delivery, interlibrary loan, has been in operation since the early 1900s (*6*). As a supplement to ownership, this form of access has been extremely successful from the beginning, even when library users were expected to wait two to three weeks for requested materials. Modern developments have made the interlibrary loan process even more efficient. National bibliographic utilities such as OCLC and RLIN, as well as shared catalogs, have simplified the bibliographic verification process and the transmission of requests. New transmission systems such as Ariel have made the receipt of requests a much speedier process than ever before.

The effectiveness of interlibrary loan is measured by turnaround time and fill rate. Turnaround time has been defined as a "measurement of the elapsed time between the initiation of a request and the fulfillment of that request." The fill rate is "the relationship between the total number of interlibrary loan requests and the number of requests successfully completed" (*4*). Thanks to the effectiveness of interlibrary loan technology, turnaround time and fill rate among libraries has been steadily improving. What is alarming, however, is the steady increase of interlibrary loan transactions that takes place each year. Figure 2 indicates that interlibrary lending and borrowing among ARL libraries have been climbing consistently since 1986. Each year libraries are handling an escalating number of interlibrary loan transactions. This requires additional staff time and, of course, added costs. This is an example of one of the problems associated with access. As fewer materials are being "owned," libraries must rely more and more on other sources for these materials.

Document delivery suppliers are commercial vendors who provide journal articles to libraries under contractual agreements. These commercial document delivery (CDD) services are being utilized as an alternative to the interlibrary lending process. Many libraries, under pressure from having to cancel print subscriptions, are in the process of testing various CDD services to determine whether or not they are viable substitutes for ownership of journal titles. In a recent study, a university library

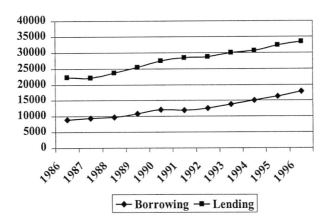

FIGURE 2. *Interlibrary borrowing and lending in ARL libraries: average per library (1986–1996). Data from Ref. 17.*

"sought to test how well—and at what cost—a CDD supplier could fill requests for articles from canceled journals in order to determine whether CDD was economically feasible as a way to compensate for canceled journals" (*22*). The study resulted in a 93 percent fill rate with a turnaround time of three to five days. It was concluded that CDD was indeed a viable way to compensate for subscriptions that had been canceled, as well as to supplement the existing collection. Evidence from a different two-year study on CDD supports the conclusion that document delivery "can be more cost-effective than ownership for high-cost science journals, and for low-cost science journals that receive low to medium levels of use" (*23*).

Document delivery, including both interlibrary loan and CDD, is a widely accepted form of access. It does, however, spark its share of controversy. There are many who argue that no matter how efficient interlibrary loan or CDD services may be there is still no substitute for owning the physical journal (*24*). Still others claim that "access delayed is access denied." The argument is that access through document delivery will only be acceptable if items can be delivered as quickly as it takes patrons to walk to the shelf and retrieve items themselves. More realistic is the view that, while ownership of journals is preferred, a turnaround time of twenty-four to forty-eight hours is accepta-ble in cases in which access is expected to replace ownership (*25*).

ABSTRACTING AND INDEXING DATABASES

Abstracting and indexing (A&I) databases are perhaps the most widely accepted and heavily used forms of electronic access. Print indexes were effective research tools in the past, but the electronic versions surpass the print in accessibility and ease of use. Whereas medical citations were once located within the onerous multivolume *Index Medicus*, they can now be retrieved and printed quickly and easily through the online equivalent called *Medline. Reader's Guide to Periodical Literature* is available in an electronic version, as are *Social Science Index, ERIC, Business Periodicals Index, Humanities Index, General Science Index*, and many others. *Books in Print* is now more efficient, less cumbersome, and more frequently updated in its new format, *Books in Print on Disc*. Such A&I databases have proven to be so much more efficient than the print versions that they have become the research tools of choice among patrons of academic libraries (*8*). Without a doubt, A&I databases are the least controversial forms of access.

ELECTRONIC MONOGRAPHS

In the 1970s and 1980s, the idea of the "DynaBook" emerged. It was predicted that by the turn of the century a revolutionary device would be developed that would replace the printed monograph. This device would offer better readability than a book and easier navigation. It would be lightweight and portable, would run on a long-life battery, and would be moderately priced. Its contents could be rapidly replaced so that it would function as a universal book (*9*). To date the DynaBook is not yet in existence, nor will it be anytime in the near future.

Certainly monographs have been converted to digital format. Many science and technology textbooks are now available on CD-ROM and are fully searchable. For example, *Scientific American Medicine* is now available on CD-ROM and is called *SAM-CD*. Many households are now purchasing CD-ROM encyclopedias that are updated every year or two. This is a vast improvement over the costly multivolume sets that were too expensive to update. Some monographs are even available through the Internet. Production of digitized monographs has not been prolific, however, because there still remain many drawbacks.

Few people will deny that reading from digital devices, whether portable or desktop, is problematic. Conditions such as poor light, low resolution, and slow speed often make people less inclined to read long passages onscreen. These conditions have not improved much in the last five years, and until they do the production of digitized monographs will remain minimal.

The most complex argument associated with the electronic monograph deals mainly with works from the humanities. Scholars contend that authors "can only envisage the dissemination of their works in the physical form that is the normal product of the techniques available at the time of writing" (*3*). When the form of a written work undergoes a major change, the reader's perception of that work is profoundly different. Whereas technical and scientific works are generally not subject to a reader's interpretation, most works within the humanities are. The idea of reading Margaret Mitchell's *Gone with the Wind* or Leo Tolstoy's *War and Peace* on a digital device is unappealing to scholars and laypersons alike.

Within libraries, arguments concerning the "death of the printed book" have continued for years. In the meantime, the publishing industry has continued to grow (*9*). More books are being published and purchased, and public libraries continue to circulate books to a large percentage of the population. Clearly, the printed book is still a desired medium. Though many technical and scientific monographs will be converted to digital format for ease of use and convenience, the idea that the printed book will disappear altogether is no longer a valid concern.

ELECTRONIC JOURNALS

There was a time when the ability to retrieve citations online from indexing databases was a remarkable achievement. Then came a period when citations were no longer enough, and library users demanded online abstracts as well. Now there is a great urgency for what can easily be deemed the most complex and controversial form of access—the electronic journal: "For more than three centuries, the journal has played a crucial role in the creation, transmission, and storage of knowledge, as the primary medium of communication among scholars" (11). Despite its successes, however, the factors involving rising journal prices and increased scholarly publication have led publishers to seek out alternatives to the printed journal. The electronic journal (e-journal) has emerged in the 1990s as a solution to these problems; however, the e-journal has become less a solution to those problems than the origin of an altogether different set of difficulties.

Before 1993, e-journals were distributed as ASCII text files through electronic mailing lists. Gopher and FTP protocols were also used to provide additional access to this new journal format. The introduction of the first World Wide Web (WWW) browser in 1993 had a significant impact on both the number and distribution mechanisms of e-journals. Now, e-journals have developed far beyond the simple ASCII text format: "Journals published on the WWW can include hypertext links connecting references, tables and other parts of an article as well as links to other Web files. In addition, they can use powerful new features such as graphics, sound, video, and even miniprograms" (11). It would seem that the benefits of e-journals outweigh the problems associated with the traditional print journals. It requires detailed examination of the various advantages and disadvantages of the e-journal to determine whether this assumption is true.

Format

Traditional print journals have been in existence for hundreds of years. The format has been tried, tested, and accepted by scholars as an effective method of the communication of knowledge. The e-journal, on the other hand, is a format that is still in the early stages of development, and the many issues related to them are in constant change (11). In theory, the format of the e-journal is much more versatile than the print. Graphic capabilities and hypertext link features would greatly enhance the effectiveness of the transmission of information. Most of the e-journals available today are experimental, however. Until more data have been gathered and more issues resolved, publishers are unwilling to pour large amounts of resources into the development of this journal format.

Training and Equipment

Print journals are fairly straightforward and require very little training to use. No special equipment, aside from perhaps a photocopier, is needed to utilize them effectively. This is not the case with e-journals. Hefty hardware and software requirements accompany their use, and upgrades are a constant necessity. In addition to the basic requirements such as computers, modems, and WWW access, there is a need for peripheral equipment such as printers. Libraries must ensure that adequate workstations are available for users.

Training in the use of such equipment is no small task. Library staff members need to be able to deal with daily maintenance of computers and printers and to respond to "the inevitable technical snafus that accompany any electronic service" (*24*). The users themselves require a fair amount of computer skills to use e-journals. Training courses are frequently offered to library patrons not only in the use of equipment, but also in the use of the individual e-journal interfaces. Thus far, no standards have been established regarding user interfaces for e-journals. Until that happens, user training will continue to rest heavily upon libraries.

Limits of Use and Ease of Access

If shelved properly, print journals are easy to locate within libraries. They are limited, however, to one user at a time. Electronic journals may be accessed by multiple users simultaneously. This kind of use, though, is strictly limited by detailed licensing agreements and by copyright laws.

In this early stage of development, access to e-journals is disturbingly unreliable. In a recent study on accessing e-journals, many pitfalls were encountered (*11*). Of the 131 journals used in the study, more than half could not be accessed on the first try. The list of factors that can negatively influence the access of e-journals is a long one. Incorrect uniform resource locators (URLs) cause a large percentage of the problems. Any slight error in the URL such as a missing letter or symbol will result in a connection failure. Often a URL for an e-journal is changed, and if the subscribers are not notified promptly they are not able to access the e-journal. Internet connection problems, server problems, and high volumes of traffic on the WWW can also affect access. Other issues concerning licensing agreements can cause obstacles. For instance, if an e-journal is password-accessible, libraries must determine ways to distribute the password to users while still adhering to the license agreement. If the password changes, notifying users of that change is often sporadic. The same kinds of troubles arise when e-journals rely on user IDs or IP addresses to allow access.

Harter and Kim writes, "if e-journal articles cannot be accessed by the target audience when they are needed, their value is diminished. Unstable or limited access to e-journals cannot help but affect their acceptability among scholars as a legitimate medium of formal scholarly communication" (*11*). Access problems associated with e-journals must be resolved if this format is to be widely accepted.

Archiving

The archiving of print journals is not a complicated procedure. If a library purchases a subscription to a serial, that library is responsible for storing back issues of that journal title, whether they are bound, in offsite storage, or converted to microform. This issue of archiving e-journals is complex. If a journal is being accessed online, who is responsible for maintaining the back issues? Is it the publisher or the library? Libraries do not own the actual physical journal but rather the right to access that journal. If an e-journal subscription is canceled or temporarily suspended, will the library be allowed to access the issues it had previously paid to access? What will happen if the e-journal publisher goes out of business? Will all the archives be lost?

In the e-journal study mentioned earlier, 55 percent of the e-journals in the sample could not be accessed on the first try. One-fifth had incomplete archives, and one-fourth had ceased publication. For some of the e-journals it was impossible to identify whether articles were missing from the archives because no index to published articles was provided (*11*).

The archiving of e-journals is a troublesome predicament for both libraries and publishers. The procedure for the archiving of e-journals, as well as which format they will take (paper, microfilm, microfiche, floppy disk, CD-ROM, or on local servers), remains to be determined. It is crucial that these issues be resolved in order for the evolution of e-journals to be successful.

Cost Factors

It has already been determined that libraries can no longer afford print subscriptions to the extent that they have in the past. Operating costs, including processing and binding, are also considerable. Whether or not e-journals will alleviate these cost constraints has yet to be determined.

Currrently there are a number of "free" e-journals available on the Internet. In this experimental phase, some publishers are giving libraries and scholars the opportunity to test the capabilities of the new journal format by offering them at no charge. This is convenient at present, but it would be delusional to assume that these e-journals will continue to be given away at no cost. As for-profit businesses, publishers must survive. If e-journals are the wave of the future, they must be able to support the academic publishing industry. Publishers will find a way to make this happen. In the study on access to e-journals, there were significantly more problems with free e-journals than with fee-based ones (*11*). Access, performance, and archival qualities were poor. This indicates that these free journals cannot be sustained.

At the opposite end of the spectrum are those publishers who are allowing access to e-journals only under rigid requirements or exorbitant costs. A few are offering free access to e-journals when a library subscribes to the print version. Many, however, require that a library purchase a print subscription before allowing access to the electronic version, and then append an additional charge for the e-journal. Still others offer access to the electronic version at the same price as, or higher than, the print version. Many librarians have accused publishers of price gouging and of unfairly limiting the libraries' ability to copy and redistribute information from e-journals. Publishers argue that the development of electronic materials is expensive and that they must protect their products from being distributed so freely that sales evaporate (*26*).

A recent statement released by the International Coalition of Library Consortia calls for an end to the excessive pricing of electronic publications. The coalition agrees that "current pricing models for e-information, which are developing during a period of experimentation, are not sustainable," and that libraries should not be asked "to support in full the cost of the research and development to bring such products to market" (*16*). The statement suggests that publishers must reduce the cost of e-journals to reflect the savings accrued through the production of the new format. Since it is cheaper for the publishers to produce an e-journal than a print journal, libraries should benefit from this reduction in production costs. The coalition also states that libraries should be given the option to purchase the electronic product without the paper subscription, and that the electronic product should cost less than the printed subscription price.

In response, publishers argue that while developing the new electronic products that are in such demand among libraries, they must at the same time continue to provide the costly printed versions of scholarly journals (*27*). In addition, publishers claim that the "fair-use" guidelines that applied to print publications must not apply to electronic products. With a few clicks of a mouse, electronic products may be copied and distributed as many times as the user wishes. "It is unreasonable to expect publishers to survive... if they face the possibility of a single copy being sold, then distributed universally" (*9*).

Clearly, the current pricing models for e-journals will not alleviate the problems associated with the soaring costs of print subscriptions. Since open discussions on this issue have begun, it is hopeful that publishers and libraries will be able to reach a compromise, however, there are other expenses involved with e-journals besides subscription and access costs. One such expense involves printing. Because of the difficulty in reading from digital devices with poor lighting and resolution, library users tend to print out any text that is longer than about 500 words. If every long article within an e-journal is printed out each time it is used, a typical public library "would use at least 50 times as much paper as present" (*9*). This is a serious economic and ecological disadvantage, and it is one that must be considered when discussing the costs associated with e-journals.

In-House Maintenance

One of the problems with print journals is that they occupy a considerable amount of space. For decades, libraries have had to contend with diminishing shelf space for the storage of journals. Some libraries have resorted to the relocation of old or discontinued titles to remote storage facilities, which naturally impedes access. Another distinct disadvantage of print journals is that they are often mutilated, stolen, or misshelved.

E-journals do not occupy any physical space within the library facility. The only space considerations are the workstations used to access them. There is no shelving required for e-journals, nor can they be stolen or mutilated.

Speed of Delivery

The delivery of print journals has proven to be unreliable. Because the publication of a print issue is dependent upon so many different factors, issues are frequently released later than expected. Even when released on time, issues are often received by libraries weeks after the date of publication. Sometimes issues are lost in the mail, mutilated by the mail-sorting process, or missing from the library shelves. Claiming is a costly, time-consuming process, as is the procurement of replacement copies.

E-journals are published decidedly faster than print journals. For many e-journals, articles are released as they are accepted. This accelerates the publication process because there is no need to wait until enough articles are ready before publishing an issue (*11*). Even for those e-journals released as whole issues like regular journals, the "delivery" process is faster and more reliable. There is no concern that these e-journal issues will be lost in the mail. Provided the archives are available, no issues are ever "missing," which eliminates the claiming process altogether.

Other Issues

There are a few less obvious but equally important issues to consider when comparing print journals to e-journals. Cataloging is one of them. Print journals are easily cataloged within most online catalogs because there are established rules and standards for doing so. E-journals are a new format and must therefore be treated differently within the online public catalogs. The rules and standards for the cataloging of e-journals and their representation within public catalogs are still being discussed, however. At present, the cataloging of e-journals is a complicated and time-consuming issue.

Usage statistics of journals have long been employed in libraries to determine such things as which journals to renew and which to cancel. Most libraries have devised methods for keeping track of how often journal issues have been used. An effective method for gathering such statistics on the use of e-journals has not yet been established. There has been some experimentation with counters on WEB pages, but these have proven to be unreliable.

Unfortunately, not even an in-depth discussion on the pros and cons of the e-journal can help determine conclusively whether it is an acceptable replacement for the print journal. Table 3 offers a brief comparison between the two formats. The check marks, which indicate perceived advantages, seem to be fairly balanced. It will require a resolution of all the numerous problems associated with e-journals before a true comparison can be made.

The Ongoing Debate

Considering the copious problems associated with the various forms of access, and taking into account the historic view of libraries as storehouses, it is no wonder that the access versus ownership controversy continues to simmer. One group insists that the library of the future will be completely digitized. Another decries that electronic access will eliminate libraries and librarianship altogether. A third group maintains that the traditional library must not be compromised, and that ownership should continue to be the primary focus of libraries.

It is difficult to take a stand on an issue when not all of the facts are available. As demonstrated in the discussion on e-journals, the electronic format of information is still in its early stages of development. Arguments against access are based on the current performance of digitized information. It could be assumed that as the electronic format is developed and perfected, performance will improve considerably. Still, it is important to consider the various arguments that are in opposition to access.

TABLE 3

Comparison of Print Journals to Electronic Journals

Traditional print journals	Electronic journals
✓ Format is tested and standardized.	Format is in the early stages of development.
✓ Easy for patrons to use.	Requires some training for patrons to use.
✓ No special equipment needed.	Special equipment required (hardware, software, printers, etc.).
✓ Easy to locate (if shelved properly).	Access is currently unreliable (URL problems, Internet connection problems, etc.).
✓ Use is limited only to copyright laws.	Use is limited by copyright laws *and* licensing agreements.
✓ Archiving is effective and permanent.	Archiving is "up in the air."
Operating costs are considerable (ordering, cataloging, claiming, binding).	✓ Operating costs are minimal (no cataloging, binding, or claiming).
Requires shelving.	✓ No shelving required.
Often mutilated, stolen, or misshelved.	✓ Cannot be mutilated, stolen, or misshelved.
Requires extensive storage space.	✓ Saves considerable storage space.
Allows only one user at a time.	✓ Allows for multiple users with simultaneous access.
Slow delivery via "snail mail."	✓ Immediate receipt of issue.
Issues are easily lost in the mail or missing.	✓ No more missing issues.
Slow publication.	✓ Fast publication.

Note: ✓ = an advantage.

"Access delayed is access denied"—this statement has become the battle cry for supporters of the traditional library. At first glance, the statement is an accurate one. If a library patron must wait for an item because the library does not own it, immediate fulfillment of that information need has been denied, however, the fallacy in this argument lies in the fact that interlibrary loan, which is a form of "delayed access," has been accepted by library patrons for decades. Libraries rely on interlibrary loan when they do not own a book or a journal title, and although it may take days or weeks for a patron to receive the information he or she seeks, it is still a viable and acceptable form of access. It may also be argued that delayed access to digitized information, when caused by technical difficulties, might only be a matter of hours rather than days.

"Access does not guarantee availability." Providing access to an item through interlibrary loan or in electronic format does not guarantee that the information sought will be available. Lending libraries may have already lent the item elsewhere, and Internet connections or server problems may cause the item to be unavailable. The same holds true for items that are actually owned in-house, however. Books and journals may be on loan, in use, misshelved, missing, or lost, thus it can also be said that ownership does not guarantee availability.

"Browsing is compromised when journal titles are canceled"—a recent study on the effectiveness of access versus ownership revealed that browsing a physical item is still a primary need for academic library patrons (*23*). Often current awareness in a field of study is achieved by browsing the table of contents of various journals in that field. It may be argued that when ownership of journal titles is suspended in favor of access, the browsing feature is lost. There are alternatives, however, to browsing the physical item. Table of contents (TOC) and alerting services are now available from many publishers. TOC subscribers are alerted electronically when a new issue is available. The subscribers may then "browse" the TOC of the new issue or of previous issues. An advantage to this service is that some allow hypertext links to the full-text articles or to related articles. Some protest that TOC services are limited to periodicals with a high volume of use, and that those journals with low use are not included (*28*). This may change once the electronic format has gone beyond the experimental stage. In any case, electronic alerting services can be utilized to achieve the same purpose as the browsing of a physical item.

"Access is limited to one's ability to pay"—this brings into play the highly debated "fee versus free" issue. It has been common in the past for libraries to charge patrons for interlibrary loans and for database searching. Since these services have until recently been supplements to ownership, the charges seemed justified. It was reasoned that these were "extra" services, and that it was appropriate to charge for them (*29*). When access is favored in place of ownership, the justification for charging fees is no longer valid. Many agree that library users should not be penalized for the shift from ownership to access. The American Library Association's *Handbook of Organization* asserts that "the charging of fees and levies for information services, including those services utilizing the latest information technology, is discriminatory in publicly supported institutions providing library and information services" (*30*). When emphasis shifts from ownership to access, libraries will need to find an alternative to charging fees for information that was once owned.

"In order for one library to access an item, another must have acquired it" (*6*)—this is perhaps the most difficult statement to deny in the access versus ownership debate. If libraries purchase fewer materials and turn to other sources for information, who will provide that information? This question is especially relevant when discussing monographs and interlibrary loans. Each year, libraries are buying a smaller percentage of the total number of books published. If all research libraries continue with this trend, the interlibrary lending of books will become defunct. A book cannot be borrowed or lent if it is not owned by someone. As such, libraries are in a position of dependency. This quandary will only be resolved through cooperation between libraries and shared collection development.

The Compromise

There has been a considerable amount of discourse within the past ten years on the access versus ownership dispute. Authors of early literature on the issue commonly took a decisive stand in one direction or the other. More recently, though, librarians are migrating toward a "middle-of-the-road" stance that indicates that the debate is nearing a compromise.

The phrase "And, Not Or" is the backbone of the compromise. Rather than making a choice between ownership and access, libraries should consider building a collection comprising both materials that are owned and materials that are accessed. One author's vision for the library of the future is as follows:

- The future means both print and electronic communication.
- The future means both linear text and hypertext.
- The future means both mediation by librarians and direct access.
- The future means both collections and access.
- The future means a library that is both edifice and interface (9).

Another author states, "The time has come to look upon library materials as divided into classes of available and not available; to cherish physical collections because they meet real needs and make possible a variety of services; and to integrate electronic resources into our idea of 'collection'" (20). Yet another maintains that the success of the library of the future "should be redefined to reflect, not quantity, but provision for need" (7).

Most librarians agree that libraries, particularly academic and research libraries, need to abandon the traditional "tonnage" model, which emphasizes the sheer number of volumes and journal subscriptions a single collection contains (15). It is also agreed that the possibilities that technology presents cannot be long denied. While not being able to purchase a large portion of the resources being published, libraries today are able through electronic access to make available more resources than at any other time in the history of libraries (4).

In order to be successful today and in the future, libraries need to be able to fulfill the information needs of patrons, regardless of the method by which this is done. The decision of whether to own information or to provide access to information should first be based on the needs of the community and the content required to meet those needs. Only then should the package (whether owned or accessed) be considered (7).

"What will matter in a library, what has always mattered in a library, is the quality of the collection, and, of course, the public's ability to access it and use it" (14)—library users are primarily concerned with whether or not they are able to locate the information they need. To patrons, the method of locating this information is irrelevant.

The demand for information and the need for specific knowledge has driven libraries for centuries. This demand will never disappear. To ensure that libraries continue to meet this demand is to secure the future of librarianship. Libraries must find a way, through cooperation and resource sharing, to make use of the best features from both the traditional warehouse library model and the contemporary access model. Based on the needs of the library community, a careful balance should be made between owned materials and electronic materials. This access *and* ownership library model is a challenge for all librarians today. Once this challenge is met, libraries will remain secure in their status as the hub of the information community of the future.

REFERENCES

1. J. Thompson, *A History of the Principles of Librarianship*, Clive Bingley, London, 1977.
2. S. Jackson, *Libraries and Librarianship in the West: A Brief History*, McGraw-Hill, New York, 1974.

3. J. P. Feather, "The Book in History and the History of the Book," in *The History of Books and Libraries: Two Views,* Library of Congress, Washington, D.C., 1986, pp. 1–16.

4. I. Owens, "Issues of Ownership, Access, and Document Delivery: Considerations for the Humanities." *Ac. Librar.,* **9**(17/18), 45–62 (1997).

5. M. A. Coffey, "The Evolution of Librarianship into a Profession," Ph. D. thesis, St. Louis University, St. Louis, MO, 1990.

6. J. M. Smith, *A Chronology of Librarianship,* Scarecrow Press, Metuchen, NJ, 1968.

7. B. Harloe and J. M. Budd, "Collection Development and Scholarly Communication in the Era of Electronic Access." *J. Acad. Librar.,* **20**(2), 83–87 (May 1994).

8. R. Pikowsky, "High Serials Prices Lead to the Debate Over Access vs. Ownership." *Serials Librar.,* **32**(3/4), 33–37 (1997).

9. W. Crawford, "Paper Persists: Why Physical Library Collections Still Matter." *Online* (Jan. 1998); available at WWW site: <http://www.onlineinc.com/onlinemag/JanOL98/crawford1.htm>.

10. W. R. Perryman, "The Changing Landscape of Information Access: The Impact of Impact of Technological Advances Upon the Acquisition, Ownership, and Dissemination of Informational Resources Within the Research Library Community." *J. Librr. Admin.,* **15**(1/2), 73–93 (1991).

11. S. P. Harter and H. J. Kim, "Accessing Electronic Journals and Other E-publications: An Empirical Study." *College Res. Librr.,* **57**(5), 440–455 (Sept. 1996).

12. "The 1997 National Survey of U.S. Public Libraries and the Internet: Summary Results, November 1997," American Library Association Office for Information Technology Policy, Washington, D.C., 1997.

13. K. Coyle, "Why Librarians Should Rule the Net," 1997; available at WWW site: <http://www.dla.ucop.edu/~kec/texas/index.htm>.

14. C. T. Corcoran, "Are We Ready for the Library of the Future?" *Salon 21st* (Dec. 2, 1997), available at WWW site: <http://www.salon1999.com/21st/feature/1997/12/02feature.html>.

15. Association of Research Libraries, "To Publish and Perish." *Policy Persp.,* **7**(4), 1–12 (March 1998).

16. "Statement of Current Perspective and Preferred Practices for the Selection and Purchase of Electronic Information," International Coalition of Library Consortia, March 1998; available at WWW site: <http://www.library.yale.edu/consortia/statement.html>.

17. "Association of Research Libraries Statistics: Descriptive Statistics for Academic Institutions," Association of Research Libraries, 1998; available at WWW site: <http://arl.cni/org:80/stats/arlstat/index.html>.

18. V. J. Payne and M. A. Burke, "A Cost-Effectiveness Study of Ownership versus Access." *Serials Librar.,* **32**(3/4), 139–152 (1997).

19. L. T. Kane, "Access vs. Ownership: Do We Have to Make a Choice?" *College Res. Librr.,* **58**(1), 59–67 (Jan. 1997).

20. M. Gorman, "Ownership *and* Access: A New Idea of 'Collection.'" *C&RL News,* **58**(7), 498–499 (July/Aug. 1997).

21. S. S. Intner, "Differences Between Access vs. Ownership." *Technicalities,* **9**(9), 5–8 (Sept. 1989).

22. J. Hughes, "Can Document Delivery Compensate for Reduced Serials Holdings? A Life Sciences Library Perspective." *College Res. Librr.,* **58**(5), 421–431 (Sept. 1997).

23. S. Beardman, "The Cost-Effectiveness of Access Versus Ownership: A Report on the Virtual Library Project at the University of Western Australia Library." *Austr. Librr. Rev.,* **13**(2), 173–181 (1996).

24. C. A. Hawbaker and C. K. Wagner, "Periodical Ownership Versus Fulltext Online Access: A Cost-Benefit Analysis." *J. Acad. Librar.,* **22**(2), 105–109 (March 1996).

25. C. B. Truesdell, "Is Access a Viable Alternative to Ownership? A Review of Access Performance." *J. Acad. Librar.,* **20**(4), 200–206 (Sept. 1994).

26. L. Guernsey, "Libraries Call Academic-Publishing System 'Dysfunctional' and Attack Price Policies." *Chronicle Higher Ed.,* (March 27, 1998); available at WWW site: <http://chronicle.com/data/internet.dir/itdata/1998/03/t98032701.htm>.

27. L. Guernsey, "Library Groups, Decrying 'Excessive Pricing,' Demand New Policies on Electronic Journals." *Chronicle Higher Ed.,* (April 10, 1998); available at WWW site: <http://chronicle.com/data/articles.dir/art-44.dir/issue-31.dir/31a03301.htm>.

28. M. B. Line, "Access Versus Ownership: How Real an Alternative Is It?" *IFLA J.,* **22**, 35–41 (1996).

29. I. B. Hoadley, "Access vs. Ownership: Myth or Reality." *Librr. Ac. Prac. Theory,* **17**, 191–195 (1993).

30. *American Library Association Handbook of Organization,* American Library Association, Chicago, 1996–1997, p. 41.

SELECTED BIBLIOGRAPHY ON ACCESS VERSUS OWNERSHIP

Alexander, A. W., "Access vs. Ownership: Strategic Implications for Agents." *Serials Librar.,* **24**(3/4), 125–127 (1994).

Barwick, M., "Interlending and Document Supply: A Review of Recent Literature." *Interlend. Doc. Supply,* **25**(3), 126–132 (1997).

Beardman, S., "The Cost-Effectiveness of Access versus Ownership: A Report on the Virtual Library Project at the University of Western Australia Library." *Austr. Libr. Rev.,* **13**(2), 173–181 (1996).

Bennett, D. C. et al., "To Publish and Perish." *Policy Persp.,* **7**(4), 1–12 (March 1998).

Brin, B. and Cochran, E., "Access and Ownership in the Academic Environment: One Library's Progress Report." *J. Acad. Librar.,* **20**(4), 207–212 (Sept. 1994).

Buntin, A., "Life Between a Rock and a Hard Place: The Transition from Print to Electronic," Jan. 1997; available at WWW site: <http://www.nnlm.nlm.nih.gov/psr/alison.html>.

Caswell, J. V., "Building an Integrated User Interface to Electronic Resources." *Inform. Tech. Libr.,* **16**(2), 63–72 (June 1997).

Commings, K., "Access Over Ownership." *Computers Libr.,* **17**(4), 24–27 (April 1997).

Corcoran, C. T., "Are We Ready for the Library of the Future?" *Salon 21st* (Dec. 2, 1997); available at WWW site: <http://www.salon1999.com/21st/feature/1997/12/02feature.html>.

Crawford, W., "Paper Persists: Why Physical Library Collections Still Matter." *Online* (Jan. 1998); available at WWW site: <http://www.onlineinc.com/onlinemag/JanOL98/crawford1.htm>.

Feather, J. P. and McKitterick, D., *The History of Books and Libraries: Two Views,* Library of Congress, Washington, D.C., 1986.

Ferguson, A. W. and Kehoe, K., "Access vs. Ownership: What Is Most Cost Effective in the Sciences." *J. Libr. Admin.,* **19**(2), 89–99 (1993).

Gorman, M., "Ownership and Access: A New Idea of 'Collection.'" *C&RL News,* **58**(7), 498–499 (July/Aug. 1997).

Harloe, B. and Budd, J. M., "Collection Development and Scholarly Communication in the Era of Electronic Access." *J. Acad. Librar.,* **20**(2), 83–87 (May 1994).

Guernsey, L., "Libraries Call Academic-Publishing System 'Dysfunctional' and Attack Price Policies." *Chronicle Higher Ed.,* (March 27, 1998); available at WWW site: <http://chronicle.com/data/internet.dir/itdata/1998/03/t98032701.htm>.

Guernsey, L., "Library Groups, Decrying 'Excessive Pricing,' Demand New Policies on Electronic Journals." *Chronicle Higher Ed.,* (April 10, 1998); available at WWW site: <http://chronicle.com/data/articles.dir/art-44.dir/issue-31.dir/31a03301.htm>.

Harter, S. P. and Kim, H. J., "Accessing Electronic Journals and Other E-publications: An Empirical Study." *College Res. Libr.,* **57**(5), 440–455 (Sept. 1996).

Hawbaker, C. A. and Wagner, C. K., "Periodical Ownership Versus Fulltext Online Access: A Cost-Benefit Analysis." *J. Acad. Librar.,* **22**(2), 105–109 (March 1996).

Hoadley, I. B., "Access vs. Ownership: Myth or Reality." *Libr. Ac. Prac. Theory,* **17**, 191–195 (1993).

Hughes, J., "Can Document Delivery Compensate for Reduced Serial Holdings? A Life Sciences Library Perspective." *College Res. Libr.,* **58**(5), 421–431 (Sept. 1997).

Intner, S. S., "Differences Between Access vs. Ownership." *Technicalities,* **9**(9), 5–8 (Sept. 1989).

Jackson, S., *Libraries and Librarianship in the West: A Brief History,* McGraw–Hill, New York, 1974.

James, S., "Ownership and Access, Database and OPAC: Present and Future Opportunities for Academic Libraries." *Libr. Rev.,* **39**(4), 21–32 (1990).

Jankowska, M. A., "Economic and Technological Aspects of Electronic and Printed Recorded Knowledge," in *Encyclopedia of Library and Information Science,* vol. 61, suppl. 24, Marcel Dekker, New York, 1997, pp. 121–130.

Kane, L. T., "Access vs. Ownership: Do We Have to Make a Choice?" *College Res. Libr.,* **58**(1), 59–67 (Jan. 1997).

Kingma, B. R., *The Economics of Access versus Ownership: The Costs and Benefits of Access to Scholarly Articles via Interlibrary Loan and Journal Subscriptions,* Haworth Press, New York, 1996.

Kleiner, J. P. and Hamaker, C. A., "Libraries 2000: Transforming Libraries Using Document Delivery, Needs Assessment, and Networked Resources." *College Res. Libr.,* **58**(4), 355–374 (July 1997).

Line, M. B., "Access versus Ownership: How Real an Alternative Is It?" *IFLA J.,* **22**, 35–41 (1996).

Marshall, G., "Libraries and Educational Reform: Access Is Ownership." *Bookmark*, **49**, 111–113 (winter 1991).

Matheson, N. W., "The Idea of the Library in the Twenty-First Century." *Bull. Med. Libr. Assoc.,* **83**(1), 1–7 (Jan. 1995).

Moyer, R. W., "Monopoly Power and Electronic Journals." *Libr. Q.,* **67**(4), 325–349 (1997).

Miller, R. H., "From Warehouse to Gateway: A New University Library and a New Paradigm." *Libr. Ac. Prac. Theory,* **17**, 319–331 (1993).

Owens, I., "Issues of Ownership, Access, and Document Delivery: Considerations for the Humanities." *Ac. Librar.,* **9**(17/18), 45–62 (1997).

Pastine, M., "Ownership or Access to Electronic Information: A Selected Bibliography." *Collec. Mgt.,* **22**(2), 187–217 (1997).

Payne, V. J. and Burke, M. A., "A Cost-Effectiveness Study of Ownership versus Access." *Serials Librar.,* **32**(3/4), 139–152 (1997).

Perryman, W. R., "The Changing Landscape of Information Access: The Impact of Technological Advances Upon the Acquisition, Ownership, and Dissemination of Information Resources Within the Research Library Community." *J. Libr. Admin.,* **15**(1/2), 73–93 (1991).

Pikowsky, R., "High Serials Prices Lead to the Debate Over Access vs. Ownership." *Serials Librar.,* **32**(3/4), 33–37 (1997).

Saunders, L. M., "Transforming Acquisitions to Support Virtual Libraries." *Inform. Tech. Libr.,* **14**(1), 41–46 (March 1995).

Shaughnessy, T. W., "From Ownership to Access: A Dilemma for Library Managers." *J. Libr. Admin.,* **14**(1), 1–7 (1991).

Smith, J. M., *A Chronology of Librarianship,* Scarecrow Press, Metuchen, NJ, 1968.

Thompson, J., *A History of the Principles of Librarianship,* Clive Bingley, London, 1977.

Truesdell, C. B., "Is Access a Viable Alternative to Ownership? A Review of Access Performance." *J. Acad. Librar.,* **20**(4), 200–206 (Sept. 1994).

Tyckoson, D., "Access vs. Ownership: Changing Roles for Librarians." *Ref. Librar.,* **34**, 37–45 (1991).

Von Wahlde, B., "Access vs. Ownership: A SUNY University Center Libraries Study of the Economics of Document Delivery." *Resource Sharing Inform. Networks,* **12**(2), 19–30 (1997).

Weingarten, F. W., "Technological Change and the Evolution of Information Policy." *Inform. Tech. Policy Outlook,* **1**(1), 1–8 (Dec. 1997).

Weston, B., Reinke, C., and Morgan, E. L., "Methods for Collecting, Processing, and Providing Access to Electronic Serials." *Serials Librar.,* **25**(3/4), 327–331 (1995).

LAURA TOWNSEND KANE

AN ALGORITHM FOR ABDUCTIVE INFERENCE IN ARTIFICIAL INTELLIGENCE

Introduction to Abduction

Abduction, inference to the best explanation, is a form of reasoning first identified by the philosopher C. S. Peirce and more recently applied to a variety of problems in artificial intelligence. Abduction is a technique used to explain the appearance of findings. As a process, it requires a means of generating plausible domain hypotheses to explain the findings, evaluating those hypotheses, and composing some of those hypotheses into a coherent explanation.

In artificial intelligence researchers have successfully applied automated abduction with varying results to problems such as medical diagnosis, test result interpretation, theory decision making, legal reasoning, natural language understanding, and speech recognition. Different researchers have used widely different implementation approaches to solve abduction problems. These approaches have included automated theorem proving using logic, Bayesian probabilities, neural networks, and rule-based symbolic systems. In most cases, the problem-solving systems using these approaches perform the processes of hypothesis generation, evaluation, and composition.

Since abduction is taken to be inference to the "best" explanation, researchers have felt that such an explanation can only be derived by generating all possible combinations of explanatory hypotheses and selecting the most plausible combination. This is inherently intractable. Forming and evaluating each of the possible combinations of explanatory hypotheses is a formidable task. The human ability to perform abduction seems to be simplified in cases in which the term *best* more often means "best within reason, but not necessarily optimal." Algorithms that assume this latter attitude will often perform as well as methods that resort to intractable approaches, and they will perform in a reasonable amount of time.

One approach to abduction is to solve the overall explanation problem by decomposing it into smaller abduction problems, called local abductions, and then uniting the solutions into a single composite explanation. This simplification of the problem into smaller problems requires the additional consideration of the dependencies that exist between the local abduction problems. The local abduction method therefore utilizes a variety of "propagation" techniques to maintain consistency and to handle hypotheses' dependencies. The local abduction approach has been successfully applied to the various types of problems mentioned earlier. Furthermore, the algorithm is extendible to a layered abduction approach for problems that use a multitude of knowledge and hypothesis sources, such as natural language understanding and speech recognition.

This article presents abduction as a class of problems. It describes several examples of abductive problems. It briefly examines various approaches and then presents the local abduction algorithm in detail. The article then describes layered abduction and the various control strategies that can be applied. Finally, the article examines several different automated abduction systems that range in the problems that they solve from legal reasoning to natural language understanding and speech recognition.

Abduction Explained

Philosopher C. S. Peirce first coined the term abduction to be a kind of deduction in reverse (*1*). Standard deduction works as follows. If it is known that A → B and it is known that A is true, then one can conclude B is true (the symbol → is taken to convey implications or causation). Abduction turns this around to say that given A → B, and that B is true, then we might conclude A is also true. How can this form of reasoning be used? Consider a situation in which it is known that A causes B. If B has appeared, one might conclude that A is its cause. It is more reasonable, however, to assume that there are multiple rules that might apply to a given situation. Consider instead the following facts:

$$A \rightarrow F$$

$$B \rightarrow F$$

$$C \rightarrow F$$

$$D \rightarrow F$$

$$E \rightarrow F$$

and F is true (has been observed).

The abductive inference tells us that A or B or C or D or E caused F. If there is information available to conclude that A, B, C, and D are unlikely, then the best explanation for F is E.

Abduction is a form of inference along with deduction and induction. Deduction is an infallible form of inference. Given true premises, the conclusion of a deduction must be true. Induction is a fallible form of reasoning. The predominant type of induction is "inductive generalization," which determines from some sample set of cases some characteristic to apply to a larger population. Induction is an example of ampliative inference since the conclusion may represent more information than what was presented in the premises. Abduction, like induction, is both fallible and ampliative. Abduction infers a best explanation for an experience. Given a set of data, the hypotheses that can best account for or explain the data are concluded. In abduction, the conclusion explains the premise, it explains *why* the data occurred. Abduction seems to be an ubiquitous form of processing (*2*).

Figure 1 illustrates a generic abductive problem in which there are a set of findings and a set of plausible hypotheses to explain those findings. In this figure, arrows indicate explanatory coverage, and hypothesis plausibilities indicate how likely each hypothesis is given the data. This figure does not show the output of abduction, a conclusion that *best* explains the data. One explanation for the data is the collection of hypotheses {H1, H4, H6}. This may be the best explanation if the decision is based on the hypotheses that have the highest individual plausibilities, although there are other important factors that might make other explanations better, such as simplicity, parsimony, and consistency. Notice in this example that the best explanation itself is made up of a collection of hypotheses. One problem with abductive problem solving is

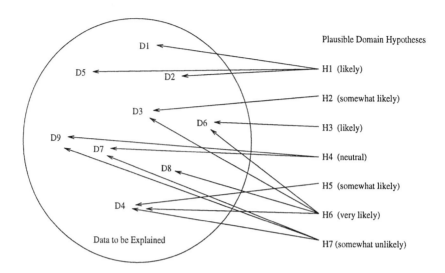

FIGURE 1. *Example of abduction: explaining the appearance of findings.*

that the need to find the best explanation implies selecting the explanation that is most plausible. In situations in which multiple hypotheses are required to form the explanation, finding the most plausible explanation requires evaluating all or many combinations of the plausible hypotheses. This makes abduction intractable.

Recent research in artificial intelligence has demonstrated the use of abduction to solve a variety of interpretive reasoning problems in a large number of domains. These problems include diagnosis (both medical and mechanical), test data interpretation (in many domains), natural language understanding, legal reasoning, and theory formation. Some of the approaches taken are intractable, while other approaches have found ways to avoid the intractability.

Abductive Problems

An abductive task is one that has input that requires explaining and output that represents the best explanation of the input. The steps taken to arrive at the output, given the input, is the abductive process. Abductive problems exist everywhere: a driver trying to explain the odd sound his car is making, a scientist trying to explain why people cannot walk through walls, a student trying to explain (internally) what the teacher is saying in her lecture, a detective trying to explain how and why a person was murdered, a juror deciding if the accused is innocent or guilty, and a child trying to identify the image in an optical illusion. In each of these examples, the agent is given findings and must first hypothesize the cause of the findings, and then attempt to derive the best single cause or collection of causes until that agent is satisfied.

A concrete example of abduction is the diagnostic process. In the case of medical diagnosis, a medical practitioner will attempt to explain the symptoms of a sick patient with some disease or illness. First, the patient's symptoms evoke possible disease hypotheses. These hypotheses are evaluated, possibly by running various tests. The explanatory power of each hypothesis is considered. The hypothesis (or set of hypotheses) that best explains all of the symptoms is then selected and a treatment devised. In the case of automobile mechanical diagnosis, a mechanic will attempt to explain the observed problems of the machine by identifying the malfunctioning component(s). The input is a set of findings that consist of odd behaviors and poor automotive performance and the output is the hypothesized malfunction (or malfunctions) that best explains all of the findings (or at least the important ones).

Philosophers and psychologists have long suggested that perception relies on some form of inference, with recent suggestions claiming that it is an abductive task (2). A speaker intends to convey some information and produces auditory and/or visual stimuli that encode the information. The recipient then transforms this information into an internal representation of meaning. To make this transformation from auditory and/or visual stimuli to an internal representation of meaning, some form of inference is used. In visual perception, the eye receives information in the form of lines and edges, and explains these with (after several stages) volumetrics. In natural language understanding the input is an acoustic signal or a visual image of text, and the goal is to process these data to create a description that captures the semantics and pragmatics of the input. In perceptual problems, the abduction is performed in layers in which different forms of knowledge are applied at the different levels of the problem.

Abduction in Artificial Intelligence

Applying abduction to artificial intelligence problems began with Harry Pople and his system, Internist. Pople identified that the diagnostic task was one of inference to the best explanation. Since then, researchers in artificial intelligence have applied abduction to diagnostic problems as well as to many other types of problems. The methods of implementation for abduction have varied greatly from symbolic rule-based approaches to automated theorem proving to Bayesian probabilities to neural networks. In this section, five approaches are described.

POPLE AND INTERNIST

Pople implemented a medical system, Internist (and later Caduceus), to diagnose internal diseases (3). Internist uses explicitly represented disease hypotheses in the form of disease classification tree. The goal of Internist is to come to the best complete and parsimonious explanation for the input data. Parsimony means that the explanation has no overlapping or superfluous hypotheses. The abduction is accomplished through a method of hypothesization—scoring and covering (or explaining) the given data using a hypothesis-driven approach.

Internist begins by evaluating the available hypotheses in the disease classification tree. Scores are computed based on the amount of the data a given hypothesis can explain. The score includes weights that represent the importance of each finding. The score computed for a given hypothesis consists of the importance of the findings that can be explained and are present, findings that are expected but are not present, and findings that are present but not explained by the hypothesis. Next, the scored hypotheses are sorted from highest scoring (most likely) to lowest scoring. *Competing* hypotheses (those that can account for some of the same findings) are compared and the highest scoring competitor is selected. If only one hypothesis is selected from this process, it is considered true. If several hypotheses are considered, differentiation between the top competing hypotheses takes place by determining the explanatory differences between the hypotheses and rescoring each hypothesis. The cycle then begins again until all findings have been explained or the only remaining findings to be explained have low importance.

Internist takes into account the explanatory power of a hypothesis and the expectations of that hypothesis in creating a diagnostic conclusion. One of the problems with Internist is that hypotheses might not have been scored appropriately, causing incorrect hypotheses to be accepted as true. Another problem is Internist's lack of ability to critique the set of accepted hypotheses because it ignores the possibility of alternative explanations once an explainer is found. In spite of these problems, Internist is considered a successful attempt at medical diagnosis and the earliest attempt at automated abduction.

HOBBS AND TACITUS

Jerry Hobbs developed a system called the abductive commonsense inference text understanding system (TACITUS, *4*). TACITUS is a system for interpreting natural language texts, and in particular, malfunction reports, although it is intended to be domain- and application-independent.

TACITUS performs its task by producing logical forms in first-order predicate calculus and backward-chaining across them. It creates an abductive conclusion or explanation by determining the best subset of predicates that can explain the sentence. The backward-chaining process results in an abductive conclusion that is composed of the least costly predicates necessary to generate a proof corresponding to the "explanation." The best subset is determined by the sum of the costs that are associated with the predicates. Costs for predicates are determined by their specificity and their semantic contribution to the overall proof. The best explanation is the least expensive complete explanation. In TACITUS it is important to weigh the specificity of a single predicate against the semantic contribution made by the combination of several less specific predicates. It is possible that a single, highly specific predicate is cheaper to conclude than some number of less specific predicates that explain the same text.

The basic operation of TACITUS is to start with the input text and express it in its logical form. The sentence is then interpreted with respect to a knowledge base that reflects the shared knowledge of the speaker and the previously interpreted sentences. The system attempts to resolve four pragmatic problems: syntactic ambiguity, metonymy, references, and compound nominal interpretation. Assumptions are made as necessary. The system's goal is to prove some subset of predicates that represent the text; that which is not proven is assumed to be "new" information.

REGGIA AND PENG

Reggia and Peng (5) combine a variation of Bayesian probabilities and the general set covering model to solve medical diagnosis. Knowledge is provided in two forms: explanatory knowledge that specifies what possible medical symptoms each hypothesis can explain, and probabilistic knowledge that specifies the probability of each hypothesis given the present symptoms.

Generating an explanation requires first identifying which hypotheses can explain the given finding and then calculating each hypothesis' evidential probability using the Bayesian formulas. This computation requires considering two probabilities: the prior probability of the disease occurring and the causal probability that the disease will cause the given symptoms. Hypotheses then form a set cover to explain the findings. The criteria for choosing the best set cover is based on principles of minimality (or parsimony), consistency, complete coverage, and highest degree of plausibility (highest probability).

Reggia and Peng assume that hypotheses are mutually independent so that covering the data can be accomplished in a piecemeal fashion and that the hypothesis probabilities will not change because of the acceptance of other hypotheses. Without this assumption, the problem becomes intractable because causal probabilities are required for every possible combination of findings and hypotheses. With this assumption, however, there is no mechanism applied to allow for dependencies that might exist between hypotheses.

A more recent extension to the Bayesian approach is to use intermediate states in the model that allow for pathophysiological states. The approach taken by Reggia and Peng has become popular and used in other areas, including language processing (6), error classification (7), and memory modeling (8).

PEARL AND BELIEF NETS

Judea Pearl (9) has solved abduction problems by combining Bayesian probabilities and causal networks. Pearl's belief network method models diagnostic knowledge as a network of hypotheses and symptoms. Hypotheses that can explain symptoms are directly connected together. Two forms of probabilities are used to connect hypothesis and symptom nodes: evidential probabilities and causal probabilities (representing the probability of the symptom appearing given the disease, and the probability of the disease given the symptom, respectively), with prior probabilities additionally ascribed to each hypothesis node. Probabilities are computed both for links between nodes and for hypotheses.

To use the belief network, the nodes corresponding to symptoms that are present in the given case are activated. Evidential knowledge is propagated to the connecting hypothesis nodes. Hypothesis nodes then update their own probability of presence by combining the evidential probability and prior probability. The belief of a hypothesis node is the probability that the hypothesis node is true based on the values propagated to it and the prior probability stored in that node. Once a hypothesis node computes its own belief, it propagates this new probability to all connecting symptom nodes and any other causally related hypothesis nodes. These nodes then update their own probabilities. Beliefs continue to propagate through the network until a stable state is reached. Those hypotheses that have a sufficiently high belief are considered true and can be used to explain the activated symptoms. All other hypotheses are considered false.

One restriction with this approach is in the connectivity of the belief network. If the network is cyclic, then the network might never reach a stable state. To remove cycles from the network, some hypotheses nodes must be preinstantiated as true or false. The network can then be executed to find a best explanation; however, this explanation will have assumed some of the hypotheses were true and some false. To adequately determine which series of preinstantiations is best, the network must be run for each possible combination of true and false values for these hypotheses. The combination that yields the highest overall set of confidences is then selected as the solution and the best explanation is composed of those hypotheses that were preinstantiated as true along with those hypotheses that had sufficiently high belief values. Because of the need to run the network on all possible combinations of preinstantiated hypotheses, the method is intractable for any domain that has a cyclic belief network (and most real-world diagnostic problems will have cyclic belief networks).

THAGARD AND NEURAL NETS

Paul Thagard (*10*) has developed a mechanism for abduction to be used in deciding between two (or more) competing explanatory theories. He has used this method to implement a variety of systems, including legal reasoning and theory evaluation (as will be described later in the article). His implementation uses neural networks that are trained based on a set of evidence. The neural network contains hypothesis and finding nodes. In this approach, hypotheses are divided into sets supporting one of the possible theories. Each set can have potential explainers for a given data item. Explanatory knowledge is given by connecting hypothesis nodes to finding nodes where a hypothesis is able to explain that datum. The network propagates activations around the network until it stabilizes. Hypothesis nodes that are still active are considered as part of the composite explanation, while hypothesis nodes that are not active are ruled out.

Thagard is able to capture a variety of knowledge (other than explanatory) in his networks by adding links between different nodes. Hypothesis interaction knowledge (incompatibilities, associations) is given by connecting some hypothesis nodes to others. Incompatibility connections are made with inhibitory links while association connections are made with excitatory links. Analogy, simplicity, and "unification" (where two or more hypotheses must unite to explain a finding) are all possible. Weights for the links are determined based on the amount that a hypothesis can cause a finding or the degree of association or incompatibility between hypotheses.

There are limitations that are inherent with this approach. All hypotheses and their explanatory knowledge must be captured at the time the system is developed and not at run time. The system tends to be inefficient because of lengthy training. There is no mechanism available to generate an explanation for the results of the system finding a best explanation. Finally, this approach is only applicable in problems that have competing sets of theories to select from rather than as a general tool for diagnosis or natural language understanding.

The Local Abduction Approach

In this section, a problem- and domain-independent approach to performing abduction is presented. This approach is based on decomposing the abductive problem into three separate tasks: hypothesis generation, hypothesis instantiation, and hypothesis composition.

- *Hypothesis generation* is the process of obtaining plausible domain hypotheses that can potentially explain findings. Generation may be accomplished by any number of possible methods. Hierarchical classification (*11*) generates plausible domain hypotheses by traversing top-down through a taxonomic hierarchy of hypotheses (e.g., malfunctions) organized by specificity. Cueing uses associative knowledge to generate hypotheses that are related to the given findings. Hypotheses may be generated from first principles using some functional or causal model. Heuristic search strategies can be used to navigate through some organized hypothesis search spaces selecting promising hypotheses. A neural network may be able to suggest hypotheses by using the findings as the initial conditions and having the network spread activations to generate hypotheses.
- *Hypothesis instantiation* is the process of determining each hypothesis's relevance for the current case. This includes assigning an initial plausibility to the hypothesis (hypothesis scoring) and determining hypothesis-specific information such as explanatory coverage and hypothesis interactions. Similar to generation, instantiation can be realized through a variety of methods. The plausibility may be obtained by using routine recognition (*12*; matching knowledge and searching for the presence and absence of features of interest), Bayesian probabilities, statistical matching, judging the strength of a neural network activation, or some other method. The explanatory coverage and hypothesis interaction knowledge may be static information of what a hypothesis will always be able to account for, may be derived from first principles, or may be some combination of the two.
- *Hypothesis composition* is the process of generating a composite explanation to account for the data using previously generated and instantiated hypotheses. Composition may be accomplished by generating all possible combinations of explanatory hypotheses that were previously generated, evaluating each combination, and selecting the best. Another approach, as seen with Pearl and Thagard, is a holistic composition through some belief or neural network. A simpler approach to either of these is to incrementally build a composite hypothesis out of the explanatory parts, critiquing the composite hypothesis as it grows.

HYPOTHESIS COMPOSITION USING LOCAL ABDUCTIONS

The article now concentrates on a tractable algorithm for the construction of a composite hypothesis using an incremental construction method. This approach is based on finding *local abductions*. Each finding is explained by selecting the best available hypothesis. The selected hypothesis is then combined with other hypotheses that have been selected to explain other findings. As a hypothesis is selected, any other findings that it can explain are removed from the set of findings to be explained. By removing all findings that the newly accepted hypothesis can explain, the composite is constructed to be parsimonious (i.e., no superfluous or overlapping hypotheses). A mechanism is used to ensure consistency among hypotheses included in the composite by propagating any forms of hypothesis interactions to the hypotheses that still remain as plausible explainers for any remaining findings. The local abduction approach, unlike many of the approaches mentioned earlier, is tractable. It is also extensible toward problems requiring multiple abductions (as described later). What follows is a description of the local abduction algorithm.

- *Generate and instantiate hypotheses* and generate or obtain findings to be explained.
- *Include* in the composite any hypotheses *predetermined* to be part of the best explanation (an optional step). *Expand any expectations from a higher level.* This step may occur during layered abduction when higher-level problem solvers have generated expectations for the level for which an explanation is being generated. *Propagate the effects* of hypotheses being accepted into the composite. Propagation will be described in the next section.
- *Loop* on the following until either all findings are accounted for *or* until no more progress is made in the explanatory coverage.
  - *Find all confirmed hypotheses* and add them in the composite. A confirmed hypothesis is one that receives the highest confidence plausibility possible during the instantiation subtask and is assumed to be present in the case. *If confirmed hypotheses* are found *then propagate the effects* of the lastest additions and go back to the loop beginning, otherwise continue.
  - *Find all essential hypotheses* and add them to the composite. An essential hypothesis is a hypothesis that is the *sole* explanation for some finding. *If essential hypotheses* are found, *then propagate the effects* of their inclusion into the composite and go back to the loop beginning, otherwise continue.

At this point, the hypotheses included in the composite are those that are almost undeniably a part of the best explanation because they have been implied from other problem solving, are so highly rated that they are certain, or are the only means of explaining some finding(s). Explaining the remaining findings will require including more tentative hypotheses, thus lessening the overall confidence in the composite.

  - *Find all clear best hypotheses* and add them to the composite. A clear best hypothesis is one that explains a finding better than any other hypothesis and has a reasonably high plausibility. *If clear best hypotheses* are found, *then propagate the effects* of their inclusion into the composite and go back to the loop beginning, otherwise continue.
  - *Find all of the weak best hypotheses* and add them to the composite. Weak best hypotheses are similar to clear best hypotheses, but the requirements are relaxed to allow for less superior hypotheses. *If weak best hypotheses* are found, *then propagate the effects* of their inclusion into the composite and go back to the loop beginning, otherwise continue.
- *End loop*
- If there are still some unaccounted findings, *attempt to guess* from from the remaining hypotheses that have not been ruled out. This step is optional and only used if the need to explain the remaining data over is more important than the risk of guessing incorrectly. Guessing may be accomplished by letting unexplained findings vote on the hypothesis by which it is most likely explained. This allows hypotheses that explain more to have better chances of being chosen than hypotheses that explain less. *If any guessed hypotheses* are found, *then propagate the effects* of their inclusion into the composite and go back to the loop beginning, otherwise end.

As a result, all of the findings will be accounted for, or there will be no more hypotheses available to explain unaccounted findings, or the only remaining hypotheses are too close in plausibility and explanatory coverage to allow for a confident decision. In the last case, the unexplained findings could be left unexplained or guessing could take place. One can control the minimum confidence of the final composite by limiting the loop to essentials and clear bests, or allow for a more complete but less confident conclusion by allowing for weak bests and even guessing. Additionally, one can provide for levels of "clear best" and "weak best" thresholds allowing for additional steps in the process of constructing the composite hypothesis.

HYPOTHESIS INTERACTIONS AND PROPAGATION OF LOCAL ABDUCTIONS

It is a mistake to assume that hypotheses are independent. The local abduction strategy as described above treats hypotheses as unrelated. In order to handle hypothesis dependencies, a propagation mechanism is included. As hypotheses are added to the composite, any dependencies are identified and handled. These dependencies and the methods by which they are handled take on many forms.

An *implication* occurs if one hypothesis directly implies a second hypothesis (logically or causally). If the first hypothesis is true (previously accepted), then the second hypothesis is true (should be accepted). A negative implication occurs if the second hypothesis is false (rejected or ruled out), implying that the first hypothesis is also false. Implications can be thought of as truth preserving. The result of an implication is that the implied hypothesis is added to the composite and the negatively implied hypothesis is ruled out.

A weaker form of an implication is an *expectation,* which occurs when multiple hypotheses are related in such a way that if one hypothesis was accepted to be true then the related hypotheses might be expected to be true as well. Expectations may also be positive or negative. A positive expectation is one in which one hypothesis expects another so that the second hypothesis can be reconsidered and given higher plausibility. A negative expectation is one in which one hypothesis does *not* expect another hypothesis. In this case, the plausibility of the second hypothesis is lowered.

Hypotheses may also be *incompatible,* so that two or more hypotheses are mutually exclusive. If a hypothesis is accepted and is incompatible with another hypothesis, then the incompatible hypothesis can be ruled out and removed from future consideration.

The propagation steps in the local abduction algorithm perform these actions whenever hypothesis interactions are identified. It should be noted that other forms of interactions are possible, such as refinements of hypotheses into more detailed hypotheses and combining hypotheses for additive coverage (in which two hypotheses may together explain more than the hypothesis could explain apart). For more details on this algorithm including propagation mechanisms, see Refs. *13, 14,* and *2.*

D(1) is a collection of data
H(1) is the best explanation of D(1)
Let D(2) = H(1)

D(2) is a collection of data
H(2) is the best explanation of D(2)
Let D(3) = H2()

.

.

.

H(n) is the final explanation

FIGURE 2. *Layered abduction: an explanation at one level becomes the next level's findings.*

LAYERED ABDUCTIONS

Layered abduction means multiple abductive processes used in conjuction to come to an abductive conclusion. This form of reasoning is useful when the abductive explanation must be provided in a vocabulary of hypotheses only achievable through a series of cascaded inferences. This is the case in perceptual problems such as visual understanding, speech recognition, and natural language understanding. This form of processing can also be used for diagnosis and other problems.

In bottom-up layered abduction processing, the explanation produced by one abductive process becomes the findings to be explained at the next level. Passing the explanation between two levels can occur after an entire composite has been accepted, as each hypothesis is added to the composite, as a subset of hypotheses reaches a certain level of confidence, at predetermined time intervals, or when processing at one level stalls and might benefit from some outside guidance. The schema for layered abduction is illustrated in Fig. 2.

In addition to bottom-up processing, processing from a higher level to lower levels can occur. This downward flow of information can generate expectations to aid the lower-level abductions, question ambiguous data, and help determine the level of plausibility of higher-level hypotheses. By combining bottom-up and top-down processing, a layered abduction mechanism can generate a partial conclusion at one level to leverage further problem solving at the same level of inference as well as at neighboring levels.

To perform layered abduction, the knowledge necessary to solve the problem must be organized in such a way that the results at one layer can be used as input to another layer. For example, a medical expert system determines the cause of a disease based on the symptoms of the patient. The system might have a pathological (disease) hierarchy and an etiological (disease cause) hierarchy. The input is the set of patient symptoms. A first abduction would generate a disease or set of diseases to explain the symptoms. These diseases and perhaps other patient information become the input to be explained by a second abduction. This second abduction would use the etiological hierarchy to generate plausible hypotheses. This abduction explains why the patient contracted the disease by considering the patient's diseases along with the patient's medical history and other relevant patient information. In summary, the disease composite was created from the symptoms, and based on the diagnosis, the cause of the disease was ascertained. In speech recognition, layers might pertain to phonetic information, lexical information, and syntactic information. In natural language understanding, layers might pertain to syntax, semantics, pragmatics, and discourse.

Examples

This section will demonstrate the abductive algorithm by describing four different abductive systems in the areas of legal reasoning, speech recognition, theory evaluation, and natural language understanding. In order to keep the section brief, the examples are described at a high level.

PEYER: LEGAL REASONING

Peyer is a knowledge-based system that performs legal reasoning. The system (originally formulated by Thagard, *10*) is based on a court case involving California highway police officer Craig Peyer who was tried for the murder of Cara Knott on December 27, 1986. Knott was a woman that Peyer had pulled over the night of her death. During the trial, twenty-two women, all young and attractive, testified that they had been pulled over by Peyer. Furthermore, they testified that Peyer spoke with them longer than was necessary for just a ticket, and they were all pulled over near the stretch of road where Knott's body was found. The trial in San Diego ended in a hung jury on February 27, 1988.

Peyer is an abductive system that models findings and hypotheses to explain those findings. As with Thagard's implementation, hypothesis generation and instantiation are omitted with all of the case findings and hypotheses already present and the explanatory information and initial plausibility scores predetermined. Peyer has seventeen findings to explain and sixteen explanatory hypotheses. Hypotheses are divided into two categories: those reflecting innocence and those reflecting guilt. Both guilt and innocence hypotheses can offer to explain findings. Some findings have only a single hypothesis that can explain them, while others can be explained by both guilt and innocence hypotheses. In many cases, guilt and innocence hypotheses are incompatible. For instance, the hypothesis "Peyer killed Knott" is incompatible with "Someone other than Peyer killed Knott," but both hypotheses explain the finding "Knott was killed." All hypotheses are provided with an initial plausibility of "neutral" with the hopes that hypothesis interactions (expectations, implications, and incompatibilities) can allow the system to make progress in explaining the findings. The system is able to come to a quick explanation of the findings based on the various evidence, finding Peyer to be innocent because of enough "reasonable doubt." Peyer's real court case ended in a hung jury and Thagard's implementation ended with a decision leaning toward guilt. Details of the Peyer system can be found elsewhere (*14, 15*).

ARTREC: SPEECH RECOGNITION

ARTREC is a layered abduction articulatory recognition system (*15*). It takes microbeam pellet data (motions of the speaker's vocal tract) as input and attempts to infer what was spoken using two levels of abduction. The first level of abduction hypothesizes articulatory gestures (qualitative vocal tract motions) to explain individual and groups of motions found in the pellet data. Gestures such as "alveolar closure" represent phonetic events that arise during an utterance. ARTREC generates hypotheses based on cues from findings. For instance, the tongue tip being raised to the roof of the mouth would generate hypotheses for alveolar closure, "rhotization," and "frication," as found in the sounds "n" and "t," "r" and "s," respectively. Hypotheses are instantiated by using routine recognition, searching the various pellet data motions for expected motions. Knowledge that is instantiated includes the motions that each hypothesis can account for and hypothesis interactions of incompatibilities and expectations. Besides gestural hypotheses, ARTREC also generates "noise hypotheses" that can be used to explain some of the motions as random, spurious, or unintentional motions arising during the utterance. This process of hypothesis generation and instantiation will typically produce 150 to 200 gesture and noise hypotheses to be used to account for the motions of the given one-sentence utterance. The hypothesis composition process is run to generate the best explanation for the motions in terms of gestures, resulting in fifty to seventy-five accepted gesture and noise hypotheses.

Since articulatory gestures are not a satisfactory level of response, a second level of abduction takes place. Previously accepted gestures are now explained in terms of syllables. (Noise hypotheses accepted at the prior level are not passed on to this level.) For instance, the syllable "nine" consists of an alveolar closure followed by a motion of "tongue tip and blade lowering" and a final alveolar closure. If these three gestures have been accepted from the previous abduction and appear in this order and in close temporal proximity, then the hypothesis "nine" can be used to explain these motions. Again ARTREC performs a sequence of hypothesis generation (by cueing based on the previously accepted gestures), hypothesis instantiation, and hypothesis composition. Between fifty and seventy-five syllable and noise hypotheses are generated at this level. The result of this second abduction is an explanation composed to ten to twenty syllable and noise hypotheses that are used to account for the vocal tract motions of the original one-sentence utterance. The current version of ARTREC has only monosyllabic words in its lexicon, which makes an explanation in terms of syllables sufficient. Additional levels of abduction would be added if the final explanation were needed in a vocabulary of words or syntactic units.

The ARTREC system has a limited lexicon (approximately ten words) and simple grammar. (All utterances have the form "is it five nine five pine street? no its five nine nine pine street" with variations of five, nine, no, and yes being used.) It was tested on some 400 utterances from five different speakers. Most interesting were a series of experiments demonstrating different aspects of the abduction algorithm. Using a single-level abduction system that mapped motions directly to syllables resulted in a 90 percent word recognition accuracy. With layered abduction, accuracy improved to 94 percent. A "pessimistic" layered version was run in which only essential and clear-best hypotheses were accepted. This version yielded a 96 percent accuracy rate, although it only explained about two-thirds of the words. Finally, a pessimistic version was run with top-down processing in the form of expectations to help disambiguate processing at the first abduction level. This last version achieved an accuracy of 97 percent.

CREATIONISM VS. EVOLUTION: A THEORY EVALUATOR

Another layered abduction system was constructed, again based on an implementation from Thagard (*10*), that attempts to decide which of two theories, evolution or creationism, can better explain life on Earth. This system, the theory evaluator, expands on Thagard's implementation by including a greater number of findings and hypotheses (*16*). Similar to the Peyer system, all hypotheses, findings, explanatory information, and initial hypothesis plausibilities are programmed into the system. The system performs hypothesis composition only. Unlike the Peyer system, however, and like ARTREC, the theory evaluator performs two levels of abduction.

The system has twenty findings to be explained. In order to explain these findings, there is a set of nine "low-level" hypotheses. Some of these hypotheses are pro-evolution (e.g., "speciation," "extinction," and "natural selection"), some are pro-creationism ("God created all species roughly 10,000 years ago," "transition records of fossils contain inaccuracies"), and some are neutral (e.g., "all terrestrial life is related"). None of these hypotheses is specifically equivalent to either of the two theories. The result of the first hypothesis composition is a list of accepted hypotheses that best explain the given twenty findings. These in turn can then be explained by appealing to the two theories. A second hypothesis composition is performed and the theory that best explains the previously accepted hypotheses is selected.

There were four versions of the system, each using a different form of creationism with varying degrees of explanatory power. In two of the four cases, one based on nonscientific creationism, and one in which the age of life on Earth was used as a datum, evolution was the clear choice because evolution alone could plausibly explain a majority of findings about life on Earth, including that species have been noted to change (speciation) and die out (extinction). In a third run, the Bible was used as a source of evidence in favor of creationism. In this case, since there was clear evidence (the Bible) for the creationism theory, the choice was clearly for creationism even though it could not explain all of the hypotheses previously accepted (such as extinction), leading to a partially unexplained solution. The final version added a third theory, that God started the process of evolution. In this version, the system could not differentiate between the new theory and evolution because, based on explanatory coverage, they are essentially the same.

SAPI: UNDERSTANDING SEMANTICS AND PRAGMATICS IN NATURAL LANGUAGE

In the SAPI (semantic and pragmatic interpretation) system, layered abduction is used to perform natural language understanding within the domain of travel agency reservations (*17, 18*). The SAPI system has linguistic knowledge represented in the form of systemic grammar. (For a complete overview of systemic grammars, refer to

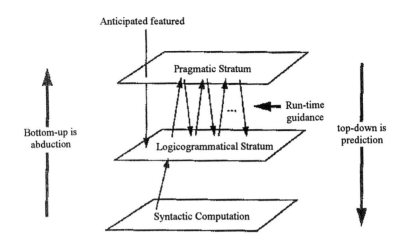

FIGURE 3. *Graphical view of layered abduction and top-down guidance for SAPI.*

Winograd, *19.*) The SAPI system uses two layers (referred to as strata): the *logicogrammatical stratum* used to create the semantic interpretation of a given sentence by using information about semantics, grammar, and some discourse; and the *pragmatic stratum* used to provide top-down guidance, to determine if the semantic interpretation previously generated is correct, and to create a pragmatic interpretation by using pragmatic and sociolinguistic information. Both strata represent linguistic knowledge in the form of classification hierarchies (or sets of hierarchies in the case of the logicogrammatical stratum), which are used as means of generating hypotheses, and realization rules, which define a mapping between the strata. See Figure 3 for a graphical view of SAPI.

The input to the system is the systemic grammar, a structural analysis of the sentence in question, and any anticipated logicogrammatical features.* These are all assumed to be correct. The anticipated features, the features in the logicogrammatical stratum that explain the structural analysis, the subconstituent features that are required by the aforementioned features, and the parents of all these features are added to the composite with a high degree of confidence.

The next step is to determine if any of the sociopragmatic features can account for a logicogrammatical feature in the composite. This is an example of bottom-up layered abduction, in which hypotheses at the lower level become findings to be explained at the higher level. If any such sociopragmatic feature is found, all of its preselections of logicogrammatical features are included in the composite. These new members of the composite have their status propagated through the logicogrammatical hierarchy and

---

*Features, whether logicogrammatical or pragmatic, are used as the hypotheses to form the explanation or interpretation of the input sentence.

the pragmatic stratum is again evaluated. When no sociopragmatic features can add to the explanation, processing returns to the logicogrammatical stratum.

The next step is to make decisions between competing siblings' features in the systemic grammar hierarchy. If one child is a default feature, it is put in the composite first. Default features are those that are assumed to be likely until proven otherwise. Whenever a feature is put into the composite, its realization rules are posted as constraints to be propagated. Realization rules define the structure of the sentence in terms of surface and deep roles. When an inconsistency occurs among these constraints, backtracking takes place, removing previously accepted features. Additional hypotheses are placed in the composite until a complete and consistent path is made through the logicogrammatical stratum, where completeness implies that a choice has been made for each system traversed and consistency implies that no realization rules conflict.

Top-down guidance from the pragmatic stratum to the logicogrammatical stratum is manifested in two forms: anticipatory guidance and run-time guidance. Anticipatory guidance represents the listener's expecations and is realized in the system by selecting expected pragmatic features and instantiating their associated logicogrammatical features at the beginning of processing. Run-time guidance, which occurs during processing as a result of accepting logicogrammatical features, is realized by having the pragmatic analyzer attempt to explain a partial semantic explanation and having the effects of the pragmatic level composite propagated down into the logicogrammatical stratum.

The SAPI system was tested on eleven sentences of varying complexity. It could create a complete and correct interpretation for each of the sentences with or without any top-down guidance. The computational implication of including top-down guidance was that anticipatory guidance caused a processing speedup in 94 percent of the experiments and run-time guidance caused a processing speedup in 56 percent of the experiments. The amount of speedup ranged from a very small fraction to 55 percent. In general, the more anticipatory knowledge available, the less difference the run-time guidance made. Also, in situations in which the top-down and bottom-up processing were in conflict, SAPI determined which was the more reliable source of information and included its features in the composite and discarded the unreliable source's features.

Conclusion

In this article, a domain- and problem-independent strategy for performing abduction has been shown. The strength of this strategy lies in its ability to combine local abductions to come to a global abduction. It is both tractable and highly useful. Further research has led to the development of other useful features such as layered abduction with top-down guidance and noise hypotheses. The result has been the creation of a number of disparate problem-solving systems, all based on the same strategy, yet all solving highly different problems. This article has described several abductive systems in an attempt to demonstrate the complete domain independence of the algorithm and its usefulness for solving perceptual problems.

REFERENCES

1. C. S. Peirce, "Abduction and Induction," in *Philosophical Writings of Peirce,* J. Buchler, ed., Dover, New York, 1955, pp. 150–156.
2. J. Josephson and S. Josephson, eds., *Abductive Inference: Computation, Philosophy, Technology,* Cambridge University Press, New York, 1994.
3. H. Pople, "The Formation of Composite Hypotheses in Diagnostic Problem Solving: An Exercise in Synthetic Reasoning," *Proceedings of IJCAI Five,* San Francisco, 1977, pp. 1030–1037.
4. J. Hobbs, M. Stickel, D. Appelt, and P. Martin, "Interpretation as Abduction." *AIJ.,* **63**(1-2), (1993).
5. J. Reggia, "Diagnostic Expert Systems Based on a Set Covering Model." *Internat. J. Man-Machine Stud.,* **19**, 437–460 (Nov. 1983).
6. V. Dasigi, *Word Sense Disambiguation in Descriptive Text Interpretation: A Dual-Route Parsimonious Covering Model,* Ph.D. thesis, University of Maryland, College Park, 1988.
7. S. Ahuja, *An Artificial Intelligence Environment for the Analysis and Classification of Errors in Discrete Sequential Processes,* Ph.D. thesis, University of Maryland at Baltimore County, Nov. 1985.
8. J. Reggia, "Virtual Lateral Inhibation in Activation Model of Associative Memory," *Proceedings of International Joint Conference on Artificial Intelligence,* San Francisco, 1985, pp. 244–248.
9. J. Pearl, "Distributed Revision of Composite Beliefs." *AI,* **33**(2), 173–215 (Oct. 1987).
10. P. Thagard, *Computational Philosophy of Science,* Bradford Books/MIT Press, 1988.
11. T. Bylander and S. Mittal, "CSRL: A Language for Classificatory Problem Solving and Uncertainty Handling." *AI Mag.,* **7**(3), 66–77 (Aug. 1986).
12. T. Bylander, T. Johnson, and A. Goel, "Structured Matching: A Task-Specific Technique for Making Decisions." *Knowl. Ac.,* **3**(1), 1–20 (1991).
13. R. Fox and J. Josephson, "Peirce: A Tool for Abductive Inference," *Proceedings of the Sixth International Conference on Tools with Artificial Intelligence,* IEEE Press, Los Alamitos, CA, Nov. 1994, pp. 571–577.
14. J. Josephson and R. Fox, "Peirce-IGTT: A Domain-Independent Problem Solver for Abductive Assembly," technical report, the Ohio State University, Columbus, OH, 1991.
15. R. Fox, *Layered Abduction for Speech Recognition from Articulation,* Ph.D. thesis, the Ohio State University, Columbus, OH, 1992.
16. R. Fox, J. Josephson, and B. Trusko, "Automated Theory Decision Making: A Case of Evolution vs. Creationism," technical report, Laboratory for Artificial Intelligence Research, the Ohio State University, Columbus, OH, 1992.
17. J. Hartigan, *Semantic and Pragmatic Parsing Based on Systemic Grammar and Layered Abduction,* Ph.D. thesis, the Ohio State University, Columbus, OH, 1994.
18. T. Patten, M. L. Geis, and B. Becker, "Toward a Theory of Compilation for Natural Language Generation." *Computa. Intell.,* **8**(1), (1992).
19. T. Winograd, *Language as a Cognitive Process,* Addison Wesley, London, 1983.

RICHARD FOX
JULIE HARTIGAN

THE CLIENT SIDE OF THE WORLD WIDE WEB

Introduction

By the mid-1990s, the World Wide Web (or simply the Web) became the most active part of the Internet. According to the National Science Foundation Network (NSFNET) backbone statistics, the Web moved into first place both in terms of the percentage of total packets moved (21%) and percentage of total bytes moved (26%) along the NSF backbone in the first few months of 1995. This placed the Web well ahead of the traditional Internet activity leaders, FTP (14%/21%) and Telnet (7.5%/2.5%), as the most popular Internet service.

Figure 1 plots the recent evolution of the Web, Gopher, and FTP as a percentage of overall network packet transmission and volume of information along the NSFNET backbone. This is the most recent data available since the NSFNET has subsequently changed to a distributed network architecture involving multiple network access points (NAPs).

The rapid escalation of Web use seems to be the result of at least three characteristics.

> The Web is an enabling technology. The Web was the first widespread network technology to extend the notion of a virtual network machine to multimedia. While the ability to execute programs on remote computers distributed throughout the digital networks was not new (e.g., Telnet), the ability to produce, distribute, and view multimedia on remote networked computers was new to the Web.

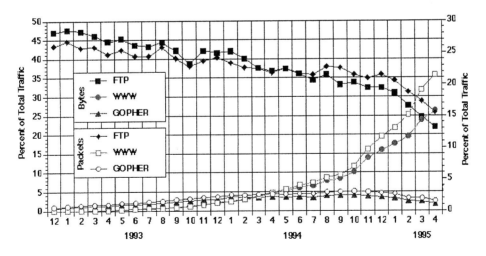

FIGURE 1. *Comparison of three popular Internet protocols by volume of information and number of packets transmitted along the NSFNET backbone. Comparison based on percentage of total. (Adapted from J. Pitkow, "GVU NSFNET Backbone Statistics," 1995.)*

The Web is a unifying technology. The unification came through the Web's accommodation of a wide range of multimedia formats. Since such audio (e.g., .WAV, .AU), graphics (e.g., .GIF, .JPG) and animation (e.g., MPEG) formats are all digital, they were already unified in desktop applications prior to the Web. The Web, however, unified them for distributed network applications. One Web "browser," as it later became called, would correctly render dozens of media formats regardless of network source.

The Web is a social phenomena. The Web social experience evolved in three stages. Stage one was the phenomena of Web "surfing." The richness and variety of Web documents and the novelty of the experience made Web surfing the de facto standard for curiosity-driven networking behavior in the 1990s. The second stage involved such Web interactive communication forums as the Internet relay chat (IRC), which provided a new outlet for interpersonal but not-in-person communication. The third stage, which is in its infancy as of this writing, involves the notion of virtual community. Neither the widespread popularity nor the social implications of such network-based interactive communication have been well documented at this writing.

Web Protocols

The Web is an application of the client-server model for networked computing systems that support Internet protocols. The client, to be discussed below, handles all of the interfacing with the computing environment and temporarily stores information for presentation to the user. The networked servers are the information repositories and hosts of the software required to handle requests from the client.

The Internet, a nearly ubiquitous collection of packet-switched digital networks, supports dozens of communications and networking protocols. Table 1 lists some of these protocols. The Web uses the protocol pair hypertext transfer protocol (HTTP) and hypertext markup language (HTML). The former establishes the basic handshaking procedures between client and server, while the latter defines the organization and structure of Web documents. At this writing, the current HTTP version is 1.0, while adoption of version 4.0 of HTML should take place by late 1998.

A typical Web client-server transaction would take place in a sequence similar to the following:

1. The client establishes a connection with a server identified by a uniform resource locator (URL) and passes information to the server.
2. The server sets the environment variables that identify the important parameters for the transaction [e.g., time/date stamp, Internet protocol (IP) number of the client and server). These variables are available for client and server use at any time during the transaction either as common gateway interface (CGI) program variables or as server-side includes (SSIs) in HTML documents.
3. The server passes any command line input or standard input that came from the client on to the appropriate CGI programs (if any).
4. The CGI programs on the server execute.
5. The CGI programs return output to the server (if any).
6. The server resets the environment variables for output.
7. The server sends output back to the client and closes the connection.
8. The client renders this output for the user.

TABLE 1

Brief Descriptions of Some Common Internet Protocols

PROTOCOL NAME (abbreviation/version or standard): DESCRIPTION

- Internet protocol (IP/IPv4): Basic communication (or data-delivery) protocol for packet-switched computer networks (e.g., Internet). IP pakcets prefix headers of at least 20 bytes, which specify source and destination IP addresses as well as format information, to the actual data. IP is a potentially lossy and verbose transmission protocol.

- Transmission control protocol (TCP/STD7): Protocol for ensuring reliable transmission of IP packets. TCP checks for lost or duplicate packets (alt: datagrams), requests retransmission of packets when required, and puts the packets back in order on receipt.

- Hypertext markup language (HTML/2.0): Protocol for implementing a simplified application of ISO standard 8879:1986 standard generalized markup language (SGML) for the Web. HTML defines the organization and structure of Web documents. HTML uses primitive ASCII "tagging" convention to define elements and features.

- Hypertext transfer protocol (HTTP/1.0): Transactions protocol for client-server communication on the Web .HTTP relies on TCP/IP for transport/routing across the Internet. HTTP is said to be a "generic" and "stateless" protocol, meaning, respectively, that it accommodates non-HTTP protocols (e.g., FTP) and disconnects client-server connection immediately after each transaction (vs. FTP and Telnet).

- Domain name system (DNS/STD14): Protocol for the implementation of a global distributed database on Internet servers which, collectively, map symbolic Internet names onto specific IP addresses. The client interface to DNS is a program called a "resolver," which traverses the DNS servers until it can return the appropriate address record to the client.

- File transfer protocol <ftp,RFC959): Platform-independent, command-response protocol for transferring files between computers. Initial client-server connection exchanges control information. Subsequent connection exchanges data in generic form.

- Telnet (Telnet/STD8): Interconnection protocol that establishes a remote client as a virtual extension of a server following the network virtual terminal (NVT) model. Both client and server behave as if connection is local, even though connection is via the Internet.

This defines the general case in which the client specifically requests information that must be computed from the server. In the much simpler case, in which the client only requests media on the server, steps 3 through 6 don't apply.

The connection that is established between client and server relies on the unique IP numeric addressing scheme. Each node of the Internet is currently identified by a four-byte address (e.g., 128.328.18.5), defining a total address space of $256**4 = 4,294,967,300$, which is rapidly becoming depleted because of the enormous popularity of the Internet and the Web. For convenience, the Internet has a domain name server (DNS) system which translates URLs into unique IP addresses. (See above.)

The networking aspects of Internet communications will not be dealt with here except to mention that the Internet's communications metaphor is packet switching (vs. the circuit-switching metaphor of basic telephony), which is managed by the Internet's communication software suite, transmission control protocol/Internet protocol (TCP/IP). Plans are currently underway to modify this suite to accommodate higher-bandwidth networking. The new communication protocol, Internet protocol next generation (IPNG), will extend the capabilities of the current IP version 4 to include packet tunneling (by which Internet paths to the destination are specified in the packets as well as the destination addresses), 128-bit IP addresses (eight 8-bit segments vs. the present four 8-bit segments), $2**32$ individual multicast addresses, and support of connection-oriented, asynchronous transfer mode (ATM) networks. This will bring about many changes in the use of the Internet early in the next century.

While many other Internet protocols (e.g., FTP, Gopher, network news transfer protocol—NNTP) have multiprotocol capability, only the native Web "killer" protocols (HTTP and HTML) have provided versatility and robustness sufficient to generate and retain the interest of large numbers of major media providers and software developers. As a result, in just a few years the Web has become the medium of choice for general-purpose network information exchange.

The Origins and Uses of the Web

The Web was conceived by Tim Berners-Lee and his colleagues in 1989 as a shared information space that would support collaborative work. Berners-Lee defined HTTP and HTML at that time. As a proof of concept prototype, Berners-Lee developed the first Web client navigator-browser in 1990 for the NeXTStep platform. Nicola Pellow developed the first cross-platform Web browser in 1991, while Berners-Lee and Bernd Pollerman developed the first server application—a phone book database. By 1992, interest in the Web was sufficient to produce four additional browsers—Erwise, Midas, and Viola for X Windows, and Cello for Windows. The following year, Marc Andreessen of the National Center for Supercomputer Application (NCSA) wrote Mosaic for X Windows, which soon became the browser standard against which all others would be compared. Andreessen went on to cofound Netscape Communications in 1994, whose current browser, Netscape Navigator, is the current de facto standard Web browser.

Despite the original design goal of supporting collaborative work, Web use has become highly variegated. The Web is now extended into an incredibly wide range of products and services offered by individuals and organizations, for commerce, education, entertainment, and even propaganda. A partial list of popular Web applications includes the following:

- Individual and organizational home pages
- Sales prospecting via interactive forms-based surveys
- Advertising and the distribution of product promotional material
- New product information, product updates, product recall notices
- Product support—manuals, techical support, frequently asked questions (faqs)
- Corporate record keeping—usually via local area networks (LANs) and intranets
- Electronic commerce made possible with the advent of several secure HTTP transmission protocols and electronic banking, which can handle small charges (perhaps at the level of millicents)
- Religious proselytizing
- Propagandizing
- Digital politics

Most Web resources at this writing are still set up for noninteractive, multimedia downloads. This will change in the next decade as software developers and Web content providers shift their attention to the interactive and participatory capabilities of the Internet, the Web and their successor technologies. For the moment, however, the dominant Web theme seems to remain static HTML documents, not infrequently augmented with arguably gratuitous animations and sound.

We observe that in the mid-1990s the Web environment was complemented in two important respects, first, with the development of "plug-ins," which behave in much the same way as spawnable perusers and players but which don't require the use of the browser launchpad, and second, with the advent of executable content made possible primarily by the Java development language, whose binary object modules are executable on the client directly from Java-enabled Web browsers. Not surprisingly, this latest extension, which involves executing foreign programs that have been downloaded across the networks, is not without security risk.

A Survey of Web Use

The first extensive reporting on Web use began with the first World Wide Web survey in January 1994, conducted by Jim Pitkow and his colleagues at the Graphics, Visualization and Usability (GVU) Center at Georgia Tech. These surveys continue to this day at six-month intervals, the latest of which is the sixth survey, which is summarized here.

The average age of Web users is 34.9 years, steadily increasing over the past few years from 32.7 years in the fourth survey. Approximately one-third of the users are female (31.4%), up from 5 percent for the first survey in 1994. Over half (56.1%) have college degrees, and 52.5 percent of all users have either computing or educational vocations. European users tend to be slightly more male (80.2%) and most likely to be in education or computing (68%). English remains the primary language of Web users (93%).

From the client's perspective, 66 percent of all Web users claim a Microsoft Windows client as their primary computing platform, followed by Macintosh (26%) and Unix (3.6%). Over half have monitors (1) at or above 800×600 resolution (53.4%), and (2) 15 inches or larger (53.9%). The majority of platforms (58.4%) support at least 16-bit color. In excess of 80 percent of the users surveyed indicated a preference for Netscape's browser, while 12.2 percent preferred Microsoft's Internet Explorer. Internet Explorer's 9 percent gain in market share from the previous survey corresponds to an equal loss in market share by Netscape during the same interval.

Direct Internet connections are still in the minority, with 71.6 percent of all Web users using modems with transmission speeds of 28.8 Kb/second or less.

Just 36.1 percent of users have begun their Web use in the past year, down from 43.1 percent, 60.3 percent, and 50.2 percent in the fifth, fourth, and third GVU surveys, respectively, reflecting the first-time Web utilization may have peaked. The fact that 42.4 percent have been using the Web for one to three years may signify a level of technology maturation. Most Web use now takes place in the home (63.6%), a

TABLE 2

Surveys of Adult Internet Use

Name and date of survey	Estimated Internet users
CommerceNet/Nielsen (1995)	37 million
Find/SVP	8.4 million
O'Reilly & Associates (1995)	5.8 million
Times/Mirror (1995)	25 million

significant increase over previous surveys. This suggests that the Web has achieved a significant level of acceptance and pervasiveness within the computer-use community. Primary Web use includes

- Browsing or "surfing" (77.1%)
- Entertainment (63.8%)
- Education (53.3%)
- Work (50.5%)
- Business research (41.6%)
- Academic research (35.7%)
- Shopping (18/8%)

Primary Web-related problems include

- Download delays (76.6%)
- Difficulty in locating known resources (34.1%)
- Organizing collected data (31.0%)
- Difficulty in revisiting known resources (13.4%)
- Expense of use (7.8%)

It should be emphasized that the GVU user-profile surveys are nonrandom and self-selecting, and their results should therefore be conservatively and cautiously interpreted. Random surveys of Web use have been conducted, however, but with mixed results. The data in Table 2 corroborate the difficulty inherent in producing reliable Internet use data from such random surveys. For further insight, see Hoffman, et al.

Client-Side Web Software

Client-side software for the Web remains primarily browser-centric. Web browsers provide the stability and evolutionary momentum to continue to bring together vendors of new multimedia perusers and executable content. This trend began in 1994 with the advent of so-called helper apps, multimedia perusers and players that could be spawned via the Web browser's built-in program launchpad. By year's end most Web browsers included generic launchpads that spawned prespecified multimedia players based on the filetype/file extent (.WAV designated MS Window's audio file, .QT designated Quicktime, etc.).

The generic launchpad was a significant technological advance for two reasons. First, it decoupled the evolutionary paths and hence the development paces of browsers and multimedia. The first multimedia Web browsers relied entirely on internal media perusers, thereby creating a bottleneck as the pace of the development of new multimedia formats exceeded that of the internal perusers. By decoupling, both browser and multimedia developers could advance independently without fear of incompatibility.

Second, generic launchpads spawn external processes that execute independently of the Web browser and hence render the multimedia in an external window. This process independence discourages the development of helper apps that are proprietary to a particular browser, which led to the rapid growth of freeware, shareware, and commercial helper apps that are now available for popular client platforms. That the helper apps could be used in isolation of the browser became a collateral advantage for easy perusal of local multimedia files as well.

This generic, browser-independent approach toward rendering multimedia would be challenged twice in 1996 by plug-ins and by "executable content."

Plug-ins (or add-ons), as the name implies, are external applications that extend the browser's built-in capability for rendering multimedia files. Unlike helper apps, however, plug-ins render the media "inline"; that is, within the browser's window in the case of video, or with simultaneous presentation in the case of audio. In this way the functionality of the plug-in is seamlessly integrated with the operation of the browser. Plug-ins are proprietary and browser-specific because of this tight integration. Some of the more popular current plug-in technologies are Web telephony, virtual reality and 3D players, and real-time (or "steaming") audio and video.

Executable content continues the theme of tight integration between multimedia peruser and browser, but with a slight twist. In the case of executable content, the multimedia and the peruser are one; that is, an enabled browser will download the executable files that render the multimedia and execute them as well, all within the browser's own workspace on the client. The practical utility of having both media and player in one executable file stimulated the rapid development of this technology despite growing concerns for security.

Since in theory at least foreign executables may be malevolent as well as benevolent, well-behaved executable content binaries are "hobbled" to prevent malevolent programs from achieving client-side execution. By early 1997, however, security breaches of executable content-enabled browsers were still being routinely reported. While there are several competing paradigms for Web-oriented executable content, including JavaScript, Telescript, and ActiveX, the cross-platform language Java was the clear environment of choice in early 1997.

Search Engines and Information Overload

By the mid-1990s, an ever-increasing array of available Web resources began to work against efficient access in a significant way. By mid-decade, the number of Web

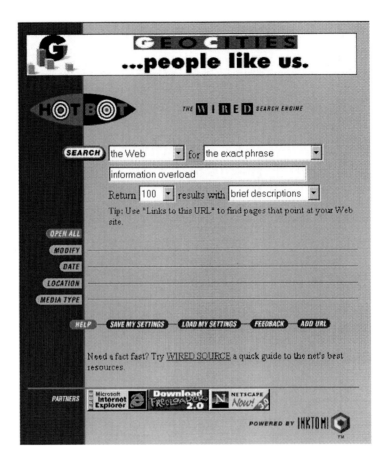

FIGURE 2. *The interface of one of the more advanced current search engines, HotBot. This search produced 54,466 matches.*

sites indexed by the popular search engines approached 100 million, thereby flooding the Web with a veritable tidal wave of information. Information overload—having to deal with more information than one could comfortably process—became a Web reality.

At this writing, there are more than 125 search engines (see Fig. 2) available to Web users, each with its own search characteristics. A recent addition to the Web has been the "metalevel" search engine, which utilizes several other search engines to locate the information. There are also special-purpose indexing tools that categorize Web resources (as a home page, by document type, etc.).

In operation, search engines behave like the search utility in a typical desktop productivity tool. Most search engines support Boolean queries through an interface that is built around a CGI form. Typically this involves passing the query parameters from the form to the server as a CGI query_string variable. The server then searches the index database and reports matches to the user in the form of a dynamically created HTML document. This index is produced by the server's network indexer, which utilizes a variety of utilities for traversing the Web in search of indexable (if not always useful) information (e.g., spiders, wanderers, crawlers, ants, and robots).

The strength of today's powerful search engines actually works against their successful deployment. The exponential growth of the Web (as measured in terms of clients connected, number of sites, and number of files) has produced a great deal of information that is of little utility or long term benefit to the overwhelming majority of Web information consumers. The Web now consists of an enormous number of vanity homepages, narrow-interest documents, and insubstantial and inaccurate information resources which inhibit productive searching. The most efficient searching would result if the Web's resources were indexed, graded and carefully categorized as they were being posted. But such prescriptivism runs counter to the Web philosophy of fostering an open, uninhibited, free exchange of information, it is unlikely to ever take hold.

Thus, while search engines may achieve some additional effectiveness by refining their indexing behavior through careful document parsing integrated with full use of the HTML <META> and <TITLE> tags, the free-wheeling spirit behind Web resource development will likely prevent search engines, as they are now designed, from ever becoming reliable, stand-alone Web information retrieval tools.

Future Information-Retrieval Enhancements

Information retrieval tools which can mitigate against the problem of information overload may be categorized broadly by the nature of their computing host—server-side or client-side. We illustrate these categories of tools with an example of each.

One server-side approach that holds great promise is information agency. "Agents" (also known as software robots, softbots, and bots) are computer programs that roam the Internet on behalf of an owner, ferreting information and taking actions as situations warrant. If such agents are competent and trustworthy, they may free the owner from much of the actual navigation and searching involved in locating Web resources.

Information agents of many types are currently being deployed for the location, manipulation, monitoring, and transmission of a variety of Web and Internet resources. They operate within several Internet protocols. If current research is successful, it is entirely possible that information agency will be one of the major growth industries in network computing by the turn of the century.

While there is nothing to prevent agents from being deployed on the client, there seems to be a general feeling that it is wise to do as much screening as possible on the servers in order to diminish the volume of information reported to the user and to minimize bandwidth drain on the networks. As a result, server-side agency is predominant at the moment.

One proposed enhancement for the client side is information customization. As we use the term, information customization has five basic characteristics: (1) it is always performed on the client side, (2) it is specifically designed to maximize information uptake rather than filter or retrieve, (3) it "personalizes" documents by such techniques as extraction, (4) it is never done autonomously, and (5) the capability of nonprescriptive, nonlinear document traversal is always added by the software—that is, for the specific user. Condition 2 sets information customization apart from traditional information filtering and retrieval, while 4 would set it apart from client-side agency and 5 would distinguish it from traditional nonlinear document traversal systems (e.g., hypertext).

Information customization software as envisioned here would make it possible for users to "speed read" documents through nonlinear traversal in much the same way as with hypertext, but with information customization, the nonlinearity would be nonprescriptive—that is, added for the user by the client software rather than by the information provider at the time that the document is created. Prototypes of information customization clients integrate with Web browsers as well as other desktop applications and are document format-independent.

Push-Phase Information Access

Typically Web information access is "pull-phase," meaning that the information is sought after by the user. The navigation through cyberspace by URL is a paradigm case of pull-phase access. During 1996 several experiments in "puch-phase" access were undertaken.

Push-phase or, more properly, "solicited" push-phase access, involves the connection of clients to netcasting network information providers. As one example, Pointcast (www.pointcast.com) users connect to a central digital "transmitter" that connects the end user to a variety of different information feeds (Reuters, Business Wire, *People* magazine, etc.) integrated on Pointcast's server. On the client side, the Pointcast peruser operates as an autonomous window providing downloaded information from selected feeds. Pointcast follows in the tradition of the cable television industry by consolidating and distributing information (including advertising) from one distribution source to many subscribers.

Marimba Corporation's (www.marimba.com) approach to solicited push, however, is quite different. Here an analogy with direct broadcast television satellite systems is closer. Marimba's proprietary client-server software, Castanet, allows the end user to connect to an arbitrary number of third-party server transmitters from the client side. The connection between a Castanet client "tuner" and each of the Castanet server transmitters is called a "channel." In basic terms the channel amounts to network access to some server's file structure. Where Pointcast may be thought of as a 1:many network transmitter, Castanet would be many:many. An illustration of Castanet appears in Fig. 3.

Push-phase information access is an interesting extension of the Web because it is the first Web application that departs from the browser-centric model, where the Web browser either spawns other applications or runs the application as an extension of itself. Both Pointcast and Castanet are browser-independent. Castanet is the most supervenient with respect to the browser in that each channel application (1) performs

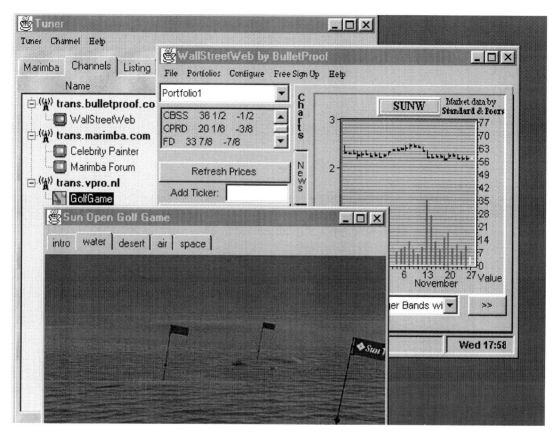

FIGURE 3. *Marimba's Castanet Client. Note three channels are established, the first and third of which are active in separate windows. Interactivity between client and server is automatic and autonomous for each channel.*

autonomous local processing, (2) enjoys persistent, client-resident storage, and (3) updates both data and program upgrades differentially, by sending only those files that are new or have been changed. Castanet differential updating is client-initiated (vs. Pointcast), which facilitates authorized transmission through server firewalls. Castanet is both a significant and robust departure from the browser-centric approach to client connectivity. (Exactly the opposite was true of the short-lived Java-enhanced browser, Hot Java.)

At this writing, Netscape, Marimba, and Pointcast have announced plans to collaborate on meta-push technology that will integrate all three technologies and services in a common intranet client, Constellation. If successful, this technology should be well entrenched by the end of this century.

Conclusion

The overwhelming popularity of the Web produced development of client-side Web products at a breathless pace in the 1990s. This caused a race-for-features competition between browser developers that became known as the "browser war." It is interesting to note that the early, pioneering Web browsers, Erwise, Midas, Viola, and Cello were early casualties of the war. Even Mosaic, the Web browser that made the Web viable, lost its leadership role by 1994 when rival Netscape offered a succession of more feature-rich freeware alternatives. According to the GVU Web surveys, Mosaic went from a 97 percent market share in January 1994 to less than 3 percent two years later. This illustrates just how unforgiving the Web audience is regarding perceived technology deficiencies in their Web browsers. It also illustrates that product life cycles can be very short in cyberspace. At this writing, the Web browser market is dominated by Netscape, with a secondary presence held by Microsoft's Internet Explorer.

Although Web browser technology is mature, it remains in a state of flux as new Internet and Web technologies (e.g, plug-ins, push-phase access tools, integrated e-mail) are put forth. This will continue for the foreseeable future as additional media formats and applications are seen as useful complements to the Web experience. In the main, Web browsers have converged on HTML 3.2 and HTTP 1.0 compliance, differing primarily in terms of the nature of the extensions beyond those standards that they seek to implement. Even desktop "office suites" (e.g., Microsoft Office, Lotus SmartSuite, Corel Office Professional) are now HTML- and executable content-enabled.

Although not covered here because of the browser-centricity of client-side Web software, it should be mentioned that scores of other Web utilities exist for the client side. These include but are not limited to browser enhancers and accelerators, which employ "look-ahead" download strategies, Internet fax utilities, off-line browsers and automated downloaders, client-side search utilities (vs. server-side search utilities, covered above), and Web site backup tools.

There is no question that the enormous popularity of the Web will continue in the near term. The commercial potential of the Web will also continue, encouraging even more innovation. Much of that innovation will take place on the client side as developers seek to market these tools to the burgeoning numbers of computer users.

BIBLIOGRAPHY

Berghel, H., "Dealing with Information Overload." *Commun. ACM,* **40**(2), 19–24 (Feb. 1997).

Berghel, H., "The Client Side of the Web." *Commun. ACM,* **39**(1), 30–40 (Jan. 1996).

Berleant, D. and H. Berghel, "Customizing Information." *IEEE Computer,* part 1—**27**(9), 76–78 (Sept. 1994); part 2—**27**(10), 76–78 (Oct. 1994).

Berners-Lee, T., "WWW: Past, Present and Future." *Computer,* **29**(10), 67–77 (Oct. 1996).

Comer, D., *Internetworking with TCP/IP,* vol. 1, 3rd ed., Prentice Hall, Englewood Cliffs, NJ, 1995.

Internet Protocol Next Generation, Internet Engineering Task Force, for current status see: http://www.ietf.cnri.reston.va.us/html.charters/ipngwg-charter.html and http://playground.sun.com/pub/ipng/html/ipng-main.html.

Hoffman, D., W. Kalsbeek, and T. Novak, "Internet and Web Use in the U.S." *Commun. ACM,* **39**(12), 37–46 (Dec. 1996).

NSFNET Backbone Traffic Distribution Statistics, April 1995, http://www.cc.gatech.edu/gvu/stats/NSF/merit.html.

Pitkow, J et al. "GVU's WWW User Surveys," online at http://www.cc.gatech.edu/gvu/user_surveys/.

Pitkow, J., "GVU NSFNET Backbone Statistics," URL = http://www.cc.gatech.edu/gvu/stats/NSF/merit.html/e (1995).

Wellman, B. and M. Gulia, "Net Surfers Don't Ride Alone: Virtual Communities as Communities," in *Communities in Cyberspace*, P. Kollock and M. Smith, eds., University of California Press, Berkely (1998); digital preprint at http://www.acm.org/~ccp/references/wellman/wellman.html/.

HAL BERGHEL

COLLECTING HUMAN RIGHTS EVIDENCE: A MODEL FOR ARCHIVAL COLLECTION DEVELOPMENT

By conservative estimates, the twentieth century has witnessed more than 170 million murdered by state action, excluding soldiers killed in war (*1*). The scale of government atrocities has been almost beyond comprehension and seemingly beyond control. Since the fall of Nazi Germany, appalling violations of human rights and humanitarian law have continued unabated throughout the world—in the Soviet and Chinese gulags, in the killing fields of Cambodia, Rwanda, and the former Yugoslavia, and in many other countries in which millions have perished under brutal regimes. These events have occurred despite the adoption of numerous protocols, resolutions, treaties, agreements, and other international instruments on behalf of human rights by the global community. This era of worldwide violence and genocide has represented one of humanity's darkest hours. Commentators and scholars have termed this epoch the "century of genocide," nevertheless, in response to the plague of violence, this century has also seen the rise of a historically unprecedented global movement on behalf of human rights and humanitarian law, which has left in its wake an extraordinary trail of uncollected primary evidence.

The recorded memory of the international human rights movement depends on the collection of this archival evidence. The global human rights movement consists of thousands of nongovernmental organizations that act to investigate and publicize violations in order to compel governments to comply with international law and recognized norms of human rights. In essence they serve as investigators of crime, compilers of evidence, disseminating agents of information, and in the end, recorders of memory regarding victims and perpetrators of atrocities. Human rights organizations also draft and lobby on behalf of new human rights instruments in international and regional forums, assist in developing new civil institutions in fragile emerging democracies, and provide legal and medical assistance to victims of human rights abuses. Most important, they act to hold governments and the international community accountable to their own laws, constitutions, and agreements in the face of indifference, selectivity, and self-interest.

These actions have served to discredit the frequent claim by governments that the treatment of their own citizens is an internal affair and of no concern to the international community. As a result, the world has witnessed a remarkable occurrence—the gradual erosion of sovereignty and the inviolability of borders in favor of growing insistence on international scrutiny and humanitarian intervention in cases concerning the most extreme abuses. In addition, the emerging recognition of the centrality of human rights in formulating peaceful settlements of armed conflict has reflected a growing consensus that such principles are critical to a stable and secure world order. Despite the dangerous challenges in the rise of "exclusionary" ideologies and the quest for ethnic, linguistic, and religious "purity" manifested in brutal intolerance and mass bloodshed, the human rights movement is gaining momentum. These developments in global human rights affairs, therefore, make the acquisition of primary evidence regarding one the most profound sociopolitical movements and issues of the twentieth century a necessary endeavor.

This documentation enterprise, however, requires an analysis or taxonomy for viewing the global human rights movement and formulating a collection strategy with which to delineate the universe of human rights groups. More than 1,000 human rights organizations exist in the United States and Canada alone, and thousands more operate worldwide. Rather than a homogenous movement, however, the international human rights movement encompasses a constellation of differing causes, goals, ideologies, and constituencies with sometimes contradictory functions and purposes. These circumstances pose difficulties in discerning how many such organizations exist and the nature of their actions. A series of human rights directories published by the Human Rights Internet, however, offer a starting point for ascertaining the vast array of these groups. The North American directory delineates more than a 1,000 human rights groups in the United States and Canada. The Western Europe directory lists almost 1,400, and the Third World directory more than 600. Numerous groups are not listed, however, for fear of retribution. In compiling the directories, the editors have emphasized human rights organizations that act in the international arena, thus excluding the numerous civil groups in the United States, Canada, and Europe (2).

The Internet directories, however, provide only a listing of international human rights groups, offering little analysis on the international human rights movement. In addition, although the scholarly literature regarding human rights is large, few articles contain critical analyses on the significant contributions of international human rights organizations (3). This absence stems largely from the paucity of archival evidence in research universities and other educational institutions, and illustrates the danger to the historical record when significant materials on leading worldwide social and political movements remain uncollected. A few scholars, however, have conducted extensive studies on human rights nongovernmental organizations, including Laurie S. Wiseberg, Henry Scoble, and Lowell W. Livezey. These analyses provide an important conceptual framework by which to view and interpret human rights groups and thus to develop a rational collecting scope and strategy (4).

Nongovernmental Organizations: Exclusive and Nonexclusive

International human rights organizations may be classified according to their "exclusive" or "nonexclusive" nature concerning activities in the human rights arena. Several groups, including Amnesty International, the International Commission of Jurists, and Human Rights Watch, are devoted solely to promoting and defending worldwide norms of human rights conduct. These organizations consider autonomy from government affiliation or influence essential to their credibility, nevertheless, their work is inherently political since they lobby governments and the international community to curb violations of human rights and humanitarian law. Exclusive human rights organizations routinely monitor the actions of governments and armed groups and seek to curb violations of human rights through fact finding and disseminating information to the world community. Their credibility therefore rests largely in nonpartisanship, in objective and verifiable fact finding, and in the integrity of applying international human rights standards. Although these elite groups compose a small minority of the international human rights movement, they wield considerable influence on the world stage, constitute its core, and set the agenda for the movement as a whole (5).

The nonexclusive segment of the internatonal human rights movement comprises many more numerous and diverse organizations that also devote substantial resources to the promotion and defense of human rights and humanitarian law. These various groups include trade unions, religious institutions, professional associations, women's organizations, civil rights groups, political organizations, refugee groups, single-issue and policy groups, ethnically based and ideological entities, solidarity groups, organizations concerned with the elderly, children, the handicapped, and the poor, and other similar organizations. While serving as important proponents of human rights, these organizations encompass a range of other interests, thus human rights issues constitute an important but not exclusive part of their activities (6). The most active nonexclusive groups tend to be international professional associations whose members and interests span national borders. In the past fifteen to twenty-five years, especially during the Cold War, these associations established human rights committees to monitor the treatment of foreign colleagues. The American Bar Association, for example, established a committee on international human rights to work on behalf of colleagues suffering from political repression or other forms of degradation. The legal profession has become actively involved in providing assistance regarding legal defenses, filing writs of habeas corpus, preparing amicus curiae briefs, sending observers to public trials, training villagers or indigenous peoples in their rights, and offering advice to individuals with little or no access to legal resources. The Committee on Scientific Freedom and Human Rights instituted by the American Statistical Association also seeks to curb persecution of colleagues and provides opportunities for staticians to give assistance to human rights groups and policy makers. In the literary field, the International Association of Poets, Editors, Essayists, Playrights, and Novelists (PEN) supports writers silenced or imprisoned by repressive regimes by mobilizing world opinion on their plight, providing assistance, and writing to government officials. PEN also on occasion sends representatives abroad to obtain information on imprisoned writers (7).

The science and medical fields also have acted in strong support of international human rights. The Human Rights Committee of the Academy of Sciences has campaigned vigorously on behalf of overseas colleagues. In the 1970s and 1980s the committee became involved in cases of repression concerning the former Soviet Union, Chile, Syria, and China. During this same period, the Science and Human Rights unit of the American Association for the Advancement of Science denounced human rights violations of South African medical professionals and Latin American technicians. In addition, the medical and scientific professions have provided some of the most vitally important services pertaining to the gathering of forensic evidence, identifying remains of victims, and reuniting families through genetic analysis. Forensic anthropologists have assisted in identifying the remains of the "disappeared" in Argentina and gathered forensic evidence in the former Yugoslavia and Rwanda for war crimes tribunals, as well as performed other investigative work regarding those murdered by state action or by armed groups. Physicians and others in the medical community have strongly lobbied against the use of medicine for purposes of torture and provided treatment for victims of human rights abuse (8).

Most human rights groups in the United States and overseas focus on domestic political and civil liberties in their own countries. In the United States, these groups are typified by the American Civil Liberties Union, the National Urban League, the National Organization for Women, the National Association for the Advancement of Colored People, and B'nai B'rith. Although these organizations formed in response to specific conflict situations, they have since pursued other activities and issues beyond their original mandates in an attempt to further democratic pluralism. Although always active in the domestic arena, these groups have only marginally become involved in international human rights. Because these groups advance civil and political rights in their own societies they comprise part of the larger human rights field. The international community has broadly recognized and codified the principle that civil and political rights are inextricably part of human rights under the United Nation's Universal Declaration of Human Rights and other worldwide agreements and instruments. The fundamental difference between civil rights and human rights organizations is that the former focus on their own societies while the latter act specifically in the international arena. Both types of organizations seek to secure the rights of the individual against state abuse and work on the principle that governments must be held accountable to their own laws and constitutions (9).

Another nonexclusive category includes solidarity groups that support the human rights of co-religionists, ethnic nationals, or others in a particular overseas country. In North America and Europe numerous groups have arisen to monitor human rights in many countries throughout the world. Labor unions also have played an important role in promoting the rights of workers overseas to organize freely, to bargain collectively, and to improve health and safety conditions (10).

Both exclusive and nonexclusive organizations have played influential roles in international human rights affairs. As political actors, however, they have pursued different aims. Although they may join forces regarding particular issues, nonexclusive organizations typically work on behalf of members or constituents. Exclusive groups, however, promote the rights for all members of society. In addition, while nonexclusive organizations largely promote their own interest and programs, major exclusive organizations are more nonpartisan in nature and focus on advancing democratic pluralism among all legitimate forces.

Nongovernmental Organizations: Rights of Democratic Governance and Rights of the Person

The human rights movement also may be classified according to groups concerned primarily with rights of democratic governance and political freedom and those concerned largely with the rights of the security of the person, such as the right not to be tortured, arbitrarily detained, or killed. The rights of individual security have not only been the focus of leading "exclusive" U.S. human rights groups, but also of many liberal Protestant and Catholic agencies, religious orders, the National Council of Churches (NCC), and other secular and religious agencies. Although these groups also seek political freedom for societies suffering under repressive conditions, their main goal is to deter extralegal killings, torture, disappearances, arbitrary detention, and other egregious forms of human rights violations directed against individuals or whole groups. Human rights organizations that advocate on behalf of political freedom primarily focus on the extent that citizens can freely participate in the political process, including the ability to associate, speak, and disseminate information without retribution. These organizations tend to view the rights of individual security as a logical extension of democratic pluralism and fundamental civil liberties (*11*).

This analysis provides insight concerning how both types of organizations fell on opposite sides of the political divide of American foreign policy during the Cold War. International human rights groups concerned with individual security rights often investigated and publicized the atrocities of right-wing military regimes in Latin America allied with the U.S. government. Because of American attempts to curb Soviet influence, the reporting of these violations of human rights frequently clashed with U.S. foreign policy, sometimes prompting considerable criticism from White House officials. In the 1980s, the reporting of human rights atrocities in El Salvador provoked charges from the Reagan administration that the human rights community was deliberately exaggerating the extent of abuses to undermine U.S. foreign policy (*12*). In such cases, however, human rights reporting stemmed primarily from attempts to curb ongoing atrocities rather than from political or ideological motives to discredit the American government. Prior to the move toward democratic pluralism in Latin America, these military regimes constituted the main perpetrators of state-sponsored human rights abuses on a continuing basis, thus these organizations responded more to the violent nature of government-sponsored human rights abuses and the frequency with which they occurred (*13*).

On the other side of the political spectrum, organizations concerned primarily with civil and political rights focused their activities largely on the communist regimes of the former east bloc and the Soviet Union. These activities both complemented and supported U.S. foreign policy. Although many of these human rights groups possessed varying political ideologies and mandates, they held mostly a unified view in seeing the Soviet bloc's totalitarian nature as profoundly antithetical to the fundamental principles of democratic pluralism, universal sufferage, open elections, freedom of speech and association, and independent media. During this time, numerous major Jewish organizations actively campaigned on behalf of co-religionists in the former Soviet Union, which officially denied religious and cultural rights and freedom of movement to the Jewish population. Other organizations formed to support the rights of Soviet Pentacostals, Christians, scientists, writers, dissidents, and others suffering under repressive state policies. Although many human rights groups and others worked on behalf of political freedom in numerous countries throughout the world, the predominate focus was on the Soviet bloc. As a result, the activities of these organizations considerably helped to legitimize U.S. foreign policy objectives regarding the Soviet Union (*14*).

Selection Criteria

These two systems of classifying human rights organizations provide a fundamental basis from which to formulate a collecting scope and strategy. The formulation of collection criteria should be based on two primary considerations: first, whether the primary focus should be on organizations that have common goals or mandates or whether materials should be collected from a cross-sampling of groups with varying ideologies and strategies; and second, whether or not collecting parameters should encompass groups that also focus on U.S. domestic issues in addition to international concerns. These issues should be addressed by defining both a collecting field and priorities according to the following criteria: (1) that the primary focus should encompass U.S.-based organizations that promote international human rights; (2) that priority should be given to core elite groups such as Human Rights Watch or Amnesty International over less prominent groups; (3) that emphasis should be given to groups that act to support political freedom and civil liberties overseas; and (4) that consideration should be given to acquiring materials that document human rights issues pertaining to other countries, regions, and political systems throughout the world.

This collection field therefore includes organizations that advance and defend international human rights and excludes the numerous domestic advocacy and civil rights groups. Although civil rights groups are vitally important in the domestic arena, they have peripheral significance to international human rights affairs. This scheme also places low priority on labor unions, the records of which are already being collected by numerous archival institutions. In addition, this collecting field also excludes groups that support the international recognition of social and cultural rights, since their activities tend to be considerably more limited in scope in comparison to more influential organizations.

Because exclusive organizations comprise the vanguard of the movement and wield the most influence, these groups should constitute first priority for any collecting strategy documenting the international human rights movement. Furthermore, since the concern of international human rights groups span numerous issues and individual cases, their records will provide a broad representation of human rights and political issues throughout the world. At the same time, these elitist or core groups largely represent one facet of the movement, pertaining mostly to rights of individual security.

Other groups that have focused on the medical and legal aspects, political rights, religious entities, single-issue and solidarity groups, and others that have developed special expertise should also be given significant attention. In many cases, the records of these organizations provide the most precise data or evidence regarding particular human rights issues. Elite organizations, including Amnesty International and Human Rights Watch, sometimes consult smaller human rights groups that have expertise on specific issues or cases. Because these smaller organizations have often intensely focused on a single cause and have become an authoritative source on specific issues, their records have considerable documentary value (15). The Union of Councils for Soviet Jews, which organized on behalf of freedom of emigration and religion for co-religionists, acted primarily as a single-issue entity for more than thirty years. During this time, the organization compiled a vast array of materials on the subject, and served as one of the most authorative sources on the issue to the U.S. government, the international community, and other groups before the collapse of the Soviet Union (16). Many other single-issue organizations have developed expertise on a range of other human rights issues. Archival institutions therefore need to formulate collecting strategies based on analyzing groups according to specific issues and the extent of influence that these single-issue nongovernmental organizations have wielded in international relations.

Designing a collecting field pertaining to human rights should thus consider organizations concerned with the security of the person as well as groups that primarily support the right of democratic governance overseas. This approach also will cover elite organizations that focus on human rights exclusively as well as those that work on behalf of this issue part-time. The mandates of these various types of organizations may overlap since there can be no political rights without basic guarantees of the security of the individual. Within this collecting field, nongovernmental organizations should be ranked regarding their international prestige and influence, the significance of the issues they support, and the effectiveness of their campaigns and strategies. This approach will provide archival programs with a fundamental starting point with which to view the human rights field and define an effective acquisitions strategy. Furthermore research concerning the mandates and strategies of individual rights groups will provide significant supplementary information in determining priorities for a successful archival collection program.

Critical Issues of Concern

The issue of sensitive information represents the primary concern for international human rights organizations considering the archiving of materials. In conducting investigations and overseas missions, human rights groups derive information from various confidential sources, including informants, relatives of victims, and other contacts. Because of the sensitive nature of prisoner dossiers and confidential sources, human rights organizations have considerable concern that releasing such information may endanger the lives of victims and survivors of egregious human rights violations, their relatives, descendants, and informants. Political conditions in many countries remain volatile, fragile democracies may collapse or revert to totalitarian systems, and military coups, new dictatorships, and other changing political conditions may put past victims of human rights violations and their descendants at substantial risk. These realities make it imperative that highly sensitive material be restricted for lengthy periods to protect individuals and sources from exposure and retribution; nevertheless, the necessity for these closure provisions can be balanced with appropriate access provisions, including the use of screening application procedures to ensure the availability of confidential materials to legitimate and serious scholars and researchers during the restriction period. This petition procedure should include requirements for applicants to provide academic references, an abstract of the proposed research project, and other identifying information that can be verified. Within the closure period, the access process should be based on submitting applicant data to an information screening committee either at the institution housing the materials if the collection has been donated, or directly to the human rights organization if the materials have been placed on deposit. In either case, with appropriate guidelines the screening committee can determine whether or not to grant access. Although such screening procedures may raise the spectre of bias in granting access, it provides a workable method of availability to material that would otherwise remain closed during the designated restriction period. After the closure period expires, however, the materials would be opened to public scrutiny without qualification.

Another issue requiring consideration concerns whether to base negotiations for human rights materials on gift or deposit arrangements. Because international human rights nongovernmental organizations have an acute concern regarding sensitivity of information, negotiations based on deposit arrangements have already been shown to help alleviate doubts about archiving material with external archival institutions, thus if gift arrangements appear problematic, deposit agreements should be negotiated providing organizations with the right to retain ownership over their materials with the option of later transferring title to them. Deposit agreements embody both advantages and disadvantages. One disadvantage is that archival institutions assume the risk of expending considerable time, labor, and funds to acquire, process, conserve, store, promote, and provide reference services to collections that may have only transitory status if an organization later decides to withdraw its collection. Although a deposit agreement may include a protection measure providing for remuneration for costs incurred if the depositing organization decides to withdraw its materials, this measure constitutes no guarantee that such removal will not occur. Even with these disadvantages, deposit agreements have been in standard use as legal instruments in the archival profession for many years, and depositors rarely tend to void these agreements without good cause. In this sense, deposit agreements tend to impose discipline on the host institution to abide by the deposit agreement's terms and conditions. Furthermore, when dealing with human rights organizations, deposit agreements often pose the only way to acquire and preserve these materials, thereby making them accessible for scholarly research.

Although sensitivity issues represent the main impediment to acquiring archival material relating to international human rights affairs, these concerns continue after the acquisition of such records. The collection of this evidence, however, is important, as it contains significant data concerning human rights in various regions and political systems in the world, and the responses of nongovernmental organizations, the international community, and official international human rights bodies to curb violence and further democratic governance. Furthermore, the imposition of access restrictions for designated time periods is common practice within the archival profession to protect confidential information. Although donor agreements also may typically include access restrictions, many nongovernmental organizations exhibit acute concern regarding transferring title to their archival materials. Deposit agreements therefore provide a critical and legitimate alternative by assuring human rights organizations a continuing and ultimately controlling interest in their files. These terms have been shown to help alleviate sensitivity concerns and have proved successful in convincing several major international human rights nongovernmental organizations to deposit their archives with external institutions (*17*).

Human Rights and Contemporary World Affairs

The legacy of human rights has taken a new turn with the collapse of the Soviet Union and the end of the Cold War. In place of the Cold War has risen a new, albeit more chaotic, world order. Although many nations have moved toward accepting democratic pluralism and respect for human rights, others have fractured along ethnic, religious, and lingustic hatreds. Through the mass killings in Rwanda and Bosnia, the world has witnessed the return of genocide as a political solution, different in nature, but reminiscent of the killing fields of Cambodia. Despite the attempts to curb the tide of worldwide violence and promote democratic pluralism, international human rights organizations are at a loss over how to respond to genocide; nevertheless, investigators human rights groups continue to serve as witnesses and recorders of memory regarding international accountability and the crimes of individual governments and armed groups. The evidence gathered by human rights organizations becomes critical when considering how governments around the world have responded to atrocities. Many governments express respect for human rights, and in fact international action in response to human rights crises has risen considerably. At the same time, political motivations, self-interest, and selectivity continue to be the norm for governments in dealing with human rights issues. Such motivations reveal that not even the best of democratic governments can always be relied on to fulfill their commitments to human rights. Obligations to international treaties may be ignored when convenient, self-interest may prevent action in countries in which intervention is desperately needed, and human rights violations of allies may be (Amnesty International Report 1993) "greeted with silence while those of declared enemies are met with public condemnations, sometimes backed with action." The recording of these events therefore has made the work of human rights organizations a grim endeavor, ever revealing to the world the inconsistencies, abject failures, and double standards of governments in their respect for human rights. Each year, organizations such as Amnesty International and Human Rights Watch publish world reports on the status of human rights, a bleak reminder that throughout the world tens of thousands of individuals are imprisoned, disappear, are brutally murdered by state action, or are tortured for their political beliefs or because governments want to suppress all dissent. These reports represents an indictment of the international community's cumulative failure to make human rights a priority. As Amnesty International stated in 1993, "When governments knowingly shirk their obligation to protect rights themselves and to hold other states to their international commitments, their seeming indifference becomes complicity. When the international community remains silent, it provides a shield behind which governments believe they can order the secret police, the torturers, and state assassins into action with impunity" (*18*).

Conclusion

International human rights organizations have been the persistent voice for the forgotten victim, the attester of government depravity, and the primary driving force for civilized conduct and accountability throughout the world. The numerous human rights nongovernmental groups that have arisen in the past twenty years have produced an extraordinary mass of evidence regarding the truth behind government efforts to conceal their heinous crimes behind veils of secrecy and deception. During Simon Wiesenthal's ordeal in the Nazi Lagers, SS officers gloated, Primo Levi, *The Drowned and the Saved* (Summit Books, New York, 1988), pp. 11–12. "However this war may end, we have won the war against you; none of you will be left to bear witness, even if someone were to survive, the world will not believe him. There will be suspicions, discussions, research by historians, but their will be no certainties, because we will destroy the evidence together with you." Similarly, Alexander Solzhensitsyn lamented that no record of the crimes of the gulag would ever come to light, Alexander Solzhenitsyn, *The Gulag Archipelago* (Harper and Row, New York, 1974), p. X. "Those who do not wish to recall have already had enough time—and will have more—to destroy all documents, down to the very last one." The historical circumstances of the fall of Nazi Germany in 1945 and the collapse of the Soviet Union in 1991 preempted the complete destruction of evidence concerning either the Holocaust or the gulags. Even so, there are those who have advanced claims that these two heinous crimes either never occurred or were not as inhumane as the historical evidence shows. Governments have made revisionist claims of their own; in effect, have tried to rewrite history through disinformation, concealment or destruction of evidence, and liquidation of witnesses and brutal suppression of dissent. The careful documentation of international human rights organizations and the collection of this evidence by archival institutions provide one effective counterforce to such attempts (*19*).

REFERENCES AND NOTES

1. R. J. Rummel, *Death by Government*, Transaction Publishers, New Brunswick, USA, 1994

2. See L. W. Livezey, *Nongovernmental Organizations and the Idea of Human Rights*, Center of International Studies, Princeton University, Princeton, NJ, 1988, p. 19; L. Wiseberg and H. Sirett, eds., *North American Human Rights Directory*, Human Rights Internet, Washington, DC, 1984; *Human Rights Directory: Latin America, Africa, Asia,* Human Rights Internet, Washington, DC, 1981; *Human Rights Directory: Western Europe,* Human Rights Internet, Washington, DC, 1982.

3. C. Warbrick, review of *Nongovernmental Organizations and Ideas of Human Rights, Internat. Aff.,* **65**, 536–537 (summer 1989).

4.   See H. M. Scoble and L. S. Wiseberg, "The Importance and Functions of Human Rights Organizations," *Human Rights Internet Project,* Human Rights Internet, Cambridge, MA, 1980; "Human Rights and Amnesty International." *Annals Amer. Acad. Polit. Soc. Sci.,* **413**, 10–26 (May 1974). Also see Livezey, Ref. *2*.

5.   L. S. Wiseberg, "Human Rights Nongovernmental Organizations and the Idea of Human Rights," in *Human Rights in the World Community,* Univ. of Pennsylvania Press, Philadelphia, 1992, pp. 372–373.

6.   Ref. *5*, p. 373.

7.   Ref. *5*, pp. 374–375. Also see Richard P. Claude and Burns H. Weston, eds., *Human Rights in the World Community: Issues and Action* (University of Pennsylvania Press, Philadelphia, 1992), pp. 362–363, 365.

8.   Ref. *5*, p. 375.

9.   See D. P. Forsythe, *The Internationalization of Human Rights*, Lexington Books, Lexington, MA, 1991, p. 40

10.   See Wiseberg and Sirett, *North American Human Rights Directory* (Ref. *2*) and the *HRI Reporter: Master List of Human Rights Organizations and Serial Publications*, Human Rights Internet, Human Rights Centre, University of Ottawa, Ottawa, Canada, 1991.

11.   Livezey, "Human Rights and NGOs," *The Center Magazine* vol. xvii, no. 3 (May/June 1984), p. 19, p. 34.

12.   See D. Orentlicher, "Bearing Witness: The Art and Science of Human Rights Fact-Finding," pp. 87–89.

13.   Ref. *11*, p. 35

14.   Ref. *11*, p. 36.

15.   "AI's Relations with Non-Governmental Organizations," report from the Secretary General's Office, May 15, 1985, Barbara Sproul papers, Amnesty International USA, AIUSA, archives of the University of Colorado at Boulder.

16.   The Union of councils for Soviet Jews constitutes the umbrella organization for the various and largely autonomous councils around the country. The Union of Councils constituted a single-issue political organization that focused exclusively on securing freedom of emigration and cultural rights for co-religionists inside the former Soviet Union. The archives of the Union of Councils are located at the archives, University of Colorado at Boulder.

17.   Such organizations include Amnesty International USA, Physicians for Human Rights, Human Rights Watch, and the Union of Councils of Soviety Jews. The papers of these human rights organizations have been deposited at the archives, University of Colorado at Boulder.

18.   See *Amnesty International Report 1993*, London, 1993, p. 2.

19.   See P. Levy, *The Drowned and the Saved*, Summit, New York, 1988, pp. 11–12; and A. Solzhenitsyn, *The Gulag Archipelago*, Harper & Row, New York, 1974, p. X.

BRUCE P. MONTGOMERY

CONDUCTING RESEARCH ON THE INTERNET

Introduction

The purpose of this article is to outline the approach for conducting research on the Internet. This article will begin with an overview of the Internet, discuss primary and secondary research approaches, and provide a note about the validity of the results. The appendices include various sample sites available on the Internet to aid the researcher and sample information concerning Internet research tools.

The Origins of the Internet

For many years computers were large mainframes that were operated by experts in isolated rooms away from the individuals who actually generated or utilized their information. With the introduction of the personal computer in the early to mid-1980s, computing power came to an individual's desk (*1*). The lack of easy computer connection capability, however, resulted in workstations operated by the provider or user of the computer's information. Stand-alone machines meant that sharing of information was extremely difficult, however. This changed when Xerox Corporation developed a standard approach called Ethernet that allowed computers to share information through a cable connection. While it was definite progress, this approach focused on sharing data between computers at a single site. The next significant advance came with the funding provided by the U.S. military's Defense Advanced Research Projects Agency (DARPA), which focused on allowing computers at various sites to share data over the telephone lines. This new approach allowed computers to seek out data on the network given a machine address. This new capability, termed the Internet, became the backbone for sharing data. This data-sharing capability became even more powerful with the advent of tools such as browsers.

Today the Internet consists of thousands of computers linked together over the phone lines. Conceptually it can be viewed as the largest collection of diverse information in the world—essentially as a globally accessible world library. It also contains an equally diverse population of individuals keen on participating in this information realm. For example, according to Nielsen Media Research (www.nielsen media.com), of the 220 million people over the age of sixteen in North America, 23 percent use the Internet, 17 percent use the World Wide Web, and 73 percent (6 million people) of the World Wide Web users search for information about products or services.

Conducting Primary Research

The Internet is an ideal area in which to conduct primary research in that there tends to be a large number of helpful individuals who enjoy offering assistance to other users, assuming that the request is not overly commercial in nature. While it has been estimated that only 10 percent of Canadians have access to the Internet (2), that still means that approximately 3 million people are online. The Internet makes an ideal inexpensive place to conduct research. The following presents a methodology to conduct primary research, beginning with an exploratory data collection stage and followed by a questionnaire (3).

A NINE-STEP METHODOLOGY FOR CONDUCTING PRIMARY RESEARCH ON THE INTERNET

1. Define the ideal target market or unit of analysis.
2. Search UseNet to find and subscribe to relevant discussion (news-) groups. UseNet News is similar to a global "community bulletin board"; when someone posts an article users all over the world can access it. Over 250,000 articles are posted each day. There are 15,000 newsgroups, and 40 million people participate in Internet forums (4).
   Most browsers have an option called newsgroup that gives a listing of electronic forums divided by topic. Here the users post questions or opinions or information related to their topic. For a listing of newsgroups try http://www.dejanews.com or www.reference.com.
3. Find an electronic E-mail topic list (sometimes referred to as mail reflectors). Similar in concept to newsgroups, a user enters his or her E-mail address onto a master database. In this type of forum users can post a message to a central location and it is then broadcast to all addresses on the mailing list. These E-mail lists are sometimes related to products, companies, magazines, and the like. For example, E-mail to listproc@educom.unc.edu and the sender will be placed on a newsletter that summarizes technology news from a variety of sources. Try http://www.neosoft.com/internet/paml for an extensive list of possible E-mail groups. In order to develop sample sets, it is possible to get the mailing list of all those in the forum (5).
4. Find the appropriate Web forum. Web forums are relatively new, are similar to E-mail groups, and are attached to a particular Web site. Although not used as much, there are more than 25,000 Web forums in operation (4).
5. Use a filtering system to monitor Internet forums. A filtering system scans the forums for certain keywords and returns those entries that match. For example, the Standford Information Filtering Technology (http://www.reference.com) or commercially available services are available for $145 per month and at $.50 per reference. eWatch in the United States monitors 33,000 Internet public discussion areas and 8,000 E-mail discussion lists and message boards on America On-Line and CompuServe on behalf of clients, or for $310 per month Web Alert will monitor specific Web sites (2).
6. Once the relevant forums have been discovered the next step is to send an inquiry to the forum to find if other relevant groups exist.
7. Devise a series of strategic queries and send to a few relevant forums. This begins the process of gathering responses to general questions of interest.
8. The next step begins an active research approach by devising and posting a detailed survey on your Web site.
9. Post a note to discussion groups about the survey.

METHODS FOR RESEARCHING VISITORS TO THE WEB SITE

Given that visitors are coming to the Web site, perhaps to fill out the survey mentioned in the previous section, the next step is to post a "guest book" or Web site survey to encourage visitors to provide a profile of themselves. While this is an active data collection approach there are automated tools available to gather various data about such visitors (6, 7).

Various software products are available that will monitor the Web site and generate the following types of statistics.

Statistics that can be gathered without actual visitors' data	Statistics derived from visitors' URL[a]
Number of download requests	Number of visits
Number/percentage of successful/failed requests	Average number of requests per visits
Most popular documents or files	Average duration per visits
Number of document transfers by day	Average number of visits per week/day
Most downloaded files by type	Number of visits per hour
Most popular submitted forms and scripts	Visits from organizations
Least popular documents or files	Visits from countries
Most popular documents by directory	Most popular visit entry page
Most popular directories accessed	Most popular exit page
Average number of requests per week	Average number of users per day/week
Average number of requests per day	Most frequent cities
Total bytes transferred	Most popular referring URLs
Average bytes transferred by day	Most popular user operating systems
Average bytes transferred by hour or day	
Average number of hits on weekdays and weekends	
Most/least active day of the week	
Most/least active day ever	
Activity level per day of week	

[a]Universal resource locator—essentially an address or unique identifier of a particular computer.

Conducting Secondary Research

Keeping in the mind the concept of the diverse nature of topics on the Internet, it is no surprise that it has a large potential for conducting secondary research.

SEARCH ENGINES

The Internet can be regarded as a huge database sorted into categories, each of which is defined by keywords. The primary tool is thus one that retrieves the Web sites that are in the appropriate category. A number of search tools are available through any browser. These tools are called search engines, and hundreds exist. The primary search engines, such as Infoseek, Altavista, Yahoo!, and Excite, have different approaches to gathering information Web sites and providing classification of the results (*5, 8, 9*). For example, some only search on a supplied keyword, and others search the entire document on the Web site. Most provide a scoring as to the appropriateness of the retrieved sites to the desired search word. Some will also examine related words. In some search engines, the developer of the Web site decides the keywords relevant to his or her Web site. In other search engines a software package automatically indexes the pages.

There is no standard keyword categories approach; the challenge for the researchers is to determine which keywords should be used in order to find the proper sites. There are many other different kinds of search engines, including the following:

- Some search engines accept phrases and logical AND OR combinations or look in the Web site address (URL) for such things as search words.
- Some will search with the keyword and the context (e.g., Windows as referring to house windows or Microsoft Windows).
- Search engines of more complexity are arriving. For example, WebCompass (www.quarter back.com) purports to use language processing technology to better classify data into logical categories. In addition, it can perform this task automatically at given intervals to continuously monitor the Internet for specific topics.
- Some search engines will submit the search parameters to many search engines and rank the results.
- Meta-engines will search not only Web sites but Usenet and published content sites.

For information about search engines see http://www.searchenginewatch.com.

Directories provide the searcher with prequalified Web sites; only those websites that have passed a content screen are slotted into a category. These online directories have the sites found during a search of a higher relevant likelihood.

CONTENT

The content provided on the Web sites is diverse. For example, statistics of all kinds can be found at corporate Web sites, various publications, government organizations, and so forth by searching on the keywords *population, demographics,* or *census*. A site such as http://www.census.gov/ would be found and offer access to various related databases.

For those attempting to gain information about the latest trends, most popular magazines, journals, and so on have Web sites offering online versions of their magazines and searchable archives of articles.

One of the best methods to keep updated on technological trends is through patents. These published patent and trademark databases can also be searched online through Micropatents Patent Searcher (U.S.—http://www.micropat.com).

To locate books try http://www.amazon.com to search on a word or author. Also one can subscribe to their newslist which provides notification when a book from an author or topic is released.

Various sites even provide the researcher with dictionaries, thesauri, translators, currency exchange tables, ZIP codes, area codes, and translators. For example, try http://www.itools.com/research-it/research-it.html.

See Appendix A for some useful Web site addresses.

A SIX-STEP METHODOLOGY FOR CONDUCTING SECONDARY DATA COLLECTION

1. Review the online news content publications for key concepts.
2. Use a search tool to look for related books or view the patent databases if relevant.
3. Compile the list of relevant keywords and phrases. Derive both general keywords and phrases and specifically more narrowly focused ones. For example, a general keyword could be one that the general public would use, such as *mouse*, and a more specific one could be *one button Macintosh mouse*.
4. Review the search tools for the most relevant search technique (e.g., title search, document search, Usenet, or published content).
5. Decide on the appropriate search tools that come with the browser or a commercially available search meta-engine.
6. Conduct the search with the general keywords or phrases, then conduct the search again on the retrieved list with the specific keywords and phrases.

Cautionary Note on Validity

Essentially anyone with the proper equipment can put data on the Internet, thus the question of the validity of information is always important. There is no central authority approving published materials, thus individuals can purposely put on misleading or false material. For example, individuals have placed information that cookie maker Mrs. Fields was linked to O. J. Simpson or tried to manipulate share prices with false data. Some even put on the Internet Web sites that appear to be a legitimate site but are copies of legitimate sites (*2*).

Conclusions

The Internet provides a connection to a massive amount of information, either directly by finding the right content or indirectly by finding the site where the appropriate material can be ordered. As it continues to grow it will provide the preliminary tool for conducting data collection. A researcher can easily envisage compiling an E-mail list of research subjects to try experiments on. It may be possible to first conduct entire business research studies without leaving the office and at costs far less than currently possible. Since finding the secondary data and the subjects to conduct primary research could all be available on the Internet. In fact, it's easy to envisage an E-mail list of subjects being available for download off the Internet. As the Internet grows, categorization of the sites and so forth might become more standardized with companies offering online research services making data collection easier in the ever-growing diverse set of information.

The final word is validity, however, in that Internet data and subjects are more difficult to qualify.

Appendix A: Useful Web Site Addresses

SEARCH ENGINES FOR WEB SITES

http://www.hotbot.com
http://www.excite.com
http://www.architext.com
http://www.lycos.com
http://www.infoseek.com
http://www.webcrawler.com
http://www.search.com (pointer to hundreds of search engines)
http://www.albany.net/allinone (has hundreds of search engines)

DIRECTORIES OF REGISTERED WEB SITES

http://www.opentext.com
http://www.magellan.com
http://www.yahoo.com
http://www.gnn.com/wic/newrescat/toc.html
http://www.w3.org/hypertext/DataSource
http://cuiwww.unige.ch/w3catalog

META-ENGINES THAT SEARCH WEBSITES, USENET, AND PUBLISHED CONTENT

http://www.metacrawler.com
http://www.informktibm.com

PUBLISHED NEWS CONTENT

Clarinet News: http://www.clarinet.com
Computers and technology: http://www.elibrary.com
Electronic Newstand: http://www.enews.com
IBM InfoSage: http://www.infosage.ibm.com
Net News: http://mcaca.com/netnwhpg.htm
Newspage: http://www.newspage.com
Pathfinder: http://pathfinder.com
Computer News Daily: http://www.technweb.cmp.com
Techweb: http://www.technweb.cmp.com
ZD Net: http://www.zdnet.com
CompuBooks: http://www.compubooks.com/bokks.html

WEB SITES OF COMPANIES WITH WEB ANALYSIS SOFTWARE

Bien Logic www.bienlogic.com
E.G. Software www.egsoftware.com
Group Cortex www.cortex.com
Interse www.interse.com
I/Pro www.ipro.com

Jupiter Communications
www.jup.com
NetCount www.netcount.com
Nielsen Media Research www.nielsenmedia.com
Open Market www.openmarket.com
Real Media www.real.media.com
Stream www.stream.com
Webthreads www.webthreads.com

REFERENCES

1. A. Newman et al., "Special Edition Using Java," Que Corporation, Indianapolis, pp. 6–7.
2. K. MacGregor, *Ottawa Citizen*, Sept. 6, 1997, p. E1.
3. T. Vassos, *Strategic Internet Marketing,* Que Corporation, Indianapolis, 1997
4. http://www.reference.com.
5. J. Snyder, "Stop Thief," *Internet World*, **7**(8), 102–104 (Sept. 1996); www.jw.com.
6. R. Stout, "Web Site Traffic Reports: A Simple Analysis." *NetGuide*, **4**(3), 147–150 (March 1997); www.netguide.com.
7. I. Westmacott, "WebAdmin: All the Information That's Fit to Log." *Webserver*, **1**(4), 14–21 (Nov./Dec. 1996), www.cpg.com.
8. A. Sternbergh, "Facts of Demand." *Profit*, 79–80 (Sept. 1977).
9. J. Easton, "Secrets of Successful Web Stories." *ZD Internet*, **2**(10), 91–98 (Oct. 1997).

JAMES BOWEN

THE DESIGN OF DOCUMENT INFORMATION SYSTEMS

Introduction

Information technology (IT) is ubiquitous in offices nowadays. In the 1980s IT was used mainly for well-structured, mainly numerical data: electronic data processing, management information, and decision support, but since the beginning of the 1990s the importance of automated support for document handling and document information management has increased enormously.

Information* in former centuries was scarce and precious, and should be preserved carefully; our appreciation is more complex today. We are drowning in information on the one hand, but thirsty for knowledge on the other (*1*). Information is rated highly: "the fundament of mankind, the fourth production factor, the essence of economy". Lack of information will be a valid reason for bitter complaint, but the flood of

---

*There are several definitions of information. Information denotes in this article an entity from the series data-information-knowledge-wisdom. It should be recorded, have meaning, and be able to change a person's knowledge: "Information is a body of data on a semantic level".

documents is leading to information overload. Apparently millions of people have the feeling that they underuse information, have difficulty separating essential information from what is nice to know, and think that the Internet will exacerbate obsessive information gathering. Some would like to become a member of "Dataholics Anonymous!"

Documents are the most important source of information. Documents prove to be far more important information sources than structured numerical data for most office staffs.* Such document-based organizations as insurance companies, governments, communities, and banks are flooded with documents, but also the headquarters of such action-based organizations as police organizations or chemical companies are flooded with documents. Office staff members may spend 75 percent of their working time on document-bound tasks, creating, retrieving, and filtering documents.

Documents are the most valuable information sources for the decision-making top management as well (see, e.g., Ref. 2), and of course, last but not least, libraries, archives, and record management departments have a deep interest in automated support for document handling and document information management. There is enormous interest in IT support.

Documents contain text and other ill-structured information. This was (and is) more difficult to handle for the computer than well-structured data, but it has become feasible now. Software for document storage and retrieval and for the control of document collections and document flows has developed more or less separately from facilities for management information (3). Software for document information systems (document IS)† should be able to function without major failures or breakdowns, although it is not perfect, and the user-friendliness can often be improved. Electronic document databases may demand an enormous amount of electronic storage space, but the prices for mass storage, data communication, and other necessary hardware for document IS are considerably lower than previously.

Organizations face tight margins, and the competition between organizations is fiercer than ever. The economic motive, savings in the document sector, is very welcome. Organizations face increasing demand for quality in their products and services, which gives rise to the need for improved quality of document handling—a quality motive for document IS. The amounts of word-processed documents have become unmanageable without IT support—a manageability motive. Vulnerable precious documents must be preserved—the preservation motive. Apparently various motives exist for interest in document IS, and, of course, the classical methods of information handling simply cannot answer today's needs.

---

*The word document traditionally is used for hard copies only. Due to the use of IT this concept is no longer applicable. A document is defined as "any object which has the purpose, or to which the purpose is given, to serve for the perusal of the data of which it is the carrier". The object may be a book, report, journal article, form, contract, letter, etc.; the data carrier may be paper, CD-ROM disk, microfiche, etc.

†A document IS is defined simply as an information system of which the data are of document nature. The database of a document IS contains references to documents, and it may contain (parts of) documents in the form of texts and/or document images.

Former ideals of the paperless office have vanished. Books, documents, reports, and paper will still be used. They are cheap and easy to use in the proper circumstances. In many cases, however, IT is needed to support document information and document-bound tasks, thus many pilot studies for document IS are carried out, prototypes are being tested, and document IS are being implemented. Many more will follow. According to the 1998 national survey on IT in the Netherlands, document IS are in most business branches only in the introduction stage, and nowhere further than the growth stage (4).

The design of a document IS does not boil down to the choice and finetuning of a software package. That is not the only thing needed to get a good document IS, and it is often not even the most important problem of the design.

In this contribution three design projects on three different cases are given. Thereafter general methodological design aspects are described for document IS, as well as specific aspects to be regarded on document IS design.

Some Cases of Document IS Design

CASE 1: THE DESIGN OF A DOCUMENT IS AT ASSIST

The mission of Assist, an organization with some 160 staff members, is to assist its member organizations (unionlike organizations) with periodical negotiations on working conditions and everything that can be related thereto. For this purpose several informational tools are in use: automated data collections (a few document IS were operational already), spreadsheets, graphical tools, and structured subject lists of subjects that are to be discussed by representatives of Assist with the member organizations. Assist receives documents on all kinds of subjects. Some are stored, some are forwarded, and some must be treated as classified. Assist produces and publishes documents, as well.

In order to improve the services of the organization, to give better access to the document information and to gain efficiency, it was decided to introduce a new document architecture. In fact, Assist wanted companywide IT support by an electronic document architecture, based on rather qualitative factors.

- Information is sometimes only poorly accessible.
- A lot of valuable information is present, but this is unknown to those who might need it.
- The document flow is large and not well managed.
- Communications could be improved.

The need to improve the document handling and document information management in the Assist organization was growing as the number of member organizations was increasing. Moreover, Assist had set up five regional offices in the country, which will gradually take over parts of the work of the central organization. The conversion of one centralized organization to a distributed organization may lead to a further reduction of the capacity to manage documents.

As always in this type of organization

- A part of the document process is time-consuming, and support of it by electronic means could lead to increase of efficiency.
- The work is not well structured, the primary processes of the organization cannot be described in a detailed, general valid way.
- The advisory work of the staff of Assist is done more or less separately. It depends upon specific persons, each with his or her own specific knowledge. IT support could lead to an improvement on knowledge sharing.

Situation Analysis and Definition Study

The approach consisted of the following steps:

- Make a situation analysis (three months).
- Select suitable software and hardware (three months, in time overlapping with the situation analysis).
- Write a report with recommendations for management, with an overview of the new situation with document IS and indicate a path to reach the new situation.
- Make operational prototypes and demonstrations for the staff.

The situation analysis describes the current organization structure, the current way of working, the collections, and the bottlenecks. The bottlenecks were identified by consulting reports of the organization and by looking around and talking with the staff. The list of desiderata to be solved by the document IS contained such items as diversity in the index structures and overdependence on the expertise of specific staff members.

In the situation analysis scheme such techniques as those in the Information Systems work and Analysis of Change methodology (ISAC) have not been used. We find that such schemes offer hardly any help to the design process.

The definition study describes the following:

- The document information collections: of the contents, either the relation to the administrative processes or the subject category of interest; the format and the place where paper documents are stored.
- The index data: an index with attributes and the relation to the documents; an index structure and an index of words in documents plus synonyms.
- The functions: structured searching, unstructured searching; the updating of index data after documents have been added and a scheme of user group authorizations.
- The norms and standards to be maintained.

The participation of the management and the staff is an extremely important point. Management, the advisors, and the staff are not computer experts. "Our staff should not only be able to work with it, they should be glad with it" is sometimes formulated. This needs a lot of attention. In the course of the design, three organizations with more or less related problems were visited, and their experiences were used.

A software package has been chosen. For this goal several document packages for groupware and document management were tested in-house. Workflow management software may be acquired in the future. A decision on a succeeding workflow project will be taken only after the document IS project has been finished. After the tests, a groupware basis package with excellent retrieval facilities for electronic document support, good document management facilities, and connection possibilities for workflow support was chosen. A scheme has been drawn of the migration path for current information systems and standard software.

Further decisions with regard to document data entry have to be taken. Conversion of electronic data is a lot of work. Conversion of old paper document information may be very costly indeed.

Costs and Benefits

The main one-time costs are the costs of new equipment (PCs, a server with more storage space, increased capacity of the network, etc.; total $350,000). The costs of software, application software, education, and training are less, although not negligible. The costs of data entry will be spread over years. Permanent costs (every year) include service and equipment renewal as well as systems management and information management (one full-time equivalent).

The most important benefits are: better access to the collections of information, improved possibilities for sharing information, the use of modern search strategies, fast and improved maintenance of electronic indexes, and the reproduction and exchange of tables and graphic representations. The benefits prove to be difficult to quantify. The avoidance of "disasters" alone, to avoid faulty information provision that costs members and goodwill should be worth this money, although that has not been proven. The investment seems to be worthwhile.

CASE 2: THE DESIGN OF A DOCUMENT INFORMATION SYSTEM AT PRESS LTD.

The costs of document information handling should be reduced for Press Ltd., an industrial firm, so this organization was interested in possible cost reductions by means of a document IS. High-quality document information handling is important as well, and this should also be improved. A pilot project for a document IS was carried out at one of the business units of Press Ltd. The chosen business unit was small, well organized, and stable.

In response to the preference expressed by Press Ltd., a design methodology was chosen based upon project control. The design route was divided into a series of phases through which the project must progress, including the following:

- Situation analysis and definition study
- Quotation request for the selection of an existing software package
- Installation, testing, and use

The phases can be subdivided further. After each (sub)phase, the results are to be approved by Press Ltd.

Situation Analysis and Definition Study

This stage is very important for assessing the balance between the organizational needs and wants and the use of IT. As cost reduction was a goal, the foreseen benefits must justify the costs.

Included in the description of the desired new situation were the following:

- The new tasks when the document IS would be in use, based on the description of the current process and tasks
- Information storage and retrieval (ISR) and document image facilities, and an overview of the access structures to the documents, including keywords and indexes to the documents
- Various strategies with respect to the conversion of part of the "old" paper documents to electronic documents
- Specification of the storage requirements (amounts, times) both for the electronic and the paper documents
- Specification of further technical requirements, for instance, network capacity, a scanner, optical character recognition (OCR), and printing devices

The current and new situations as presented were based upon data on the following:

- Static document characteristics
  = Total numbers of documents, numbers of copies per document, numbers of pages per document, sizes, black-and-white, grey, or color, one-sided or two-sided pages
  = Source or sender of each document
- Dynamic document characteristics: document data entry needs, selection data for documents to be saved, the time span over which these documents have to be kept machine-readable
- Document-handling data, registration of the working time spent on document-based tasks and the use of documents

Automatic indexing tools and intelligent OCR-processing (see, e.g., Refs. 5–7) will not be used yet. In this case, the index terms are formed by a classification of the documents, a hierarchical structure by which the documents can be searched. Examples of general index terms include: firm name, address, city, client-number, date, whether the document is incoming or outgoing, business unit, and document-type. Examples of document-specific indexes include for a quotation request document: quotation number, salesperson, machine type; for a sales document: order number, salesperson, machine type, quotation number; for a purchase document: purchase number, machine type; in general: correspondence number, date. The users are not allowed to assign free text identifiers to documents.

Business Process Redesign?

On automation, the business processes can fundamentally be restructured. This is called business process redesign (BPR). In this case there was interest in BPR. A report on the possibilities of BPR for this case was made. We calculated that the combination of both implementing a document IS and BPR would be profitable, but Press Ltd. decided to postpone formal changes in its way of working and to start a BPR project at some other time. Simultaneously implementing the document IS and BPR aims at the benefits of both, but means double trouble at one time. The choice was made not to rush matters. Often a phased IT introduction is preferred to a big bang approach, in which all applications are implemented in the target system at once. A phased introduction reduces the risk of failure; moreover; the flexibility of an organization in implementing change is a critical factor. This flexibility and bearing power of the organization must not be overestimated, and a pilot project is a sensible approach.

Benefits

In this case the benefits were the following:

- The foreseen expansion of the staff with one staff member could be avoided ($40,000 per year).
- Fewer photocopies, less storage space, and fewer envelopes and other materials needed in the mail room and the office (several thousands of dollars per year).
- Immediate response to customers' questions becomes possible; all relevant documents are available, and if one staff member is absent a colleague may answer the question. This probably leads to satisfied customers and is assumed to lead to more orders for Press Ltd. This factor cannot be translated unambiguously into money, but may correspond to $20,000 per year. This figure was accepted (!).
- Various other factors are of minor importance. They may correspond to amounts in the order of magnitude of a few thousand dollars per year. We have, in fact, neglected them.

In this case, the acquisition costs of hardware and software are about $70,000. The benefits were estimated to be $60,000 per year. Taking into account the necessary service license, employee training, and operating costs, the return on investment time was some eighteen months. Extension of the document IS over the whole company will presumably make the figures more favorable. The implementation of a document IS provides increased growth potential to the organization. It is a step toward BPR and/or other possibilities, but the growth potential is regarded as an unestimable extra. The financial survey was based on a restricted economic view.

A quotation request (or shortened to quotation or invitation to tender—several terms are in use) was sent out. Its generalized contents are described later. Various quotations were received. As was foreseen, none met all wishes. In one quotation a few requested items were missing. In another the specifications were not completely met. In the third the price was markedly higher for the complete IS.

Both the presentations of the proposed document IS and a visit to a reference site with a similar system gave a clear view of the skills of the suppliers and the suitability of a document IS. After presentations, discussions, and some adjustments of the specifications of the system and of the prices, one supplier was selected.

During the contract negotiations, the following points received attention: subject of the contract; prices of the components and the services; intellectual ownership of the software; implementation of the contract; acceptance of the system; supply, risk, and guarantee; payment arrangements; responsibilities; and disbandment and disagreement arrangements. The possibilities of buying, renting, or leasing the necessary hardware and software components for the test period were analyzed, too. Some of these points may seem unnecessary, but it was regarded as sensible to be careful with contracts (*8*).

CASE 3: ELECTRONIC DOCUMENT MANAGEMENT FOR THE INVESTIGATION SERVICE

One of the services of the Ministry of Housing, Spatial Planning and Environment is the investigation service. Its main responsibility is the investigation of alleged fraud. The investigation service obtains its cases from other executive departments of the ministry. In the preliminary research stage the investigation service gathers information. This stage ends with advice about the way in which an investigation will be conducted. Before an investigation is conducted, more information from a wide range of sources is collected. If needed, an investigator will question witnesses. Finally, the findings are compiled in a written report. If there is enough evidence the report will be handed over to the public prosecutor and the case will be brought to court.

The investigation office has an office at the ministry in The Hague and the supporting staff is located here. There are regional offices as well, distributed over the country.

The government gives high priority to the suppression of fraud. This leads to an increasing number of cases that are handed over to the investigation service. The number of employees grew from some thirty-five to some seventy in three years.

Problems include the following:

- The span of control of the managers grows. Because of the size of the service, they are forced to change from a co-working style to control-style management.
- There is only limited insight in the status of the work. Too many cases processed by the investigation service passed the terms. Moreover, this makes it difficult to plan work in the future.
- Changes in the tasks of employees and internal education of new employees result in the idea that the efficiency could be improved.
- There is not sufficient space to store information.
- The document management level does not seem to fulfill the growing demands for support from the investigators.

As is clear from the description, during the process many documents are consulted, created, exchanged, and updated. Documents may be in electronic or hard-copy form. The supporting staff is not capable of maintaining an appropriate level of services. The management of the investigation service sees IT as a tool to solve the problems. It also sees opportunities for IT with respect to the management of information flows (both electronic and hard-copy) and the control of work flows within the organization.

A table was made showing the characteristics of the documents involved during the process of investigation. It contains the document categories, tasks, type of carrier (paper, electronic file, diskette, spoken word), and the amounts involved.

The investigation process is one that uses a lot of information types from several information sources. It is a poorly structured process that depends highly on both the character of the case and the investigator conducting the case.

The choice of software did not contain too many technical details. The main requirements prove to be the following:

- Document management facilities
- Retrieval functions and tools
- Loan facilities
- Compatibility with other packages, especially with the word processor used
- Electronic archive management issues

This last one includes: it must be stated when certain information may be deleted, which persons are allowed to access which information, and how information is kept accessible in the long term given the technological developments.

The choice of a software package was quickly decided (weeks). When one package was found that met the required functions, it was accepted.

Documents will be stored in the electronic repository. Dedicated applications, supporting tools for process control, and tools for document manipulation have access to documents in the repository. The repository contains the electronic documents and it has facilities for version control and access checking. The latter is of importance for dealing with confidential information. The repository contains the document descriptors as well as the indexes to the documents.

The document management functions of the repository include functions to

- Control the document descriptors
- Control the documents
- Control the user's rights
- Control the applications that have access to the electronic repository

A major effort concerns the procedures. The procedures require the support of the management of the investigation service. It also requires the cooperation of the investigators. This is evident for hard-copy documents given on loan to an employee. It is just as essential that an employee makes documents in his regional office machine readable. If investigators do not cooperate, these documents will not be added to the electronic file. One can buy costly scanners for the offices, but that is not the end of the solution. The procedures are essential. A strictly technical solution for document management will not work. Management support for procedures was needed.

The shift in responsibilities in this case is striking. Investigators will become partly responsible for registering the documents and for the progress of the ongoing work. The record management unit will no longer be needed to decide on the retention of documents, and its required skill shifts from "high routine information selection" to "organizing document management".

Employees working at the record management unit may regard this shift as a threat to their jobs. This may lead to resistance. To avoid this, the record management unit was asked to participate in the design. By becoming involved, they became aware of the possibilities the new situation offered.

Document data conversion demands attention in this case, too. The main questions are

- What documents are converted from hard copy to electronic documents?
- What criteria shall be used to make the electronic repository accessible?
- When and how will documents be deleted from the electronic repository and in what cases will they be added to an electronic archive?

Informational and procedural grounds lead to the answers to these questions. They are not described here. The point is that the answers are based upon informational and organizational reasons instead of technological ones (*9, 10*).

How to Design Document IS: Methodological Aspects

The cases of Assist, Press, and the ministry differ in various respects. The goals and benefits are quite different. Other kinds of cases could have been added. There is a wealth of problems in practice. Due to the difference between them, it will not be possible to write a cookbook on the design of document IS; IS design is always an engineering process (*11, 12*). It is possible, however, to draw guidelines and to point to pitfalls in the design process. The described cases are the basis of this article, but other experiences have been used, too.

DESIGN METHODOLOGY

For the design of any IS other than a very simple one, a design methodology is used.* The main reasons for using a design methodology are twofold.

- Expertise: the experiences of other designers are used, tested and proven ways may be used to describe an organization (top-down, bottom-up, processes, actors); there are checklists; there is less chance that vital parts of significant organizational and technical problems or solutions are overlooked.
- Communication: representations of the design, documentation, and software can be shown in a standardized way to the customers, to problem owners, and to other members of the design team; communication enables work to be shared among colleagues.

The use of a design methodology has disadvantages as well. Methodologies are made for problem solving in general, for a class of practical problems, but in practice each design problem is different. Whatever methodology is chosen, it will miss views and tools on some of the problems, some actions will be described too globally, and other actions needlessly receive much attention. Van Rees wrote in the 1980s: "Help! The methodology doesn't work." A good designer with an open eye is needed for the actual problems to get a good design. An appropriate methodology will work well only in the hands of a designer who is aware of specific circumstances in a problem situation.

Some twenty-five design methodologies are regularly used for all kinds of IS. A comparison is given in Refs. *13–15*. The design methodologies differ considerably. The elements of one design methodology may even have no counterpart in another methodology. This leads to the question of what kinds of elements exist and what elements should be provided to ensure that a document IS can be effectively designed. The Delft framework (*16*) is used to evaluate design methodologies and to adjust

---

*A methodology is defined as a coherent collection of methods and techniques to solve a class of practical problems.

theoretical views to practical needs. It characterizes design methodologies in the following ways:

- Way of thinking (the *Weltanschauung*—the perspective on the problem domain—from which can be derived what objects are pertinent)
- Way of control (what successive stages are distinguished in the progress of the design and what happens after each stage)
- Way of working (what steps and actions must be taken by the designer)
- Way of modeling (what models are made and what their mutual relations are)
- Way of support (what kinds of diagrams or other scheme techniques are to be used)

The way of support is a derivative of the four other ways. There are tools to support the modeling for all kinds of models. They are not discussed here.

WAY OF THINKING

The objects that are pertinent for the document IS will be found in a document that describes its purpose (if that has been written). In many cases the top terms to be assigned to that document would be documents, information, document and information bases, and flows, users, and usage. They then must be the main objects in the methodology and/or in the actual design.

Occasionally other terms appear here: times to complete, action sequences, queuing, and flexibility. In these cases, document routing and workflow management play a role and the design should be focused on it.

WAY OF WORKING

The way of working is the core of the expertise of the designer. The steps and actions that have to be taken for solving the ill-structured problem of the design of a document IS include five subjects to be discussed in more detail. They are

- Selection of IT resources
- Design of index structures
- Outsourcing
- Document data conversion
- Cooperation by interorganizational document IS

They are so important that separate sections are dedicated to them. This section contains other aspects of the way of working. In a given case they may be just as important as the five subjects treated in separate sections.

1. A document IS with one big database is expensive to build and expensive to maintain. If possible, downsizing must be pursued. An analysis must point out ways to make smaller units, to make database parts. The use of documents may pinpoint ways to make database parts. It requires an analysis of business processes for which information provision is demanded. As in the case of Press Ltd., the resulting scheme is a matrix of document groups vs. task groups (categories of documents split up because of subject and/or because of use vs. use or users or tasks).

2. For the growth path there is choice for a phased, controlled growth path or a big bang approach, in which a complete IS is put into use at once. A strong argumentation for a controlled growth path is the limited predictability of any system design. One should always be prepared for unprepared setbacks. A strong argument for a big bang approach is of an economic nature; the big bang approach will bring benefits soon after the complete document IS has been installed, while in a controlled growth path the benefits will evolve only gradually. The choice is difficult; both approaches occur. In practice document IS tend to be complex. That may be the reason that more organizations choose gradual growth rather than the big bang.

3. To get an impression of the sizes and amounts the document IS will contain, an inventory must be made up of the document data.
    a. Data on the static document database (numbers, sizes, colors in the documents, document storage space, index storage space).
    b. Data on the dynamic requirements (numbers of incoming documents per day, period of record keeping, printing capacities).
    c. The technical infrastructure (server requirements, workstations, printers, other peripherals, network requirements for data communication).
    d. The index structures.

4. Communication to users and training of users. Users differ in their level of education, their familiarity with computers, and the frequency with which they will use parts of the IS, but they decide on its success. In one case the following actions were taken: announcement of what was going to happen, a formal introduction, informal demonstrations to those who seemed to be interested, and a test with some users. The communicative talents of the designer were extremely valuable.
    A more formal approach distinguishes three consecutive stages.
    a. Communication before the document IS will be built (give an introductory course; ask users who will want to participate for how much in design stages).
    b. Communication during design and development (manage some participation, make reports on the progress, show a prototype, let users work with an experimental IS).
    c. Communication afterwards (training for all, system management, information management, a help desk).

5. Man–machine interaction aspects form an important part of user-friendliness. Document information is ill-structured. Still, the context of the information on the screen must be easy to perceive. Screen functionality and screen layout are even more important than usual.
    The dialogue for retrieval should contain command shortcuts for experienced users, informative feedback during an operation (e.g., "please wait"), closed dialogues, and simple error messages.
    Surprisingly, the man–machine interface does not always get the attention that seems necessary. As a consequence, after the implementation, users sometimes rate the user-friendliness as only "poor". As text is sensitive to context, users should not be too easily satisfied. Maybe in the future users will be used to work with only restricted awareness of the informational environment. It is more likely that in the future improvements will follow from current or future research on the visualization of the information environment in the document IS.
    It is useful to test the user interface. Criteria for the quality of the user interface are
    a. The result of inquiries on the user interface.
    b. The percentage of potential users that are willing to work with it.
    c. The percentage of potential users that are able to work with it after training or after a specified time.
    d. The average number of mistakes of competent users per hour or per 1000 actions.
    e. The number of times that a user cannot give the command that corresponds to his or her needs.
    f. The number of times a user utters his or her annoyance.

g. The part that is used by the user of the language and the syntax that the document IS would accept.
6. For management purposes it must be possible to obtain static and dynamic data from the document IS. Document use and process control appear to have a managerial dimension. Getting data to manage, however, is not needed only for *document* IS.
7. Document IS tend to be complex. Their design is complex, too. Reduction of complexity should be a goal. There are various ways to reach this: user participation, attention to the functions the IS must offer (sufficient ISR facilities!), access protection, privacy, backup facilities, a clear decision-making process, time control and budget control, and so forth. Again, however, reduction of complexity is not a problem to *document* IS design only; we refer to standard works on IS design.

WAY OF MODELING

A model is a reduction of some part of reality to something that can more easily be understood. Modeling is thus "the science and art of leaving out". The models and their mutual relations are the core of the expertise of the designer, just as the way of working is. Management, department managers, department staff, IT consultants, and others all have their own ideas of their own relevant parts of reality. If document structures are complex, the usage of documents is unclear, workloads of office employees seem to be unbalanced and working times are irregularly spent, then models for them are indispensable for a successful design.

1. For structured data, models are often supported by a scheme technique. As Rowley (*14*) points out, those tools are not applicable to document information problems. As an example, entity relation diagrams (ERDs) are a way of support used to describe static structured data. In a document IS, the entities could be documents. These ERDs are not of much help for the purpose of communicating possibilities of document IS to a problem owner. For structured data, data flow diagrams (DFDs) are often used to describe the flow of data. For document IS this comes down to document flow diagrams, but again they are rarely used. Especially for complex tasks, drawing correct DFDs in great detail involves a lot of work. Even then, these DFDs are not much help in representing the problem and the alternatives and getting feedback.
    To business process modeling applies the same thing.
    If the problem is of a document nature, the document problem and document solutions have to be modeled.
2. In the design phase the attention is usually directed to the new situation, however (first), one needs a valid and sufficiently detailed description (a model) of the current situation. This is a necessity for a proper problem-solving cycle including conceptualization and validation and verification of a given problem situation. Only after the current situation has been described (second), one or more models of new situations including situations with a document IS are presented. These new situations correspond to attempts to solve problems and thus to benefits (to be described in the section on costs and benefits).
3. Modeling is difficult. Experience shows that it takes students considerable time to understand modeling. The fact that a problem (or a solution) has to be modeled and that problems (and solutions) are widely different implies that the models are widely different. We are reluctant to generalize. A few examples of choices for modeling in a document environment are given.
    a. For the document database, fields are often used as entities. The modeling technique, then, is a data model indicating which fields must be present and which of them should be searchable.
    b. For the design of the search structure, thesaurus building is a modeling technique.

    c. For the document information reuse or republishing, the logical document structure can be modeled in a document-type definition according to the standard generalized mark-up language (SGML).

    d. Modeling user groups to document categories (described in the way of working) was performed in Press and Assist.

    e. For dynamic situations, at Delft University of Technology and elsewhere, simulation and animation are used in addition to static models. This is suited for document use, for instance. Excellent results have been reported with techniques of dynamic modeling in various cases (*17*).

WAY OF CONTROL

The way of control indicates how the design process should be managed and controlled.

1. Overall, the organizational aspects are important. A change in document information provision affects an organization so pervasively that organizational understanding and rethinking are vital. Organization redesign may not be necessary, but organizational aspects are a main feature rather than of secondary importance.

2. User acceptance is too weak an approach for the design of document IS. In the design of a document IS, user participation should be required rather than mere user acceptance. Various design methodologies adhere to this principle. The document sector has, in fact, been aware of this need for a long time. Mumford's design methodology, ETHICS, a thoroughly participative methodology published around 1980, was based on experiences in the document sector.

3. Document IS software is rarely built *ab initio* nowadays. In most cases, standard tested and proven software is bought and tailored. Consequently, the fact that software quality management remains important and that software engineering receives a lot of attention in many methodologies is not our main concern.

Selection of IT Resources

The hardware for a document IS contains few surprises. Most of the hardware is well known from other IT applications. Scanning equipment, CD-ROM, or WORM disk or other kinds of data storage devices are relatively common. Twenty-one-inch monitors, a powerful server, and printers are often used. Document data require much data communication, so additional network capacity may be required. Documents contain text, graphics, tables, and photos. Motion video and sound will eventually add to the "media richness", but they were not present in the cases described above.

The document-biased nature of the data leads to more specific requirements for the software. The way of thinking in document information and document-bound tasks differs to a certain degree from other areas. This is obvious from the main sources on document handling and document information management.

Document software must have specific features.

- Variable field lengths of records
- Multiple fields
- Binary large objects (blobs)
- Thesaurus relations between index terms

- An inexact query language with facilities for truncation and masking of arguments, for proximity and similarity operators, for set manipulation facilities, and/or for relevance ranking and relevance feedback
- Hyperlinks in the document data
- Image enhancement

Workflow management requires other functions, of which the most prominent are

- Document routing
- Business process building facilities
- Item status facilities

These elements do not have a clear equivalent in numerical data processing.

The design of a document IS often includes the selection of an appropriate tested and proven standard software package for configuration and tailoring. It reduces the requirements for software engineering. Often units in an organization demand many tailor-made adjustments of the software. Essentially the reasons for those demands boil down to: we are different, we know better, we cannot wait, and we want to be on our own. These reasons have been put forward for twenty years now. Sometimes we have to be warned to be careful with adjustments. Every adjustment carries the burdens of increasing service costs, difficulties to upgrading existing software, and making work procedures more rigid. The actual selection of software, then, remains an interesting design problem. First, there are many packages. An experienced person will know some packages for a given situation, but you cannot know everything. Second, the differences in situations, requirements, and sizes of document collections make it difficult to predict whether a package that performs well in one case will do in some other case.

There are bibliographic tools to help select a package. They are given in online and CD-ROM databases: Business Software Database, Buyer's Guide to Micro Software, Datapro Software Directory, and Microcomputer Software Guide Online. A reference visit to an organization with a similar kind of document IS may wind up the selection procedure.

Document-bound tasks to be supported by IT are: document creation and production, document dissemination, information retrieval, document processing, and document management tasks in libraries, archives, and records management offices. This range of tasks can be supported by technologies that have evolved either from document image processing or from ISR functions.

ISR and document image-processing facilities tend to integrate. On the one hand, document image information must be retrievable, and so document image software packages increasingly are being equipped with retrieval facilities. On the other hand, textual information is supplemented increasingly by graphics, drawings, and photos. Currently the majority of hosts of online bibliographic databases offer the display of document images. This trend is not only technology-driven. Users ask for it, as they may require the combination of several data types. For instance, Ref. *18* describes the need to support police information staff with multiple data types.

The palette of functions betrays the origin of different packages. Although each package has functions in every area, on a first classification the following groups of document packages can be distinguished:

- Above all functionality on ISR, an elaborate query language: Zyindex, AskSam, BRS/Search, Topic, Excalibur, and so forth
- Library document management, large collection, borrowing facilities: Adlib, Star, Vubis, and so forth
- Document image packages: OPEN/Image, Imageplus, Imagelink, and so forth
- Document management packages: Docs Open, Saros Mezzanine, Soft Solutions, and so forth
- Packages for workflow: Staffware, Flowmark, Teamware, and so forth
- Packages for information sharing and knowledge management (groupware): Lotus Notes (Domino), Novell Groupwise, and so forth

The trend toward integration is somewhat reminiscent of the separate development in former days of machine-readable library catalogues on the one hand and online ISR on the other. Now they are often supplementary or integrated. The next trend toward integration is the provision of data export facilities between document image and ISR applications and electronic data processing (EDP) and management information facilities. Users with a networked PC on their desk, and with word processor and spreadsheet facilities do not need a separate IS for their document data, especially those who use parts of existing documents as building blocks for new documents. The hardware, the software, and the data representation of our document IS must thus be compatible with other IS.

For the support of electronic document management a wide range of software packages exist. The choice depends on the kind of support that is needed. In Table 1 neighbors of document packages in related areas are given. For instance, EDP software is required if the data, the task, and the process are well structured. Work Flow Automation (WFA) software is optimal if the process is relatively well defined. If the task and the process are undefined, then groupware for knowledge management should be used. (By the way, the class of groupware programs includes videoconferencing and group decision rooms, too.)

Access Structure of the Documents

For document IS this is an important design step, the importance of which should not be underrated by system designers without experience in information science, libraries, archives, and record management. The growing flood of documents leads to increased demands on sharp tools to select the necessary from the unwanted documents. Moreover, the use of filtering techniques in addition to retrieval leads to requirements on the access structure of documents (*19*). Last but not least, quality requirements lead to increased needs for index terms. There are questions like "We

TABLE 1

Survey of Types of Software Packages

	Structure of data	Structure of task	Structure of process
EDP (electronic data processing)			
MIS (management information systems)	+	+	+
DSS (decision support systems)			
EIS (executive information systems)	+	+	+/–
WFM (workflow management)			
WFA (workflow automation)	+/–	+/–	+
Forms processing			
Ad hoc WFA			
E-mail	+/–	+/–	–
DIP (document image processing)	–	+	+/–
ISR (information storage and retrieval)	–	–	+/–
Groupware for information sharing	–	–	–

Note: + = high level of structure; +/– = indifferent; – = low level of structure.

have had a similar situation before, how did we react to it?" In the "paper" situation, if the pertinent documents could not be found quickly they were not searched for at all. Such a question would be answered from memory, not always very precisely. The enhanced quality requirements for tasks are precisely the reason these questions cannot be neglected but have to be answered today. The paradigm for information retrieval is still developing (20). In practice, it is difficult to foresee whether full-text search engines will ever be able to retrieve the majority of the relevant documents for all cases. Currently an improved set of index terms, both in static and in dynamic environments, may be preferred. Extended possibilities for document retrieval will be welcome, but extra indexes require extra storage space, and an extensive indexing effort costs money. Requirements engineering of the index structure and comparison of current keyword sets must be studied in an early phase of the project. Here information science expertise must come in.

Outsourcing

The design and implementation of a large project in a complex situation is often outsourced to a document IS supplier. The selection of such a supplier has far-reaching consequences. The future information provision of the company depends on it. Many established suppliers of electronic document systems have developed software that is widely applied in governmental and commercial organizations; specialized systems for specific problems with pros and cons exist; existing hardware infrastructure may restrict the possible solutions.

These facts make it difficult to choose the right supplier. It demands a thorough investigation. Moreover, few have the detailed expertise to ensure the proposed document IS can technically be implemented in the foreseen way and offers the best value for money. Many organizations therefore send out a quotation request or invitation to tender. It takes a lot of work and a lot of time to make the quotation request, nevertheless it is essential to do this work. A quotation request containing only a general survey of possibilities and ideas will surely result in fundamentally different quotations. Worse, the requirements of the document IS have evidently not been agreed upon in the organization. Such a selection process can result in a software package that uses sophisticated technology, is furnished with a most impressive user interface, but unfortunately does not fulfill the real needs and wants. A request based upon good preparation is essential to receive quotations that can correspond to the needs of the organization.

Hiring an external expert may help, but the problem owner cannot export the problem. The more expensive the expertise that is hired, the more time the problem owner has to spend to ensure that the expertise is used in the best way.

The contents of the request must contain a complete and clear summary of the preliminary research. In order to receive good quotations, the following steps must be made:

1. Find information on suppliers from business partners, magazines, visits to suppliers, exhibitions, or advice from external experts.
2. Establish a short list of potential suppliers that are expected to be able to satisfy one's requirements in the short and long term.
3. Compile a quotation request and send it to these suppliers.

The following subsections give an indication of the contents of the quotation request.

PURPOSE SECTION

The problems of the current situation are explained. Also explained is how it is expected that these problems will be solved. It should be clear to the supplier why a document IS will be wanted.

ADMINISTRATIVE SECTION

The rules according to which the suppliers are supposed to act are described in the administrative section (e.g., the time and place to which the quotation must be submitted, the way in which it will be reviewed, the schedule for the total project, and the details of the contact persons).

TECHNICAL SECTION

This section presents the current and the designed future situation. It includes the company processes and task structures, the requirements for hardware and data communication facilities based upon static and dynamic aspects, the document image facilities and ISR facilities needed, and an indication of the software license policy of the organization.

In view of the necessary data exchange with other applications (the integration issue), an overview must be given both of the hardware that is already in use and of document formats. The technical section also describes the demanded functions of the workstations. Examples are: rotate documents on the screen, enlarge a part of a page, keep several pages on the screen, remove pages, store pages locally for fast turnover, and provide annotation facilities and image enhancement.

MANAGEMENT SECTION

This section contains requirements for the project plan, the preparation of the installation and the responsibilities, the criteria for the test plan, requirements for education of the staff, and the required documentation as well as the qualifications, experience, references, and financial data of the supplier.

COST SECTION

In this section the suppliers are asked to provide information about the prices and costs of the document IS, including all necessary hardware. The suppliers are asked to subdivide cost data into categories: hardware, system software, applications software, installation, maintenance, staff education, documentation, and project management. This subdivision highlights differences in prices and omissions of the suppliers.

An example of a possible problem is the license of software for a limited information system—for instance, a prototype. If licensed software will be used, the license must be valid for the whole corporation, not only for the prototype. This may give rise to unexpected costs.

LEGAL SECTION

This section gives a description of all the arrangements that have to be made, such as contracts and licences. Examples of contracts are buying agreements, service contracts, software licenses, payment agreements, and secrecy agreements. A quotation request contains company information that must not become public. It is thus useful to have a secrecy agreement stating that the company information may only be used in the quotation. In the case of Press Ltd., the secrecy agreement was sent out at the start of the process. Only if the potential supplier had signed this secrecy agreement was the complete quotation request sent to it.

SELECTION

The evaluation of the quotations is not only based on the submissions of the suppliers, but also on the perceived skill of the suppliers in completing the whole project successfully. The quotations should be evaluated rather objectively by evaluation criteria that are drawn up in advance. Examples of evaluation and selection criteria are: satisfy the requirements (goals of the project) and the quality of the design, meet the technical requirements, determine the qualifications and experience of the supplier, and present the quotation and the prices of the proposed document IS.

Document Data Conversion

The importance of document data conversion should not be underestimated. Incoming mail (new documents) must be made electronic. The documents that are present already in the organization (old documents) have to be considered as well.

CONVERSION OF OLD DOCUMENTS

This is a difficult subject to decide on, as the costs of a large conversion of "old" paper documents are substantial. Conversion of a card catalogue may be an enormous job. The data conversion costs from paper to electronic documents may be much more than the costs for hardware, software, education, and training together. In the case of an insurance company it turned out to be necessary to convert 70 percent of all the folders in the dynamic archive.

In terms of design in the conversion of old documents, one can choose to convert none of the old documents, all of the old documents, or all since a specified date. There is a case in which it was decided to enter electronic data exclusive of the documents that had been borrowed. This seems a sensible solution. The disadvantage is that the documents that have not been borrowed from the closed stacks in the period with both an electronic catalogue and a card catalogue will never be found again as soon as the card catalogues are out of use and removed to some cellar.

Quality requirements are a design question as well. There may be faulty or unusable indexes. One may choose to improve the quality. The data entry or OCR data have to be corrected anyway. In that case it may be recommended that the indexes be corrected as well, and at the same time. Keywords and so forth need not be corrected during this stage; this can be postponed to some later stage.

Conversion from one electronic format to another is a big problem as well. The use of standards makes this problem manageable. In some situations in which several IS are used, data conversion is performed by screen scraping or such techniques.

CONVERSION OF NEW DOCUMENTS

Often new documents are scanned to make images in the mail room. This is an archive procedure. It includes the selection step: What will have to be kept? A scanner at the workplace can be used to make other documents machine-readable.

The images are put on temporary magnetic media until they are indexed, then they are put on permanent media. Indexing new documents in the new situations may be performed by end users but even so, information management (i.e., the responsibility for the maintenance of the collection of index terms for all types of documents) tends to be centralized; it is a library/information officer function. This view was implicit in Lewis's Doomsday scenario (21).

Interorganizational Cooperation

Should automated support for cooperation with other organizations be aimed at? It is an interesting question. There are many healthy interorganizational document IS; for instance, online bibliographic databases, common catalogues with contents from several sources and/or with more than one owner and many others. Advantages are that the costs of system design, a server, a data communication network, document data entry, and/or maintenance of the index structure are shared by many organizations.

There was no choice for Assist or for the investigation service; it was a necessity. There are examples in which automated support of interorganizational cooperation goes further. Usually this is caused by strategic terms. All kinds of organizations (not only libraries and archives) face the demand for interoperability, short lines for supply of products or services, and the possibility to get together into new products and new services for new markets. They are in turn a response to the trend to globalization and the ongoing competition between organization networks. Common use of document information, as shown above, tends to be followed by the exchange of electronic information and the integration of applications between organizations (*22, 23*).

Not only organizations without a common authority, but also business units within one big corporation with only remote common authority may face this situation; for instance, in the case of a relatively independent business unit that contributes to one common corporate process.

In the cases of common catalogues the participating organizations are rather alike, partly colleagues and partly competitors, so that some horizontal integration originates. The above situation is a form of vertical integration, however; suppliers of information and customers of information cooperate to form organization networks. Especially if one of the partners is dominant, the speed of the design and implementation of an interorganizational document IS will be markedly higher than in the case of horizontal integration.

The stakes in this case of implementation of document IS are higher, but the costs are higher as well. Management issues are the tensions between parties, especially as the relations between the partners in the network may be subject to change, the distribution of costs and benefits in the network, and the complexity of the document IS design for a group of organizations without common authority.

The following problems appear to exist on the design of an interorganizational document IS:

- There is a problem (e.g., poor service, poor coordination, high costs of the end product, long times to complete products), but the fact that there is a problem does not automatically lead to collaboration.
- A conceptual and empirical model of the new situation at the business level is not made.
- As a corollary, the model of the new situation at the employee level is not made.
- Technical issues.

Some of the technical issues for cooperation can be circumvented by adherence to standards and norms. There are quite a few subjects for standardization specific for document IS, and the use of a standard may then be necessary.

For compression of text there were and are various "document archivers". Examples are ARJ, LHA, ZIP, and Compress. There are several standards for compressed document images—TIFF, JBIG, GIF, and JPEG—and others may follow.

In the case of interorganizational cooperation based on document information interchange, three more standards demand special attention: SGML, ODMA, and Z39.50.

1. Reuse of information becomes easier with a standard logical document structure. For this standardization the current development of SGML is promising (*24*). SGML and the related standards aiming at standard document layout are used by publishers, printers, and so on, along with other organizations with a lot of documentation. Related standards are standard generalized interchange format, SDIF, ISO 9069; Document Style Specification and Semantics Language, DSSSL, ISO 10179; and Standard Page Description Language, SPDL, ISO 10180.

2. A different kind of standard aims at improving interoperability between applications. The open document management API (ODMA) translates instructions such as "open" and "save" of an application to the document management system. Updated lists of document management systems that have implemented ODMA appear regularly on the Internet (*25*).

3. A very important standard for information retrieval in distributed environments is the Z39.50 query language standard (*26*). The Z39.50 protocol specifies formats and procedures governing the exchange of messages, enabling the client to request that the server searches databases for information that meets specified criteria, and to retrieve some or all of the identified information. It is meant to control the search session as well. The list of standards to enable interorganizational cooperation based on document information should be expanded with IT standards from outside the document area. Examples are DDE (dynamic data exchange), DLL (dynamic link library), ODBC (open database connectivity), CORBA (common object request broker architecture), and X.400 or TCP/IP for messaging. Of course, the subject access structure of documents may have to be agreed upon between the cooperating organizations.

Document standards can reduce problems, however, the process to get the standards into use will take a lot of time and effort.

Why Design a Document IS?: Economic Factors and Quality Requirements

To design an information system requires identifying the profits and advantages of its use and finding a balance between the specific needs and wants of an organization on the one hand, and IT possibilities on the other. Achieving this balance is very important. Too little attention to organizational requirements will generally result in systems that have limited value to the problem owner; too little attention to IT may lead to unrealistic and expensive demands on available technology.

Why were (and why are) organizations interested in document IS, what were their goals, and what were the results of the implementation of a document IS? We have analyzed the following aspects: advantages and benefits and disadvantages and costs in these cases and in other organizations (*12*). "Enabling good document handling and document information management" contains aspects of an economic and

TABLE 2a

Advantages and Benefits of a Document IS at the Management Level

— Fewer staff members are needed; for instance, to manage and transport documents (physically).

— Generation of income by making electronic document information available to third parties, database publishing for publishers and other organizations.

— Flexibility through guaranteed access to documents, several staff members can answer a customer's telephone inquiry immediately, the documents are not at the desk of a colleague, documents are not lost or misfiled.

— Integration of all relevant information sources for corporate purposes.

— Guarantee of the possibility to confirm or challenge a statement at the top level of the organization or to society by referring to the pertinent documents.

— Reduction of lead times to produce new documents: manuals, product catalogues, etc. (e.g., instance by cut and paste).

— Saving on archive space, keeping only one copy of the original document, and keeping it elsewhere (as a matter of fact this often-quoted benefit proves to be small).

— Fewer photocopies need to be made; an electronic copy is used in most situations. (Organizations tend to underestimate their photocopy figures. In the Netherlands 30.10^9 photocopies are made per year. Both in industrial and governmental environments each original document may be regularly photocopied 10 to 100 times!).

— Protection of vulnerable, valuable, rare, unique documents.

— Enables the introduction of workflow management.

— Generation of management information (for process control and company management).

TABLE 2b

Disadvantages and Costs of a Document IS at the Management Level

— The analysis phase of the design is difficult, it is a large shift from the paper-based situation; relative uncertainty exists about the outcome of a project. (Note that in spite of this, prototyping must not be used as an excuse for poor reflection on the design of the document IS.)

— Acquisition costs and operational costs for equipment, network, software, and education of staff are far from negligible.

— Staff is needed for system management and for automated information management.

— Work restructuring has to be managed; reorganization fuzz.

— Standardization issues are not yet quite solved. This may result sometimes in unexpected problems with coupling of IS and data transport between IS.

TABLE 3a

Advantages of a Document IS at the Employee Level

—	Fewer piles of uncompleted work waiting for documentation or document files;
—	Carryover of work; a task can be completed, no need to wait for a colleague who has the relevant documents on his/her desk.
—	Better access to documents, more index terms to documents.
—	Integration of text, figures, and graphics from several documents for a task.
—	More documents are accessible or available in a distributed environment.
—	Satisfied users if the information system functions well and if the users have been informed and have participated in the design and/or implementation. Working with a modern complex user interface seems to contribute to one's status (!).

TABLE 3b

Disadvantages of a Document IS at the Employee Level

—	Education, reeducation of the staff: a "computer driving license" for a multifunctional system asks somewhat more than an afternoon of training.
—	Change of work, new relations between staff members, uncertainty about the future of the office.
—	Better document retrieval in the electronic situation than in the manual situation, but it is not perfect.
—	New procedures based on automated task support tend to be more strict than the old manually controlled ones.

managerial nature on the one hand and quality and usability aspects on the other. Not surprisingly, the aspects of an economic and managerial nature are of more interest to the executive staff, which is responsible for the organization in the broader context, at the management level of an organization. The quality and usability aspects refer to the employee level (i.e., to the staff members who will be using the document IS every day).

Tables 2a and 2b show generalized benefits and advantages, as well as costs and disadvantages, respectively, at the management level. Tables 3a and 3b show generalized advantages and disadvantages at the employee level.

The tables give a kaleidoscopic view. The factors in them are admittedly of a different type and size for any one organization. They have been identified at different organizations (not only the cases given here) with different problems and opportunities and with different needs and wants for their electronic document management. For instance

- A reduction of the number of staff for records management was demanded at some industrial firms.
- Flexible and multiple-user access to documents at an industrial firm and at a hospital.

- Generation of income from their collection at libraries and documentation organizations and at a publishers.
- A reduction of the number of photocopies was a goal of many.

In many cases, these organizations found other benefits, indicated in the tables, to further influence the financial results.

Things are not as easy as they look, however. Information economy is, in our opinion, a field that is not yet sufficiently understood. Information is a queer element in the economic paradigms to which mankind is accustomed. Information does not disappear when it is used. The costs to multiply and distribute information are very small compared to the costs to generate and acquire it. These and other strange qualities of the object "information" lead among other things to disputes on cost accounting and on pricing mechanisms for IT support for document information provision. In practice, they are assigned more or less arbitrarily.

We found two other aspects as well for evaluating the benefits of document IS. An ex ante representation of the financial consequences of a document IS is rarely fully correct, even if costs and income have been properly calculated. In each of the three cases, during the design and implementation of the document IS or shortly afterwards, staff members came up with ideas for minor task restructuring or additional services, so the original foreseen prototype was adapted. The problem of the benefit measurement is *what* to measure. Moreover, the introduction of IT is a step in the development path of the organizations. Step 1: computers are introduced for numerical data; step 2: a document IS is implemented; step 3: a workflow package or knowledge management support is tested. The steps can be subdivided if some business units follow and others trail, and if various versions follow one another. The problem with benefit measurement is *when* to measure. The ability to grow and to change with the help of IT is a vital condition for an organization. (More succinctly, the implementation of a document IS is only a battle in a war. This sounds less kind but it is not completely incomprehensible.) The benefits may partly be the results of other circumstances. In restricted economic terms they can hardly be unambiguously assigned.

Nevertheless, many document IS seem to be worth the expense. For several cases return on investment times have been calculated, with some assumptions. They tend to range between one and two-and-a-half years.

Important at the employee level is that users will be happy to work with the document IS if it is functioning well. Most staff members in any organization will be proud of their work. They will be proud to perform good quality work, and the challenge for the information system designer is to enable the staff to do so.

Conclusion

The design of document IS apparently has a special character. Differences exist between separate cases of document IS design, as is shown in the three cases and elsewhere. There is a wealth of problems in practice and one should be careful to generalize results.

It is well to combine expertise from the library and information field, the archives and records management fields, and the informatics and computer science fields. In this way the document nature of data is taken into account in the design of a document IS. The expertise must be fine-tuned to the needs in each case, as each case has its specialties. We are one methodology. We prefer to use elements on the way of thinking, the way of working, the way of modeling, the way of control, and the way of support and add that to any methodology that is used by or known to the user organization.

The way of working and the way of modeling are the core of the success of the design. They include downsizing, the design growth path, and an inventory of document data. User education and training is important. Man–machine interaction does not always seem to receive sufficient attention.

Explicit models are indispensable for a successful design. Data models often are not very impressive. A few examples of modeling choices have been given. For dynamic situations, simulation and animation are useful.

User participation is a time-consuming aspect, but it helps to achieve a good product. Moreover, for the designer it is a rewarding way of working.

It is not difficult to choose a database system that can handle multiple data types in an adequate way.

It is necessary to give sufficient attention to the access structure and indexing of documents, both maintenance and renewal of the access structure itself and the procedures.

In the case of outsourcing of the design, a quotation request takes considerable time and effort. A clear and complete quotation request, including more than just technical requirements, is necessary to allow the suppliers to submit good quotations in a short time (a few weeks). After the presentations of the quotations by the suppliers it is possible to judge them quickly and rather objectively, using predefined selection criteria.

Document data conversion is costly. The decision to convert from paper to an electronic form or from one electronic format to another has far-reaching consequences. Steering is possible by the decision about what part to convert, what facilities will exist for conversion in the operational phase, and quality requirements.

The use of document data by other parties leads increasingly to document exchange. As a consequence, the design of interorganizational document IS receives more and more attention. The problems in this area have been described shortly. Standards for document formats and functions are essential, however, some of the problems are not solved by these standards.

The benefits of the document IS are not easy to measure. Information is a queer element in economic theories. Readjustments and minor changes during the design and development affect the foreseen benefits. A document IS often is only a step during the development of the organization. Attention has been drawn to the problems of when to measure and what to measure; nevertheless, costs and benefits have been described. A list of costs and benefits at two levels has been drawn. It is dangerous to generalize about costs and benefits. Each case is represented by only a few entries in those lists: a nice corollary to the remark on the use of only one methodology for the wealth of differences in the cases in practice! In the cases presented here and in many cases elsewhere, however, the document IS seem to be well worth the expense.

Acknowledgment

We thank R. van der Leij, G. Rosman, and J. J. M. Uijlenbroek for their cooperation on the projects. We thank Assist, Press Ltd., and the Investigation Service for their enthusiasm and many valuable discussions.

REFERENCES

1. P. Königer and K. Janowitz, "Drowning in Information, but Thirsty for Knowledge" *Internat. J. Inform. Mgt.,* **15**(1), 5–16 (1995).
2. R. H. Sprague, "Electronic Document Management: Challenges and Opportunities for Information Systems Managers." *MIS Q.*, 29–49 (March 1995).
3. G. W. van Putten and R. Smedinga, "The Possibilities and Limitations of Document Information Systems and Text Management Systems in Organizations." *Electronic Libr.,* **10**(1), 33–39 (1992).
4. B. Derksen, P. Noordam, and A. van der Vlist, "De IT-antenne: Volgen van Ontwikkelingen in een Dynamische Markt," KPMG Management Consulting, Utrecht, 1998 (in Dutch).
5. W. Sun, L.-M. Liu, W. Zhang, and J. C. Comfort, "Intelligent OCR Processing." *JASIS*, **43**(6), 422–431 (1992).
6. S. V. Rice, F. R. Jenkins, and T. A. Nartker, *The Fifth Annual Test of OCR Accuracy,* Information Science Research Institute, Las Vegas, NV, 1996.
7. H. Bunke and P. S. P. Wang, eds., *Handbook of Character Recognition and Document Image Analysis,* World Scientific, Singapore, 1997.
8. G. Rosman, K. van der Meer, and H. G. Sol, "The Design of Document Information Systems." *J. Inform. Sci.,* **22**(4), 287–297 (1996).
9. K. van der Meer and J. J. M. Uijlenbroek, "The Possibilities of Electronic Document Management for Supporting Ad Hoc Processes: A Case Study," in *Proceedings of the DLM Forum on Electron. Records,* Brussels, 1996, pp. 249–259.
10. J. J. M. Uijlenbroek, "Designing Electronic Document Infrastructures," doctoral dissertation, Delft University of Technology, Delft, the Netherlands, 1997.
11. H. Saiedian, "Information Systems Design Is an Engineering Process," in *Encyclopedia of Library and Information Science,* vol. 60, 1997, pp. 120–133.
12. K. van der Meer, *Documentaire Informatiesystemen,* 3rd rev. ed., NBLC, The Hague, 1998 (in Dutch).
13. D. J. Flynn and O. F. Diaz, *Information Modelling,* Prentice-Hall, Englewood Cliffs, NJ, 1996.
14. J. E. Rowley, "Information Systems Methodologies: A Review and Assessment of Their Applicability to the Selection, Design and Implementation of Library Information Systems.", *J. Inform. Sci.,* **19**(4), 291–302 (1993).
15. T. W. Olle, J. Hagelstein, I. G. Macdonald, C. Rolland, H. G. Sol, F. J. M. van Assche, and A. A. Verrijn-Stuart, *Information Systems Methodologies: A Framework for Understanding,* 2nd ed., Addison-Wesley, Wokingham, U.K. 1991.
16. P. S. Seligmann, G. M. Wijers, and H. G. Sol, "Analyzing the Structure of I.S. Methodologies—An Alternative Approach," in *Proc. of the First Dutch Conf. Inform. Sys.,* R. Maes, ed. Amersfoort, 1989, pp. 1–28.
17. G. J. de Vreede, "Facilitating Organizational Change: The Participative Application of Dynamic Modelling," doctoral dissertation, Delft University of Technology, Delft, the Netherlands, 1996.
18. M. J. Hoogeveen and K. van der Meer, "Integration of Information Retrieval and Database Management in Support of Multimedia Police Work." *J. Inform. Sci.,* **20**(2), 79–87 (1994).
19. N. J. Belkin and W. B. Croft, "Information Filtering and Information Retrieval: Two Sides of the Same Coin?" *Commun. ACM,* **35**(12), 29–38 (1992).
20. S. Dominich, "The Interaction-Based Information Retrieval Paradigm," in *Encyclopedia of Library and Information Science,* vol. 59, 1996, pp. 218–236.
21. D. A. Lewis, "Today's Challenge–Tomorrow's Choice: Change or Be Changed or the Doomsday Scenario Mk2." *J. Inform. Sci.,* **2**(2), 59–74 (1980).
22. A. L. M. Cavaye and P. B. Cragg, "Factors Contributing to the Success of Customer Oriented Interorganisational Systems." *J. Strat. Inform. Syst.,* **4**(1), 13–30 (1995).

23.   D. T. T. van Eijck, "Designing Organizational Coordination," doctoral dissertation, Delft University of Technology, Delft, the Netherlands, 1996.

24.   Y. Marcoux and M. Svigny, "Why SGML? Why Now?" *JASIS,* **48**(7), 584–592 (1997).

25.   ODMA (url): http://www.activedoc.com/odma.

26.   M. St. Pierre, "Z39.50 for Full-Text Search and Retrieval," in *Z39.50 Implementation Experiences,* P. Over, W. E. Moen, R. Denenberg, and L. Stovel, eds. NIST special publication 500–229, U.S. Department of Commerce, NIST, Gaithersburg, MD, 1995, pp. 1–9.

BIBLIOGRAPHY

Blair, D. C., *Language and Representation in Information Retrieval,* Elsevier, Amsterdam, 1990.

Bikson, T. K. and Frinking, E. J., Preserving the Present: Toward Viable Electronic Records, SDU Publishers, The Hague, 1993.

Blokdijk, A. and Blokdijk, P., *Planning and Design of Information Systems,* Academic, London, 1987.

Cooper, M. D., *Design of Library Automation Systems,* Wiley Computer Publishing, New York, 1996.

Fidel, R., Hahn Bellardo, T., Rasmussen, E. M., and Smith, P. J., eds., *Challenges in Indexing Electronic Text and Images*, ASIS, Learned Information, Medford, NJ, 1994.

Marchionini, G., *Information Seeking in Electronic Environments,* Cambridge Series on Human–Computer Interactions, vol. 9, Cambridge University Press, Cambridge, U.K., 1995.

Newman, W. M. and Lamming M. G., *Interactive System Design,* Addison-Wesley, Wokingham, U.K., 1995.

Over, P., Moen, W. E., Denenberg, R., and Stovel, L., *Z39.50 Implementation Experiences,* NIST special publication 500–229, U.S. Department of Commerce, NIST, Gaithersburg, MD, 1995.

Salton, G., *Automatic Text Processing: The Transformation, Analysis and Retrieval of Information by Computer,* Addison-Wesley, Reading, U.K., 1989.

Schneiderman, B., *Designing the User Interface: Strategies for Effective Human–Computer Interaction,* 2nd ed., Addison-Wesley, Reading, 1993.

Sol, H. G., *Simulation in Information Systems Development,* University of Groningen, Groningen, U.K., 1982.

Sprague, R. H. and McNurlin, B.C., *Information Systems Management in Practice,* 3rd ed., Prentice-Hall, Englewood Cliffs, NJ, 1993.

Witten, I. H., Moffat, A., and Bell, T. C., *Managing Gigabytes: Compressing and Indexing Documents and Images,* Van Nostrand Reinhold, New York, 1994.

KEES VAN DER MEER
HENK G. SOL

ELECTRONIC COPYRIGHT

Introduction

The 1990s will be remembered as a decade when the world's information became accessible on the Internet and World Wide Web to anyone owning a computer. Global computer networks are a reality, the transfer of information is executed instantaneously with a simple keystroke, and every personal computer has the potential to become a powerful desktop information factory.

Interpretations of national and international copyright laws and treaties are consequently more muddied than ever, with most of the world struggling to apply copyright laws from the 1970s and earlier (written with printed works in mind) to instantaneous transmissions across telephone lines and cable networks. As one observer noted, "Computer executives, publishers, artists and authors are trying to reconcile 21st century computer technology with 19th century laws protecting intellectual property" (1).

Major electronic copyright dilemmas abound. There is a lack of clarity about whether or not content on the Internet is free, especially when terms and conditions and/or copyright statements are elusive to locate and difficult to interpret when they are discovered. The inconsistency of copyright statements between print and electronic versions of the same material is troublesome.

Although print versions of many digital journals are registered with the Copyright Clearance Center (CCC), Web sites lack explicit statements about whether or not royalty payments for electronic copies can be paid to the CCC if the reproductive use is of a commercial nature.

Intranets and legal dissemination of Web-based information to multiple sites in the same corporation is a recent quandary that concerns corporate librarians and intranet developers. Current standards of licensing do not seem to apply; site licenses are being rewritten in favor of enterprisewide licenses, and transaction-based fees are being exchanged for annual usage fees.

Rightsholders and users of copyrighted works have always differed over reproduction rights. Owners demand to be fairly compensated for the "sweat of their brow," to recoup their costs, and to earn reasonable profits in bringing information to the public's attention. Creators of Web pages are worried about preserving their own intellectual property in cases in which their pages are either linked without permission or imported into frames of someone else's Web pages. Ownership, even of noncommercial materials such as personal home pages, is an important concern of publishers.

Users wish to honor intellectual property rights, but are frustrated over what they view as exorbitant fees to acquire content or restrictions on how information can be disseminated and shared. Recent court cases have encouraged an underground movement whose members' philosophy is a "use it and lose it" attitude toward copying and downloading (2).

Those who utilize Internet services can reasonably argue that publishers who provide marketing or promotional material on Web sites implicitly encourage downloading, printing, and copying of the material for distribution to more than one individual within an organization. Some information professionals define reproduction as a matter of intent. If a Web page is informative, then copying the page may not be perceived as a misuse of the owner's copyright. Other intermediaries suggest that if the "safest" recourse at this time is to provide URLs to users rather than download or forward content, then the profession may be obstucting access to information.

Staying informed about the various copyright policies of document suppliers is problematical for the information professional. Collection policies vary among document delivery clearinghouses, electronic vendors, database producers, and academic libraries providing interlibrary loan services. Some have direct agreements with publishers; others use the CCC's transactional or annual authorization reporting services; several offer flat fees for all documents provided; and a few do not collect fees at all, giving the full responsibility of seeking permission or paying royalties to the requestor. Potential copyright violations may exist all along the chain, from the document requestor, to the intermediary who handles the requisition, to the document supplier who takes the order, and to the specific individual who makes the reproduction.

The library profession is speculating about whether or not the electronic age will end the availability of physical collections and archives or encourage publishers to mount retrospective coverage on the Internet. Intermediaries are monitoring worldwide ramifications of how older material remains available and how intellectual rights for accessing and copying this information will be handled (*3*).

Ever-evolving issues raised by the availability of digital content make it nearly impossible to provide a comprehensive overview of electronic copyright. For the first time in nearly two decades, significant changes in worldwide copyright legislation and treaties are being proposed; the ultimate outcome of litigation over fair use rights on the Internet and the archiving, linking, and framing of Web sites are to be determined; and new technologies proposed by publishers and authors to control and protect content are in their infancy.

This review of electronic copyright emphasizes significant copyright laws in the United States and worldwide intellectual property rights treaties; highlights how these laws and treaties are being applied to digital content; underscores major court cases that have rendered clear-cut guidelines or added confusion to reproductive rights; and notes current issues that are likely to have an impact on the future of copyright. A list of resources to monitor electronic copyright issues is also supplied.

Copyright Law: A Historical Perspective

A discussion of electronic copyright cannot be complete without a review of international laws exercising authority over intellectual property rights. Most laws were drafted before the advent of electronic media. Although CD-ROM and computer hardware and software technologies are now incorporated into many national laws and international treaties, determining how to protect Internet technology and content remains a hotly debated issue among worldwide copyright governing bodies. Much of the current debate is about whether or not existing laws must be changed to encompass Web-based technologies.

UNITED STATES: COPYRIGHT LAW

The U.S. government has recognized the importance of protecting copyright holders' works since 1790, when Congress approved a copyright clause in the Constitution "to promote the progress of science and useful arts, by securing for limited times to authors and inventors the exclusive right to their respective writings and discoveries" (*4*). The enactment of the Copyright Act of 1976, its revision on January 1, 1978 (U.S. Public Law 94-553, General Revision of the Copyright Law), the Computer Software Act of 1980, and the Semiconductor Chip Protection Act of 1984, strengthened federal copyright legislation. Additionally, in 1990, Congress amended the Copyright Act to ensure that state and private institutions would be subject to monitory damages if they violated the intellectual property rights of others.

Section 106 of the Copyright Act outlines five separate rights of authors to protect published and unpublished original works (defined as literary, dramatic, musical, artistic, and "certain other intellectual works"), including the following:

1. The right to reproduce the copyrighted work in copies or phonorecords
2. The right to prepare derivative works based upon the copyrighted work
3. The right to distribute copies or phonorecords of the copyrighted work to the public by sale or other transfer of ownership, or by rental, lease, or lending
4. The right to perform the work publicly, in the case of literary, musical, dramatic, and choreographic works, pantomimes, and motion pictures and other audiovisual works
5. The right to display the copyrighted work publicly, in the case of literary, musical, dramatic, and choreographic works, pantomimes, and pictorial, graphic, or sculptural works, including the individual images of a motion picture or other audiovisual work (5)

A work created on or after January 1, 1978, is automatically protected from the moment of its creation and remains in effect during the author's lifetime plus fifty additional years after the author's death. When it is a collaborative work, the term lasts for fifty years after the last surviving author's demise. Works made for hire and anonymous and pseudonymous works are protected for seventy-five years from the date of the first publication or 100 years from the date of creation, whichever expires first.

Works created but not published or registered for copyright before January 1, 1978, are also protected for the life of the author plus fifty-, seventy-five-, or 100-year terms. (Note previous paragraph.) Under no circumstances will the term of copyright expire before December 31, 2002, and for works published on or before December 31, 2002, the term of the copyright will not expire before December 31, 2027.

Works published prior to 1978 are protected for twenty-eight years, and can be renewed for an additional forty-seven years. Public law 102–307, enacted on June 26, 1992, amended the Copyright Act of 1976 to automatically extend to forty-seven years the copyright term of works published from January 1, 1964, through December 31, 1977 (6).

On March 3, 1995, Congress proposed the Copyright Term Extension Act of 1995, which would extend the terms of copyright in the above-stated clauses by twenty years. To date, the recommended changes have not been enacted (7).

Works created by U.S. government employees during their employment are in the public domain, but works created by outside contractors for the U.S. government may or may not be. State and local governments may claim copyright to their works.

Fair use doctrine as designated in section 107 of the Copyright Act and the additional copying rights permitted librarians in section 108 are the most confusing for those seeking to reproduce works legally. While it is specifically unlawful to violate these five rights, the Copyright Act provides exemptions from copyright liability, including fair use doctrine, compulsory licensing, and library rights. Section 107 states

Notwithstanding the provisions of sections 106 and 106A, the fair use of a copyrighted work, including such use by reproduction in copies or phonorecords or by any other means specified by that section, for purposes such as criticism, comment, news reporting, teaching (including multiple copies for classroom use), scholarship, or research, is not an infringement of copyright. In determining whether the use made of a work in any particular case is a fair use the factors to be considered shall include:

1. the purpose and character of the use, including whether such use is of a commercial nature or is for nonprofit educational purposes;
2. the nature of the copyrighted work;
3. the amount and substantiality of the portion used in relation to the copyrighted work as a whole; and
4. the effect of the use upon the potential market for or value of the copyrighted work (*8*).

Compulsory licensing permits the use of copyrighted works if royalties are paid to owners and statutory conditions are observed.

Section 108 provides additional copying rights to libraries: (1) the reproduction or distribution is made without any purpose of direct or indirect commercial advantage; (2) the collections of the library or archives are (a) open to the public, or (b) available not only to researchers affiliated with the library or archive or with the institution of which it is a part, but also to other persons doing research in a specialized field; and (3) the reproduction or distribution of the work includes a notice of copyright (*9*).

COPYRIGHT CLEARANCE CENTER

In 1978, at the suggestion of Congress, the CCC was established to plan and implement an efficient mechanism for the licensing of photocopying. As a nonprofit clearinghouse, the CCC licenses users to photocopy registered titles, publishes fees that are authorized by the participating publishers, and collects the fee and forwards them to the publishers. Five licensing services are available to users. Under the Transactional Reporting Service (TRS), individuals pay a royalty fee per publication photocopied. The Annual Authorization Service (AAS) is available to organizations with more than 750 employees. Corporations pay an annual license fee based on a survey of photocopying activity to determine the number and type of copies being made. A similar arrangement for companies and nonprofit organizations with fewer than 750 employees is offered by the Photocopy Authorizations License (PAL). The Federal Government Photocopy License (FEDLINK) extends to federal government employees the right to photocopy items from the CCC's collection of titles.

The Academic Permissions Service (APS) provides precleared permissions for academic coursepacks and classroom handouts. The Electronic Rights Service (ERS), implemented in 1997 by the CCC, is a direct result of Web-based content. For a fee, the CCC will approach copyright holders on behalf of academic institutions for permission to reproduce digital works.

In 1995, the CCC announced a new Internet service to aid commercial organizations, academic institutions, and individuals in receiving copyright permissions. This rights clearance system, called CCC Online, provides access to 1.75 million titles distributed by over 9,200 participating publishers in the CCC. A user of CCC Online searches for specific titles; determines if the publisher allows photocopying, and if so, the amount of royalty fees; files electronically for permission to photocopy; and pays for that permission online (*10*).

Not all publications of each publisher registered with the CCC are covered by licensing arrangements, and copying of individual articles within the CCC collection of titles is not always permitted to users of the TRS. The copyright permission of a publisher may only extend to personal use, in which copying for resale or for commercial purposes is not allowed. Document delivery services especially must check a publication's copyright statement to ensure that resale is authorized by the publisher.

The recording and disbursal of royalty fees is labor-intensive. At the moment, the CCC is the only major centralized collection agency available to users in the United States. In 1995, however, the National Writers Union was a major force in organizing and launching a second collection bureau, the Authors Registry (*11*).

NATIONAL INFORMATION INFRASTRUCTURE

No major copyright legislation has been enacted in the United States for nearly twenty years. The 1978 law continues to govern the rights, privileges, and disputes of authors, publishers, teachers, librarians, researchers, and scholars. Beyond a doubt, electronic transmissions of data and Internet delivery of information introduce issues and concerns not conclusively answered by the Copyright Act. Although Congress has refused to provide additional clarification or revision to the act, in February 1993, President Bill Clinton formed the Information Infrastructure Task Force (IITF) "to articulate and implement the Administration's vision for the National Information Infrastructure (NII)" and "to develop comprehensive telecommunications and information policies and programs that best meet the country's needs" (*12*).

Three committees are organized within the IITF to formulate "Administration positions on key telecommunications issues . . . to develop, demonstrate and promote applications of information technologies in key areas; [and to address] critical information policy issues that must be dealt with if the NII is to be fully deployed and utilized" (*12*). One of these committees, the Information Policy Committee, established the Working Group on Intellectual Property Rights to specifically examine the intellectual property implications of the NII. In July 1994, recognizing that there is no central organization to set standards and rules of operation for digital media and communications, the working group proposed a new copyright regulatory structure that would provide an interpretation of copyright law and acknowledge the existence of new technology. The administration's final report, entitled "Intellectual Property and the National Information Infrastructure," was released on September 5, 1995, and is often referred to as the "white paper" (*13*)

The white paper recognizes technological advances and developments that control the delivery of information, and encourages "effective copyright protection promot[ing] a new Cybermarketplace of ideas, expression and products" (*13*); consequently, major legislative changes to the Copyright Act are proposed. The categories of technology currently outlined in the law would be broadened to cover and protect digital information and its transmission. The definitions of *transmit* and *publication* would be amended so that current and future technologies developed by copyright owners would be protected. The "importation, manufacture, or distribution of any device or product, or the provision of any service" that deactivates a copyright owner's technological protection system would be prohibited. The "dissemination of copyright management information known to be false and the authorized removal or alteration of copyright management information" would be unlawful (*13*).

The IITF also advised that the "unauthorized browsing of a work in digital form would be considered an infringement of the owner's copyright; strict liability of online service providers for copyright infringement by users would be imposed; and application of copyright's fair use doctrine in digital networked environments would be limited." The report encourages the enactment of legislation that would "make it a criminal offense to willfully infringe a copyright by reproducing or distributing [copyrighted material] with a retail value of $5,000 or more" (*13*).

Additional recommendations from the white paper include proposals to grant libraries greater privileges in reproducing copyrighted, digitized works for preservation; to allow nonprofit groups to prepare Braille or large-type editions of copyrighted works for visually impaired persons if "the owner of the exclusive right to distribute the work in the United States has not entered the market for such editions during the first year following first publication...; to prohibit the importation, manufacture or distribution of any device or product, or the provision of any service," that defeat anticopying systems (without the copyright owner's authority); and to regulate the "fraudulent" alteration of copyrighted information (*13*).

The report does encourage communication between copyright owners and libraries and schools "to assist" in the purchase and licensing of digital works, but states that "it is...premature to reduce the liability of any type of service provider in the NII environment." There is a strong implication that online service providers especially will be held liable for copyright infringements by their users (*13*).

Since the word *work* is used in the Copyright Act, some industry experts insist that no modification to the law is necessary. Publishers of electronic media generally maintain that existing laws and international treaties are adequate to protect their works against copyright infringement. While the writers of the U.S. Constitution and the Copyright Act of 1976 could not anticipate new media innovations—radio, film, television, microfilm/fiche, CD-ROM, online databases, and the Internet—supporters of the current law state that the Copyright Act is "format-neutral" (*14*), protecting the works of authors regardless of the medium used.

In response to the white paper, library groups—including the Association of Research Libraries, the American Library Assocation, the American Association of Law Libraries, the Medical Library Association, and the Special Libraries Association—issued a statement and commissioned a legal "review and analysis" of the IITF report (*15*). In part their evaluation of the white paper states

> the Report has a subtle but meaningful impact on libraries and educational institutions. By emphasizing the economics of copyright over the public interest in accessibility to copyrighted works, it underscores what may be the increasing difficulty of nonprofit institutions to secure or grant access to works for little or no cost ... While its legal initiatives appear modest, the core thrust of the Report is far-reaching. It posits the thesis that copyright is an economic right of owners to be exploited. In its view, the copyright law as a code of regulation should facilitate economic exploitation of works which is in the commercial interest of the United States and its citizenry ... Since the pervasive theme of the recommendations is enhancement of the economic exploitation of copyrighted works, less heed is paid to the public interest

aspect of copyright law or established exceptions to copyright rights...The weakest part of the Report is its assessment of the relationship of fair use to digital use (*16*)

To counter opposition to changes, the IITF quoted from Thomas Jefferson.

I am not an advocate for frequent changes in laws and constitutions. But laws and institutions must go hand in hand with the progress of the human mind. As that becomes more developed, more enlightened, as new discoveries are made, new truths discovered and manners and opinions change, with the change of circumstances, institutions must advance also to keep pace with the times. We might as well require a man to wear still the coat which fitted him when a boy (*13*).

On February 7 and 8, 1996, the U.S. House of Representatives conducted hearings on copyright in the digital age. The members of the Subcommittee on Courts and Intellectual Property held opposing viewpoints regarding the white paper's legislative recommendations (*17*).

The most disputed issue involved the liability of service providers for their customers' use of electronic information. Those against such a provision in the Copyright Act emphasize the impossibility of implementing a system to monitor users. Supporters underscore the need for increased protection for copyright owners.

The perceived elimination of fair use was also debated during the House hearings. Since the white paper highlights the commerciality of computer and communications technology, with proposed legislation stressing the economics of copyright over the public's interest in securing and accessing copyrighted works, library and scholarly groups responded with position papers and statements urging the government to rethink its stance on the fair use doctrine.

UNIFORM COMMERCIAL CODE

The Uniform Commercial Code (UCC) was adopted in the 1950s as a means for states to protect the sale of goods, the leasing of personal property, and other commercial transactions between merchants. The primary focus of the UCC has been the protection of tangible property. Currently under review is a new law, UCC article 2B–Licensing, which would protect the sale of intangible property (i.e., software, not only between merchants, but also between retailers and consumers). The implementation of article 2B would validate shrinkwrap licenses and any other license covering the use of electronic infomation (*18*).

International Treaties

UNIVERSAL COPYRIGHT CONVENTION AND THE BERNE CONVENTION

The United States belongs to the Universal Copyright Convention (also known as the UCC) and the Berne Convention for the Protection of Literary and Artistic Works. The UCC was written in Geneva, Switzerland, in 1952, enacted on September

16, 1955, and revised in Paris in 1971. Administered by UNESCO, the UCC protects the works of authors who reside in member countries if the works bear the notice of copyright in the form (generally a copyright symbol, name of the copyright owner, and year of first publication of the work) and position specified by the UCC (*19*).

The Berne Convention was signed by September 9, 1886, with the United States joining on March 1, 1989 (the U.S. Congress needed over 100 years to revise the Copyright Act so that U.S. laws would be more harmonious with Berne). The World Intellectual Property Organization, headquartered in Geneva, Switzerland, governs the treaty. The Berne Convention guarantees copyright protection in all member nations for its authors, and guards against copyright infringement of foreign members' works in the United States. Unlike the UCC, the Berne Convention does not require registration or notification of copyright on authors' publications. The Berne Convention protects more inclusive rights than does the UCC, including those of translation, reproduction, public performance, adaptation, paternity, and integrity. (The UCC recognizes rights to reproduce, adapt, and publicly perform or broadcast a work.)

The UCC recognizes the Berne Convention, and contains provisions for countries that are signatories of both treaties. When issues of copyright infringement are raised, the Berne Convention prevails. If a country has signed both treaties and withdraws from Berne, it will not be protected by the UCC (*20*).

WORLD INTELLECTUAL PROPERTY ORGANIZATION (WIPO)

On December 20, 1996, the participating countries of the Berne Convention adopted the WIPO Copyright Treaty and the WIPO Performances and Phonograms Treaty to establish copyright protection for digital literary and artistic works and to address the rights of performers and producers of phonograms. Thirty countries must ratify the individual treaties before they become effective internationally (*21*).

In part, the contracting parties recognized "the need to introduce new international rules and clarify the interpretation of certain existing rules in order to provide adequate solutions to the questions raised by new economic, social, cultural and technological developments," as well as acknowledged "the profound impact of the development and convergence of information and communication technologies on the creation and use of literary and artistic works" (*22*).

GENERAL AGREEMENT ON TARIFFS AND TRADE (GATT)

In 1996, the U.S. Congress enacted new legislation as part of the General Agreement on Tariffs and Trade (GATT). Works produced in 120 countries during the previous seventy-five years were automatically restored to copyright, as long as the works were still under copyright protection in their countries of origin. The GATT legislation affects nonprofit and for-profit sectors, as well as individuals who unwittingly download online graphics. Those in jeopardy of copyright infringement include users who download graphics for duplication in their own published materials (electronic or print) and any individual or organization recreating artwork or performing musical compositions to earn revenue (*23*).

Copyright Legal Precedent: Notable Cases

COMMERCIAL VERSUS FAIR USE: THE TEXACO CASE

The most antagonistic and watched case on copyright infringement during the past decade is *American Geophysical Union et al.* v. *Texaco Inc.* (*24*). While the litigation addressed unauthorized photocopying of printed works by a commercial organization, the case has widespread implications for reproduction of digital works.

In 1985, a Texaco researcher's files were randomly selected for review to determine copyright infringements. The plaintiffs—originally six publishers of scientific and technical journals and later expanded to eighty-three publishers—selected eight copies of complete copyrighted articles, notes, and letters from the *Journal of Catalysis*, a monthly publication of Academic Press. These eight copies were among a number of photocopied articles published in several journals and discovered in the researcher's files; for purposes of reaching a decision in this case, the publishers chose to focus their litigation on copies made from the *Journal of Catalysis*.

Texaco maintained that the photocopying was allowed under the fair use clauses of section 107 of the Copyright Act. In 1992, the Federal District Court of New York ruled that the publishers prevailed on factors one, three and four of section 107. The purpose and character of the photocopying was found to be commercial; the copyrighted work was photocopied in its entirety; and the publishers' market revenues were reduced by lost sales of paid subscriptions and licensing income. The second factor—the nature of the copyrighted work—favored Texaco, in that the court determined that the scope of the photocopied articles were in essence factual. A few days after this decision, the judge, in a footnote to the opinion, wrote that even if Texaco's purpose in photocopying was considered research (in effect, upholding the first factor of purpose and character of use as specified in section 107 of the Copyright Act), the plaintiffs would still prevail (*24*).

Texaco pledged to appeal the decision to the U.S. Supreme Court, applauded by many library associations, research groups, and business organizations that supported Texaco's position. In 1994, the 1992 ruling was upheld in the U.S. Court of Appeals for the Second Circuit. The court concluded that "Primarily because of lost licensing revenue, and to a minor extent because of lost subscription revenue, we agree with the District Court that 'the publishers have demonstrated a substantial harm to the value of their copyrights through [Texaco's] copying'...and...conclude that three of the four statutory factors, including the important first and fourth factors, favor the publishers." The Court also affirmed the importance of the CCC's licensing systems (*25*).

To the disappointment of researchers and librarians, Texaco settled the case in May 1995, by agreeing to pay $1 million settlement and a retroactive licensing fee to the CCC, by taking responsibility for a significant portion of the legal fees, and by entering into a five-year standard licensing agreement for its photocopying activities through the CCC. Despite the settlement, Texaco denies any wrongdoing (*26–28*).

In July 1995, the same U.S. Court of Appeals for the Second Circuit amended its 1994 opinion of the case, stating that its findings were predicated on "institutional, systematic copying," not copying done by individual researchers or professors. The amended majority ruling did restate that the original opinion of the court addressed the specific circumstances of the Texaco case and not the broader issue of fair use as it applies to the photocopying of scientific articles. What is confusing to the library and research communities is the following statement by the court:

> We do not deal with the question of copying by an individual for personal use in research or otherwise (not for resale), recognizing that under the fair use doctrine or the de minimis doctrine, such a practice by an individual might well not constitute an infringement...In other words, our opinion does not decide the case that would arise if Chickering [the researcher named in the case] were a professor or an independent scientist engaged in copying and creating files for independent research, as opposed to being employed by an institution in the pursuit of his research on the institution's behalf (*29*).

The second circuit court declined to explain its new opinion, causing further uncertainty to watchers of copyright infringement cases. Photocopying within non-profit organizations and academic institutions engaged in research activities seems to be a widespread practice, yet these groups have yet to be singled out by publishers for copyright violations. Commercial companies remain particularly vulnerable to publisher lawsuits when they reproduce individual articles from paid subscriptions without seeking permission or paying licensing fees to the CCC.

At this juncture, commercial research organizations have little option but to comply with the findings of the Texaco case. Photocopying for future personal reference appears to be off-limits to the for-profit sector, with nonprofit research groups and educational institutions monitoring the legal literature for parallel litigation among their own ranks.

Although the Texaco decision was not handed down by the U.S. Supreme Court, the case is significant because the site of the adjudication (i.e., the U.S. Court of Appeals for the Second Circuit resides in New York) is also the location of many major publishers.

DIRECTORY AND LEGAL PUBLICATIONS

In 1991, the Supreme Court ruled that a Kansas telephone directory was not protected by copyright laws because it was a factual work compiled from public domain information and lacking any originality. In reversing the decision of the U.S. District Court for the District of Kansas, the Supreme Court

> held that (1) the names, towns, and telephone numbers listed in the white pages were not protected by the telephone company's copyright in its combined white and yellow pages directory, because the listings in the white pages were not original to the telephone company, since (a) the listings, rather than owning their origin to the telephone company, were uncopyrightable facts, and (b) the telephone company has not selected, coordinated, or arranged these uncopyrightable facts in an original way sufficient to satisfy the minimum standards for copyright protection—either under the Federal Constitution's Article I, [Section 8, Clause 8], which authorizes Congress to secure for limited times to authors the exclusive right to their respective writings, or the Copyright Act of 1976..., which provides copyright protection for original works of authorship—given that the telephone company's selection and alphabetical arrangement of the listings lacked the creativity necessary to

demonstrate originality; and (2) because the telephone company's white pages listings lacked the requisite originality for copyright protection, the publishing company's use of the listings could not constitute copyright infringement (*30*).

The Supreme Court ruling distressed many public domain directory publishers who assumed that copyright notice on their publications was enough to ensure protection from infringement. In the summer of 1997, the *Feist* decision was extended to legal publications, in which a federal court determined that rulings by federal judges are public documents, and therefore legal decisions can be copied from any publisher as long as the publisher's value-added features (such as headnotes, indexes, and the arrangement of information) are not copied (*31*).

In a third case, involving a CD-ROM telephone directory, a publisher attempted to protect its factual compilation with a shrink-wrap license. A state court ruled that copyrighted databases cannot be protected by contractual agreements (*32*); however, in a reversal of the decision, a federal court ruled that shrink-wrap licenses do protect copyrighted works such as telephone directories, even if the works are compilations of facts (*33*).

COURSEPACKS

In April 1991, the Federal District Court in New York City ruled that Kinko's Graphics Corporation exceeded its rights of fair use when it photocopied textbook chapters to create "anthologies" of scholastic materials for use at local universities. The court was not persuaded that the copying was done for educational purposes, and reached its decision against Kinko's because the profit motive was seen as the overriding factor for the company's conduct. The amount copied from each textbook was substantial, and photocopies made by Kinko's eroded potential sales of the textbooks. While publishers urged the court to ban photocopying of any publication for the creation of anthologies, the Court declined, stating its preference to evaluate the fair use of each item in photocopied collections (*34*).

In July 1994, a federal district judge ruled that Michigan Document Services willfully infringed publisher's copyrighted materials by photocopying them for use in coursepacks (*35*). In February 1996, the U.S. Court of Appeals for the Sixth Circuit overturned the lower court's decision, ruling the Michigan Document Services' unauthorized use of copyrighted coursepacks was fair use. The use was nonprofit and educational. Since only 5 percent to 30 percent of each item was copied, the amount and substantiality did not substitute for sales of the originals. The publishers did not prove that they had been harmed by lost sales, only by lost permission fees (*36*).

In April 1996, the same U.S. Court of Appeals agreed to rehear the case, and in November of that year, upheld the lower court's ruling that Michigan Document Services violated copyright (*37*). In March 1997, the Supreme Court refused to review the case (*38*).

AUTHORS AND PUBLISHERS: AN ADVERSARIAL RELATIONSHIP

Authors who retain their own copyright are not generally reimbursed by online service providers or the CCC. Many publishers remain resistant to compensating authors for electronic versions of their works.

In 1993, a lawsuit was brought by the National Writers Union against Time Warner, Times Mirror, Reed-Elsevier, and University Microfilms in an attempt to secure royalty payments for freelance writers whose works have been reproduced in electronic databases (*39*). In an August 1997 decision, a federal court ruled that the publishers can republish printed works on CD-ROM's and in electronic databases without obtaining permission from the authors. The ruling did not specify Internet/Web republishing (*40*).

In 1996, *Harper's* magazine announced that it would become the first publisher to share profits from electronic publishing with its authors. Royalties from CD-ROM earnings and online articles will be split evenly, and writers will be paid retroactively for electronic articles published since January 1994. *Harper's* will make future payments through the Authors Registry, supported by major writers' groups and nearly 100 literary agencies representing more than 50,000 writers. To track earnings, the Information Access Company will require its online services to provide a per-article accounting (*41*).

Publishers Weekly also announced that it would pay its authors back and future royalties for electronic works, and the Carl Corporation entered into an agreement with the National Writers Union to establish a transaction-based writers' royalty system for articles ordered on the UnCover database. On the other hand, while K-III Communications will compensate writers for articles published in several of its titles from 1993 to 1995, the publisher has developed contracts demanding free future electronic rights from its authors (*41*).

In October 1997, five freelance writers filed a lawsuit against Knight-Ridder Information Inc., arguing that the online vendor distributed excerpts from their books on the UnCover service without compensating the authors who retain copyright (*42*). As mentioned above, UnCover had reached an agreement with the National Writers Union to compensate writers for reproduced works, so many industry experts will be watching the outcome of this case with interest.

INTERNET SERVICE PROVIDERS

Late in 1995, CompuServe, in a class-action lawsuit, reached a settlement with the National Music Publishers Association. Prior to the legal action, CompuServe allowed subscribers to download over 550 copyrighted songs owned by Frank Music Corporation. Under the agreement, CompuServe must pay the association a rights fee and provide a mechanism for other content providers to license music rights from the association agent (*43*).

Two suits, brought by the Church of Scientology against former members and their Internet providers for disseminating Scientology documents on the Web, were dismissed in court. (The *Washington Post* was also named in one of the suits for including in an article two sentences from Scientology publications.) A northern Virginia federal judge dismissed one case against the defendants, citing "that a much broader motivation prevailed [by the Church of Scientology]—the stifling of criticism and dissent of the religious practices of Scientology and the destruction of its opponents" (*44*). The judge in the second case ruled that users' postings are not the responsibility of their Internet providers, a decision that goes against recommendations in the white paper (*45*).

Copyright Law in the Digital Age

Rightsholders and users of information differ in their opinions about whether or not the Copyright Act grants protection for electronic transmission of content. In contention is a publisher's tendency to protect its copyrights by adding shrink-wrap licenses to software or terms and conditions to online databases and Web sites. Such licenses tend to impose restrictions on the use, copying, lending, selling, and transmission of software programs and content, generally preventing any fair usage as specified in the Copyright Act.

The online consumer is generally unaware of copyright, so the trend seems to be to prosecute Internet service providers for their users' infringements. Listserv and newsgroup users are beginning to specify their conditions for retransmissions by attaching statements to their messages indicating whether or not messages may be freely copied and distributed.

In an effort to clarify divergent interpretations of what is or is not protected, the U.S. Copyright Office and the Register of Copyrights have issued a number of statements regarding electronic content.

> The copyright law protects works of authorship, published or unpublished, in any tangible medium of expression...The Copyright Office would readily register a work as published that was posted to an electronic bulletin board by or under the authority of the copyright owner...posting on an electronic bulletin board could constitute publication. A delivery of the means by which any member of the public may obtain a copy of a work by downloading it, is in effect the same as if one had actually delivered a copy. There is a distinction between "general" publication and "limited" publication. The definition given above is that of "general" publication. A "limited" publication occurs when there is an effective restriction on the class of persons who can obtain a copy of the work and a restriction on the purpose for which that copy can be used (*46*).

ELECTRONIC MAIL AND LISTSERVS

Too few end users or consumers are aware that electronic mail messages are protected by the Copyright Act as original works of authorship or that the Berne Convention safeguards authors' rights in member countries. Yet without seeking author permission, Internet users fequently make copies of personal mail messages for transmission.

Since the Berne Convention does not require authors to register or provide notification of their copyright, the information and publishing industries widely acknowledge that electronic mail communications and listserv postings are protected, as they are considered original works of authorship. So far, an international tribunal to resolve individual copyright disputes has not been established. When potential copyright infringements arise, plaintiffs tend to file lawsuits in countries favorable to their position. Disparate state or country law and jurisdictional control to hear copyright infringement cases further complicate the right to copy or not to copy messages or files.

WEB-BASED CONTENT

Those who publish on the Web seem to be protected by the Copyright Act and Berne if the design and arrangement of text, graphics, audio, and video are original works. Public domain information is not always apparent; the information itself may not be protected by copyright law, but the page, if originality is evident in its creation, may be protected. The saving of Hyper Text Markup Language (HTML) source code to reuse as a template for a Web page is probably also in copyright violation. If the HTML source code is used for personal reasons, however, then this may be a fair use application and copyright has not been violated.

There is yet to be a clear-cut adjudication about the copyrightability of links. Linked lists may not be copyrighted, but if original thought was used to create the links, they may be protected by copyright law. Many industry experts believe that the Internet was established to link individuals and organizations with common interests, and to copyright links and collect royalties would severely hamper the Internet's great strength. On the other hand, there are many organizations that do not want certain individuals or groups to link into their Web sites, and are therefore imposing threats of lawsuits or requiring annual royalty or licensing payments. Some legal experts feel that there is "implied permission" allowing unlimited linkages from and to Web sites.

Framing is a form of linking, in which a Web site owner will place the content of other Web sites within its own site. In mid-1997, TotalNews settled a lawsuit over the display of outside news sites alongside the TotalNews logo, menu, and advertising banners. The news providers, including Time Inc., CNN, Dow Jones, Times Mirror, the Washington Post Co., and Reuters, sued TotalNews for not first seeking permission to frame their copyrighted sites. The media companies objected to the importation of their content without the advertising, and negotiated a link license with TotalNews to compensate the news Web owners (*47*).

COMMERCIAL DATABASES: TERMS AND CONDITIONS

By imposing fees and conditions of use on nearly all content, owners have narrowed, perhaps eliminated, the concept of fair use as conceived in the Copyright Act. Dialog's 1994 announcement of its Electronic Redistribution and Archiving (ERA) Service, allowing online searchers to redistribute a specified number of copies only within the user's organization (and thereby permitting enterprisewide copying of electronic information if royalties are paid), was widely hailed by information professionals. Advocates of this service support similar electronic rights mechanisms for all commercial and noncommercial database and Internet services.

Electronic rights are not generally specified by other commercial database produc-ers. A searcher does sign a subscription agreement with LEXIS/NEXIS. The "license" permits fair use distribution as specified under the Copyright Act of 1976. Allowable copying beyond the fair use provisions is detailed in the "Supplemental Terms for Specific Materials." Public domain databases on LEXIS/NEXIS generally do not contain copyright notices. Dow Jones News/Retrieval permits "personal, noncommer-cial use only" of its copyrighted information. Reproduction, retransmission, and any dissemination require written consent.

Most online providers that offer numerous databases for searching do copyright each record in a database. Since the database provider and online service have "added value" by "creatively" compiling the record, arranging the record information for retrieval and adding field names so individual parts of the record can be searched, the record becomes protected by copyright laws. It does not matter if the record contains public domain information or information from commercially produced works.

To ensure that search results are not in violation of copyright infringement, information professionals are advised to conduct one search for one user at a time (i.e., do not duplicate the results of each search for several users). If current awareness services are provided to users in which more than one copy is distributed, librarians should negotiate licensing arrangements with the online services that allow duplica-tion of search results to more than one individual. When downloading online search results, intermediaries must keep all copyright notices with each record when postpro-cessing search results. Cover sheets, outlining a user's responsibility to honor copy-right laws, should be developed for each delivered search.

WEB DATABASES: TERMS AND CONDITIONS

It is often a struggle to locate publishers' copyright statements on their Web sites; when terms and conditions are uncovered, they lack clarity about what can or cannot be reproduced. For example, publishers tend to differentiate between personal use and commercial use of copyrighted materials, restrictions are established for interme-diary searchers that are not applicable to end users, notifications are absent on whether or not royalty payments to the CCC for electronic copies are allowed, and higher prices are imposed for content retrieved on commercial databases that are not in place for duplicate content found on the Internet.

In part, the lack of clarity has to do with how end users are defined. Consumer end users have been referred to as "inept but happy information consumers" who do not seek help from a librarian or pay an independent to retrieve information. The consumer end user is probably not the person addressed in copyright and terms and conditions statements posted by database providers on their Web sites. The profes-sional end user, on the other hand, employs the Internet as an information tool to further advance the services and/or product line of a nonprofit or for-profit organiza-tion. This type of end user typically has access to a corporate or special library or employs a librarian or pays an information broker to retrieve information faster and more reliably on commercial online systems. The professional end user works in an organization that can afford to pay for its information and is therefore considered the target of any restrictions on the use of information found on the Internet (*48*).

Intermediaries who conduct searches on commercial databases at the request of professional end users review contracts and negotiate database terms with vendors. By contrast, "click here" contracts do not present similar opportunities to negotiate terms of use. If a user agrees to terms, many contract law experts are likely to advise that an enforceable contract has been created.

Until terms are clarified and royalty payment mechanisms are in place for duplicating Web content, intermediaries should click on terms and conditions policies, read them, and try to determine when it is legal to reproduce the needed information or when it is "safer" to contact the publisher for "pass-along" commercial rights. The rights and permissions departments of each Web site should be contacted for permission, or the CCC should be asked to secure rights from the publishers for the use of digital copies.

The Future

COPYRIGHT LEGISLATION

Discussion and debate about the NII report and its recommendations to revise existing copyright, trademark, patent, and trade laws will probably persist well into the next century. For now, it appears that current legislation and federal adjudications on copyright infringements must be accepted. Until the U.S. Congress enacts clarifying changes, the Copyright Act of 1976 and future court decisions will remain subject to interpretation.

If the U.S. government's intent is to ultimately commercialize the NII, however, public domain works—now copyright-free and available at low or no cost—could be restricted by the private sector to users who pay licensing or royalty fees to access these materials. The capability of individuals to freely communicate with each other globally could be diminished by threats of copyright violations. The ease with which research is documented may be jeopardized if publishers forbid users to combine information from a number of sources into single comprehensive reports.

The future of copyright legislation is unpredictable; issues surrounding fair use and the commercialization of information remain cloudy. Although authors, researchers, publishers, librarians, and consumers strive to safeguard their own copyright security, they recognize the importance of delivering information to the public without the imposition of inappropriate restrictions. Finding the suitable equilibrium is daunting.

DATABASE PRODUCERS

In March 1996, the European Commission adopted a directive requiring member states to implement database protection laws by January 1, 1998. The directive would protect factual databases from "extraction" and "reutilization" for a period of fifteen years (*49*). The U.S. Copyright Office held sixteen meetings in the spring of 1997 to discuss legislation that would provide greater legal protection to databases. Proponents and opponents had an opportunity to voice their opinions about the need for revised or new laws (*50*). In summarizing the views of divergent groups, the Copyright

Office acknowledged that there is agreement about two key principles: "databases are vulnerable to copying, and adequate incentives are needed to ensure their continued creation...[and] 'free riding' in the form of substantial copying for commercial, competitive purposes should not be permitted" (*50*). The Copyright Office is not authorized to make recommendations, but its report is being closely scrutinized by Congress with producers continuing to lobby for stricter laws to protect their databases from copyright infringement.

NONPROFIT ORGANIZATIONS AND EDUCATIONAL INSTITUTIONS

Teachers, who previously were comfortable legally distributing photocopies of selected publications to their students under guidelines established in section 107 of the Copyright Act (i.e., single copying for teachers and multiple copies for classroom use), face uncertainty about electronic distribution rights that may or may not be granted as educational fair use.

Many college and university libraries, particularly those that belong to the American Research Libraries (ARL), are becoming increasingly frustrated over not being able to "afford to buy access to the knowledge which they paid to have created." They are seriously contemplating the establishment of a new "rights-management organization to retain a royalty-free right for the use...of faculty-produced journal articles. Such an organization would permit [universities] to offset the power of any publisher who wished to price university libraries out of the market." A second option being considered by the academic community is "turning over the production and pricing of their journals to the private sector, while retaining editorial control" (*51*).

Publishers generally hold authors' copyrights "in perpetuity," provide a limited number of complimentary reprints to authors, and maintain rights to reproduce in all future formats authors' works. In bypassing publishers, authors hope to retain their individual copyrights by directly authorizing reproduction permissions and receiving royalties. The research and library communities are concerned by the possible lack of peer review and indexing control should authors publish their own works (e.g., scientists conducting similar research may find it difficult to access and scrutinize works written by their counterparts). Authors respond by insisting that electronic evaluations and classification schemes can be implemented; these electronic mechanisms are as effective as current traditional practices.

PUBLISHER INITIATIVES

In contrast to the academic community, publishers are testing a digital system to "organize and track material, charge for purchases and secure copyrighted material with high-tech envelopes or 'wrappers.'" The tagging system is called "digital object identifier" (DOI), and is intended "to protect digital material from unauthorized copying." A user will be able to read content on a computer screen, but will not be able to download or print the material without authorization (*52*).

ARCHIVING THE INTERNET

The Copyright Act is very specific about archiving. Section 108, Reproduction by Libraries and Archives, states that

> It is not an infringement of copyright for a library or archives, or any of its employees acting within the scope of their employment, to reproduce no more than one copy or phonorecord of a work, or to distribute such copy or phonorecord, under the conditions specified by this section, if (1) the reproduction or distribution is made without any purpose of direct or indirect commercial advantage; (2) the collections of library or archives are (i) open to the public or (ii) available not only to researchers affiliated with the library or archives or with the institution of which it is a part, but also to other persons doing research in a specialized field; and (3) the reproduction or distribution of the work includes a notice of copyright (9).

Internet caching (in which frequently requested Web pages are copied into a user's browser) and the storage of favorite Web sites in bookmarks could be considered forms of archiving. To date, no rights holder has sued a user, Internet provider, or browser software company over the caching of Web site URLs. With mixed reaction from Web site owners, some companies have begun the laborious process of archiving the Internet. The information community seems to advocate Internet archives, pointing out the necessity to preserve a historical record of the world's intellectual property, while many rights holders express concern that permission or licensing agreements are not being sought from them to create the archives. The debate may intensify over the next few years, with a clear-cut resolution only being provided when a significant case is litigated.

A Cautious Approach

At least two major courses of action can be taken by libraries, for-profit corporations, nonprofit organizations, and independent information professionals. First, a conservative position can be maintained regarding duplication of copyrighted works, forbidding any reproduction, preparation, distribution, performance, or displaying of works without first seeking written permission from the copyright holder or paying royalty fees for such rights. Seemingly an extreme viewpoint, considering the current climate of litigation, this is a "safe" policy. Perhaps a riskier second approach is to continue duplication practices as "protected" by the fair use sections of the Copyright Act. Organizations or individuals faced with legal suits over interpretations of these sections will need substantial financial resources to cover lengthy judicial battles.

Librarians and independent information providers have not as yet been sued over copyright infringement, but there is concern about what their users and clients are doing with copyrighted works after searches of online and CD-ROM resources have been submitted. As intermediaries, it is important that vendors' mandates are followed by the placement of copyright notices on all materials forwarded to a second party, by cautioning users about limitations imposed on the reproduction of copyrighted works, and by educating users about royalty payment mechanisms that compensate publishers and authors for copying beyond the fair use provisions.

In using the Internet and other systems furnished by online service providers, care must be taken not to infringe upon the rights of copyright holders of electronic mail messages and data files. To prevent this, the best safeguards are the following:

1. Read and follow vendor licensing agreements.
2. Look for copyright notices (keeping in mind that works do not have to have such notices in order to be protected).
3. Seek written permission from the publisher to download information when there is uncertainty about what is allowed.
4. Give patrons or clients Internet URLs to retrieve information. If each individual logs on and downloads his or her own version, then reproduction may be viewed as personal use copying.
5. Although a universal mechanism is not in place to pay royalties, contact the CCC to seek permissions from publishers when copying is for commercial purposes.
6. If a user *must* click on a terms and conditions agreement in order to view or retrieve an Internet document, then the contract is probably enforceable, similar to hard-copy agreements signed with commercial vendors.
7. Information brokers, librarians, or other intermediaries conducting research on behalf of another individual or company are advised to search commercial databases for full-text articles and *not* the Internet, or use a document supplier who pays royalties to the CCC. Content is not free, but signed terms and conditions are quite clear about reproduction rights.

REFERENCES

1. J. Markoff, "In a World of Instant Copies, Who Pays for Original Work?" *New York Times*, 4:18 (Aug. 9, 1992).
2. S. C. Ardito, "Electronic Copyright Under Siege." *Online*, **20**(5), 83–88 (Sept./Oct. 1996).
3. S. C. Ardito and P. Eiblum, "Conflicted Copyrights—Inevitability: Death, Taxes, and Copyright." *Online*, **22**(1), Jan./Feb. 1998).
4. U.S. Constitution, Article I, Section 8 (patents and copyrights).
5. U.S. Code, Title 17, Copyrights, "Section 106. Exclusive rights in copyrighted works."
6. U.S. Code, Title 17, Copyrights, "Sections 301–305. Duration of copyright."
7. United States, 104th Congress, 1st Session, "S.483: Copyright Term Extension Act of 1995," March 3, 1995.
8. U.S. Code, Title 17, Copyrights, "Section 107. Limitations on exclusive rights: fair use."
9. U.S. Code, Title 17, Copyrights, "Section 108. Limitations on exclusive rights: reproduction by libraries and archives."
10. "Open Market, Copyright Clearance Center Announce Online Rights Clearance System." *Inform. Today,* **12**(6), 6 (June 1995).
11. American Society of Journalists and Authors, "Authors and Agents Launch 'ASCAP'-Style Agency for Writers." *ASJA Contracts Watch* (May 18, 1995).
12. U.S. Department of Commerce, Information Infrastructure Task Force, "A Preliminary Draft of the Report of the Working Group on Intellectual Property Rights," U.S. Patent and Trademark Office, Washington, DC, July 1994.
13. U.S. Department of Commerce, Information Infrastructure Task Force, "Intellectual Property and the National Information Infrastructure: The Report of the Working Group on Intellectual Property Rights," U.S. Patent and Trademark Office, Washington, DC, Sept. 5, 1995.
14. "What You Need to Know about Copyright." *Inform. Adv.,* **7**(2), 1 (Feb. 1995).
15. "Fair Use in the Electronic Age: Serving the Public Interest." *College Res. Libr. News*, **56**(1), 24 (Jan. 1995).

16.   A. P. Lutzker, "Commerce Department's White Paper on National and Global Information Infrastructure: Executive Summary for the Library and Educational Community," Washington, DC, Sept. 20, 1995.

17.   J. Shiver, "Lawmakers Debate Internet Copyright Bill." *Los Angeles Times*, D:2 (Feb. 8, 1996).

18.   National Conference of Commissioners on Uniform State Laws, Uniform Commercial Code, Article 2B, Licenses (draft), Sept. 22, 1997.

19.   Universal Copyright Convention as revised in Paris on July 24, 1971.

20.   Berne Convention for the Protection of Literary and Artistic Works, Paris Act of July 24, 1971.

21.   S. R. Englund and R. L. Horton, "Bills to Implement WIPO Treaties Ignite Debate." *Nat. Law J.,* **20**(8), C34 (Oct. 20, 1997).

22.   WIPO (World Intellectual Property Organization) Copyright Treaty, adopted by the Diplomatic Conference on Dec. 20, 1996.

23.   P. Dorbrin "Using Works of Foreign Artists? Free Ride is Over." *Phila. Inquirer*, C:1–2 (Jan. 28, 1996).

24.   *American Geophysical Union et al.* v. *Texaco Inc.*, 85 Civ. 3446 (PLN), S.D.N.Y., July 24, 1992.

25.   *American Geophysical Union et al.* v. *Texaco Inc.,* U.S. Court of Appeals for the Second Circuit, No. 92–9341, Oct. 28, 1994.

26.   "Texaco Will Pay $1M to Settle Copyright Suit." *Pub. Weekly* **242**(21), 12 (May 22, 1995).

27.   "Publishers, Texaco Settle Suit." *Editor Pub.,* **128**(26), 52 (July 1, 1995).

28.   "Photocopying Action Is Settled by Texaco." *New York Law J.,* **214**(87), 11 (Nov. 3, 1995).

29.   D. Pines, "Aim to Narrow Circuit Ruling on 'Fair Use'; Amended Decision Issued in Controversial Case." *New York Law J.,* **214**(12), 1 (July 19, 1995).

30.   "Feist Publications, Inc., Petitioner v. Rural Telephone Service Company, Inc.," U.S. Supreme Court Reports, 499 US 340, 113 L Ed 2d 358, 111 S Ct 1282 [no. 89–1909], argued Jan. 9, 1991, decided March 27, 1991.

31.   *Hyperlaw Inc.* v. *West Publishing Co.,* no. 91–0589, U.S. District Court of New York, May 20, 1997.

32.   *ProCD, Inc.* v. *Zeidenberg*, no. 95–C–0671–C, U.S. District Court for the Western District of Wisconsin, Jan. 4, 1996.

33.   *ProCD, Incorporated* v. *Matthew Zeidenberg and Silken Mountain Web Services, Inc.,* no. 96–1139, U.S. Court of Appeals for the Seventh Circuit, June 20, 1996.

34.   *Basic Books, Inc.* v. *Kinko's Graphics Corp.,* 758 F. Supp. 1522, S.D.N.Y., 1991.

35.   *Princeton University Press* v. *Michigan Document Services Inc.,* 855 F. Supp. 905, 910, E.D.Mich., 1994.

36.   *Princeton University Press* v. *Michigan Document Services,* U.S. Court of Appeals for the Sixth Circuit, no. 94–1778, Feb. 12, 1996.

37.   *Princeton University Press, MacMillan, Inc., and St. Martin's Press, Inc.,* v. *Michigan Document Services, Inc., and James M. Smith,* U.S. Court of Appeals for the Sixth Circuit no. 94–1778, Nov. 8, 1996.

38.   "Supreme Court Refusal to Hear MDS Case Welcome News for Publishers." *AAP News*, March 31, 1997.

39.   J. Matthews, "Writers Sue on Story Use by Data Services." *Washington Post,* C:3 (Dec. 17, 1993).

40.   *Jonathan Tasini, Mary Kay Blakely, Barbara Garson, Margot Mifflin, Sonia Jaffe Robbins, and David S. Whitford* v. *The New York Times Co., Newsday Inc., Time Inc., The Atlantic Monthly Co., Mead Data Central Corp., and University Microfilms Inc.,* 93 Civ. 8678 (SS), S.D.N.Y. Aug. 13, 1997.

41.   American Society of Journalists and Authors, "Harper's Is First to Pay All Contributors for Past E-use and Pledge Split for Future; PW to Follow; Both to Use Authors Registry as Payment Agency; K-III Also to Pay for Unauthorized Use but Won't Commit on Future." *ASJA Contracts Watch,* Feb. 2, 1996.

42.   S. Herhold, "Five Freelance Writers Allege Copyright Violations on Internet." *San Jose Mercury News,* C:3 (Oct. 24, 1997).

43.   *Frank Music Corp. and The Harry Fox Agency, Inc.* v. *CompuServe Incorporated,* Civ. No. 93–Civ–8153–JFK, S.D.N.Y., Nov. 8, 1995.

44.   *Religious Technology Center* v. *Arnaldo Pagliarini Lerma, Digital Gateway Systems, The Washington Post, Mark Fisher, and Richard Leiby,* 908 F. Supp. 1353, D.Va., Nov. 29, 1995.

45.   *Religious Technology Center* v. *Netcom On-line Communication Services, Inc.,* 907 F. Supp. 1361, No. C–95–20091 RMW, 1995 WL 707167, N.D.Cal., Nov. 21, 1995.

46.   U.S. Copyright Office, "Publication via Electronic Bulletin Board," Washington, DC, Nov. 1, 1994.

47.   *Digital Ink Co., Time Inc., Cable News Network, Inc., Times Mirror Company, Dow Jones & Company, Inc., and Reuters New Media Inc.* v. *Total News, Inc., Datapix Inc., Grouper Technologies Inc., Roman*

Godzich, Larry Pagni and Norman Bashkingy, 97 Civ. 1190, U.S. District Court Southern District of New York (PKL), Feb. 20, 1997.

48.   S. C. Ardito and C. Ebbinghouse, "All Rights Reserved . . . Well, Maybe Not: Copyright in a Web World." *Searcher*, **5**(5), 24–34 (May 1997).

49.   "Directive 96/9/EC of the European Parliament and of the Council of 11 March 1996 on the Legal Protection of Databases," *Official J. Euro. Comm.,* **L77**, 20 (March 27, 1996).

50.   A. L. Deutsch, "Congress to Consider Data Base Bill." *Nat. Law J.,* **20**(8), C3 (Oct. 20, 1997).

51.   D. Schulenburger, Faculty convocation speech, University of Kansas, Lawrence, KS, Sept. 9, 1997.

52.   D. Carvajal, "An Electronic Sheriff to Battle Book Rustling." *New York Times,* D:1 (Sept. 22, 1997).

BIBLIOGRAPHY

Alvarez, G., "New Legal Issues on the Net: A Technology Agenda for 1996 and Beyond." *Amer. Lawyer,* **S28**(4), 28 (Dec. 1995).

Ardito, S. C., "The Information Broker and Intellectual Property Rights." *Bull. Amer. Soc. Inform. Sci.,* **21**(3), 19 (Feb./March 1995).

Bielefield, A., Bielefled, A., and Cheeseman, L. *Technology and Copyright Law: A Guidebook for the Library, Research and Teaching Professions,* Neal Schuman, New York, NY, 1997.

Crews, K. D., "Copyright, Fair Use, and the Challenge for Universities: Promoting the Progress of Higher Education." *Pub. Res. Q.,* **12**(1), 95–96 (spring 1996).

Crews, K. D., "Copyright Law and Information Policy Planning: Public Rights of Use in the 1990s and Beyond." *J. Gov. Inform.*, **22**(2), 87–99 (March/April 1995).

"Free Speech and Copyright in Cyberspace: Legal Issues Surrounding the Internet." *Online Libr. Microcomputers,* **13**(3), 1 (March 1995).

Gasaway, L. N., *Libraries and Copyright: A Guide to Copyright Law in the 1990s,* Special Libraries Association, Washington, DC, 1994.

Gasaway, L. N., ed., *Growing Pains: Adapting Copyright for Libraries, Education, and Society,* Fred B. Rothman, Littleton, CO, 1997.

Hartnick, A. J., "White Paper on Info Superhighway." *New York Law J.,* **214**(82), 5 (Oct. 27, 1995).

Hartnick, A. J., "White Paper on Info Superhighway: Part 2." *New York Law J.,* **214**(87), 5 (Nov. 3, 1995).

"The New Copyright-Driven Economics of Document Delivery." *Searcher,* **4**(7), 28–30 (July/Aug. 1996).

Nimmer, R. T., *Information Law: Rights, Licenses, Liabilities,* Carswell Thomson, Scarborough, Ontario, Canada, 1996.

Noer, M., "Policing Cyberspace—US Copyright Laws Need Updating." *Forbes*, **155**(8), 50 (April 10, 1995).

Rose, L., *Netlaw: Your Rights in the Online World,* Osborne McGraw-Hill, Berkeley, CA, 1995.

Rose, L., *Netlaw: Internet Law in Plain English,* Osborne McGraw-Hill, Berkeley, CA, 1998.

U.S. Copyright Office, *Copyright Basics,* Washington, DC, Sept. 1995.

SELECTED COPYRIGHT INTERNET SITES

American Association of Law Libraries: http://www.aallnet.org/committee/copyright/
American Research Libraries: http://arl.cni.org/scomm/copyright/copyright.html
Coalition for Networked Information: http://www.cni.org
Copyright Clearance Center Online: http://www.copyright.com
The Copyright Website: http://www.benedict.com/
The Creative Incentive Coalition: http://www.cic.org/
Cyberspace Law Center: http://www.cybersquirrel.com/clc/ip.htm/
Digital Future Coalition: http://www.ari.net/dfc/
DOI (Digital Object Identifier System): http://www.doi.org/
Electronic Frontier Foundation: http://www.eff.org
FindLaw: http://www.findlaw.com
Franklin Pierce Law Center's Intellectual Property Mall: http://www.ipmall.fplc.edu/
Information Property: Copyrights, Trademarks & Patents: http://www.brint.com/IntellP.htm
Intellectual Property and the National Information Infrastructure: The Report of the

Working Group on Intellectual Property Rights—http://www.uspto.gov/web/offices/com/doc/ipnii
KuesterLaw: The Technology Law Resource—http://kuesterlaw.com
The Legal Information Institute, Cornell University: http://www.law.cornell.edu
Special Libraries Association—http:www.sla.org/membership/irc/copyright.html
Stanford University Libraries: Copyright and Fair Use—http://fairuse.stanford.edu
U.S. Copyright Office: http://lcweb.loc.gov/copyright
U.S. Patent and Trademark Office: http://www.uspto.gov
University of Texas—http://www.utsystem.edu/ogc/intellectualproperty/
WIPO (World Intellectual Property Organization): http://www.wipo.org/

STEPHANIE C. ARDITO

FLEXIBLE WORKING IN U.K. LIBRARY AND INFORMATION SERVICES

Introduction

The drive for flexibility has been a characteristic feature of U.K. library and information service management for the last decade. Flexible work patterns have been embraced by library and information service managers in the United Kingdom as a way of coping with uncertainty and responding to change. As service managers respond to customer demands for new services on the one hand, and staff demands for different ways of working on the other, the nature of the library and information workforce has been transformed.

Although flexibility has become a "'buzz-word' for what many see as positive or exciting long-term changes to the world of work" (*1*), flexible work patterns have long been a feature of library and information services in the United Kingdom. In 1879, for example, Thomas Baker, addressing the Second Annual Meeting of the Library Association, explained that the publicly funded Manchester free libraries were using women workers employed as: "half-timers, from five o'clock P.M. to nine every evening at the wages of ten shillings per week, with the prospect of appointment as full assistants as vacancies occurred" (*2*).

Similarly, in the 1960s, Layzell Ward campaigned for the increased availability of part-time work in U.K. library and information services so that women with child-care responsibilities could continue with their careers (*3*). The term *flexible worker* may thus be of recent origin, but the concept of employees working other than on a full-time, permanent basis is not. The recent upsurge in interest in flexible working does have some substance behind it, however; new and different working patterns have emerged, the scale of flexible working has increased, and the attitudes of library and information service managers toward their flexible workers have changed as they realize that new strategies and practices are needed if they are to take full advantage of the benefits flexible workers offer.

Definitions

The term flexible work is often used to describe a whole range of work patterns that do not conform to the standard, permanent, full-time employment contract. Flexibility is difficult to define comprehensively and can refer to functional flexibility or multiskilling. The more common uses of the term, however, refer to

- Numerical flexibility, whereby employers vary the number of staff members to meet labor needs by, for example, the use of temporary workers, agency staff, workers on fixed-term contracts and casual workers
- Temporal flexibility, whereby employers vary the hours or days worked by employees to respond to daily or weekly production pressure by, for example, the use of part-time workers or job-sharers

In the United Kingdom, there are a variety of work patterns that fall within both these categories, the most common being

- *part-time work*—although the U.K. Equal Opportunities Commission suggests that part-time work means different things to different people (*4*), employers generally define part-time workers as those working less than "the standard working week." This itself can vary from one workplace to another, however.
- *Job-share*—by which "two or more people voluntarily shar[e] the responsibilities of what is normally a full-time job" (*5*).
- *Temporary work*—the employment of workers on daily, weekly, monthly, or short-term contracts that end at the employer's discretion.
- *annualized hours contracts*—"a system whereby the period of time within which employees must work is defined over a whole year" (*6*); thus, the average 37.5-hour work week becomes 1702.5 hours (after holiday and bank holiday entitlements), which are worked in the course of the year after agreement between worker and manager.
- *Term-time only contracts*—common in universities, colleges, and schools, employees work only when the academic institution is in session, and not during the vacations.
- *Flextime*—which allows employees to choose, often around fixed "core hours," when they start and finish work.

Flexibility of location is also important and becoming increasingly common with the development of communications technology. Teleworking and other forms of home working have increased steadily and involve staff members spending all or some of their work week at home using equipment such as telephone, fax, and computer to carry out their tasks.

The Nature of the Workforce

THE NATIONAL PICTURE

The last twenty years have been characterized by a huge expansion in the use of flexible workers in the United Kingdom, particularly in the service sector. It is difficult to trace the growth of some flexible work patterns as data on job-sharing, flexitime, annual hours contracts, and term-time working was first systematically collected in the spring 1993 *Labour Force Survey,* but it has been estimated that flexible workers constitute 38.2 percent of all those in employment (*1*). This trend is likely to continue; the Department for Education and Employment predicts that the share of employees working part-time, for example, is expected to increase from 29 percent in 1996 to 31 percent in 2006 (*7*). The most recent *Labour Force Survey* data (from the summer of 1997) show that around a quarter of employees in the United Kingdom work part-time and almost 7 percent are temporary workers (*8*).

These changes in the nature of the labor market may be attributed to four developments (*9*). First, globalization and increased competition have forced organizations to scrutinize the effectiveness and efficiency of their operations in a quest for greater price/cost flexibility, which has led to more extensive use of temporal flexibility. Second, technological changes have created a demand for new working arrangements. Third, demographic changes have altered the makeup of the U.K. labor force, with a vast increase in the number of married women participating in paid labor market activity (*10*). In order to accommodate their other traditional responsibilities such as child care, different work patterns have been adopted to entice women into the workforce. Finally, British government policies since 1979 have encouraged labor-market flexibility.

THE U.K. LIBRARY AND INFORMATION SERVICE WORKFORCE

A variety of work patterns are in use in U.K. library and information services, reflecting in part at least what is happening in the general labor market. At a national level, there are few historical statistics to provide comparative data, but a picture of an increasing use of flexible workers does emerge, and the significance of flexible work patterns in U.K. library and information services is beyond doubt. According to one study, 87 percent of library and information organizations taking part in a national survey of flexible work practices used some form of flexible working (*11*). Just 13 percent of respondents said their organization had no flexible workers and was staffed by permanent, full-time workers only. Workers employed on permanent part-time, temporary part-time, job-share, home working, temporary full-time, term-time, and annualized hours' contracts represented 40 percent of all workers. (See Table 1.)

TABLE 1

U.K. Library and Information Service Workers on
Flexible Work Patterns (as Percentage of All Workers)

Working pattern	Percent
Permanent part-time	29
Job-share	3
Temporary part-time	4
Temporary full-time	1
Homeworker	<1
Term-time only	2
Annual hours	1

Source: Data from Ref. *12*.

The following sections give an overview of the more common flexible work patterns in U.K. library and information services.

Part-Time Work

Within the national expansion of the flexible workforce, the rapidly increasing number of part-time workers has been significant, and library and information services have been no exception to this rule. As Table 1 illustrates, extensive use is made of part-time working patterns in library and information services in the United Kingdom. One study found that 21 percent of library and information services had increased the number of part-time workers over a twelve-month period in 1994 and 1995 (*12*). Part-time workers are the most common form of flexible worker in library and information services and have traditionally been used as the most efficient method of ensuring staff levels are maintained for the duration of the service's long opening hours. In public libraries in the United Kingdom, however, part-time staff members are often employed for the opposite reason; that is, that smaller branch or community libraries are open for less than "full-time" hours and therefore only need part-time staff. Part-time workers are also often recruited for specific purposes (e.g., evening and weekend services, and shelving; *13*).

It has been suggested that some types of work may be better suited to part-time employment than others (*14*), and library work is arguably one of these. From the employer's point of view there is considerable scope for part-time work in libraries, with variable working hours and workloads making part-time work very attractive. From the employee's point of view, part-time work may be a useful way of coping with the routine duties of library work, as there is less danger of boredom if the worker knows he or she will be engaged on a particular task for a limited time only.

In the United Kingdom, part-time contracts are offered most often to support staff. Although there are significant numbers of part-time workers who are professional staff members, the figures in Table 2 suggest that there is some resistance to professional librarians not working full-time. Despite the widespread use of part-time staff, there is still a common view among library and information service managers

TABLE 2

Percentage of U.K. Library Information Services Organizations Using
Part-Time Workers, by Employee Status

	Professional librarians	Support staff
Permanent part-time	30	65
Temporary part-time	12	30

Source: Data from Ref. *11*.

that any employee working less than permanent full-time hours lacks the necessary commitment to his or her work and the organization (*13*). This can lead to negative views of the part-time worker's ability and promotion potential. Although legislation in the United Kingdom has to some extent "leveled the playing field" for part-time workers (see below), restrictions relating to terms of employment, career advancement, and the variety of posts available for part-time workers persist. These difficulties have encouraged employers and employees to look for alternatives to part-time working. Job sharing has emerged as a partial solution to the problems of equity in employment and promotion prospects that part-time workers often face.

Job Sharing

Job sharing has existed in some form in the United Kingdom since the 1940s, when Barclays Bank ran a "twinning" scheme (*15*). The implementation of job sharing in U.K. library and information services did not, however, begin until the 1970s (*16*). The opportunity to job share, it is argued, halts the downward occupational mobility of women workers with child care responsibilities, and in general gives women a better chance of reaching senior management positions as they can maintain their position in the library management hierarchy (*17*). Job sharing thus extends opportunities to work less than full-time hours in a professional post at a senior level. In one survey, 26 percent of library and information services indicated that they used job sharing (*12*). The acceptability of senior and professional posts for job share (or any other flexible working pattern) is, however, a matter for debate, and the adoption of flexible working at higher levels is still dependent on the attitudes and decisions of individual managers. There is therefore no consensus of opinion among library and information service managers in the United Kingdom about the appropriateness of all posts in all circumstances for flexible working. Although there is no automatic right to be able to job share, many organizations in the United Kingdom, especially those in the public sector, have instituted policies of job sharing as part of their implemenation of equal opportunity policies.

Job sharing is therefore quite widespread within U.K. library and information services, but there is some confusion about when posts are "truly" job share, and when they are merely "job splits"; that is, two members of staff doing different tasks within, notionally, one post, almost like part-time work. Job sharers should have a period of overlap at least once a week, when they are both at work to exchange information about the job and make sure that each job-share partner knows what the other is doing or planning.

Temporary Contracts

The establishment of specialist recruitment agencies for the library and information sector, TFPL and Instant Library to name just two, bears testament to the growing demand for temporary workers in library and information services in the United Kingdom. The employment of temporary workers may result from uncertainty about the organization's long-term future or financial status, or may be used to cover vacancies, maternity leave, long-term sickness leave, and holidays. Their use is no longer limited to library assistants but increasingly includes professional library positions (*18*).

Generally these workers do the same work as permanent staff members and are often paid the same wage as permanent workers. The employer, however, has the advantage of terminating the contract when necessary. This is an example of employer-led flexibility in which the need to cut labor costs has resulted in the creation of "core" and "peripheral" workforces and the development of a corresponding status divide.

Included in the category of temporary workers are casual workers, sometimes referred to as "as and when staff," "reserves," or "relief staff." Public libraries in the United Kingdom, for example, often maintain registers of local workers ("relief panels"), usually support staff, who can be called in at short notice to cover for unexpected absences in the workplace. In situations of minimum staffing levels, casual workers of this nature are an essential element in the maintenance of services and are generally expected to undertake the full range of library assistant duties. Casual workers are also often employed as a crisis measure when organizations need to respond to an unforeseen change (*13*). Changes in higher education in the United Kingdom for example, have resulted in an increase in routine work, concentrated at certain times of the year. Casual workers can help organizations cope with these busy periods. Casual and temporary workers are a cost-effective source of labor because employers in the United Kingdom often feel no obligation (and are under little legislative responsibility) to offer them holidays, sick pay, training, pensions, and other benefits (*19*). Also, by being able to control to the hour when these workers are on the job and by paying for these work hours only, staffing costs are not only kept to a minimum, they are also controllable. In an area in which budgets can change radically from one year to another, this type of control and the manager's flexibility to react to imposed changes are essential.

Casual workers are often recruited from the ranks of previous employees who want to return to library work after a career break, for example. Regular customers are another potential pool of recruits (*13*). Casual workers are generally not considered by managers as reliable as permanent employees. They often have other part-time or casual jobs and therefore cannot be as flexible as the library or information service manager would like them to be. Although casual workers usually have the option of refusing work, should they refuse it too often they will be considered unreliable and will not be offered work regularly. The balance of power is weighted firmly in the employer's favor and the ambiguous nature of the contract in these cases means that should a worker fail to meet the standard of work required there is no termination process like that protecting permanent staff; the organization simply does not contact the worker involved, implicitly ending the employment contract.

Casual workers are, however, in a good position to become permanent members of staff should they wish and should the opportunity arise. No only do they have inside knowledge of vacancies, but they also have experience of organizational systems, policies, and procedures. Over a period, casual workers can build a relationship with the permanent workers, who may specifically request individuals who they know are efficient and who work well with other staff members and customers.

Term-Time Only Contracts

Term-time work has been advocated in the United Kingdom as an effective and cost-efficient method of staffing services in academic institutions, especially in school libraries, in which the work of the library or information service is, or has traditionally been, term-based and there is a limited amount of work during the vacations. Although these services benefit by economizing on staffing costs when the libraries are relatively quiet, the opportunity not to work during school holidays is clearly advantageous for carers of school-aged children. This can, however, lead managers to question term-time workers' commitment to the organization and their attitude toward their work (*13*).

There is also a risk that term-time workers can become alienated from the rest of the organization during the long summer school holidays when they are not working. In academic libraries, for example, major changes to the organization of stock and services are generally carried out in the summer when the library is at its quietest. Term-time workers are in danger of missing out on vital operational details that will affect them and how they work.

Attitudes to Flexible Work

The preceding sections give an indication of the challenges facing the manager of a flexible workforce in U.K. library and information services, and the advantages and disadvantages of flexible work from the perspective of both employer and employee. The following sections explicitly identify the pros and cons of flexible work by drawing on research into the flexible library and information workforce in the United Kingdom. Although the work on which this is based was limited to the United Kingdom, many of the basic concepts, problems identified, and lessons learned transcend national boundaries.

MANAGERS' OPINIONS OF FLEXIBLE WORKERS

Although an overwhelming majority of managers in one survey stated that they were satisfied with certain types of flexible workers (see Table 3), there are still a number of negative stereotypes that exist about these employees.

TABLE 3

Managers' Satisfaction with Flexible Workers (%)

	Very satisfied	Satisfied	Dissatisfied	Very dissatisfied
Permanent part-time workers	54	44	<1	1
Temporary part-time workers	35	59	4	2
Job-share	41	53	4	2

Source: Data from Ref. *11*.

Part-time and temporary workers have career and work patterns that generally diverge from the long hours and the continual career trajectory culture of western societies. Because of this, these workers are often considered by managers as "different" from permanent full-time workers in a number of ways, including assumptions that

- They have different reasons for working.
- They devote most of their energy to activities away from the workplace.
- The type of work contract is more important than the type of job they do.
- Their commitment to and interest in their work is less than that of their full-time colleagues (*13*).

There are, perhaps, elements of truth in some of these assertions. Part-time workers do have responsibilities and activities away from the workplace. As a result of this, they tend to look for jobs that will allow them to continue to meet their other commitments. There is little hard evidence to support the last assumption, however. The research that has been undertaken into flexible workers in library and information services suggests they enjoy being part of a working environment and are interested in and dedicated to their jobs (*13*).

Despite reservations about flexible workers' commitment and interest, library and information service managers in the United Kingdom use temporary contracts, part-time employment, casual employment, and job sharing as important tools in their labor use strategies because flexible working schedules enable them to manage daily and seasonal peaks and troughs in demands for services and ensure that trained staff are available at all times of their nonstandard opening hours (*12*). They also enable them to recruit and retain skilled workers who, for whatever reason, need to work nonstandard hours (*20*). Financial uncertainty has also had a huge impact on the labor use strategies of U.K. library and information services, particularly those in the public sector (*12*). Library and information service managers have to make staffing decisions within their budget, and in the harsh financial climate of the 1990s, many are choosing to use flexible workers as part of a cost-effective workforce strategy.

FLEXIBLE WORKERS' ATTITUDES TOWARD THEIR WORK

Despite the growth of flexible work over the last two decades, stereotypes of flexible workers persist. Evidence from research conducted in this area of workforce planning would dispute these negative stereotypical assumptions about flexible workers, however, and instead suggests that flexible workers are as concerned about the quality of their work, job satisfaction, and the effectiveness of their service as their permanent, full-time colleagues (*13*).

The preceding discussion indicates that the adoption of flexible work practices in U.K. library and information services is generally employer-led and exists primarily for the benefit of the organization. Library managers' need for part-time and temporary workers is, however, complemented by the need or desire of some workers to work less than full-time hours. Like any group of workers, those on flexible work schedules are by no means homogeneous and will have a variety of reasons for working part-time or in a temporary position. Child care responsibilities are the main reason for working part-time (*21*), but those who initially start to work on a part-time basis because of, for example, child-care commitment may find that as their children grow, other activities take up their time away from work. Part-time work can be an attractive option for those nearing the end of their working lives but who still want to be active and supplement their pensions. Other workers might positively opt for part-time work as a way of escaping the pressure and strain of a full-time job. In contrast, workers with demanding caring responsibilities in the home may consider a part-time job a legitimate opportunity to get out of the house and make social contact. People may also decide to work part-time to accommodate study.

Temporary workers may feel they have little choice over their work pattern, although temporary positions are not necessarily a dead end. For those unsure about their future career direction, temporary work can be a useful means of taking stock, and individuals with little chance of a full-time job to develop their skills profile may view a temporary contract as a way of gaining valuable experience. Workers seeking a job in times of high unemployment or wanting to expand their experience in times of low turnover may therefore opt for the financial insecurity of temporary work in a bid for long-term benefits. Generally, however, temporary contracts are a second choice made in desperate circumstances, and there have been concerns expressed about the "casualization" of the U.K labor market and the lack of full-time work opportunities (*22*).

Flexible workers therefore need to reconcile a number of inherent contradictions associated with the nature of their contracts. Permanent full-time work provides adequate financial return, but limits the time available to attend to caring responsibilities, domestic duties, social activities, or other commitments. Part-time contracts, on the other hand, leave workers with adequate time away from work to fulfill their various obligations but offer less in the way of monetary reward. Temporary contracts can bring anxiety and frustration as the worker waits to hear about his or her future with the organization, but in certain circumstances they can act as a convenient stopgap in which individuals gain experience and have the opportunity to think seriously about the direction of their future careers.

Library and information service managers' need for a cost-effective and efficient workforce is thus complemented by the desire or need of some individuals to work less than full-time hours. Despite the obvious advantages of flexible work from both the employer's and employee's perspectives, however, flexible work is not necessarily an easy option for managers or workers seeking new ways of working. The administrative and management issues that accompany an increase in the numbers of flexible workers in any organization need to be given careful thought.

The Management Challenges of the Flexible Workforce

While, as indicated above, library and information service managers in the United Kingdom value flexible workers as team members that enable the service to meet its commitments, areas of concern still remain.

COMMUNICATION

Communication is often cited as the most intractable problem facing managers with large numbers of flexible workers (*12*). Organizations that hold team briefing meetings on fixed days at fixed times will find that certain part-timers or job sharers are invariably absent because they do not work that day or at that time. Missing important communications can particularly affect those workers who do not work full-time hours, as there may be significant periods of time when they are not in the workplace. They are also vulnerable to missing news "through the grapevine", as, compared with their full-time colleagues, they have less extensive social contact at work. Although managers can ensure that workers are kept up to date through a variety of communication media (newsletters, memos, etc.), face-to-face communication is preferable and ensures that the worker gains a complete picture of organizational conditions and plans.

Problems with organizational communications are recognized by both workers and managers alike. Part-time workers, for example, may find that they hear about issues that involve them in a roundabout manner, or more by accident than design. This can be detrimental to team spirit and may leave flexible workers feeling alienated from the rest of the organization. Exclusion from informal social networks can also be a problem for flexible workers with the danger of a wide gulf emerging between part-time and full-time staff members, or perhaps between temporary and permanent workers (*13*).

COORDINATION

The logistics of coordinating work, timetables, and meetings for certain types of flexible workers (e.g., part-time staff) can be aggravating for all involved. Those organizations using large numbers of flexible workers find that the number of individuals in the organization can double, meaning that there are a lot of "bodies" to look after (*11*). Similarly, Morris reported how, from the manager's perspective, job-sharing amounts to a "doubling-up" of staff problems and increased staffing costs (*18*). As well as the heavier administrative workload, training needs also increase. The coordination of training for large numbers of flexible workers can, however, be problematic. Timetables may also cause problems from the workers' point of view. Casual workers, for example, may find the erratic nature of this type of work very frustrating, and the uncertainty of their future within the organization can be unsettling for workers on all types of short-term contracts (*13*).

TRAINING

Training may be difficult for flexible workers because a number of barriers exist, from the point of view of both the workers and the managers. These barriers may exclude flexible workers from organizational training opportunities. Broad differences in the training received by different types of workers in the United Kingdom are clearly identified by McGiveney, who suggests that most training offered by employers is available to their full-time employees, while their part-time employees are offered little training (*19*). Similar findings were reported in a Confederation of British Industry report which found that "Companies are more prepared to accept responsibility for training their full-time than for their part-time employees; similarly they accept responsibility for training more readily for permanent than for temporary staff" (*20*).

There is evidence that flexible workers in library and information services in the United Kingdom do not receive the same amount and/or type of training as their full-time permanent colleagues (*13*). Table 4 suggests that training opportunities vary according to the permanence of the worker's contract and there is some evidence that it varies according to the number of hours worked, although this is not as marked. In fact, according to this survey of training and flexible workers in the United Kingdom, job sharers fare the best of all categories of workers except in relation to external training.

Evidence suggests that the two main barriers to training that managers find most difficult to overcome are first, the inability to release workers from their usual duties, and second, problems in matching training time with hours worked. Other problems

TABLE 4

Library and Information Services Offering Different Types of Training,
as a Percentage of Those Using Specified Working Patterns

	Induction	In-house	On-the-job	Off-the-job
Permanent full-time	92	86	94	94
Permanent part-time	91	84	94	86
Temporary full-time	81	74	95	53
Temporary part-time	81	70	92	43
Job share	94	90	98	85
Term-time	86	78	89	68
Annual hours	75	63	88	51
Casual	67	43	88	18

Source: Data from Ref. *13*.

include financial constraints and reluctance on the part of the worker and the manager to participate in or initiate training (*13*).

As far as flexible workers are concerned, a frequent complaint in one study was that they did not have the training they considered necessary to perform their jobs to what they considered an acceptable standard (*13*). As Table 4 shows, some types of workers are more likely to have access to training than others. This can leave workers with the impression that they are not valued and can leave the organization open to charges of neglect and discrimination. (See below.)

Problems Releasing Workers

The minimal staffing levels maintained in many library and information services in the United Kingdom can make it difficult for managers to release workers to attend off-the-job training sessions *and* maintain adequate staff cover, and while this is a consideration for all workers, it is particularly problematic for flexible workers, as they are frequently deployed to provide for peak-service demand periods, which makes it more urgent that these periods are fully staffed.

Matching Working and Training Hours

Flexible workers can face considerable difficulty if training sessions are scheduled outside their regular working hours. Services may depend on workers being able to rearrange their other commitments to participate, perhaps taking time off in lieu. This, however, is of limited help to workers who have second part-time jobs or other commitments scheduled around their regular working hours. Matching training with working hours can be particularly problematic in relation to external training opportunities, for which training time is controlled by another organization. As noted above, flexible workers often work a double shift or some sort, usually combining labor-market employment with domestic/caring labor, or less frequently, with studying, further part-time jobs, and self-employment. Ensuring that all commitments are met means that a delicate balance has to be maintained. Training organized outside regular working hours disturbs that balance and can be a significant barrier preventing participation. Difficulties in rearranging child care for day-long training courses, for example, can cause severe problems. Considerations such as these make the scheduling of training particularly sensitive.

Financial Constraints

Financial constraints can mean that the more expensive types of training are unavailable to flexible workers because the employing organization cannot or will not pay their fees. This is of particular concern in those organizations that employ large numbers of part-time or job-share workers because external courses, for example, may be a very effective method of training in specialized areas but their cost for a large number of workers may be prohibitive.

Reluctance to Train

Managers may feel that it is not worthwhile investing a great deal of training in flexible workers, particularly those on casual or very short-term contracts. Furthermore, research has found that temporary workers are unlikely to be included in staff review/appraisal processes so a further factor behind managers' reluctance to train these workers might be the manager's ignorance of the workers' training needs (*13*). Managers might also perceive reluctance on the part of the workers themselves to take part in training due to, for example, a lack of time, a lack of interest, or the expectation of being refused training, all of which make it easier for managers to ignore flexible workers when considering training their staff.

Communication of Training Opportunities

Communication difficulties have already been mentioned, but a lack of timely communication of training activities can mean that flexible workers are unable to attend because it is too late for them to rearrange their other commitments. Flexible workers are therefore often "information poor," lacking knowledge of training opportunities. Although this might not be deliberate, a comparative lack of contact with their supervisor and other staff members means that they are often "out of sight and out of mind."

The Effective Management of Flexible Working Practices

As the discussion above suggests, flexible workers are perhaps different in a number of significant ways from their full-time, permanent colleagues, but by accepting this, library and information service managers should not take it as an excuse to treat flexible workers in an adverse manner. On the contrary, managers should be alert to the fact that they may have to modify their management policies and procedures to ensure that flexible working patterns are fully integrated into the library or information service, and that they are administered effectively and fairly. After all, there is an interdependency between the organizational needs for efficiency and the workers' need for flexibility. Workforce planning is concerned with the quality as well as the quantity of staff employed, which means that as well as ensuring that the appropriate number of people on a particular working pattern are on the job, managers also need to make certain that all staff have the necessary training, development, and support to be effective in their work.

COMMUNICATION

As noted above, part-time workers in particular are vulnerable to missing important workplace communications. By using multiple communication channels managers can help ensure workers are kept up to date, but part-timers should also have the opportunity to attend meetings or team briefings. Team meetings are essential for building team spirit, which is particularly important for those workers who often feel on the periphery of the organization, and for giving workers the opportunity to contribute their ideas and opinions on plans or decisions. Letting flexible workers have their say can help them see the role they play in the service more clearly and encourage them to feel more involved. Although there will almost invariably be times when one worker or more is unable to attend a regularly scheduled meeting, managers should consider varying the day and/or time of meetings and hold them when the greatest number of staff members can attend. The importance of cascading information through the hierarchy should also be stressed as a way of overcoming communication difficulties, but this should be done on a systematic basis and not simply rely on word of mouth. Managers might also consider paying staff (or giving them time off in lieu) to attend meetings (*11*).

TRAINING

Although managers and workers can identify a number of logistical, organizational, and attitudinal barriers that prevent flexible workers' participation in training and development opportunities, the vast majority of these obstacles are not insuperable and there are actions that organizations can take to encourage workers to take part (*23*).

Access to Training

Flexible workers must be given equal opportunity with permanent full-time workers to attend appropriate training courses. Managers should also consider the establishment of facilitation systems such as offering time off in lieu of time spent training outside regular work hours, or financial assistance with additional care provision to allow workers to undertake training outside their regular work hours. As in-house training is the most accessible, managers should try to arrange training programs within the library or information service. Although financial barriers can restrict flexible workers' access to training, effective cascading of training is an alternative. This must entail setting aside convenient times and organizing an official session, however, rather than merely relying upon the person who attended the training session to pass on his or her skills or knowledge informally.

Scheduling of Training

Training should be scheduled within flexible workers' regular working hours as far as possible. This might involve repeating training sessions and ensuring that repeats are held on different days and different times so that as many workers as possible can attend.

Communication of Training

Library and information service managers should ensure that sufficient advance notice is given of training opportunities and that it goes to all workers. Additional efforts may be necessary to make sure that flexible workers are aware of training activities.

FLEXIBLE WORKERS AND EQUAL OPPORTUNITIES

Library and information services must also ensure that work practices and procedures do not contravene antidiscrimination legislation. During the 1970s and early 1980s workers in the United Kingdom made considerable gains as regards recognition of less conventional work patterns. Many U.K. organizations now officially recognize the right to opt for job sharing, for example. Acknowledgment of the prevalence of flexible work patterns was bolstered by legislation enacted after the House of Lords ruled that the unfair dismissal and redundancy pay provisions of the Employment Protection (Consolidation) Act of 1975 discriminated against part-time workers. From February 1995 the hours of work thresholds were removed from employment protection law so that now part-time workers, like other permanent workers, can claim unfair dismissal and qualify for redundancy rights as long as they have completed two years of service (24). These changes were based on the understanding that discrimination against part-time workers was discrimination against women and thus unlawful according to the Sex Discrimination Act. Although flexible workers in U.K library and information services are not all women, they are overwhelmingly women (12). As such, workplace practices that are judged to discriminate against part-timers could be judged to be sex discrimination, as the ruling states: "the application of different qualifying conditions for part-timers in employment legislation discriminated against women contrary to European equal pay and equal treatment laws" (24).

Discrimination against part-time workers in employment can thus be considered sex discrimination simply because most part-time workers are women. The ruling may also have implications for the training of flexible workers, as Leighton and ODonnell point out: "If, for example, part-timers and temporary staff who are predominantly female . . . are denied access to . . . training, this will probably be seen as discriminatory and unlawful" (25).

Neglect of this important issue could therefore leave library and information services in the United Kingdom open to charges of sex discrimination. The legislation puts a legal requirement on employers of part-time workers to ensure that they are not treated in a detrimental manner. Flexible workers can be a valuable asset in a library and information service, but they must be managed sensitively, appropriately, and fairly, paying due regard to both the spirit and the letter of equal opportunities policies and laws (26).

Conclusions

The pursuit of flexibility, both as a way of improving the organization for the employer and as a method of maximizing employee productivity, is a strategy library and information services in the United Kingdom are increasingly adopting. Service managers have been eager to take advantage of the benefits of using a range of employment contracts, including the following:

- Decreased costs due to matching staffing needs and provision more exactly
- The ability to meet short-term demands by temporarily increasing staff numbers
- The ability to retain workers who would leave if they had to remain in full-time positions

Alongside these and other undoubted advantages, however, there needs to be a consideration of the responsibilities managers assume as they embrace flexible work patterns. There is a tendency for managers to understate the organizational benefits of flexible work and to emphasize the positive features of flexible work patterns for individual workers. Managers and organizations, however, are dependent on flexible workers to keep within tight financial constraints. Flexible working patterns are also effective methods of retaining valued staff. While there may be logistical issues around communication and coordination that managers of flexible workers have to consider, these possible negative implications do not outweigh the significant organizational benefits. The organization's need for flexible workers is matched to some extent by workers wanting a variety of flexible work contracts. This interdependence of employing organization and flexible workers is, however, often ignored. This, along with the overemphasis on the benefits gained by the worker, maintain and legitimize the lower status, remuneration, training, and promotion opportunities afforded flexible workers. It does not, however, prevent the employing organization from presenting itself as an "equal opportunity" employer with "family-friendly" policies. Managers have much to gain by acknowledging the interdependence of flexible workers and the employing organization. A service that includes rather than alienates its flexible workers is one that will be open to current and future possibilities of the range of working patterns (*12*).

The decision to implement flexible work patterns should therefore only be the beginning of an organization's consideration of the matter. The implications of employing flexible workers need to be addressed by senior management with the aim of formulating policies and strategies that ensure that these workers are managed consistently. Flexible workers are an integral part of the library and information workforce in the United Kingdom, but by failing to take account of their specific requirements, managers run the risk of invalidating the valuable role they can play.

REFERENCES

1. G. Watson, "The Flexible Workforce and Patterns of Working Hours in the UK." *Employ. Gaz.,* 239–247 (July 1994).

2. K. Weibel and K. Heim, *The Role of Women in Librarianship 1876–1976: The Entry, Advancement, Struggle for Equalization in One Profession,* Oryx Press, Phoenix, AZ, 1979, p. 8.

3. P. Layzell Ward, *Women and Librarianship,* Library Association Publishing, London, 1966.

4. Equal Opportunities Commission, *Part-time Workers, Not Second Class Citizens,* Equal Opportunities Commission, Manchester, 1995.

5. New Ways to Work, *Change at the Top: Working Flexibility at Senior Managerial Levels in Organisations,* News Ways to Work, London, 1993, p. 14.

6. New Ways to Work *Changing Times: A Guide to Flexible Work Patterns for Human Resource Managers,* New Ways to Work, London, 1993, p. 27.

7. Department for Education and Employment, *Labour Market and Skill Trends,* Department for Education and Employment, Sheffield, 1997.

8. Department for Education and Employment, *Labour Force Survey: Spring 1997,* Department for Education and Employment, Sheffield, 1997.

9. M. Beatson, *Labour Market Flexibility,* Employment Department, Sheffield, 1995.

10. V. Beechy and T. Perkins, *A Matter of Hours*, Polity Press, Cambridge, 1987.

11. A. Goulding and E. Kerslake, "Flexible Working in Libraries: Profit and Potential Pitfalls." *Libr. Mgt.,* **17**(2), 8–16 (1996).

12. A. Goulding and E. Kerslake, "Flexible Working in UK Library and Information Services: Current Practice and Concerns." *J. Librar. Inform. Sci.,* **28**(4), 203–216 (1996).

13. A. Goulding and E. Kerslake, *Developing the Flexible Library and Information Workforce: A Quality and Equal Opportunities Perspective,* British Library Research and Innovation Report 25, British Library Research and Innovation Centre, Boston Spa, 1996.

14. M. W. Fields and J. W. Thakur, "Job-Related Attitudes of Part-Time and Full-Time Workers." *J. Mgt. Psych.,* **6**(2), 17–20 (1991).

15. A. Evans and K. Birkett, "New Patterns of Day-Working," in *Flexible Patterns of Work,* C. Curson, ed. Institute of Personnel Management, London, 1986, pp. 26–58.

16. C. Goddard, "Job Sharing in British Libraries: Implications for Managers." *J. Librar. Inform. Sci.,* **23**(4), 191–201 (1991).

17. R. Stennet, "Job Sharing in Librarianship," *Librar. Career Dev.,* **2**(1), 23–29 (1994).

18. B. Morris, "Surviving the Skills Shortage: Exploring the Options." *Inform. Libr. Mgr.,* **9**(2), 11–22 (1990).

19. V. McGiveney, *Wasted Potential: Training and Career Progression for Part-Time and Temporary Workers,* National Institute for Continuing Adult Education, Leicester, 1994.

20. Confederation of British Industry, *Flexible Labour Markets: Who Pays for Training?* Confederation of British Industry, London, 1995, p. 22.

21. G. Burrington, *Equally Good: Women in British Librarianship,* Association of Assistant Librarians, London, 1993.

22. A. Goulding and E. Kerslake, *Training for Part-Time and Temporary Workers,* Library Association Publishing, London, 1997.

23. A. Goulding and E. Kerslake, "Training the Flexible Library and Information Workforce: Problems and Practical Solutions." *Inform. Serv. Use,* **17**(4), 261–272 (1997).

24. "Statutory Rights for Part-Time Workers," *Employ. Gaz.,* **43** (Feb. 1995).

25. P. Leighton and A. O'Donnell, *The New Employment Contract: Using Employment Contracts Effectively,* Nicolas Brearly, London, 1995, p. 22.

26. E. Kerslake and A. Goulding, "'An Inappropriate Appetite for Training'? Equal Opportunities and Training for Flexible Information Workers," *Equal Op. Internat.,* **15**(8), 1–18 (1996).

BIBLIOGRAPHY

This bibliography includes references to work that is not U.K.-specific but that is pertinent to the subject of flexible library and information workers.

Belkin, L., "Permanent Part-Time Employment in Victorian Special Libraries: The Employee's Perspective." *Austr. Librar. J.,* **36**(3), 148–153 (1987).

Brustman, M. J. and Via, B. J., "Employment and Status of Part-Time Librarians in US Academic Libraries." *J. Acad. Librar.,* **14**(2), 87–91 (1988).

Burrington, G., "Report on the Symposium on Job-Sharing in Libraries." *State Librar.,* 41–42 (Nov. 1982).

Cunningham, A. M. and Wicks, W., *Flexible Work Styles in the Information Industry,* NFAIS, Philadelphia, 1993.

Dex, S. and McCullough, A., *Flexible Employment in Britain: A Statistical Analysis,* Equal Opportunities Commission, Manchester, 1995.

Dickens, L., *Whose Flexibility? Discrimination and Equality Issues in Atypical Work,* Institute of Employment Rights, London, 1992.

Gilbert, C. and Gray, K., "Job-Sharing in a Hospital Library." *Austr. Spec. Libr. News,* **18**(2), 51–55 (1985).

Glory, B., "Managing Information Resources in a Teleworking Environment." *Spec. Libr.,* **85**(1), 30–34 (1994).

Goulding, A. and Kerslake, E., "Flexible Information Workers: Training and Equal Opportunities." *Librar. Career Dev.,* **4**(2), 5–12 (1996).

Goulding, A. and Kerslake, E., "Continuing Professional Development and Flexible Information Workers:

Problems and Opportunities," in *Human Development: Competencies for the Twenty-First Century,* P. Layzell Ward and D. E. Weingand, eds. K. G. Saur, Munich, 1997, pp. 10–18.

Hewitt, P., *About Time: The Revolution in Work and Family Life,* IPPR/Rivers Oram Press, London, 1993.

Notowitz, C., "Job-Sharing for the 80s." *School Libr. J.,* 33–35 (Feb. 1982).

Sorby, B. and Pascoe, M., *Job-Sharing: The Great Divide,* Leeds Polytechnic, Leeds, 1982.

Vincent, I., "Academic Library Administrators and Part-Time Work." *Austr. Acad. Res. Libr.,* **10**(3), 150–161 (1979).

ANNE GOULDING
EVELYN KERSLAKE

A GENERIC TASK STRATEGY FOR SOLVING ROUTINE DECISION-MAKING PROBLEMS

Introduction

Decision making is a process in which an agent selects a series of actions to take that will fulfill the agent's needs. Decision making encompasses many types of problems such as scheduling, purchasing, disaster recovery, and policy making—any type of problem in which there is a set of alternative options to select from. A decision-making problem becomes routine with experience so that the possible actions available to the agent are represented in an efficient manner with additional knowledge available to determine how useful each action might be. The routine decision-making task then is to select those actions or choices from a pool of potential choices that might best fulfill the agent's needs.

In order to automate the process of routine decision making, a general-purpose algorithm is presented. The algorithm is based on the generic task paradigm of problem solving. Generic tasks are a set of information-processing strategies developed from artificial intelligence research and applied to a large number of problems. Each generic task is a building block of problem solving. Combining various generic tasks together, one can construct a problem-solving system to perform diagnosis, data interpretation, perception, planning, or other similar knowledge-intensive problems.

Three tasks in particular—hierarchical classification, routine recognition, and abductive assembly—form the basis for a process of generating, evaluating, and combining explanations. To solve routine decision-making problems, a similar approach is taken in which actions are first generated using hierarchical classification rather than hypotheses, then assessed using routine recognition, and finally assembled into a coherent overall decision using a variation of abductive assembly.

This article will describe this computational algorithm to solving routine decision making using generic tasks. First, the article will introduce decision making as a class of problems, concentrating on routine decision making. Next, it will introduce the generic task paradigm of problem solving with an examination of three tasks in particular, hierarchical classification, routine recognition, and abductive assembly. The article will then describe the routine decision-making algorithm as a variation of these three tasks. To demonstrate the algorithm, two routine decision-making problems and automated problem solvers will be discussed.

Decision Making

Problem solvers are often faced with making decisions. The process is one of selecting actions that might fulfill the needs of the problem solver. Actions can be any type of activity and are dependent on the particular problem. For instance, a consumer's decision-making actions are selecting purchases, whereas in scheduling, actions are assigning duties to personnel in some temporal sequence. The goal of decision making is not simply to generate a series or sequence of actions, but to find a good or possibly the best set of actions. A decision-making agent may therefore compare potential actions against each other to determine which action(s) is (are) best for the given situation.

The knowledge required for decision making includes some means of deriving potentially useful actions, some means of determining which actions might fulfill which of the agent's needs, and some means of determining how useful each action might be in the current situation. Often experience will play a role in decision making where an agent's preferences and constraints help determine the usefulness of actions.

SIMILARITIES AND DIFFERENCES WITH PLANNING

Decision making is much like planning, a task in which an agent generates plan steps that when taken will lead the agent toward desired goals. Semantically, there is a difference between a plan and a decision. In practice, however, the two problems have similar solutions.

In both planning and decision making, the input and output behaviors can be similarly characterized. The input to both problems are an agent's needs or goals. The output comprises those actions that will allow the agent to fulfill those needs or goals.

In planning, temporality (the order in which the actions are applied) is important, whereas in decision making, temporality is not always considered. In planning and decision making, constraints are used to restrict the possibilities of the agent. In decision making, preferences are used to determine how useful or desirable an action might be, but in planning, preferences may not be applied.

Since planning and decision making are similar types of problems, it follows that planning solutions can be used for decision-making problems. There have been many solutions applied to planning problems in artificial intelligence research. These include linear planning (*1*), nonlinear planning (*2*), hierarchical planning (*3*), reactive planning (*4*), case-based planning (*5*), and routine planning (*6, 7*). There are many deficiencies with the first three methods, limiting their usefulness. For instance, linear, nonlinear, and hierarchical planning all suffer from intractability (solutions take an exponential amount of time) because they rely almost solely on exhaustive search through a space of possible actions. Reactive planning is mostly used for real-time systems and robotics, in which a plan must be generated at run time and time is critical.

Both case-based planning and routine planning have solutions that can be applied to decision making. In case-based planning, a case is selected from a library of cases that most closely match the current situation, then the differences between the selected case and the current situation are determined and the case is "fixed" to handle the current situation. Routine planning (also referred to as "routine design") is a generic task (described below) used to solve planning and design problems classified as "routine" by performing plan-step selection and refinement. To solve decision-making problems, one might select a prior decision and alter it for the current situation using one of these two approaches. The decision-making algorithm described in this article is similar in ways to both the case-based and routine planning methods.

ROUTINE DECISION MAKING

A decision-making problem might be considered *routine* if the agent has had prior experience with and has previously attempted to solve the particular decision-making problem. Some decision-making problems will be novel or infrequent (buying a house, enrolling in college), however, a majority of the decisions faced by the typical person are those that have been solved numerous times before (choosing clothes for the day, planning the day's activities).

Routine decision-making problems can be characterized by the availability of certain types of knowledge. Two forms of knowledge need to be available for a decision-making problem to be considered routine. First, potentially useful actions must be available and organized in an efficient manner. This would allow the agent to bypass an exhaustive search and yet still have access to the various actions that might be used to solve the problem. Second, knowledge must be available to assess an action to determine how useful it might be in a given situation. Prior experience solving the particular decision-making problem will provide both forms of knowledge.

Aside from experience, other forms of knowledge can come into play to help one rate the usefulness of an action: preferences and constraints. Preferences describe what the agent likes and dislikes. Preferences can be stated specifically as a ranking of one action over another; for instance, ranking one particular product over another. Preferences are also commonly stated abstractly as a desire for one characteristic over another. In the case of scheduling daily activities, one might desire to perform outdoor tasks in the morning (before it gets hot) and driving tasks at nonrush hour times. Constraints, on the other hand, help the agent determine which actions are impractical because of a limitation on time, money, space, availability, or other factors.

Consider a first-time home buyer. The decision-making process is a novel experience for this agent. Since the buyer has never bought a house, that person may not know some of the steps required to deal with the bank, realtor, builder, or architect, thus the buyer may not get a good financial deal or a house that is structurally as sound as it should be. Questions regarding locality, school districts, types of materials used, and so forth are not readily available. As opposed to this, a person who schedules workers at a factory and has been doing this for years is able to know which workers prefer which time slots and duties and is able to generate a schedule that is most pleasing. This in turn may bring about higher worker productivity. A person who schedules airplane arrivals at airport gates understands the need to schedule heavily populated flights toward the middle of the concourse so that passengers have less distance to walk either to make connecting flights or to pick up luggage. Flights with short turnaround times might be parked at gates nearer the runway.

Novel decision-making problems include buying a house, selecting a career, and creating a new law. Routine decision-making problems include the airline or factory scheduler, deciding what groceries to purchase at the store, selecting clothes to wear, or scheduling one's daily activities. These problems are all characterized by having both the actions and the knowledge to rate the usefulness of each action readily available. The next section will describe an algorithm that can solve these types of problems.

Generic Tasks

Generic tasks are a collection of information-processing strategies used for the construction of knowledge-based systems in artificial intelligence and related fields (*8, 9*). Each task can be thought of as a building block toward intelligent problem solving. Generic Tasks are problem- and domain-independent processes. When combined, generic tasks can bring about complex reasoning behaviors to be applied to a large variety of problems, including diagnosis, data and test interpretation, perception and natural language processing, planning and design, and decision making (*6, 10, 11*).

A generic task is described functionally in terms of input and output with one or more associated methods or inference procedures that can accomplish the task. Because each task is described in this manner, the knowledge required for using that task is easily identifiable. It thus becomes an easy matter to construct automated problem solvers that use the various generic tasks. Among the generic tasks, three have been utilized in the past to solve "identification"-type problems such as diagnosis, test interpretation, and perception. These are hierarchical classification routine recognition, and abductive assembly.

HIERARCHICAL CLASSIFICATION

Hierarchical classification is the task of generating a particular instance or subtype of a given type by searching through a taxonomic hierarchy (*12*). Input to the classification task is a description of the object or concept in question and output is the subclass(es) or instance(s) that fit the described case. Each node in the hierarchy represents a concept or object at some level of specificity, in which a node's children are more specific than the node itself. Leaf nodes represent the most specific concepts or objects in the domain.

Classification is performed using a strategy known as *establish-refine*. Establish-refine is a top-down depth-first descent of the hierarchy. A node is considered for relevancy within the context of the current case. If found relevant, the node is established, and refinement occurs by attempting to establish any of the node's

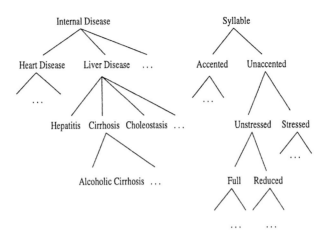

FIGURE 1. *Two classification hierarchies.*

children. A node that is not relevant to the current case is rejected, pruning away the entire subhierarchy underneath that node. A node that cannot be clearly established or rejected is suspended until there is more knowledge that allows the system to make a decision. Testing a node for relevancy can be accomplished by any number of methods, including other generic tasks.

Figure 1 shows two taxonomic hierarchies used in the task of hierarchical classification. The hierarchy on the left forms a portion of a medical diagnostic hierarchy for internal diseases. During the process of hierarchical classification, a diagnostic system would first attempt to establish that the problem is an internal disease. If established, the hypothesis would be refined by attempting to establish the form of internal disease such as heart disease or liver disease. If one of these (say heart disease) is not established, then the hypothesis along with the entire subtree is dismissed. If a hypothesis is established (say liver disease), however, then the next step is to refine that subhypothesis by trying to establish a particular form of liver disease such as hepatitis. The process continues until one or more particular leaf nodes are established. The hierarchy on the right side would be used for a speech recognition system in an attempt to identify a syllable under consideration. The classification process would start with a digitally processed signal of the acoustic sound as input. It would then attempt to classify the sound, first by establishing that the syllable was either accented or unaccented. If unaccented, it could then be refined into a stressed syllable and then a full or reduced syllable. The process would continue until a leaf node was established, in which leaf nodes represent the various syllables available in the English language.

Hierarchical classification requires two types of knowledge: a classification hierarchy that is a taxonomy of concepts or objects in the domain, and establish/reject knowledge for each node of the hierarchy. Establish/reject knowledge is the knowledge by which the classifier is able to determine if a particular node should be established, ruled out, or suspended for the given case.

ROUTINE RECOGNITION

Routine recognition is a task that allows a problem-solving agent to generate a statement of belief that a given hypothesis or concept is true or relevant (*13*). The more closely the current case matches the expectation that the agent has for the concept, the higher the belief will be. Input for the task is some description of the current case and output is a belief statement that the concept applies. Each concept in the domain requires an associated *recognition agent* that would contain the types of knowledge used to recognize whether that concept was relevant or not within the context of the current case. The recognition agent generates a statement of belief stating how plausible the concept is. The statement of belief is generated by pattern matching the current situation against features that are expected (and features that are not expected). Statements of belief, or plausibilities, are expressed in a useful qualitative vocabulary using such terms as *very likely, somewhat likely, unlikely,* or *ruled out*.

Each concept or hypothesis in the domain may have one or more associated recognition agents. Figure 2 displays an abstract recognition agent that might be used to identify some domain concept. For this concept, there are three features being sought—F1, F2, and F3. The recognition agent searches the data and other knowledge sources for these features of interest. A response is provided (either from the user, a database, or another problem solver such as another recognition agent) for each feature. The three responses are then compared against the patterns, and the recognition agent returns the associated confidence value of the first matching pattern. This confidence value denotes the recognition agent's belief that the concept

Features:
Ask Database "is F1 present?"
Ask Database "is F2 present?"
Ask Recognition Agent Y "how likely is F3?"

Patterns:
No No Unlikely = Ruled Out
No No ? = Unlikely
Yes Yes Likely = Very Likely
Yes ? Likely = Likely
? Yes Likely = Somewhat Likely
? ? Likely = Neutral
Yes Yes Neutral = Somewhat Likely

No Match Response: Unlikely

FIGURE 2. *An abstract recognition agent.*

applies to the current case. If none of the patterns match, a no-match value is given as a default. In this example, the first two features are direct queries to a database while the third feature is a call to another recognition agent.

Routine recognition is a natural way to determine if a node in a classification hierarchy is relevant or not during hierarchical classification. In a majority of the generic task research involving hierarchical classification, routine recognition (sometimes referred to as hypothesis matching or structured matching) is the knowledge used to determine if a node in the hierarchy is relevant or not for the current case. Every node in the hierarchy has an associated recognition agent. As the hierarchy is traversed, a node is considered, and its associated recognition agent is called upon. If the recognition agent returns a high enough confidence value, then the node is established. If the return value is low in confidence, the node is rejected. Some intermediate value may cause the node to suspend until further information is available.

ABDUCTIVE ASSEMBLY

Hierarchical classification and routine recognition do not differentiate between established (plausible) hypotheses or concepts. During a classification process, there may be several hypotheses or concepts that have been established, and yet some of those hypotheses or concepts may not be necessary. For instance, in a diagnostic problem, the classification process is used to determine a likely hypothesis to explain the malfunction. If the classifier finds two or more hypotheses likely, however, all of these will be returned, which is not a correct explanation. Additional processing may be required to select only those established nodes that can best explain the current situation.

Abductive assembly is a process of taking findings and generating an explanation of why the findings have arisen (*10*). This explanation may be a single hypothesis or, more commonly, a composite hypothesis of primitive or elementary hypotheses or of causally related hypotheses. The abductive process should deliver not only a composite hypothesis to explain the findings, but hopefully the *best* possible composite hypothesis. Abductive assembly may be used to further process the likely hypotheses established during hierarchical classification and return a subset of hypotheses, only those that make up the best explanation.

Figure 3 illustrates an abstract abduction problem in which there are data to be explained and plausible domain hypotheses to explain the data. In this figure, arrows indicate which hypotheses can explain which findings. The letters below the hypothesis represent its plausibility (L for likely, SL for somewhat likely, and N for neutral). The solution to an abduction problem is to find the best combination of domain hypotheses that explain the data. In this situation, best would denote a consistent composite hypothesis that is more highly rated than any other and is as simple as possible (i.e., has a few hypotheses as possible).

For the problem in Fig. 3, there are many potential explanations, but the composite of {H1, H4, H5} is probably the best because it is the simplest complete explanation with the highest degree of individual hypothesis plausibilities. Hypothesis {H4} is an

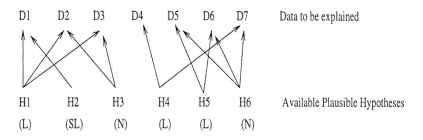

FIGURE 3. *Abstract abduction problem.*

essential hypothesis because it is the only plausible means for explaining D4. Since H4 also explains D7 and since {H5} is rated higher than {H6}, it makes {H5} a better explanation for D5 and D6 than {H6}. Hypothesis {H1} is a better explanation for D1, D2, and D3 than {H2, H3} because it has a higher plausibility and is simpler.

One of the powerful mechanisms of the abductive assembly algorithm is a propagation subtask that maintains a consistent composite hypothesis while also bringing into account knowledge of hypothesis incompatibilities, implications, and expectations. Whenever a hypothesis is included in the composite, any hypotheses that are still available but not yet included are examined. If any hypotheses are found incompatible with the newly included hypothesis, they are removed from consideration. If any hypotheses are found to be related to the newly included hypothesis (either by direct implication or indirect expectation), then their plausibilities are changed (raised if the implication or expectation is positive, lowered if the implication or expectation is negative). This allows for the possibilities that hypotheses are somehow dependent on each other. This in turn allows one to be more certain about other components of the explanation.

A Generic Task Strategy for Routine Decision Making

The combination of the three tasks of hierarchical classification, routine recognition, and abductive assembly has been applied to problems dealing with forming an explanation for the appearance of findings: diagnosis, perception, test interpretation. The process is one of generating potentially useful primitive explanations using hierarchical classification, rating each hypothesis using routine recognition, and then generating an overall best explanation using abductive assembly.

In order to solve routine decision-making problems instead of explanation problems, a variation of this strategy is used. The routine decision-making problem can be solved using plan-step generation, plan-step assessment, and plan-step assembly. Plan steps are primitive actions used by the problem-solving agent (from this point the article will refer to plan steps rather than actions). Depending on the type of the

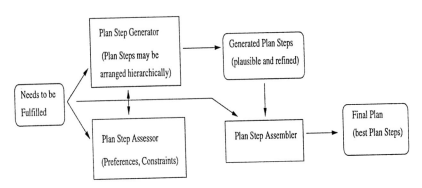

FIGURE 4. *Routine decision making as plan-step generation, assessment, and assembly.*

decision-making problem being solved, these three tasks may be very similar to hierarchical classification, routine recognition, and abductive assembly, in which plan steps replace hypotheses. Figure 4 shows the arrangement of these subtasks in order to solve routine decision-making problems.

In Fig. 4, the first step is to generate useful plan steps (that are as specific as possible). This can be done using a hierarchical classification, in which the taxonomic hierarchy is of plan steps (rather than concepts or hypotheses) at different levels of specificity. The plan step generation process can also be performed by other search-based methods, if available. Each plan step is assessed using routine recognition by appealing to specialized recognition agents, one per plan step in the domain. Plan steps that receive a positive assessment might then be used for the decision.

Figure 5 provides a recognition agent that might be used in decision making as a means for determining if the agent should plan to go to the grocery store. The "Going to the grocery store" recognition agent asks questions about the agent. Notice that the first two patterns act as "rule-out" knowledge. If the agent does not need either groceries or staples or if the store is currently closed, then there is no point in going. If, however, the agent does need either groceries or staples, has money and access to a car, and the store is open, then the plausibility of going to the store is at least "somewhat likely" or greater. If the agent needs to go to the store but has no available money or car, since there is still a need but not an easy means, the recognition agent returns a slightly negative value of "somewhat unlikely." Finally, if none of the patterns match, then the recognition agent assumes that the situation does not call for going to the store and the plausibility value is "unlikely."

The last step in the decision-making process is to use the positive assessed plan steps and have the plan-step assembler generate the best overall set of plan steps. The plan-step assembly process, a variation of abductive assembly, concentrates on one need at a time, selecting a plan step or multiple plan steps that can "best" fulfill the need. The best plan step is one that is essential (the only means of fulfilling a need) or has a higher plausibility rating than the other plan steps that might fulfill the need *and* is consistent with plan steps already selected. Two further criteria can help select plan

Features:
Does the agent need groceries?
Does the agent need staple goods of some kind?
Does the agent have money (cash, check, credit) available?
Does the agent have access to a car?
Is the grocery store currently open?

Patterns:
? ? ? ? No = Ruled Out
No No ? ? ? = Ruled Out
Yes Yes Yes Yes Yes = Very Likely
Yes ? Yes Yes Yes = Likely
? Yes Yes Yes Yes = Somewhat Likely
Yes Yes No No Yes = Somewhat Unlikely

No Match Response: Unlikely

FIGURE 5. *A recognition agent for "going to the grocery store."*

steps. A plan step that fulfills multiple needs is better than an equally rated plan step that can fulfill a single need. A plan step that is more refined (specific) than another plan step is better than a less refined plan step.

As plan steps are found and included in the growing composite of plan steps, constraints are propagated to maintain consistency and include knowledge of plan step dependencies (expectations, implications). The assembly process continues to select plan steps to fulfill each need until one of three conditions occurs. If all needs have been met by the generated plan steps than the decision is complete. If there are no more plan steps available to fulfill yet unfulfilled needs the decision is incomplete. If the only remaining plan steps that might be used are too close in desirability to choose between them, then the decision remains incomplete, although some form of tie breaking might be employed.

The routine decision-making problem can be solved by performing plan-step generation and plan-step assessment followed by plan-step assembly. These three tasks can themselves be implemented using hierarchical classification or some other search-based process for plan-step generation, routine recognition for plan-step assessment, and a variation of abductive assembly for plan-step assembly.

Examples

In order to further clarify the algorithm described in the previous section, this section will examine two types of routine decision-making problems and describe problem-solving systems that attempt to solve these problems. The problems differ greatly but use the same basic algorithm for their solution. In both problems, the decision-making task will utilize personal preferences and constraints.

The first problem is of scheduling. Scheduling is a very generic type of activity and can range from scheduling airplane arrivals at airport gates, for which the problem is one of assigning objects to locations at given times, to scheduling daily activities for which the problem is one of arranging a temporal sequence of tasks. The example used in this article will be of scheduling academic classes within a university department.

The second problem is one of consumer decision making. Consumer decision making is the problem whereby a consumer must select goods to fulfill his or her material needs. The example used here will be of deciding what grocery purchases a consumer should make to fulfill his or her nutritional needs in such a way that his or her personal preferences are applied.

A ROUTINE SCHEDULER

Routine scheduling is a process of assigning duties at particular times for a set of workers. While the problem is routine, it is complex due to an intractable number of possible combinations of duties-times-workers. Some of the possible schedules will be efficient, others will work but will not be efficient, and some will not work at all (e.g., if worker A produces a part needed by worker B, scheduling B prior to A will not work).

For the example presented here, the problem will consist of scheduling courses for a small computer science department. The goal is to find a time and teacher to assign to each of the semester's courses. In order to simplify this example, the problem will be restricted to a department of five teachers who teach between two and four classes each, covering fourteen class sections and twelve time slots of eight different computer science courses. The particular courses are three sections of computer literacy (lit), three sections of CS 1, two sections each of CS2 and CS 3, and one section each of CS 4, CS 5, CS 6, and CS 7 (which are considered upper-level courses). There are 840 possible course-time-teacher combinations, which would yield an enormous number of possible scheduling combinations.

In order to generate a useful and hopefully agreeable schedule, one should apply teacher and university constraints and preferences. This will greatly reduce the number of possibilities, greatly allowing for an easier scheduling process. Unbreakable constraints are that no teacher should teach more than their set number of classes (see Fig. 6) and that no teacher can teach two classes at the same time. Flexible constraints are that no teacher should teach both morning and evening classes on the same day, no teacher should have more than two classes in a row, and only one upper-level class should be offered at any time. A mild constraint is that each teacher should be given at most two separate courses (i.e., at most two preparations). Notice that constraints themselves come in levels so that unbreakable constraints must be be violated, flexible constraints should not be violated, and mild constraints should not be violated if there are other usable choices.

Preferences for each teacher describe what classes they like and dislike, what times they like and dislike, and whether they want back-to-back classes or not. There may be levels of preferences. For this problem, preferences are described as most preferred, preferred, mildly preferred, not preferred, and not possible (a constraint). Figure 6 shows the five teachers' preferences for this example. In this figure, after each

Mr. Lecturer (4) (btb)

	Classes	Times
Most Preferred	Lit	MW M1 / TR M1
Preferred	CS 1	MW/TR M2 / MW A1
Mildly Preferred	CS 2	TR A1
Not Preferred	CS 3	MW/TR A2
Not Possible	CS 4, CS 5 / CS 6, CS 7	MW E / TR E

Dr. Tenure (3) (btb)

	Classes	Times
Most Preferred	CS 7 / CS 5	MW/TR A1
Preferred	CS 2 / CS 4	MW/TR A2
Mildly Preferred	CS 1 / CS 3	MW/TR M2
Not Preferred	Lit	MW/TR M1 / TR E
Not Possible		MW E

Dr. Tenure Track (3)

	Classes	Times
Most Preferred	CS 3 / CS 4	MW M2 / MW A1
Preferred	CS 1	MW A2 / TR A1
Mildly Preferred	CS 5 / CS 2	TR A2 / TR M2
Not Preferred	Lit	MW/TR E / TR M1
Not Possible	CS 6	MW M1

Dr. Research Grant (2)

	Classes	Times
Most Preferred	CS 6	MW E
Preferred	CS 4 / CS 2	MW/TR A2
Mildly Preferred	CS 1 / CS 7	MW/TR A1 / TR E
Not Preferred	Lit	MW/TR M1 / MW M2
Not Possible	CS 3	TR M1

Ms. Department Chair (2)

	Classes	Times
Most Preferred	CS 1 / CS 3	MW/TR A1
Preferred	Lit / CS 4	MW/TR A2
Mildly Preferred	CS 2	MW/TR M2
Not Preferred	CS 7	MW/TR M1 / TR E
Not Possible	CS 5 / CS 6	MW E

MW - Monday Wednesday Friday or Monday Wednesday   TR - Tuesday Thursday

M1 - Early Morning, M2 - Late Morning, A1 - Early Afternoon,   M2 - Late Afternoon, E - Evening

Lit - Computer Literacy, CS 1 .. CS 7 - other Computer Science Courses   (btb) - prefers back-to-back classes

FIGURE 6. *Sample teacher preferences.*

teacher's name is the number of classes to be taught (in parentheses). Btb indicates that the teacher desires back-to-back classes (i.e., two classes in a row without a break).

Using the routine decision-making algorithm previously described, the schedule will be created as a process of plan-step generation, plan-step assessment, and plan-step assembly. For plan-step generation, a brute-force method is used to generate all possible plan steps (rather than using hierarchical classification as described in the previous section). Many of these will be discarded during the next step.

Each plan-step is now assessed for "usefulness" based on preferences. Plan steps receive high assessments if the teacher prefers both the time and course, mild assessments if the teacher prefers one of the two, or neutral assessments if the teacher has no preferences. If the teacher dislikes the class or time, a negative assessment is

TABLE 1

Some of the Plan Steps with Assessment Values

Name	Class	Time	Rating
Mr. Lecturer	Lit	MW M1	Extremely likely
Mr. Lecturer	CS 3	TR A1	Unlikely
Dr. Tenure	CS 2	MW A2	Somewhat likely
Dr. Tenure	CS 5	TR A1	Extremely likely
Dr. Tenure Track	CS 2	MW M2	Likely
Dr. Tenure Track	CS 6	MW M2	Ruled out
Dr. Research Grant	CS 1	MW E	Somewhat likely
Ms. Department Chair	CS 4	TR E	Unlikely

given. If a teacher is unable to teach a class or unable to teach at a certain time, the plan step is ruled out. Ruled out plan steps are immediately removed, although negatively assessed plan steps are kept in case they are needed. Table 1 shows a few plan steps for this example with their assessment ratings.

The third step is to perform plan-step assembly. The assembly process starts by seeking plan-steps that are essential. These are plan steps that are the only means of fulfilling a given need. For the scheduling problem, if only one teacher is capable of teaching a class, that teacher is essential (although typically there will be several times available to teach that class and so there may be no essential plan steps). If there are any essential plan steps, they are placed in the composite and the accepted plan steps are propagated by examining dependencies between these and the remaining plan steps. Propagation is described in detail below. Propagation might cause some plan steps to be discarded, and therefore more essentials may appear. The essentials step is then repeated if necessary.

If no essential plan steps have been found, the next step is to look for highly useful plan steps. These plan steps are ones that can fulfill a given need much better (are much more highly rated) than any other plan step. If any highly useful plan steps are found, they are included in the composite and their effects are propagated throughout the remaining plan steps. Again, the propagation may cause plan steps to be discarded or have other plan steps' assessments change, therefore after propagation the entire process resumes with a new search for essentials, and failing that, more highly useful plan steps.

If neither essentials nor highly useful plan steps are found, the assembler looks for less useful but still desirable plan steps. A plan step falls into this category if it is more highly rated than any other plan step that can fulfill a given class need. If any plan steps are included, then propagation occurs and the process starts again with essentials, followed by highly rated plan steps followed by useful plan steps. If no new plan steps are found that fill any of these categories, then the schedule has been filled out as much as possible with desirable plan steps. At this point, either the schedule is finished or there are classes still to be scheduled, but either any remaining plan steps are rated poorly (because no teacher wanted to teach that class) or there are ties among the plan steps. If there are any classes still to be covered, plan steps are chosen based on tie-breaking rules.

Propagation allows for constraint handling in the following ways. The remaining plan steps of teachers who have been scheduled for their maximum number of classes are discarded. If three classes have already been scheduled for one time slot, then all other plan steps at the time and day are discarded (due to classroom limitations). If a teacher has been scheduled at a particular time, then all remaining plan steps of that teacher at that time are discarded. Assessment scores for any plan steps that immediately precede or succeed an accepted plan step of a given teacher are altered, increasing the score if the teacher desires back-to-back classes, decreasing otherwise. If a teacher has been assigned a morning class for a given day, assessments for plan steps of evening classes during the same day for that teacher are lowered (or vice versa for an accepted night class). If an accepted plan step schedules an upper-level class, then assessment scores for all other upper-level classes at that time and day are lowered. Finally, if a teacher has already been assigned two *different* courses, then assessment scores are lowered for all the remaining plan steps for that teacher for a third course.

Tie-breaking rules are based on simple heuristics such as "select a plan step of a teacher who at this point has been assigned the fewest classes in the schedule." If necessary, tie-breaking rules are employed to finish the schedule.

For the example presented in Fig. 6, the assembly process does not find any essential plan steps, however, it does find several plan steps that are clearly better than any others. For instance, it determines that Dr. Research Grant should be scheduled to teach CS6 at MW evening. Dr. Tenure would be chosen for CS 7 during MW afternoon 1 and CS5 for TR afternoon 1. Dr. Tenure Track would be selected to teach CS 4 at MW morning 2. (This is chosen because MW afternoon 1 is taken by CS 7 and two upper-level classes should not be scheduled at the same time.) Mr. Lecturer will be scheduled to teach two lit classes, MW and TR morning 1. Finally, Ms. Department Chair would be chosen to teach CS 1 during MW afternoon 1.

At this point, constraints would be propagated, causing some plan steps to be removed if they are at the same time as any currently scheduled classes for that given teacher, while other plan steps have their assessments altered due to other constraints. For instance, since Dr. Research Grant is scheduled to teach a class on MW evening, any other plan steps for Dr. Research Grant that would schedule a class for MW morning would have their assessment scores lowered. The system will then go on to schedule the remaining classes. Table 2 shows the system's final schedule for this fictitious department. Notice that not everyone gets the schedule he or she most prefers (Dr. Tenure Track, for instance, must teach three different classes and teach during the TR evening, an unpreferred time), because some compromises must be made to finish the schedule.

The task of scheduling is fairly simple and yet can be extremely time-intensive due to the sheer number of possibilities. The assembly algorithm limits the possibilities to a single growing collection of plan steps. The propagation algorithm ensures consistency and utility without breaking any constraints.

TABLE 2

The Schedule for the Fictitious Computer Science Department

Course	Teacher	Time
Lit 1	Mr. Lecturer	MW morning 1
Lit 2	Mr. Lecturer	TR morning 1
Lit 3	Ms. Department Chair	TR afternoon 2
CS 1.1	Dr. Tenure Track	TR evening
CS 1.2	Dr. Tenure Track	MW afternoon 2
CS 1.3	Mr. Lecturer	MW morning 2
CS 2.1	Mr. Lecturer	TR morning 2
CS 2.2	Dr. Research Grant	TR evening
CS 3.1	Dr. Tenure	TR afternoon 2
CS 3.2	Ms. Department Chair	MW afternoon 2
CS 4.1	Dr. Tenure Track	MW morning 2
CS 5.1	Dr. Tenure	TR afternoon 1
CS 6.1	Dr. Research Grant	MW evening
CS 7.1	Dr. Tenure	MW afternoon 1

CONSUMER DECISION MAKING AND THE SHOPPER SYSTEM

The consumer problem is a situation in which there is a significant difference between what a consumer has and what a consumer desires. A solution to the consumer problem can be stated as "What should the consumer purchase to lessen this difference?" Consumer decision making is therefore the process whereby a consumer attempts to fulfill his or her needs through purchases. One specific example of this is purchasing groceries for weekly nutrition. Shopper is a knowledge-based system that performs consumer decision making based on neoclassical microeconomic theory and consumer theory (14, 15).

Shopper models a consumer whose goal is to select groceries for a number of meals. The system contains a knowledge of meals, meal ingredients, available goods, the

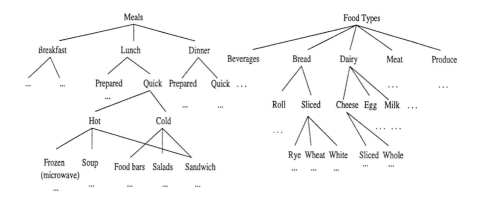

FIGURE 7. *Portion of Shopper's meal and food hierarchies.*

modeled consumer's preferences and constraints, and information pertaining to individual food items' nutrition, duration, ease of preparation, and expense. The primary knowledge groups are two classification hierarchies: meal types that form a search space of meals to satisfy meal needs, and food types that form the search space of groceries to satisfy meal ingredients. Figure 7 shows a portion of both of these hierarchies with the meal hierarchy on the left and the food hierarchy on the right. There is additional knowledge that describes the ingredients of a meal captured in an association list. Recognition agents known as "meal matchers" for the meal hierarchy nodes and "food matches" for the food hierarchy nodes represent the consumer's preferences and constraints toward meals and food items along with additional nutritional, cost, and duration information.

The input to Shopper is a list of needs stated in terms of the number of meals. Shopper's first task is to generate specific needs by generating specific types of meals. This is done by traversing the meal hierarchy and establishing meals that the consumer *might* desire. Meal matchers provide a desirability factor for each meal. Features for meal matchers ask questions of the consumer database such as "Does the consumer have access to a microwave oven?," "Does the consumer like fish?," "Is nutrition important?," and "Is cost important?" Based on the number of features that match the consumer's preferences and constraints, the meal matcher is able to assign a statement of usefulness to the meal. If the usefulness is high enough, the meal establishes and is refined by attempting to establish any child nodes.

Shopper next selects the highest-rated meals to fulfill each of the meal needs. If there are more meals than needs, only the top-rated meals are chosen. If there are more needs than meals, then some of the meals are repeated. These selected meals are then translated into specific food needs by using an association list that contains each meal's ingredients. Figure 8 shows a small portion of Shopper's association list, in this case pertaining to some of the sandwich-based lunch meals. Notice that the association list specifies food items at a very general level. They will be refined during the next step. The association list does include all components of a meal, including beverages and side orders.

Now that Shopper has determined the particular needs of the consumer, it traverses the food hierarchy searching for any food item that can fulfill any of these needs. Food matchers are used to sponsor each food type. A food type is considered by appealing to

White Meat-based Sandwich =>
  Sliced Bread, Sliced White Meat, Cheese, Leaf-Based Produce, Condiment, Side, Beverage

Red Meat-based Sandwich =>
  Sliced Bread, Sliced Red Meat, Cheese, Leaf-Based Produce, Condiment, Side, Beverage

Dairy-based Sandwich =>
  Sliced Bread, Cheese 1, Cheese 2, Leaf-Based Produce, Condiment, Side, Beverage

FIGURE 8. *A portion of Shopper's association list of meal ingredients.*

its food matcher. A food matcher represents the combined knowledge of the consumer's preference toward the food item such as taste, experience, meeting dietary considerations, consumer constraints, and consumer-independent information about that food item such as nutrition, duration, ease of preparation, and expense. Food matchers' features ask questions of the consumer and grocery knowledge bases such as "Does the consumer like white bread?," "Does the consumer like wheat bread?," "Is nutrition more important than cost?," and "Is sliced bread needed?" A food type will only establish if that item fulfills at least one need and its food matcher returns a positive desirability factor. If the food type establishes, it is refined by attempting to establish any or all of its child nodes. The classification process generates as many food items as are useful to fulfill the needs, but does not restrict the number of food items established.

A final "shopping list" is created during plan-step assembly by selecting the best food item(s) to fulfill each need. Shopper concentrates on one need at a time, selecting the best food item(s) established from the food hierarchy to fulfill that need. Some food items may fulfill multiple needs, while some needs may require multiple food items. Quantities for food items are determined by examining the number of needs a given food item will fulfill; that is, if a food item is expected to fulfill several needs, more of that food item is necessary.

A consumer *variability factor* is used so that if the consumer desires variety, a greater number of food items will be selected to fulfill common needs at the expense of desirability. The plan-step assembler will use the variability factor to decrease the rating of food items that have already been selected to fulfill other needs. In this way, other varieties of the same type of item might be selected to fulfill a similar need. For instance, if there are two separate needs for loaf of sliced bread and the consumer desires variability, the food item selected to fulfill the need will be whichever type of bread is most highly rated. Shopper would then decrease the assessment of that type of bread so that the food item selected to fulfill the second need will be a different type of bread (whichever bread was rated second highest).

An entire example of the Shopper system would take up a great deal of space. Instead, the article will now provide a reduced example to demonstrate the components without going into great depth. In this example, the modeled consumer needs one week's worth of lunches. The consumer's constraints are that he only has thirty minutes for each lunch, has access to a refrigerator but no heating source, and has preferences for meats and cheeses, although not necessarily with every meal, preferences against food bars (e.g., granola bars) and fish, prefers variety, with general nutritional preferences for healthy and low-fat foods, and enjoys both hot and cold meals. The consumer has a specific preference for white meat over red meat and for American cheese over other forms of cheese, does not like Swiss cheese, prefers lettuce over spinach for sandwiches, and prefers mayonnaise over mustard. The consumer has other stated preferences that are not relevant for this example.

Shopper first generates meals by traversing the meal hierarchy. Shopper rules out the meal branches for breakfast and dinner because there are no needs for those types of meals. Shopper descends only the lunch portion of the hierarchy, where it is able to establish "quick lunch," but not "prepared lunch" because of the time restriction. Further, "cold lunch" is established, but "hot lunch" is rejected because of the lack of a heating source (presumably at work). Based on the consumer's preferences, the selected meals will be salads and sandwiches, and in particular "vegetable salad," "white meat-based salad," "dairy sandwich," "white meat-based sandwich," and "red meat-based sandwich," but not "tuna salad," "fish-based sandwich," or "food bar."

Shopper organizes the selected meals based on the desirability. There are needs for seven lunch meals and only five selected meals, so Shoppers selects all five of them, repeating the two highest-rated meals. Next, Shopper generates the specific needs for the consumer by determining exactly what food types are required for each meal. The association list is used to identify the ingredients necessary for each meal.

The general food needs have now been identified and include "lettuce," "sliced bread," "sliced cheese," "sliced white meat," "beverage," and "condiment." The number of each type of need is determined by the number of times each food item appeared in the various association list entries. Shopper now descends the food hierarchy, selecting any food item that might be useful. To be useful, a food item must fulfill a given need (or part of a need), be acceptable by the consumer, and not violate any constraints.

Shopper descends the subhierarchies of the food hierarchy pertaining to dairy, meat, produce, and bread goods, but rejects the subhierarchies for other categories such as alcohol, frozen food, and staple goods. Shopper further refines each food item until it has established as many leaf nodes as possible in the hierarchy. Some of the nodes for this example would include "sliced American fat-free cheese," "sliced cheddar fat-free cheese," "sliced white bread," "sliced wheat bread," "iceberg lettuce," "sliced low-fat turkey," "sliced low-fat ham," and "fat-free mayonnaise." There will be more food items established than are needed, however.

Shopper selects between the established food items based on their assessment ratings provided by the food matchers. To fulfill a need for sliced cheese, Shopper would select between those cheeses available. In this case, sliced American fat-free cheese is more desirable than sliced cheddar fat-free cheese because the consumer prefers American cheese over all other kinds, whereas sliced Swiss fat-free cheese would be rejected due to an explicit dislike of that kind of cheese. Similarly, because the consumer prefers nutritional foods, sliced wheat bread would be selected over sliced white bread.

Shopper also takes into account the consumer's variability factor. If the variability factor is high, then the consumer desires variety and therefore Shopper will attempt to select different items to fulfill similar needs. For instance, if Shopper has determined that the consumer requires two packages of sliced cheese and desires variety, then it will choose both sliced American fat-free cheese and sliced cheddar fat-free cheese, even if the latter is less desired than the former. In order to determine quantities, Shopper combines similar needs, counting the number of units required. For instance, if it counts the need for twenty-four slices of cheese, then Shopper will select two packages of cheese; however, if there is only a need for twelve slices of cheese, then Shopper will only require one package. The final shopping list from Shopper to fulfill the sandwich aspect of the lunch needs for the example consumer is "1 loaf of wheat bread," "1 package of sliced American fat-free cheese," "1 package of sliced cheddar fat-free cheese," "1 small jar of fat-free mayonnaise," "1 small package sliced turkey meat," and "1 small head of lettuce."

Conclusions

This article has presented a solution to the routine decision-making problem. The solution is based on the generic tasks methodology of problem solving, combining the tasks of plan-step generation, plan-step assessment, and plan-step assembly. The three tasks can be implemented using variations of the generic tasks of hierarchical classification, routine, recognition, and abductive assembly.

The article has demonstrated the algorithm by presenting two problem-solving systems, a routine scheduler, and a consumer decision maker. In both cases, plan steps are individual actions that can be combined together to provide an overall decision that is used to fulfill the given needs. Both systems model the decision-making knowledge of consumer preferences and constraints. The two systems are highly different in purpose and knowledge, yet both use the same basic algorithm. In the routine scheduling system, plan-step generation is a simple matter and plan-step assembly is complicated by various interactions between plan steps. In Shopper, a large amount of the effort goes in the plan-step generation and there is little propagation of effects that occur in Shopper's plan-step assembly, partly because there is little interaction among groceries. The propagation is limited to two forms, the variability factor and goods that can account for multiple needs.

This routine decision-making algorithm can be applied to many similar types of problems in which there is knowledge to preenumerate the agent's actions, a means of determining what actions fulfill which of the agent's needs, and a means of evaluating how useful each action might be. If the domain has plan steps that can be arranged hierarchically, then plan-step generation can be performed using hierarchical classification. In problems in which actions contain dependencies, the plan-step assembler is able to make use of these to further the problem solving. The intent of this research is to further the abilities of automated problem-solving systems by appealing to the generic task methodology in artificial intelligence.

Acknowledgments

The author would like to acknowledge the support of the Alliance for Minority Participation at the University of Texas–Pan American for supporting several undergraduate students who have worked on aspects of Shopper. The author would also like to thank Dr. Miguel Paredes for his assistance with some of the early research into Shopper, along with the students who have provided substantial input, Gilbert Ochoa, T. J. Zecca, Karl Pankratz, and Michael Bianchi. Finally, the author would like to thank John Josephson at the Laboratory for Artificial Intelligence Research for providing the integrated generic task toolset from which Shopper was constructed.

REFERENCES

1. E. Fikes and N. J. Nilsson, "STRIPS: A New Approach to the Application of Theorem Proving to Problem Solving." *AI,* **3**(4), 189–208 (1972).

2. E. D. Sacerdoti, "The Nonlinear Nature of Plans," in *Proceedings of IJCAI-75,* IJCAII, Los Altos, CA, 1975.

3. E. D. Sacerdoti, "Planning in a Hierarchy of Abstraction Spaces." *AI,* **5**(2), 115–135 (1974).

4. P. E. Agre and D. Chapman, "An Implementation of a Theory of Activity," in *Proceedings of AAAI-87,* AAAI Press, Menlo Park, CA, 1987, pp. 268–272.

5. K. Hammond, "Chef: A Model of Case-based Planning," in *Proceedings of AAAI-86,* AAAI Press, Menlo Park, CA, 1986.

6. D. C. Brown and B. Chandrasekaran, "Plan Selection in Design Problem-Solving," in *Proceedings of AISB85 Conference,* Warwick, England, April 1985, Society for AI and the Simulation of Behavior (AISB). Springer-Verlag, London, 1985.

7. D. Herman, J. Josephson, and R. Hartung, "Use of DSPL for the Design of a Mission Planning Assistant," in *Expert Systems in Government Symposium,* 1986 IEEE Computer Society Press, Washington D.C., Oct. 1986, pp. 273–278.

8. B. Chandrasekaran, "Generic Tasks in Knowledge-based Reasoning: High-level Building Blocks for Expert System Design." *IEEE Exp.,* 23–30 (Fall 1986).

9. B. Chandrasekaran, "Towards a Functional Architecture for Intelligence Based on Generic Information Processing Tasks," in *Proceedings of the Tenth International Joint Conference on Artificial Intelligence,* IJCAII, Los Altos, CA. p. 1183–1192, 1987.

10. J. Josephson and S. Josephson, ed., *Abductive Inference: Computation, Philosophy, Technology,* Cambridge University Press, New York, 1994.

11. R. Fox, G. Ochoa, and M. Paredes, "Routine Decision Making Using Generic Tasks." *Exp. Syst. Appl.,* **12**(1), 109–117 (1997).

12. B. Chandrasekaran, "Towards a taxonomy of problem-solving types." *AI Mag.,* 9–17 (winter/spring 1983).

13. T. Bylander, A. Goel, and T. Johnson, "Structured Matching: A Computationally Feasible Technique for Making Decisions," in *Proceedings of the Fourth Knowledge Acquisition Workshop,* Banff, Canada, 1989, pp. 8:1–8:19.

14. H. Simon, *"Theories of Decision Making in Economics and Behavioral Science," American Economic Review,* p. 253–283, June, 1959, American Economic Association, Nashville, TN, 1959.

15. C. G. Walters and B. J. Bergiel, *Consumer Behavior: A Decision Making Approach,* South Western Publishing, Cincinnati, 1989.

BIBLIOGRAPHY

This article has discussed an algorithm that can be applied to a specific type of planning problem: routine decision making. Among the topics discussed were planning methods, decision making (including scheduling), and generic tasks. The following consists of a small bibliography of relevant works in these areas of artificial intelligence.

Additional References on Decision Making and Scheduling

Dologite, D., Mockler, R., and Chao, C., "The Manager's Analysis and Scheduling Consultant: A Knowledge-based System for Human Resources Workload Planning," in *8th International Symposium on Artificial Intelligence,* F. Cantu, R. Soto, M. Campbell, and J. Sanchez, ed., Instituto Tecnologico y de Estudios superiorès de Monterrey, Monterrey, Mexico, 1995, pp. 111–117.

Drabble, B., "Mission Scheduling for Spacecraft: Diaries of T-SCHED," in *Expert Planning Systems,* IEEE Press, Los Alamitos, CA, 1990, pp. 76–81.

Fox, M. S. and Smith, S. F., "ISIS: A Knowledge-based System for Factory Scheduling." *Exp. Syst.* **1**(1), 25–49 (1984).

Noronha, S. and Sarma, V., "Knowledge-based Approaches for Scheduling Problems: A Survey." *IEEE Trans. Knowl. Data Egr.,* **3**(2) 160–171 (June 1991).

Additional References on Planning

Ernst, G. and Newell, A., *GPS: A Case Study in Generality and Problem Solving,* Academic Press, New York, 1969.

Kaebling, L., "An Architecture for Intelligent Reactive Systems," in *Reasoning About Actions and Plans,* M. Georgeff and A. Lanksy ed., Morgan Kaufmann, San Francisco, CA, 1987, pp. 395–410.

Stefik, M., "Planning and Meta-planning." *AI,* **16**(2), 141–169 (1981).

Wilkins, D. E., "Hierarchical Planning: Definition and Complementation," in *ECAI '86: Seventh European Conference on Artificial Intelligence,* vol. 1, Wiley, Brighton, UK, 1986, pp. 466–478.

Barr, A. and Feigenbaum, E., eds., *Handbook of Artificial Intelligence,* vols. I and II, William Kaufman, Stanford, CA, 1981 (a survey of planning techniques).

Additional References on the Generic Task Paradigm

Chandrasekaran, B., Gomez, F., Mittal, S., and Smith, J., "An Approach to Medical Diagnosis Based on Conceptual Structures," in *Proceedings of the Sixth International Joint Conference on Artificial Intelligence,* IJCAII, Los Altos, CA, 1979, pp. 134–142.

Chandrasekaran, B., "Towards a Taxonomy of Problem-Solving Types." *AI Mag.,* 9–17 (winter/spring 1983).

Josephson, J., "A framework for Situation assessment: Using Best-Explanation Reasoning to Infer Plans from Behavior," in *Proceedings of Expert Systems Workshop,* April 1987, pp. 76–85.

Smith, J., Svirbely, J., Evans, C., Strohm, P., Josephson, J., and Tanner, M., "RED: A Red-Cell Antibody Identification Expert Module." *J. Med. Syst.,* **9**(3), 121–138 (1985).

Additional References on Specific Generic Tasks

Brown, D., *Expert Systems for Design Problem-Solving Using Design Refinement with Plan Selection and Redesign,* Ph.D. dissertation, Ohio State University, Columbus, OH, 1984.

Bylander, T. and Mittal, S., "CSRL: A Language for Classificatory Problem Solving and Uncertainty Handling." *AI Mag.,* **7**(3), 66–77 (Aug. 1986).

Johnson, T., "HYPER: The Hypothesis Matcher Tool," in *Proceedings of Expert Systems Workshop,* Defense Advanced Research Projects Agency, April 16–18, Science Applications International Corporation, Pacific Grove, CA, 1986, pp. 122–126.

Josephson, J., Chandrasekaran, B., Smith, J., and Tanner, M., "Abduction by Classification and Assembly," in *PSA 1986 Volume One, Philosophy of Science Association,* vol. 1, edition 1, Chap. VII, A. Fine and P. Machamer, eds., Philosophy of Science Association, East Lansing, pp. 458–470.

Mittal, S., Chandrasekaran, B., and Sticklen, J., "PATREC: A Knowledge-Directed Data Base for a Diagnostic Expert System." *IEEE Computer Spec. Iss.,* **17**, 51–58 (Sept. 1984).

Punch, W., Tanner, M., and Josephson, J., "Design Considerations for PEIRCE, A High-level Language for Hypothesis Assembly," in *Proceedings of Expert Systems in Government Symposium,* K. Karna, K. Parsaye, and B. Silverman eds., IEEE Computer Society, Los Alamitos, CA, Oct. 1986, pp. 279–281.

RICHARD FOX

HUMAN SUBJECTIVITY AND PERFORMANCE LIMITS IN DOCUMENT RETRIEVAL

Introduction

Much has been written in recent years regarding the faults of retrieval system evaluation based on relevance judgments. An issue of *Information Processing and Management* (1992, vol. 28, no. 4) and two issues of the *Journal of the American Society for Information Science* (1994, vol. 45, no. 3; 1996, vol. 47, no. 1) have been devoted to discussions of the nature of relevance and its use in evaluation. Excellent review articles have also been written on the subject by Saracevic (*1*) and Schamber (*2*). Notwithstanding, there is little agreement among investigators regarding the meaning and value of relevance judgments and their reliability as a means of system evaluation. Much of this uncertainty stems from individual variation observed in comparing the work of different human relevance judges. Such observations led Harter (*3*) to state that "Perhaps the single most compelling conclusion that can be reached from decades of research in information retrieval is the importance of individual differences among cases (lack of overlap)." In fact, recall and precision and similar measures, as averages over a number of queries, have the advantage that much individual variation is averaged out. The usefulness of such a standard for retrieval testing has been argued by Lesk and Salton (*4*) and more recently by Burgin (*5*), but because such summary statistics tend to ignore individual variation, they have been criticized by others as useless if not misleading (*3, 6–8*). I regard this latter assessment as overly gloomy and would like to argue for a more pragmatic view of the state of information retrieval research.

Consider for a moment another field of research altogether, namely, medical research, and in particular new drug development. Thousands of studies have been done and continue to be done that compare cure rates or rates of remission from some disease that are observed with the use of two or more drugs. Such rates of cure are summary statistics or averages very much like precision and recall in the field of information retrieval. Decisions are made regarding which drug is best based largely on such statistics. The criterion is in other words "the most good for the most people." Has such an approach benefited mankind? Without doubt, but does it not ignore a great deal of individual variation among the end users of a medication? Yes. People are very different and any particular person may respond differently from another given the same medication. Some experience minor side effects, others have none, and a few have fatal adverse reactions. Would it not be better to taylor a different medication to suit exactly the need and the genetic makeup of each individual with a disease? Yes, it would be theoretically better, but it would be economically impossible; we simply do not have the resources to do that kind of engineering. Further, even if we did, it could well take so long that many would die of their diseases before we could develop the perfect medications for them. Some individual factors are commonly considered in prescribing a medication, among them the age and weight of the patient, but many more individual variables are ignored than are taken into account, and as a consequence anyone who takes a new medication runs some small risk that he or she may be adversely affected by it.

I believe there is sufficient analogy between new drug development and information retrieval as a science to make the comparison useful. Just as new drug development largely ignores individual variation to pursue the practical goal of "the most good for the most people," so must the developers of information retrieval systems focus on a practical goal. Arguably, recall and precision are measures of "the most good for the most people" in the area of information retrieval. As such their improvement by any reasonable means seems commendable, but would it not be desirable to have a retrieval system that responded to people's individual differences? Indeed, that would be the ultimate solution to information needs. No one has shown how to attain such a goal theoretically, let alone that it is economically feasible, however. For the present we thus have retrieval systems that are largely, if not totally, unresponsive to individual differences.

Interestingly, if we could attain such a lofty goal as individualized retrieval, recall and precision may still be the best measures of our success. Both would be dramatically increased by a retrieval system that could respond optimally to the individual needs of users. This latter statement requires some explanation, however. If all performance is measured based on the judgments of a single judge for each query as is generally the case, recall and precision cannot be sensitive to individual characteristics. It is our purpose here to describe a methodology for evaluation that differs from the classical methodology largely in that multiple judges are necessary. A group or class of judges explicitly incorporates individual variation and within such a group individual variation becomes measurable by the classical measures of precision and recall. Further, by pooling the judgments of the group we can give a precise meaning to the probability ranking principle. Because the probability ranking principle defines optimal retrieval, groups of judges used in this way provide us with an improved measurement instrument that will allow us to define the limits on retrieval performance imposed by various states of knowledge about the individual.

The Probability Ranking Principle

The probability ranking principle (*9, 10*) forms a useful description of ideal retrieval.

Probability ranking principle.   Optimal performance is obtained by ranking the documents in the search space in decreasing order of their probability of relevance to the query, provided this probability is the best possible estimate based on document and query content.

As noted by Robertson (*10*), this result depends on an assumption about the nature of relevance, which we have characterized by the word intrinsic (*11*).

Intrinsic relevance.   The relevance of an individual document to a query is not dependent on the other documents in the database.

The probability ranking principle, as we have stated it here, faces two challenges to its validity. First, there is the question of whether or not intrinsic relevance is a reasonable requirement on the concept of relevance. Hypothetical examples have been constructed by Cooper (*10*) showing that if we do not insist on intrinsic relevance, but rather let the relevance of one document depend on what documents may have been examined before it, then the probability ranking principle is not valid. Such examples generally depend on the assumption that if one has found a document providing a certain piece of information then another document providing the same information may be of little interest. This may occasionally be true, but we are aware of no study showing that the so-called drop off (see Ref. *12*) in the value of documents retrieved after other documents is a major practical issue. On the contrary, we believe that most serious scholars initially want to see all the references possible on a subject. Later, when they have weighed the value of different articles, some may be judged unhelpful. In our own experience searching the MEDLINE database we have not experienced the phenomenon of "duplicate information" as a problem. If this is true, then "aboutness" is closer to the correct concept of relevance (*13–15*). In fact, the finding of Regazzi (*16*) that judges responded no differently when judging documents on a utility theoretic scale than when judging documents on a relevance theoretic scale supports the contention that usefulness and aboutness are essentially equivalent. Fortunately aboutness is quite consistent with the concept of intrinsic relevance. We are indeed satisfied to seek a retrieval system that delivers the documents about the query subject matter and that is measured by this as a standard. The ultimate utility of retrieved documents may at times have to be dealt with, but we believe that for practical purposes it should be handled as a separate issue. Were it necessary to include it in our analysis, it should be important in retrieval testing as it is commonly practiced with singly judged test sets for the same reasons. Evaluative studies in information retrieval have not generally dealt with the issue, and we shall not pursue it further here.

Another aspect of whether or not intrinsic relevance is a reasonable requirement is whether judges in practice can actually make judgments that are independent of the other documents in the database being queried. In fact this should be easier than making judgments dependent on the other material in the database because there is much less information to be considered. People have no trouble judging the value of different products when shopping to satisfy a particular need. They do not suddenly lose the ability to make a judgment once they have seen one product that could satisfy their need. After judging the available options they generally make a decision on which one to actually buy. In the same way people can decide the intrinsic value of a document to meet an information need regardless of what they have seen before provided they are adequately instructed about the nature of the task. We have found evidence that this is so for judges on one of our own test sets (*17*). Judges were given a few duplicate documents at random times and were not informed of this, yet a high level of consistency was found between the two judgments they recorded on such documents.

Another aspect of actual judging is order effects. Eisenberg and Barry (*18*) and Regazzi (*16*) have found evidence that presentation order affects relevance judgments. Judges at sporting events such as ice skating and gymnastics tend to hedge their bets and refrain from giving too high a score lest some later contestant deserve an even higher mark, thus a good performance early in a competition may not win as high marks as the same performance would near the end. The same phenomenon seems to occur with judges of relevance. Perhaps this is unavoidable. Our approach is to present the documents to be judged for a given query in a random order in an attempt to minimize any systematic affect of this type. We use the same random order for all judges so that presentation order is removed as a factor in interjudge comparisons.

The second challenge to the probability ranking principle is the lack of an objective criterion for relevance. There is a general lack of agreement among researchers on a definition that makes relevance a stable reproducible entity (1, 19, 20). We believe that the only hope of establishing a definition that fulfills such requirements is to look in the direction of relevance understood as a probability. The importance of such an approach was perceived early in the history of the field by Maron (9) and reiterated by van Rijsbergen (21). Several investigators, in contemplating the possible approaches to a practical definition of relevance, have commented on the difficulty of determining relevance as a probability (1, 7). If our concept of relevance is limited to the subjective probability assignment of a single judge, we would agree that little could be gained by such an approach. Even decision theorists find the interpretation of single subjective judgments of probability a contentious issue (22). Our approach is in accord with the perspicuous insight of Rees and Schultz (23, p. 179) that "stable, meaningful judgments of relevance will only result when groups of relatively homogeneous judges perform the task of evaluating the relevance of documents." Just as Froehlich (20) has proposed that retrieval systems should be designed for a typical user group, we see the need that test sets reflect the judgments of the expected class of users, thus we believe the only reasonable approach is to accept Maron's proposal (9) that relevance itself is a probability. We propose that relevance is what people say it is (24, 25) and that relevance can only be given a definition in a precise manner when the context of the discussion includes a specified judge or class of judges.

Definition.   The intrinsic relevance of a document to a query for a judge is the subjective probability estimated by that judge that the document, if obtained and used to answer the query in the manner envisioned by the judge, would prove useful for that purpose.

With this definition of relevance we can reformulate the probability ranking principle. As a formal statement we offer the following.

Class-based probability ranking principle.   Let q be a query to be applied to a database D and let C be a nonempty class of judges. For any $d \in D$ and judge $j \in C$, let $j(q,d)$ be the probability assigned by j that d is intrinsically relevant as an answer to q. Then

$$p_C(q,d) = \frac{1}{\|C\|} \sum_{j \in C} j(q,d) \tag{1}$$

represents the probability that an arbitrary judge from C would find d to be useful as an answer to q. If the numbers are accurate estimates, then retrieval of D in order of decreasing $p_C(q,d)$ in answer to q, will give optimal retrieval for the members of C.

To see why retrieval in order of decreasing $P_C(q,d)$ is optimal, it is only necessary to note that $P_C(q,d)$ is the probability that a randomly chosen member of C will find d useful in answer to q. We assume that all members of C are equally likely to be users and hence the probability that any particular judge $j \in C$ is the chosen user is $\|C\|^{-1}$. (Here $\|C\|$ denotes the number of judges in C.) Once the user j is chosen the probability that he finds the document d useful is $j(q,d)$, thus the probability that j is both chosen and finds the document d useful is $j(q,d)\|C\|^{-1}$. Because the choice of different judges is really made up of mutually exclusive events we must add up the probabilities of satisfaction coming from these different events to obtain the total probability of satisfaction, but the sum is just $p_C(q,d)$, as shown by Eq. 1. Because $p_C(q,d)$ is the probability of satisfaction for the randomly chosen unknown member of C, we obtain optimal retrieval for such a randomly chosen unknown member of C by ranking the documents in order of decreasing $p_C(q,d)$. If it is known that different members of C are not equally likely to be users of the system, they can as judges be given different weights in Eq. 1 to denote their different probabilities or frequencies of usage. We prefer to carry on the discussion at the simpler level where all users/judges are assumed to have equal likelihood of using the system.

The statement of the probability ranking principle just given pinpoints a weakness in that the prescribed retrieval order is only truly optimal if the subjective judgments on which it is based are accurate. It also possesses a strength, however, for in the judgment of the members of C with the knowledge and resources they have, the retrieval order is optimal. If the members of C are the customer base for a commercial retrieval system, then the satisfaction of the members of C is the first priority (*26*). If a member of C finds that for a given query she is presented with documents that include those that she believes are most likely to satisfy her needs but later she finds that she is wrong and she should have selected differently, she is educating herself in regard to her subjective judgments. When this sort of education becomes statistically prevalent in C it will make itself felt in the class-based probability ranking principle. If this principle is used to test and optimize the retrieval system, it allows the system to correct itself to the new standard of retrieval set by the population C. While we have explicitly used the concept of a subjective probability, this does not represent a departure from current practice. Even though human judgments of relevance as usually made are either 0 (nonrelevant) or 1 (relevant), they are nevertheless subjective. We have only expanded the probability scale to allow values other than 0 and 1. Judgment scales with more than two values have been used in the past (*25, 27, 28*), but have allowed the assignment of different levels of relevance rather than different levels of the probability of relevance. It is unlikely that humans can assign probabilities from more than some small discrete set of probabilities in a meaningful way. We have used a five-point scale of probabilities consisting of 0, 0.25, 0.5, 0.75, and 1.0 in most of our work, as opposed to the simple two-point (0 and 1) scale.

Optimal Retrieval: The Zero Knowledge Case and Statistics

To rank documents effectively for a user depends completely on the ability to predict what that user would like to see in response to a query. If we do not know the user and have no information about his individual characteristics (zero knowledge case), then we are left to make our predictions based on the query that has been submitted and some knowledge of the general population of users of the system. Then it is appropriate to apply the class-based probability ranking principle (CBPRP) and rank the documents in the order of decreasing $p_x(q,d)$ where the class C has been replaced by X, which stands for the whole population of potential users. To justify this statement we not that when X is truly a large population, then $p_x(q,d)$ is an average of a large set of small numbers and any one of these numbers could be omitted without a measurable effect on the value $p_x(q,d)$. When we invoke the values $p_x(q,d)$ for the purpose of ranking we thus are not making use of the knowledge of any particular individual, but only of robust characteristics of the whole population.

While $p_x(q,d)$ allows us to rank documents optimally in answer to a query, it is not practical to compute; rather, we must rely on statistical sampling theory to approximate $p_x(q,d)$. To this end we proceed by randomly choosing a sample $C \subseteq X$, then if C is large enough we can achieve any desired level of approximation to $p_x(q,d)$ by use of the function $p_C(q,d)$. This follows from a form of the central limit theorem (29) or even the fact that all the functions $j(q,d)$ are bounded. Note that is is not necessary that $p_C(q,d)$ be equal to $p_x(q,d)$ to produce the optimal ordering produced by $p_x(q,d)$. Usually it is sufficient that it be close. As a result we can produce optimal or near optimal rankings for the unknown user from a sufficient random sample of users C. How large C must be to produce a given quality of retrieval is difficult to predict from these considerations, however, we will present some data below that indicate that C may not have to be larger than four or five to see quite marked improvement in retrieval over what individuals can produce.

Optimal Retrieval: The Full Knowledge Case and Conflict

If in addition to the query we know some of the individual characteristics of the user we may be able to better predict what documents he or she would like to see. Presumably the more we know the better we can make this prediction and rank the documents. Clearly no knowledge that we could have could be more useful than knowing what the user's own judgments of the relevance of the documents are. This is what we mean by full knowledge, and if we have this knowledge any other knowledge about the individual is superseded and we can make perfect predictions and rankings for this user. When we rank the documents by the judgments of a single user j we are in fact invoking the CBPRP with $C = \{j\}$. Retrieval in order of decreasing $p_{\{j\}}(q,d) = j(q,d)$ is optimal retrieval for C; that is, for the single user j. Now suppose we add a second user j_2. If we have full knowledge of the judgments of both j and j_2 we may define $C = \{j,j_2\}$ and rank documents by the CBPRP based on this C. As a general rule the ranking thus produced will not be optimal for either j or j_2. This is because judges tend to disagree at a high level of anywhere from 25 percent to 60 percent of the time (30). Such conflict in preferences is dealt with by compromise. The CBPRP averages the judgments of j and j_2 and $p_C(q,d)$ rates as best that document that produces the highest average. This document may not be the highest rated by either j or j_2. For example, if $j(q,d_1) = 0.7$, $j(q,d_2) = 1.0$, and $j(q,d_3) = 0.1$, while $j_2(q,d_1) = 0.6$, $j_2(q,d_2) = 0$, and $j_2(q,d_3) = 0.9$, then $p_C(q,d_1) = 0.65$, $p_C(q,d_2) = 0.5$, and $p_C(q,d_3) = 0.5$. Thus j prefers document d_2 and j_2 prefers document d_3, but the best compromise document is d_1. The document d_1 is the best choice because both users are equally likely to use the system and we must rank with both possibilities in mind. In that case d_1 gives the highest probability of satisfaction, namely, $p_C(q,d_1) = 0.65$. In a similar fashion we can consider the addition of a third judge j_3 to form $C = \{j j_2 j_3\}$ and consider retrieval by the CBPRP, and so on ad infinitum. Each time we add another user to the class C we increase the conflict and the degree of compromise that is necessary, and the effect is to decrease the numerical values of the $p_C(q,d)$ for the highest-rated documents. This decrease may also be looked upon as a result of the growing uncertainty about who will use the system.

One may ask how the optimal retrieval defined by the CBPRP relates to actual retrieval by a system when the class C consists of one or a small set of users. The answer is that the CBPRP sets absolute limits on retrieval by an operational system for such a class C. The familiar case is that of relevance feedback for a single user. (C consists of a single user.) Relevance feedback seeks to use the information gained about the individual user from his ratings of several initial documents to improve subsequent retrieval (31–35). Such individual information can never prove more useful than knowing the user's actual judgments regarding the documents to be retrieved, thus the CBPRP always provides, in its ideal ranking based on the users' judgments, an upper limit to the performance that can be achieved by relevance feedback or any other method of obtaining and using individual characteristics to improve retrieval for that individual. When the class C consists of more than one user the interpretation is similar. CBPRP retrieval sets an absolute limit to the quality of retrieval that can be produced when one knows that the users of the system are restricted to C and they are all assumed equally likely to use the system. Such a limit could have meaning in the setting of a small group of users, provided information is collected about them and their preferences over time in an effort to improve retrieval for the group. While this is not a situation we observe in practice, we will see in the next section that it has considerable theoretical interest.

Estimating Limits with Real Data

If the user class X is a large class of people it will generally be impossible to have each member of X judge a set of documents for relevance to a set of queries. In this case, however, it may be possible to choose some much smaller but representative subset C of X. Judgments by members of C will define ideal retrieval for the class C and, as pointed out above, there may be reason to believe such is a good approximation to ideal retrieval for the larger class X. We shall attempt to illustrate this in what follows.

THE TEST SETS

We have constructed two test sets, which we will designate as test sets I and II. The construction of test set I was completed in 1993. It is based on a database D_I of 71,312 MEDLINE documents in the area of molecular biology, all of which have abstracts. From D_I 100 documents were randomly chosen to compose the set of queries Q. Queries are understood as "queries by example" in the search for other closely related documents in the database. One could not expect a human to judge all 71,312 documents in D_I for relevance to even one query. To make a tractable judgment task, our approach is to limit the comparison of each query document in Q to only the lexically most similar documents in D_I. This is implemented by first indexing the documents in D_I by the words in titles, abstracts, and MESH terms and then applying standard cosine vector retrieval. The vector model we use is described in Wilbur and Coffee (*36*) and Lucarella (*37*), while a general treatment of the approach is given in Salton (*38*). Vector retrieval is used to select for each query document in Q the fifty documents in D_I that are most similar to the query (The query itself is excluded.) In this way there is associated with each query a minidatabase of fifty documents with generally significant lexical similarity to the query. Any method of retrieval is tested by how well it ranks each set of fifty documents to bring the actual relevant documents among the fifty to the top of the ranking. The important gain here is that a judge must only compare each query document with its associated set of fifty similar documents for a total of 5,000 query–document comparisons or about 100 hours of work.

Test set I was completed by having a panel of five judges judge each of the 5,000 query–document pairs for relevance. This panel consisted of two physicians with experience in the literature of molecular biology, a college graduate with several years experience as a curator of databases in molecular biology, a college graduate in biochemistry currently working as a research assistant in the area of applied molecular biology, and a doctoral candidate in molecular biology. The instructions to the judges consisted of the following three requirements:

1. Judge a document relevant to a query if and only if you would wish to read the full document if you were given the task of writing the query document.
2. Make your judgments on a scale of 0–4; where 0 means the document is clearly not relevant; 1, the document has a 0.25 probability of relevance to writing the query document; 2, a 0.50 probability of relevance; 3, an 0.75 probability of relevance; and 4, the document is certainly relevant to the query-writing task.
3. When judging a document, treat it as if it were the only document available and disregard any other documents already judged for that query.

Here item 1 is intended to focus the judges toward a common and relatively time-independent task in an effort to obtain uniform results. The 0–4 scale in item 2 implements the definition of intrinsic relevance given in the preceding section. Our experience has been that in some cases judges find this freedom helpful in dealing with their own uncertainty in making judgments, while in other cases it allows them to express finer shades of usefulness for documents. The prescription in item 3 is a necessary requirement of intrinsic relevance; namely, that the probability of relevance be based only on the query and the document under consideration and be uninfluenced by other documents in the database.

We recently completed the construction of test set II obtained in essentially identical fashion to test set I, only from a much larger and more current database of 1.2 million MEDLINE documents. The 5,000 query–document pairs of test set II have been judged by a new panel of seven judges with the same instructions as those given to the panel for test set I. This panel consisted of three individuals holding a Ph.D. in molecular biology; three holding a Ph.D. in genetics; and one with a Ph.D. in chemistry, extensive experience in the field of molecular biology, and currently a doctoral candidate in molecular biology.

One point of concern about test sets I and II is the effect of limiting the search space for each query document to fifty lexically related documents. Some limitation must be accepted in order to make the judgment task tractable. We consider a limitation to lexically similar documents acceptable for two reasons. First, the probability of relevance between two documents that have no lexical similarity must be judged small. Our concept of relevance is strongly related to the "aboutness" of documents (*13–15*), and due to the detailed taxonomic and naming conventions in biology, documents (title plus abstract) about the same subject usually have some measure of lexical similarity. We do not claim that a judge will never judge a document pair without lexical similarity as relevant, but experience suggests a small chance of more than one judge making such a judgment for the same pair. Second, we know of no fully automatic retrieval system that can be deemed successful at retrieving documents relevant but lexically unrelated to the query. By lexically unrelated we mean, of course, post any thesaurus preprocessing. As a consequence, on the theoretical side we do not anticipate the need to test such a system and on the practical side we require our users to either identify a document or produce a query that is lexically related to the material they seek. The challenge of framing a query lexically related to the document one seeks can be an extremely difficult one, as noted by Blair and Maron (*39*), but this is a limitation of current systems unless the subject matter is severely restricted. Within the confines of lexical similarity the test sets do provide a broad sample of query–document comparisons and are representative of the highly nontrivial task of separating the relevant from the nonrelevant documents.

While this completes our brief description of test sets I and II, we refer the reader to Refs. *17, 40,* and *41* for additional details that are not crucial to our discussion here.

MEASUREMENT

Our analysis will require the ability to measure the quality of different methods of retrieval. Classically, performance at the document retrieval task has been measured by the complementary measures of precision and recall (*42*). Precision is defined as the fraction of documents retrieved that are relevant to the query, and recall is defined as the fraction of documents relevant to the query that are retrieved. While each of these measures is meaningful for retrieval in response to a single query, as measures of performance they are generally constructed as averages over a defined population of queries. More formally we may let Q be such a population of queries that are applicable to a database D consisting of N documents and let R denote the average number of relevant documents in D in response to an arbitrary query in Q. Now suppose M is some method of retrieval defined on D and responds to a query from Q by ranking the documents in D in a preferred order so that the document ranked first is intended as the most likely to be relevant to the query, and so on. Then by applying the (ranked) retrieval method M to each query in Q and checking the document at rank i to see if it is relevant to the query, we may calculate the probability p_i that a document retrieved at the ith rank by an arbitrary query from Q is relevant. Then if we limit retrieval to the first n ranks, the performance of M may be measured by the average precision and average recall defined by

$$\text{Precision}_n = \frac{1}{n} \sum_{i=1}^{n} p_i$$

$$\text{Recall}_n = \frac{1}{R} \sum_{i=1}^{n} p_i \tag{2}$$

It is useful to note that for a given test set the quantity R is a constant, hence if we consider a particular value of n, we can easily convert a precision to a recall value and vice versa, provided we know R. Nothing is lost, therefore, if we ignore recall values and restrict attention to precision as our measurement. This will be our approach in what follows.

In order to calculate precisions as defined in Eq. 2, it is necessary to assign values to the numbers p_i, $1 \leq i \leq n$. Classically this is done by considering the N queries in the set Q and for each $q \in Q$ examining the retrieved document d_i at rank i. As a rule each such d_i has been judged either relevant or nonrelevant to the query q. The value of p_i is just the fraction of the d_i that was judged relevant. Alternatively if a judgment of relevant is counted as a 1 and a judgment of nonrelevant is counted as a 0, then p_i is just the average of all such values over the N queries. In our setting, given a class C of users or judges (depending on how we wish to view them), we have the function $p_C(q,d)$, which assigns to each query q and document d the probability of relevance as judged by the members of C. Viewing p_i as an average, it is natural to define

$$p_i = \frac{1}{N} \sum_{q \in Q} p_C(q,d_i), \tag{3}$$

where i stands for the rank of interest. We saw above how the function $p_C(q,d)$ provided the ability to do ideal ranking according to the probability ranking principle. Here Eq. 2 and Eq. 3 show how this same function can be used to obtain the precision resulting from any ranking. It is the essence of the probability ranking principle that if $p_C(q,d)$ is used in this way to produce a precision, then the highest precision possible must result when $p_C(q,d)$ is also used to rank the documents in decreasing order of its values. In other words, when $p_C(q,d)$ is used for evaluation, $p_C(q,d)$ ranking produces an upper limit for performance by any method of ranking.

APPROXIMATING SEQUENCES

To begin, let us suppose that we are given a class C of N users about whom we have full knowledge so that we may apply the CBPRP. Then necessarily if $C_k, k \leq N$ represents any subclass of C with k users, we may also apply the CBPRP to C_k. Generally for a given k there will be more than one such subclass that could be considered. It is then often useful to take an average of whatever number we are considering over all such subclasses for a fixed k. Such an average provides a convenient way to summarize the overall behavior of the data. We are interested in two different kinds of averages that depend on k. The first is called the *upper series* and is defined by

$U_k^n(C)$ = average, for all different subclasses C_k of C, of the precision over the top n ranks, of retrieval by the CBPRP based on C_k and evaluated by $p_{C_k}(q,d)$.   (4)

The second is called the *lower series* and is defined by

$L_k^n(C)$ = average, for all pairs (C_k,j) where C_k is a subclass of C and $j \in C - C_k$, of the precision over the top n ranks, of retrieval by the CBPRP based on C_k and evaluated by $p_{\{j\}}(q,d)$.   (5)

It can be proved (*40*) that the upper series is a nonincreasing sequence as k increases; that is

$$U_1^n(C) \geq U_2^n(C) \geq \ldots \geq U_k^n(C) \geq \ldots \geq U_N^n(C) \tag{6}$$

and that all elements of the lower series are bounded above by $U_N^n(C)$; that is

$$L_k^n(C) \leq U_N^n(C), 1 \leq k < N \tag{7}$$

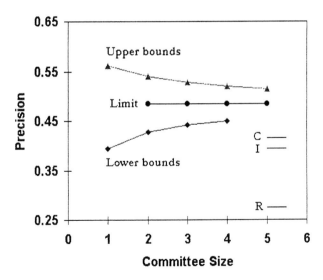

FIGURE 1. *Performance limits for test set I. The straight line represents $U_N^N(X)$ where X is the whole population of users for test set I. This limit is computed as a simple interpolation dividing equally between the upper and lower bounding series. The values of precision obtained by retrieval in random order (R), by the average of individual group members (I), and by our computer algorithm (C, a variant of the vector method; 38) are also displayed for comparison. Source: Reprinted from W. J. Wilbur, "A Comparison of Group and Individual Performance Among Subject Experts and Untrained Workers at the Document Retrieval Task." JASIS, © 1998, John Wiley & Sons, Inc. Reprinted by permission of John Wiley & Sons, Inc.*

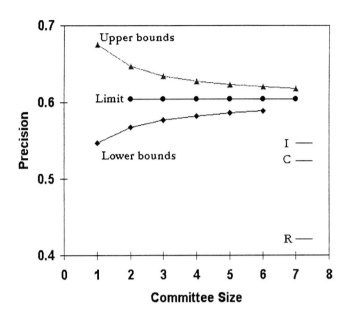

FIGURE 2. *Performance limits for test set II. The straight line represents $U_N^n (X)$ where X is the whole population of users for test set II. This limit is computed as a simple interpolation dividing equally between the upper and lower bounding series. The values of precision obtained by retrieval in random order (R), by the average of individual group members (I), and by our computer algorithm (C, a variant of the vector method; 38) are also displayed for comparison. Source: Reprinted from W. J. Wilbur, "A Comparison of Group and Individual Performance Among Subject Experts and Untrained Workers at the Document Retrieval Task." JASIS, © 1998, John Wiley & Sons, Inc. Reprinted by permission of John Wiley & Sons, Inc.*

The upper and lower series can be calculated for any class of users/judges C. The interpretation of the upper estimate $U_k^n (C)$ is the average precision a group of k members from C can achieve when they collectively rank the documents (CBPRP) and then rate those rankings themselves. As such it is an upper limit for how good retrieval can be for groups of k members from C. In accordance with Eq. 6 and what we saw previously, this upper limit progressively decreases as k increases, and the degree of compromise increases with the size of the group. The interpretation of the lower estimate $L_k^n (C)$ is the average precision a group of k members from C can achieve when they collectively rank the documents (CBPRP) and those rankings are rated by some unknown user from C but not from the group. The inequality of Eq. 7 asserts that the whole class C will rate the retrieval they do for themselves at least as high as one can expect individuals to rate retrieval done for them by any group of which they are not a member. Now if C is a large class, then the individual members of C have negligible influence on the rankings produced by the corresponding CBPRP, thus they will have no measurable preference for them over the rankings produced by any other large subclass of C of which they are not a member. This leads to the conclusion that $L_k^n (C)$ will approach $U_N^n (C)$ in the limit as k gets large. It is essentially the statistical argument shown above.

In statistics it is accepted that one may approximate the mean of a population by first taking a random sample of the population and then calculating the mean of this random sample. The larger the random sample the more assurance we have that the approximation is close to the true value. The same principle applies in our setting. The whole population of users X has N members where N is very large. We can only consider a small subclass C of X that has N_C ($<<N$) members, nevertheless it can be shown (40) that

$$E(U_k^n(C)) = U_k^n(X)$$
$$E(L_k^n(C)) = L_k^n(X)$$

$$(8)$$

so that the upper and lower numbers we can calculate from C give us an approximation to those we would obtain from X. Further it can be shown (unpublished observations) that for a fixed k as C increases in size the variance in the numbers $U_k^n(C)$ and $L_k^n(C)$ approach zero so that one can have more and more confidence in the approximations represented by Eq. 8.

In order to illustrate the foregoing equations we have calculated the upper and lower series for the set C_I consisting of five users/judges from test set I and the set C_{II} consisting of seven users/judges from test set II. The results are shown in Fig. 1 for test set I and Fig. 2 for test set II. The limit shown in each figure as a straight line is an estimate of the absolute limit on how good retrieval could be for the unknown user. In both figures the precision represented by this limit is about 50 percent higher above random than the retrieval that a single individual (L_1^{20}) could be expected to produce for the unknown user. This shows that there is a significant benefit in pooling judgments from different individuals. It also indicates that retrieval as it is currently practiced can be significantly enhanced if we can find a way to duplicate the predictions produced by groups of humans. Perhaps of just as much interest is the limit placed by U_1^{20} on the quality of retrieval that could be produced for a single user as judged by himself. This limit is, in the case of test set I, 37 percent higher above random than the retrieval that could be expected for the unknown user, while in the case of test set II it is 39 percent higher above random than the level of retrieval that could be expected for the unknown user. This level of improvement is then what can be achieved in moving from a state of zero knowledge about the individual to a state of complete knowledge. It places a limit on what can be achieved by such techniques as relevance feedback or the development of user profiles, which are based on knowledge of the individual.

We do not know how to build a practical retrieval system capable of performance at or even near the limits herein set forth either for the unknown user (zero knowledge case) or for the individual, for which one must ascertain complete knowledge of his individual characteristics (full knowledge case). We believe, however, it is helpful to have an overall view of the terrain in this area of research and some idea of what summits remain to be scaled. These results assure us that there is yet much to be done in the area of information retrieval research and that those who labor at the task are not attempting an impossibility (43–47). Finally, it is our hope that such results as these may stimulate research in an attempt to reach the limits we have described, though we believe this will be, in its entirety, no easy task.

REFERENCES

1. T. Saracevic, "Relevance: A Review of and a Framework of the Thinking on the Notion in Information Science," *JASIS,* **26**, 321–343 (1975).
2. L. Schamber, "Relevance and Information Behavior," in *Annual Review of Information Science and Technology,* vol. 29, M. E. Williams, ed. Learned Information, Inc., Medford, NJ, 1994, pp. 3–48.
3. S. P. Harter, "Variations in Relevance Assessments and the Measurement of Retrieval Effectiveness." *JASIS,* **47**(1), 37–49 (1996).
4. M. E. Lesk and G. Salton, "Relevance Assessments and Retrieval System Evaluation," *Inform. Stor. Retriev.,* **4**, 343–359 (1968).
5. R. Burgin, "Variations in Relevance Judgments and the Evaluation of Retrieval Performance," *Inform. Proc. Mgt.,* **28**(5), 619–627 (1992).
6. B. C. Brooks, "Information Technology and the Science of Information," in *Information Retrieval Research,* R. N. Oddy, S. E. Robertson, C. J. van Rijsbergen, and R. W. Williams, eds. Butterworths, London, 1981, pp. 1–8.
7. D. Ellis, "Theory and Explanation in Information Retrieval Research," *J. Inform. Sci.,* **8**, 25–38 (1984).
8. D. R. Swanson, "Historical Note: Information Retrieval and the Future of an Illusion," *JASIS,* **39**(2), 92–98 (1988).
9. M. E. Maron, "Mechanized Documentation: The Logic Behind a Probabilistic Interpretation," in *Statistical Association Methods for Mechanized Documentation: Symposium Proceedings.* Washington, DC: National Bureau of Standards Miscellaneous Publications, pp. 9–13 (1964).
10. S. E. Robertson, "The Probability Ranking Principle in IR," *J. Doc.,* **33**(4), 294–304 (1977).
11. W. J. Wilbur, "Retrieval Testing by the Comparison of Statistically Independent Retrieval Methods," *JASIS,* **43**(5), 358–370 (1992).
12. W. S. Cooper, "On Selecting a Measure of Retrieval Effectiveness, Part II. Implementation of the Philosophy." *JASIS,* **24**, 413–424 (1973).
13. W. S. Cooper, "Utility-Theoretic versus Relevance-Theoretic Measures of Effectiveness," in *Proceedings of the 1976 ASIS Annual Meeting,* Washington, DC: ASIS. p. 44 (1976).
14. M. E. Maron, "On Indexing Retrieval and the Meaning of About," in *Proceedings of the 1976 ASIS Annual Meeting.* Washington, DC: ASIS. p. 46 (1976).
15. T. Saracevic, P. Kantor, A. Y. Chamis, and D. Travison, "A Study of Information Seeking and Retrieving. I. Background and Methodology," *JASIS,* **39**(3), 161–176 (1988).
16. J. J. Regazzi, "Performance Measures for Information Retrieval Systems—An Experimental Approach," *JASIS,* **39**(4), 235–251 (1988).
17. W. J. Wilbur, "Human Subjectivity and Performance Limits in Document Retrieval," *Inform. Proc. Mgt.,* **32**(5), 515–527 (1996).
18. M. Eisenberg and C. Barry, "Order Effects: A Study of the Possible Influence of Presentation Order on User Judgments of Document Relevance," *JASIS,* **39**(5), 293–300 (1988).
19. L. Schamber, M. B. Eisenberg, and M. S. Nilan, "A Re-examination of Relevance: Toward a Dynamic, Situational Definition," *Inform. Proc. Mgt.,* **26**(6), 755–776 (1990).
20. T. J. Froehlich, "Relevance Reconsidered-Towards an Agenda for the 21st Century: Introduction to Special Topic Issue on Relevance Research," *JASIS,* **45**(3), 124–134 (1994).
21. C. J. van Rijsbergen, "Retrieval Effectiveness," in *Information Retrieval Experiment,* K. Sparck Jones, ed. Butterworths, London, pp. 32–43 (1981).
22. J. Q. Smith, *Decision Analysis: A Bayesian Approach,* Chapman and Hall, London, 1988.
23. A. M. Rees and D. G. Schultz, "A Field Experimental Approach to the Study of Relevance Assessments in Relation to Document Searching. I: Final Report," Case Western Reserve University, Cleveland, NSF contract no. C-423, 1967.
24. A. M. Rees, "The Relevance of Relevance to the Testing and Evaluation of Document Retrieval Systems," *ASLIB Proceed.,* **18**(11), 316–324 (1966).

25. S. Smithson, "Information Retrieval Evaluation in Practice: A Case Study Approach," *Inform. Proc. Mgt.,* **30**(2), 205–221 (1994).
26. W. S. Cooper, "On Selecting a Measure of Retrieval Effectiveness," *JASIS,* **24**, 87–100 (1973).
27. K. Sparck Jones, "The Cranfield Tests," in *Information Retrieval Experiment,* K. Sparck Jones, ed. Butterworths, London, pp. 256–284 (1981).
28. L. Evans, "An Experiment: Search Strategy Variations in SDI Profiles," in *Information Retrieval Experiment,* K. Sparck Jones, ed. Butterworths, London, pp. 285–315 (1981).
29. W. Feller, *An Introduction to Probability Theory and Its Applications,* vol. 2, John Wiley, New York, 1971.
30. T. Saracevic, "Individual Differences in Organizing, Searching, and Retrieving Information," in *Proceedings of the 54th Annual ASIS Meeting.* Washington, DC: Learned Information, Inc. pp. 82–86 (1991).
31. G. Salton and C. Buckley, "Improving Retrieval Performance by Relevance Feedback," *JASIS,* **41**(4), 288–297 (1990).
32. A. Bookstein, "Information Retrieval: A Sequential Learning Process," *JASIS,* **34**(5), 331–342 (1983).
33. H. Wu and G. Salton, "The Estimation of Term Relevance Weights Using Relevance Feedback," *J. Doc.,* **37**(4), 194–214 (1981).
34. C. T. Yu, W. S. Luk, and T. Y. Cheung, "A Statistical Model for Relevance Feedback in Information Retrieval," *J. ACM,* **23**(2), 273–286 (1976).
35. E. Ide, "New Experiments in Relevance Feedback," in *The Smart Retrieval System—Experiments in Automatic Document Processing,* G. Salton, ed. Prentice-Hall, Englewood Cliffs, NJ, pp. 337–354 (1971).
36. W. J. Wilbur and L. Coffee, "The Effectiveness of Document Neighboring in Search Enhancement," *Inform. Proc. Mgt.,* **30**(2), 253–266 (1994).
37. D. Lucarella, "A Document Retrieval System Based on Nearest Neighbor Searching," *J. Inform. Sci.,* **14**, 25–33 (1988).
38. G. Salton, *Automatic Text Processing,* Addison-Wesley Series in Computer Science. 1989, Reading, MA, Addison-Wesley Publication Company, 1989.
39. D. C. Blair and M. E. Maron, "An Evaluation of Retrieval Effectiveness for a Full-Text Document-Retrieval System," *Commun. ACM,* **28**(3), 289–299 (1985).
40. W. J. Wilbur, "A Comparison of Group and Individual Performance Among Subject Experts and Untrained Workers at the Document Retrieval Task," *JASIS*, **49**(6), 517–529 (1998).
41. W. J. Wilbur, "The Knowledge in Multiple Human Relevance Judgments," *ACM Transac. Inform. Syst.* **16**(2), 101–126 (1998).
42. G. Salton, "The State of Retrieval System Evaluation," *Inform. Proc. Mgt.,* **28**(4), 441–449 (1992).
43. D. D. Lewis and K. S. Jones, "Natural Language Processing for Information Retrieval," *Commun. ACM,* **39**(1), 92–101 (1996).
44. P. Norvig, "Review of Text-Based Intelligent Systems," Paul Jacobs, ed. *AI,* **65**, 181–188 (1994).
45. W. B. Croft, "Knowledge-Based and Statistical Approaches to Text Retrieval," *IEEE Exp.,* **8**(2), 8–11 (1993).
46. G. Salton, "Developments in Automatic Text Retrieval," *Science,* **253**, 974–980 (1991).
47. T. M. T. Sembok and C. J. van Rijsbergen, "Silol: A Simple Logical-Linguistic Document Retrieval System," *Inform. Proc. Mgt.,* **26**(1), 111–134 (1990).

W. JOHN WILBUR

INTEGRATING BUSINESS AND INFORMATION SYSTEMS PLANNING

Introduction

Over the past ten years, strategic information systems (IS) planning has consistently remained among the top ten issues facing senior executives (*1*). A key aspect of strategic IS planning is the integration between business planning (BP) and information systems planning (ISP), which will here be referred to as "BP-ISP integration." Webster's dictionary defines the word integrate as meaning "to bring together or incorporate parts into a whole." In the context of business and IS planning, this means that business and IS plans (that are the outputs of the planning processes) should be in harmony and consistent with each other.

Other terms that are often used synonymously with integration are *alignment coordination.* Similar to aligning things to make them neat and tidy, BP-ISP integration can be defined as the alignment of IS strategies with business goals and business strategies gained through coordination between the BP and ISP functions and activities. Although this issue has received significant attention in recent years, empirical research focusing specifically on BP-ISP integration is still relatively sparse.

Lederer and Mendelow (*2*) emphasized that coordination between ISP and BP can be achieved through three mechanisms of linkages—content, timing, and personnel. In terms of content, there should be consistency between business plans and IS plans. In other words, the relevant portions of IS plans should be included in business plans and vice versa.

Timing and personnel linkages are less often emphasized in ISP methodologies compared to content linkages. Timing refers to whether IS plans are developed before, after, or during the same time as the business plans. Coordination between business and IS plans are made easier when both plans are developed simultaneously. Furthermore, for consistency, the planning horizons for business and IS plans should be similar.

Personnel linkage is concerned with whether participants involved in business planning are also involved in IS planning and vice versa. This is important in ensuring that a common frame or reference exists between business and IS planners.

In contrast to Lederer and Mendelow's three mechanisms of linkages, Reich and Benbasat (*3*) defined linkage in term of intellectual and social dimensions. The intellectual dimension is a refinement of content linkage since it emphasizes that the content of information technology (IT) and business plans should be internally consistent (i.e., the IT mission, objectives, and plans chosen are consistent with the stated business mission and objectives) and externally valid (i.e., the plans are comprehensive and balanced with respect to external business and IT environments). Similarly, the social dimension is much broader than personnel linkage, as it

---

Note: Portions of this paper are adapted from W. R. King and T. S. H. Teo, "Integration Between Business Planning and Information Systems Planning: Validating a Stage Hypothesis." *Decision Sciences,* published by the Decision Sciences Institute, College of Business Admin. at Georgia State University, Atlanta.

emphasizes that both business and IS executives should understand each other's objectives and plans.

Researchers have also examined the strategic alignment of IT with the enterprise, rather than alignment of planning processes alone. For example, Brown and Magill (*4*) proposed a model of antecedents for IS alignment decisions. Henderson (*5*) and Henderson and Venkatraman (*6, 7*) proposed a comprehensive framework of IS strategic alignment using two fundamental dimensions: *strategic fit*, which refers to the requirement of integrating strategy formulation and implementation, and *strategic integration*, which refers to the requirement of integrating IT with the business strategy and other line and functional areas of the business. These two dimensions are defined by four domains: business strategy, IT strategy, organizational infrastructure and processes, and IT infrastructure and processes.

Why Is BP-ISP Integration Important?

The need for BP-ISP integration has been emphasized in both prescriptive (e.g., *8, 9*) and empirical studies (e.g., *10, 11*). Basically, these studies show that BP-ISP integration is important because it helps to

1. Ensure that the IS function supports organizational goals and activities at every level (*2, 12, 13*)
2. Ensure that ISP activities are coordinated with BP activities so that the IS function can better support business strategies and contribute to the achievement of business value (*14*)
3. Integrate technical issues with business issues (*15*), thereby resulting in synergy and consistency of BP and ISP efforts
4. Identify critical applications for development (*12, 16*)
5. Ensure that adquate resources are allocated to critical applications (*2, 17*)
6. Enable better management of changes in priorities of application development (*2*)
7. Facilitate information sharing and feedback during strategy formulation and implementation (*18*)
8. Ensure that the IS function becomes an integral part of the organization and not merely appended to it (*8*)
9. Enable better exploitation of opportunities to use IT for strategic purposes (*19, 20*)
10. Create a common frame of reference that is essential for internal consistency and external validity of output plans (*21*)

The Literature

Although there has been a great deal of research on ISP, relatively fewer research efforts have focused on BP-ISP integration itself. Research on BP-ISP integration is primarily at the conceptual level although there is an increasing trend in empirical work that seeks to assess the nature and impact of BP-ISP integration.

THE NATURE OF BP-ISP INTEGRATION

King (8) was among the earliest IS researchers to recognize and emphasize the importance of BP-ISP integration. He proposed an ISP methodology that can be used to integrate IS strategies with business strategies. This methodology emphasized that the IS strategy set (comprising system objectives, system constraints, and system design strategies) should be directly derived from the organizational strategy set (comprising business mission, objectives, strategy, and other strategic organizational variables). King's strategy set transformation was later adopted by IBM as part of its business systems planning methodology (22), thereby affirming the practical significance of the concept of BP-ISP integration. Note that King's conceptualization of BP-ISP integration is predominantly one way, with business plans influencing IS plans.

King and Zmud (23) expanded this conceptualization of one-way sequential integration to two-way reciprocal integration, whereby IS plans and business plans can influence each other. In doing so, King and Zmud elevated the importance of ISP in that IS plans can be proactive rather than reactive to business plans. This concept of two-way reciprocal integration was later refined by King (24), and has formed the basis for most subsequent work in this area.

Synnott (25) attempted to conceptualized the nature of BP-ISP integration into the following five types:

1. No planning: No formal BP or ISP
2. Stand-alone planning: Presence of either business plan or IS plan, but not both.
3. Reactive planning: IS function reacts to business plans and has no input in the BP process.
4. Linked planning: BP is "interfaced" with ISP. Systems resources are matched against business needs.
5. Integrated planning: BP is indistinguishable from ISP. They occur simultaneously and interactively.

An examination of Synnott's typology revealed some similarities with other conceptualization by other researchers. For example, reactive planning is similar to conceptualizations by King (8), and linked planning is similar to that by King and Zmud (23). Interestingly, for the first and second types of BP-ISP integration in Synnott's typology, BP-ISP integration is virtually absent.

The fifth type of BP-ISP integration in Synnott's typology bears some similarity to that proposed by Goldsmith (19) who emphasized that rather than separating BP and ISP activities, ISP activities should be integrated within BP activities. He further argued that in order for competitive advantage to be secured from IT applications, information and business strategies should be developed together in the same process and at the same time. This conceptualization is termed as full integration since there is no distinct separation between BP and ISP processes (similar to integrated planning by Synnott, Ref. 25).

King and Teo (26) and Teo and King (14, 27) conducted a thorough review of BP-ISP taxonomies and proposed a four-stage typology of BP-ISP integration as shown in Fig. 1. The description of each stage of integration is as follows:

(a) Type I: Administrative Integration

(b) Type II: Sequential Integration

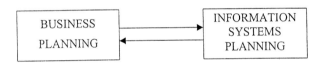

(c) Type III: Reciprocal Integration

(d) Type IV: Full Integration

FIGURE 1. *Typology of BP-ISP integration. (a) Stage I: administative integration; (b) Stage II: sequential integration; (c) Stage III: reciprocal integration; (d) Stage IV: full integration.*

Stage I: Administrative integration.   In this type of integration there is a weak relationship between BP and ISP as shown by the dotted line in Fig. 1a. Generally, there is *little* significant effort to use IT (e.g., computers, telecommunications) to support business plans.

Stage II: Sequential integration.   In this type of integration, a sequential relationship exists between BP and ISP. BP *provides directions* for ISP. This relationship is denoted above by a unidirectional arrow flowing from BP to ISP in Fig. 1b. ISP primarily focuses on providing support for business plans.

Stage III: Reciprocal integration.   In this type of integration, there is a reciprocal and *interdependent* relationship between BP and ISP. There are therefore two arrows, as shown in Fig. 1c; one arrow flowing from BP to ISP, and the other arrow flowing from ISP to BP. ISP plays *both* a role in supporting and influencing business plans.

Stage IV: Full integration.   In this type of integration, there is *little* distinction between the BP process and the ISP process. Business and information systems strategies are developed *concurrently* in the *same* integrated planning process as shown by the single box in Fig. 1d.

King and Teo (*26*) omitted the "no integration" stage proposed by other models because: (1) pretesting with IS practitioners showed that it is difficult to distinguish no integration from a "weak form of administrative integration"; and (2) with the increasing importance of IT, it is very likely that some degree of integration exists rather than no integration at all.

Furthermore, although some authors (e.g., King, Ref. *28*; Stegwee and Van Waes, Ref. *29*) have proposed a three-stage model, pretesting with IS practitioners showed that there is some distinction between reciprocal integration and full integration. In addition, Goldsmith (*19*) offered evidence that integrated planning is actually being practiced, hence the four-stage model is deemed to be sufficiently parsimonious without omitting any significant type of integration.

In summary, the above literature review shows that the extent of BP-ISP integration varies among different firms, hence in some firms ISP is primarily nonstrategic with negligible or weak integration between BP and ISP. Strategic IS applications are therefore practically unknown in these firms. The IS applications in these firms are mainly used to automate operations with minimal attention to leveraging it for competitive advantage. In other firms, BP and ISP are more tightly integrated. Here ISP is used to support (or even influence) business strategies and identify opportunities for the use of strategic IS applications.

THE STAGE MODEL FOR ISP

The stage model for ISP (*26*) suggests that not only are there different kinds of BP-ISP integration in various firms, but that firms may evolve from one level of integration to another (generally from lesser levels of integration to greater levels) as planning matures, becomes more established, and becomes more important to the organization.

This evolutionary view suggests that each successive integration level raises the strategic potential of IT and enables more effective alignment between IS and business strategies. The roles of the IS function for stages 1 and 2 are primarily reactive in nature since ISP has negligible influence on business strategies. Conversely, the roles of the IS function for stages 3 and 4 are primarily proactive in nature since the IS function plays a role in both supporting and influencing business strategies.

A portrayal of the four stages of integration described in terms of benchmark variables is shown in Table 1. Benchmark variables indicate the theoretical characteristics at each stage of integration. For example, firms at stage 1 can theoretically be expected to conform to the values of benchmark variables listed under stage 1, however, this does not mean that it is not possible for firms at stage 1 to have values of benchmark variables applicable to other stages. Rather, it means that the values of benchmark variables indicate the most likely theoretical characteristics applicable at each stage of integration.

The values of each benchmark variable in each of the four stages in Table 1 are discussed below (26).

BMK1: PURPOSE OF INTEGRATION

As shown in Table 1, for benchmark variable 1 (BMK1), the purpose of integration varies at different stages of BP-ISP integration. At stage 1, BP-ISP integration focuses primarily on the support of administrative work processes. This gradually changes as the IS function begins to support business strategy (stage 2) or influence business strategy (stage 3). At stage 4, there is joint strategy development for both business and IS strategies.

BMK2: ROLE OF THE IS FUNCTION

Table 1 shows how the role of the IS function (BMK2) may be viewed differently at the various stages of BP-ISP integration. The general transition from being technically oriented to business oriented is well documented in the literature (e.g., 30–32). At stage 1, the IS function is viewed as being primarily technically oriented. Gradually this role changes when the IS function is used as a resource to support the implementation (stage 2) and formulation (stage 3) of business strategies. At stage 4, the IS function is viewed as critical to the long-term success of the organization.

BMK3: PRIMARY ROLE OF THE IS EXECUTIVE

Clark (33) found that there seems to be a general decrease in the size of the central IS function due to end user computing (EUC) activities. This has resulted in a shift in the responsibilities of the IS function from systems design to systems integration, and from the role of a developer to that of an advisor. In addition, Boynton and Zmud (34) suggested that due to increasing decentralization, the IS function will assume a staff role analogous to a federal government in coordinating the dispersed IS resources.

The skill requirements of the senior IS executive have also changed over the years with increasing emphasis on both knowledge about changing technology and knowledge about the business. In addition, significant political and communication skills are required (30, 33). As shown in Table 1, the role of the IS executive (BMK3) gradually changes from being a functional administrator responsible for providing backroom support (stage 1), to being an IS expert who formulates IS strategy to implement business objectives (stage 2). As the firm begins to leverage IT for strategic purposes and to create business value, the rank and role of the IS executive is further elevated (35), and he or she begins to play a major role in facilitating and influencing the development and implementation of IS applications to achieve business objectives (stage 3). Finally, in stage 4 the IS executive becomes a formal and integral member of

TABLE 1

Typology of Evolutionary Stages of BP-ISP Integration

Benchmark variables	Stage1: administative integration	Stage2: sequential integration	Stage 3: reciprocal integration	Stage 4: full integration
BMK1: Purpose of integration	Administative and nonstrategic	Support business strategy	Support and influence business strategy	Joint development of business and IS strategies
BMK2: Role of IS function	Technically oriented and nonstrategic	Resource to support business strategy	Resource to support and influence business strategy	Critical to long-term survival of organization
BMK3: Primary role of IS executive	Functional administator responsible for backroom support	IS expert who formulates IS strategy to implement business strategy	IS expert who provides valuable inputs during strategy formulation and implementation	Formal and integral member of top management who is involved in many business matters
BMK4: Performance criteria for the IS function	Operational efficiency and cost minimization	Contribution to business strategy implementation	Quality of IS inputs into business strategy formulation and implementation	Long-term impact on organization
BMK5: Triggers for developing IS applications	Need to automate administrative work processes	Business goals considered first	Business goals and IS capabilities considered jointly	IS applications are critical to success of business strategy
BMK6: Top management participation in ISP	Seldom	Infrequent	Frequent	Almost always
BMK7: User participation in ISP	Seldom	Infrequent	Frequent	Almost always
BMK 8: IS executive participation in business planning	Seldom	Infrequent	Frequent	Almost always
BMK9: Assessment of new technologies	Seldom	Infrequent	Frequent	Almost always
BMK10: Status of IS executive (no. of levels below the CEO)	Four or more	Three	Two	One

Source: Reprinted with permission from King and Teo (1997).

the top management team, and provides significant inputs in both IS and non-IS related matters.

BMK4: PERFORMANCE CRITERIA FOR THE IS FUNCTION

As the IS function matures, the performance criteria for the IS function (BMK4) change from a structured focus on operational efficiency to a more unstructured concern for the impact of IS on strategic direction (*36, 37*). It follows that the early performance criteria (stage 1) delineated for the IS function are primarily concerned with operational efficiency and cost minimization (*28*). When the IS function begins to play a more strategic role, the emphasis gradually shifts to effective strategy implementation (stage 2) and then to the quality of IS inputs into business strategy formulation and implementation (stage 3). Ultimately, the performance criteria for the IS function should be its long-term impact (both financial and nonfinancial) on the organization (stage 4).

BMK5: TRIGGERS FOR DEVELOPMENT OF IS APPLICATIONS

Initially, the triggers for the development of new IS applications (BMK5 in Table 1) are opportunities for achieving greater efficiencies through process automation. As IS applications begin to be increasingly used to support business strategies, business goals become trigger mechanisms in deciding appropriate IS applications to be developed (stage 2). At stage 3, the joint consideration of business goals and IS capabilities becomes important as the firm attempts to develop systems for sustainable competitive advantage. Finally, in stage 4, IS applications are developed because they are critical to the success of the firm's strategy and the creation of business value.

BMK6: TOP MANAGEMENT PARTICIPATION IN INFORMATION SYSTEMS PLANNING

Traditionally, as in stage 1, top management had not paid attention to the IS function because it was an overhead function that generated only cost. At stage 2, greater top management participation in ISP (BMK6 in Table 1) begins when IS strategies come to be used to support business strategies. The realization that ISP can also influence business strategy motivates top management to participate more actively in ISP (stage 3). Finally, in stage 4, when the IS function becomes critical for the survival of the organization, top management and the senior IS executive jointly formulate business and IS plans.

BMK7: USER PARTICIPATION IN INFORMATION SYSTEMS PLANNING

User participation in ISP is the seventh benchmark variable (BMK7) in Table 1. Before the advent of end-user computing, user management is generally not significantly involved in ISP (stage 1), however, as end-user computing begins to proliferate and the IS function begins to influence functional units in terms of its effects on business strategies, the participation of users becomes more important in order to fully exploit the potential of IT. User participation gradually increases through the stages, until at stage 4 users participate extensively in ISP.

BMK8: SENIOR IS EXECUTIVE PARTICIPATION IN BUSINESS PLANNING

The "mirror image" of top business management participation in ISP is having senior IS executives participate in business planning (BMK8 in Table 1). The traditional role of the IS function in providing administrative support does not require the senior IS executive to participate in BP (stage 1). The senior IS executive reacts to business plans and does not have significant influence on their formulation. At stage 2, the senior IS executive participation is initiated. As the IS function becomes more important in the achievement of business objectives, it becomes necessary to include more frequent participation of the senior IS executive in BP because the traditional participants are relatively unfamiliar with the potential of IT (stage 3). With greater participation, the senior IS executive becomes more informed about business objectives (38, 39) and is better able to provide higher-quality inputs into the planning process. At stage 4, the senior IS executive becomes an integral member of the top management team and participates extensively in both BP and ISP.

BMK9: ASSESSMENT OF NEW TECHNOLOGIES

During ISP, new technologies that can impact on the film are usually assessed. The level of sophistication involved in assessing new technologies is the basis for the ninth benchmark variable (BMK9) in Table 1. In the early stages of ISP (stages 1 and 2), assessment of the impact of new technologies, if any, is usually done rather informally and infrequently. At stage 3, the need for formal and frequent procedures for assessing new technologies becomes apparent as the IS function begins to play a more important role in BP. At stage 4, an assessment of the impact of new technologies becomes an integral part of BP and ISP.

BMK10: STATUS OF SENIOR IS EXECUTIVE

The responsibilities of the IS function have changed over the years due to technological and conceptual changes that made IT more important to organizations. Benjamin et al. (30) found that the IS line responsibilities are being rapidly distributed as the IS function begins to take on more staff responsibilities. With these changing responsibilities of the IS function, the status of the senior IS executive is likely to be elevated. The position of the senior IS executive (in terms of the number of levels below the CEO) can serve as an indication of the importance of the IS function to the firm's strategy. This construct has been used successfully in previous research on ISP (e.g., 40, 35), and on chief information officers (e.g., 30, 41). Table 1 shows that as a firm moves through the stages, the IS executive moves closer to the CEO.

King and Teo (26) empirically tested the benchmark variables and found that with the exception of three benchmark variables (BMK4, BMK7, BMK9), the remaining seven benchmark variables show a moderate to strong relationship with the stage (extent) of integration.

The weak relationship of "performance criteria for IS function" (BMK4) with the stage of integration may be due to the multidimensional nature of performance. For instance, top management is often vague as to the relative importance of each performance criterion. The "frequency of user participation in ISP" (BMK7) appears to be less important than "top management participation in ISP" (BMK6) and the "IS executive participation in BP" (BMK8) as indicators of participation, probably because "users" are more likely to be involved at the project level rather than at the planning level. The "assessment of new technologies" (BMK9) has little or no relationship to the stage of integration, probably because in this era of rapid technological change the assessment of new technologies has become an integral part of planning regardless of the stage of integration.

The purpose of integration (BMK1), the role of the IS function (BMK2), the primary role of the IS executive (BMK3), and triggers for developing IS applications (BMK5) generally play a significant part in determining the appropriate role of the IS function in BP. The frequency of top management participation in ISP (BMK6), the frequency of IS executive participation in BP (BMK8), and the status of the IS executive (BMK10) are indicators of the importance of the IS function. Top management will usually participate more frequently in ISP when the IS function has a direct impact on the achievement of organizational objectives.

Similarly, the IS executive will participate more frequently in business planning when the IS function can significantly influence the success of business plans. In addition, the IS executive is more likely to be at a level closer to the CEO when the IS function plays a major strategic role in the organization. These results are consistent with previous research (e.g., *42, 10*), which found that different roles of the IS function often result in diffferent planning practices and the development of different types of IT applications.

King and Teo (*26*) also found that sequential integration (41.4%) and reciprocal integration (41.4%) occur most often, followed by administrative integration (10.8%) and full integration (6.4%). This is expected, as many firms are likely to have moved beyond administrative integration due to the increasing importance of IT, however, few firms indicated that they have reached full integration. The distribution of the stages of integration is generally intuitively appealing in that most firms are midway between administrative and full integration. Since very few firms have reached full integration, it implies that ISP has yet to become an integral part of BP.

Paths of Evolution

King and Teo (*26*) found that the paths of evolution are generally from administrative integration to sequential integration to reciprocal integration to full integration. Only 1.9 percent of the sample indicated that they had moved through all the stages to reach full integration, however. This is not surprising, since the number of firms at full integration is very small (6.4%).

Twenty-three percent of the sample did not indicate any evolution occuring. One possible reason is that some firms may bypass earlier stages and start at a later stage.

For example, given the increasing importance of IT, it is conceivable that new start-ups may begin at sequential, reciprocal, or full integration.

The occurrence of reverse evolution—that is, evolution in the direction from a stage of greater integration to a stage of lesser integration—is possible and may be due to a change in the reporting relationships due to organizational restructuring and a change in planning policy by top management. Another reason is that a firm may experiment with a more "advanced" level of BP-ISP integration, find that level to be inappropriate, and revert back to its former level. Since only 1.9 percent of the sample displayed reverse evolution, it is apparently quite unusual and probably should be considered to be an anomaly to the basic evolutionary pattern in the model.

Evolution without bypassed stages is exhibited by about 70 percent of the total sample. This provides support for the notion that bypassed stages (e.g., from administration integration to reciprocal integration, bypassing sequential integration) occur less frequently than movement without bypassed stages. Those situations in which stages are bypassed indicate, as might reasonably be expected that some firms will deviate from the model to some degree while nonetheless displaying the general evolutionary pattern described by it. Overall, these results provide support to the notion of evolution through stages as described in Table 1.

Time Spent in Each Stage of Integration

Generally, the time spent in each stage decreases as the firm moves from administrative to sequential to reciprocal integration. Teo and King (27) found evidence that the time spent in administrative integration (mean = 13.1 years) is approximately twice that spent in sequential integration (mean = 6.7 years) and thrice that spent in reciprocal integration (mean = 4.6 years). Apparently there is an acceleration in the rate of movement toward greater integration.

It seems probable that once a firm has recognized the potential role of IT, movement to greater levels of integration takes place more rapidly in order to more effectively leverage IT in the support of business strategy formulation and implementation. Another reason for this acceleration is that the movement to greater levels of integration is made easier and facilitated by learning and experience at previous lower levels of integration. In addition, rapid advances in IT have made the use of IT become more necessary in order for the organization to survive. This implies that the use of IT to support or reengineer business processes may be rapidly changing from being an option to a necessity. Consequently, the time spent at each stage decreases as the use of IT becomes more widespread, and greater levels of BP-ISP integration become necessary to the BP process.

Reasons for Movement to the Next Stage of Integration

Teo and King (27) found that the reasons for movement to the next stage of integration can be grouped into six categories: (1) the increasing need for better integration; (2) the increasing importance of IT; (3) organizational change; (4) an increase in competence; (5) the increasing need for better information; and (6) miscellaneous. The first three reasons encompass the majority of the responses. They may therefore be considered to be the primary reasons for movement to the next stage of integration.

Note that the reasons for movement seem to focus more on internal factors than external factors. This is in agreement with previous research on the progressive or strategic use of IT (*43, 44*). The reasons in the first category (i.e., increasing need for better integration) emphasize the need to use IS to support business strategy and align IS objectives to business objectives. In the second category (i.e., increasing importance of IT), leveraging IT to support business operations has become more of a necessity than an option. In the third category (i.e., organizational change), restructuring and change in senior or IS management are the most frequently cited reasons for movement to the next stage of integration.

The fourth and fifth categories, namely an increase in competence and the increasing need for better information, are less commonly cited as reasons for movement to reciprocal or full integration. It seems that prior to movement to reciprocal or full integration, basic IS competence and reliable information must be present since it is difficult for firms to have a greater level of integration between BP and ISP if the IS function is not adequately competent to contribute to strategic initiatives.

Usefulness of Stage Model

Business planners and IS executives can use the proposed stage model by King and Teo (*26*) and Teo and King (*14, 27*) as a communication tool to better understand as well as to promote consensus regarding the appropriate role of the IS function in the organization. IS executives can use the stage model to convince top management of the importance of BP-ISP integration in facilitating greater IS contributions to business strategy formulation and implementation. This would ultimately lead to more effective deployment of IT to serve business needs.

In other words, the concept of the evolution of ISP in terms of stages of growth should enable practitioners to better understand, manage, and plan for the evolution of BP-ISP integration in their firms. Better management of BP-ISP integration should ultimately lead to more successful planning systems in terms of reduced planning problems and increased organizational impact.

Since evolution is a dynamic process, however, it must be recognized that companies may deviate in terms of some of these characteristics, hence the stages of growth perspective should not be regarded as a development imperative but rather as a "central tendency" (*45*). In other words, the values of benchmark variables are not definitive guides as to the characteristics that firms are likely to possess at each stage of integration; rather, managers can use the benchmark variables as a rough guide to ISP practices in their firms. For example, if the manager believes that his or her film is currently practicing reciprocal integration, an examination of the values of the benchmark variables as a whole would either provide support or rebut this belief.

In addition, the benchmark variables may provide practitioners with a set of considerations that may deserve special attention. Specifically, these considerations may lead to more appropriate strategies and better allocation of resources in order to maximize the benefits derived from greater BP-ISP integration.

Assessment of Integration

Zviran (*11*) conducted an empirical study of 131 firms to investigate the relationships between organizational objectives and IS objectives. He found that IS objectives are associated with organizational objectives and there is a correspondence between each organizational objective and specific IS objectives. The results provide support for normative approaches to IS planning (e.g., *8*) that advocates linking IS objectives to organizational objectives.

Pyburn (*46*) proposed three ways to assess the alignment between business and IT strategy. First, assess the extent to which the organization has the capability of reaching its business goals with existing IT resources and capabilities. Lack of such means would indicate a misalignment that inhibits goal achievement. Second, the time horizon and pace of change for business and IT strategies must be consistent. For example, if the business strategy is to double sales the next year, IT resources must be provided to cope with this growth. Third, assess the objectives and values of business and IT strategies. Lack of consensus between top management and IT management regarding the appropriate role of IT in the firm is an indication of poor alignment.

Coakley et al. (*47*) proposed that strategic consensus between top management and IT management can be assessed in terms of the following domains of consensus: strategic priorities, IT contributions to strategic priorities, and ongoing impacts of IT projects and operations. Low levels of strategic consensus indicate low levels of shared understanding about the means and ends of business and IT strategies.

In a study of ten business units in three large Canadian life insurance companies, Reich and Benbasat (*3*) made use of company documents as well as conducted interviews with managers to investigate the nature of the linkage between business and IS plans. They found evidence that the social dimension of linkage can be conceptualized into two timeframes: short-term (i.e., understanding of current plans) and long-term (i.e., shared vision for the future of IT within the business unit).

Keyes-Pearce (*48*) extended Reich and Benbasat's work by examining the linkage between business plans and IS strategies across hospital networks. Based on interviews with senior management and IS directors from five business units (hospitals), she found evidence of poor linkage between business units' strategies or goals and IS strategies or plans.

Factors Influencing BP-ISP Integration

Pyburn (*16*) conducted extensive interviews with IS and senior managers from eight organizations and found that the style of senior management decision making, the volatility of the business (and the applications development portfolio), the complexity of the IS organization and management task, and the status and physical location of the IS manager influenced planning practices and consequently the degree of alignment between IS plan and corporate strategy.

Nath (*49*) carried out a field study to identify factors that IS management and general management perceived as important in aligning IS with business goals. The results showed that the top three factors identified by IS management were: education of upper management in IS, upper management commitment to IS, and a strong set of organizational goals and objectives concerning IS. Conversely, the top three factors identified by general management were: education of upper management in IS, ability of IS management to keep up with advances in IT, and education of IS management in business goals and objectives. It appears that although there is agreement with regard to the importance of educating upper management in IS, there is a lack of agreement on other issues. It is important to understand these perceptual differences so that both IS and general management can take appropriate actions to achieve alignment between the IS function and the business goals and objectives of the firm.

Lederer and Mendelow (2) conducted interviews with twenty top IS executives and found that there are four main reasons why it is difficult to achieve coordination between business and IS plans. The reasons are: unclear or unstable business mission, objectives, and priorities; lack of communication; absence of IS management from the BP process; and unrealistic expectations and lack of sophistication of user managers. The results also suggested that the presence of a top management mandate for coordinating the plans distinguishes IS executives who did not report the difficulty from IS executives who did.

Das, Zahra, and Warkentin (50) proposed that in examining the integration between BP and ISP, it is important to view ISP in terms of content and process dimensions. Content dimensions may be defined in terms of distinctive competence, IS technology, systems design, and development and infrastructure. Process dimensions describe the characteristics of the approaches a firm follows in developing and implementing a strategic IS plan, and can be defined in terms of the formality, scope, participation, influence, and coordination in the ISP process. Das, Zahra, and Warkentin (50) further emphasized that elements of each dimension should be mutually supportive and consistency should exist across both dimensions (content and process). In addition, both content and process dimensions should be integrated with business strategy. Differences in the dimensions (content and process) are likely to occur with different business strategy, hence, businesses need to ensure the compatibility of the elements within and between each dimension (content and process) in order to facilitate the overall integration of ISP with business strategy.

Broadbent and Weil (51) examined business and information strategy alignment in the Australian banking industry by using multiple sources of data, including written and interview-based information, strategic planning documentation, and annual reports. They found that the firmwide strategy formation processes of the banks, rather than their ISP methodology, were central to the alignment of business and information strategies. Specifically, a key factor in alignment is a flexible and issue-oriented strategy formation process, with concurrent processes taking place at different organizational levels. The extent and nature of the interaction between business and IS management is critical to the development of IS strategy that is aligned with business strategy.

Teo and King (27) examined the factors influencing BP-ISP integration in 157 firms and found that a single variable, namely, the "business competence of the IS executive" accounted for about 9 percent of the variation in the dependent variable (level of BP-ISP integration). The rest of the research variables tested were not significant. In other words, the results failed to confirm that the information intensity of the products/services, the information intensity of the value chain, top management's perceptions of IT importance, and the technical competence of the IS executive are significantly positively related to the level of BP-ISP integration. In addition, none of the hypotheses pertaining to environmental characteristics: dynamism (rate and unpredictability of environmental change), heterogenity (complexity that encompasses variations among the firm's markets that require diversity in production and marketing orientation), and hostility (availability of resources and the degree of competition) was supported.

These results show that the business competence of the IS executive may be more important than technical competence. Most business firms seem to intuitively understand this in the choice of a chief information officer (CIO), since most individuals selected for this position have strong business competence. These results suggest that business management seeking to improve its BP-ISP integration might focus even greater attention on ensuring that IS management is knowledgeable about the business, however. Furthermore, the results suggest that IS executives should be well versed about the business if they desire to play a more active role in BP. Note that technical competence without adequate business competence is apparently insufficient to facilitate greater BP-ISP integration.

These results provide strong empirical evidence that it is no longer sufficient for IS professionals to remain in their ivory tower and concern themselves only with the technical aspects of their jobs; rather, they should make an effort to learn about the business and think in terms of how to better use IT to improve or reengineer business processes for greater efficiency and effectiveness.

Assessing the Impact of BP-ISP Integration

Although many researchers have emphasized the importance of BP-ISP integration, very few attempt to link BP-ISP integration to performance measures. Instead, researchers commonly focus on conceptual and organizational issues. For example, Powell (52) examined the extent to which the relationship between IT and business strategy changes over time.

In terms of the empirical evaluation of the impact of BP-ISP integration, Das, Zahra, and Warkentin (50) cited an A. T. Kearney study that showed that organizations that integrated business plans and IS plans outperformed those that did not. Chan and Huff (53) found that IS strategic alignment (defined as the fit between business strategy and IS strategy) was consistently related to various dimensions of IS effectiveness. Mixed results with respect to IS strategic alignment and various dimensions of IS performance were obtained, however. Similarly, Chan et al. (54) found that business strategic orientation, IS strategic alignment, and IS effectiveness have positive impacts on business performance.

Teo and King (14) surveyed 157 companies to examine the impact of BP-ISP integration on ISP problems and IS contributions to organizational performance. The results empirically validated the importance of BP-ISP integration, since it was found to have a significant positive relationship with IS contributions to organizational performance and a significant negative relationship to the extent of ISP problems. These results suggest that the notion of IS contributions to organizational performance might only be applicable when there is high degree of integration between BP and ISP. Without such integration, it is not appropriate to expect IS to contribute significantly to organizational performance.

Concluding Remarks

In interviews with IS professionals, Lederer and Mendelow (*17*) found that coordinating (or integrating) IS plans and priorities with business plans and priorities is one of the main difficulties of ISP. This article on integration between BP and ISP should help to mitigate this difficulty by enabling a better understanding of the nature of integration as well as factors influencing such integration. Evidence of the benefits and impacts of BP-ISP integration has also been discussed.

Future research can examine the prevalence of various forms of linkages. For example, is content linkage more important than time or personnel linkages? Researchers can also examine the critical success factors in BP-ISP integration that would enable practitioners to concentrate on a small set of factors important in enhancing or facilitating greater levels of BP-ISP integration.

Since the stage model of BP-ISP integration is still in its infancy, the benchmark variables for the various stages of BP-ISP integration can be further refined. Future research can examine the factors that influence the movement from one stage to the next as well as the factors that may influence the omission of any stage. In addition, other contingency variables that may influence the extent (stage) of integration can be examined. Furthermore, attempts can be made to link the extent (stage) of integration with various performance measures to further examine the notion of whether or not higher levels of integration actually lead to greater IS contributions to organizational performance.

REFERENCES

1.   J. C. Brancheau, B. D. Janz, and J. C. Wetherbe, "Key Issues in Information Systems Management: 1994–95 SIM Dephi Results." *MIS Q.,* **20**(2), 225–242 (1996).
2.   A. L. Lederer and A. L. Mendelow, "Coordination of Information Systems Plans with Business Plans." *J. Mgt. Inform. Syst.,* **6**(2), 5–19 (1989).
3.   B. H. Reich and I. Benbasat, "Measuring the Linkage Between Business and Information Technology Objectives." *MIS Q.,* **20**(1), 55–81 (1996).
4.   C. V. Brown and S. L. Magill, "Alignment of the IS Functions with the Enterprise: Toward a Model of Antecedents." *MIS Q.,* **18**(4), 371–403 (1994).
5.   J. C. Henderson, "Aligning Business and Information Technology Domains: Strategic Planning in Hospitals." *Hosp. Health Serv. Admin.,* **37**(1), 71–87 (1992).
6.   J. C. Henderson and N. Venkatraman, "Understanding Strategic Alignment." *Bus. Q.,* 72–78 (winter 1991).
7.   J. C. Henderson and N. Venkatraman, "Strategic Alignment: Leveraging Information Technology for Transforming Organizations." *IBM Syst. J.,* **32**(1), 4–16 (1993).
8.   W. R. King, "Strategic Planning for Management Information Systems." *MIS Q.,* **2**(1), 27–37 (1978).
9.   C. J. Sass and T. A. Keefe, "MIS for Strategic Planning and a Competitive Edge." *J. Syst. Mgt.,* **41**(6), 14–17 (1988).
10. G. Premkumar and W. R. King, "An Empirical Assessment of Information Systems Planning and the Role of Information Systems in Organizations." *J. Mgt. Inform. Syst.,* **9**(2), 99–125 (1992).
11. M. Zviran, "Relationship Between Organizational and Information Systems Objectives: Some Empirical Evidence." *J. MIS,* **7**(1), 65–84 (1990).

12. A. L. Lederer and V. Sethi, "Critical Dimensions of Strategic Information Systems Planning." *Decis. Sci.,* **22**, 104–119 (1991).

13. A. L. Lederer and V. Sethi, "Guidelines for Strategic Information Planning." *J. Bus. Strat.,* 38–43 (Nov./Dec. 1991).

14. T. S. H. Teo and W. R. King, "Assessing the Impact of Integrating Business Planning and IS Planning." *Inform. Mgt.,* **30**, 309–321 (1996).

15. T. A. Byrd, V. Sambamurthy, and R. W. Zmud, "An Examination of IT Planning in a Large, Diversified Public Organization." *Decis. Sci.,* **26**(1), 49–73 (1995).

16. P. J. Pyburn, "Linking the MIS Plan with Corporate Strategy: An Exploratory Study." *MIS Q.,* **7**(2), 1–14 (1983).

17. A. L. Lederer and A. L. Mendelow, "Information Systems Planning: Incentives for Effective Action." *Data Base,* 13–20 (fall 1989).

18. K. J. Calhoun and A. L. Lederer, "From Strategic Business Planning to Strategic Information Systems Planning: The Missing Link." *J. Inform. Tech. Mgt.,* **1**(1), 1–6 (1990).

19. N. Goldsmith, "Linking IT Planning to Business Strategy." *Long Range Plan.,* **24**(6), 67–77 (1991).

20. J. M. Ward, "Integrating Information Systems into Business Strategies." *Long Range Plan.,* **20**(3), 19–29 (1987).

21. J. C. Henderson and J. G. Sifonis, "The Value of Strategic IS Planning: Understanding Consistency, Validity, and IS Markets." *MIS Q.,* **12**(2), 187–199 (1988).

22. IBM, *Business Systems Planning: Information Systems Planning Guide*, GE20-0527-4, Atlanta, GA 1984.

23. W. R. King and R. W. Zmud, "Managing Information Systems: Policy Planning, Strategic Planning and Operational Planning," in *Proceedings of the Second International Conference on Information Systems,* Boston, 1981.

24. W. R. King, "Exploiting Information as a Strategic Resource." *Internat. J. Policy Inform.,* **8**(1), 1–8 (1984).

25. W. R. Synnott, *The Information Weapon: Winning Customers and Markets with Technology,* John Wiley, New York, 1987.

26. W. R. King and T. S. H. Teo, "Integration Between Business and Information Systems Planning: Validating a Stage Hypothesis," *Des. Sci.,* **28**(2), 279–308 (1997).

27. T. S. H. Teo and W. R. King, "Integration Between Business Planning and Information Systems Planning: An Evolutionary-Contingency Perspective." *J. MIS* (1998).

28. W. R. King, "Strategic Planning for Information Resources: The Evolution of Concepts and Practice." *Inform. Res. Mgt. J.,* **1**(1), 1–8 (1988).

29. R.A. Stegwee and R. Van Waes, "The Development of Information Systems Planning Towards a Mature Management Tool," *Info. Res. Manag.* **3**(3), 8–21 (1990).

30. R. I. Benjamin, C. Dickinson, Jr., and J. F. Rockart, "Changing Roles of the Corporate Information Systems Officer." *MIS Q.,* **9**(3), 177–188 (1985).

31. R. J. Mockler, "The Intelligent Enterprise and the Changing Role of Computer Information Systems in Strategic Planning." *Inform. Res. Mgt. J.,* **4**(1), 21–28 (1991).

32. J. H. Passino and D. G. Severence, "The Changing Role of the Chief Information Officer." *Plan. Rev.,* 38–42 (Sept./Oct. 1988).

33. T. D. Clark, Jr., "Corporate Systems Management: An Overview and Research Perspective." *Commun. ACM,* **35**(2), 61–75 (1992).

34. A. C. Boynton and R. W. Zmud, "Information Technology Planning in the 1990s: Directions for Practice and Research." *MIS Q.,* **11**(1), 59–71 (1987).

35. B. Raghunathan and T. S. Raghunathan, "Relationship of the Rank of Information Systems Executive to the Organizational Role and Planning Dimensions of Information Systems." *J. Mgt. Inform. Syst.,* **6**(1), 111–126 (1989).

36. C. S. Saunders and J. W. Jones, "Measuring Performance of the Information Systems Function." *J. Mgt. Inform. Syst.,* **8**(4), 63–82 (1992).

37. C. S. Saunders and J. W. Jones, "Organizational Factors Affecting the Evaluation of Information Systems Performance." *Inform. Res. Mgt. J.,* **5**(4), 5–21 (1992).

38. A. L. Lederer and A. L. Mendelow, "Information Resource Planning: Overcoming Difficulties in Identifying Top Management's Objectives." *MIS Q.,* **11**(3), 389–399 (1987).

39. A. L. Lederer and V. Sethi, "The Implementation of Strategic Information Systems Planning Methodologies." *MIS Q.,* **12**(3), 445–461 (1988).
40. S. Y. Jang, "Influence of Organizational Factors on Information Systems Planning," unpublished Ph.D. dissertation, Katz Graduate School of Business, University of Pittsburgh, 1989.
41. E. K. Brumm, "Chief Information Officers in Service and Industrial Organizations." *Inform. Mgt. Rev.,* **5**(3), 31–45 (1990).
42. J. I. Cash, Jr., F. W. McFarlan, and J. L. McKenney, *Corporate Information Systems Management: The Issues Facing Senior Executives,* 2nd ed., Irwin, Homewood, IL, 1988.
43. E. A. Busch, S. L. Jarvenpaa, N. Tractinsky, and W. H. Glick, "External Versus Internal Perspectives in Determining a Firm's Progressive Use of Information Technology," in *Proceedings of the 12th International Conference on Information Systems,* New York, 1991, pp. 239–250.
44. W. R. King and T. S. H. Teo, "Facilitators and Inhibitors for the Strategic Use of Information Technology." *Inform. Mgt.,* **27**, 71–87 (1994).
45. D. Miller and P. H. Friesen, "A Longitudinal Study of the Corporate Life Cycle." *Mgt. Sci.,* **30**(10), 1161–1183 (1984).
46. P. J. Pyburn, "Redefining the Role of Information Technology." *Bus. Q.,* 89–94 (winter 1991).
47. J. R. Coakley, M. K. Fiegener, B. A. Leader, and D. M. White, "An Approach to Assess the Degree of Integration between an Organization's IS and Business Strategies," in *Proceedings of the First Americas Conference on Information Systems,* Pittsburgh, PA, Aug. 25–27, 1995, pp. 220–222.
48. S. Keyes-Pearce, "Linkage Between Business Plans and Information System Strategies Across Hospital Organizational Networks," in *Proceedings of the Third Pacific Asia Conference on Information Systems (PACIS),* Brisbane, Queensland, Australia, April 2–5, 1997, pp. 635–640.
49. R. Nath, "Aligning MIS with Business Goals." *Inform. Mgt.,* **16**, 71–79 (1989).
50. S. R. Das, S. A. Zahra, and M. E. Warkentin, "Integrating the Content and Process of Strategic MIS Planning with Competitive Strategy." *Decis. Sci.,* **22**, 953–984 (1991).
51. M. Broadbent and P. Weill, "Improving Business and Information Strategy Alignment: Learning from the Banking Industry." *IBM Syst. J.,* **32**(1), 162–179 (1993).
52. P. Powell, "Causality in the Alignment of Information Technology and Business Strategy." *J. Strat. Inform. Syst.,* **2**(4), 320–334 (1993).
53. Y. E. Chan and S. L. Huff, "Investigating Information Systems Strategic Alignment." in *Proceedings of the 14th International Conference on Information Systems,* Orlando, FL, 1993, pp. 345–363.
54. Y. E. Chan, S. L. Huff, D. W. Barclay, and D. G. Copeland, "Business Strategic Orientation, Information Systems Strategic Orientation, and Strategic Alignment." *Inform. Syst. Res.,* **8**(2), 125–150 (1997).

BIBLIOGRAPHY

Alter, A. E. "Business Alignment's Dirty Little Secret." *Computerworld,* **30**(20), 37 (May 13, 1996).
Baets, W. "Aligning Information Systems with Business Strategy." *J. Strat. Inform. Syst.,* **1**(4), 205–213 (1992).
Calhoun, K. J. and Lederer, A. L. "From Strategic Plan to Strategic Practice: The Communications Connection." *Mid-Amer. J. Bus.,* **5**(2), 60–64 (1990).
Chester, A. N. "Aligning Technology with Business Strategy." *Res. Tech. Mgt.,* 25–32 (Jan.–Feb. 1994).
Dutta, S. and Doz, Y. "Linking Information Technology to Business Strategy at Banco Comercial Portugues." *J. Strat. Inform. Syst.,* **4**(1), 89–110 (1995).
Henderson, J. C. "Plugging into Strategic Partnerships: The Critical IS Connection." *Sloan Mgt. Rev.,* 7–18 (spring 1990).
King, W. R. "Information Technology and Corporate Growth." *Columbia J. World Bus.,* 29–33 (summer 1985).
Lederer, A. L. and Calhoun, K. J. "Why Some Systems Don't Support Strategy." *Inform. Strat.,* 25–28 (summer 1989).
Lederer, A. L. and Salmela, H. "Toward a Theory of Strategic Information Systems Planning." *J. Strat. Inform. Syst.,* **5**, 237–253 (1996).
Lederer, A. L. and Sethi, V. "Key Prescriptions for Strategic Information Systems Planning." *J. MIS,* **13**(1), 35–62 (1996).

Luftman, J. N., Lewis, P. R., and Oldach, S. H. "Transforming the Enterprise: The Alignment of Business and Information Technology Strategies." *IBM Syst. J.,* **32**(1), 198–221 (1993).

Revell, D. "Aligning Information Resources with Business Strategy—Part I." *CMA Mag.,* **71**(2), 6 (1997).

Revell, D. "Aligning Information Resources with Business Strategy—Part II." *CMA Mag.,* **71**(3), 4 (1997).

Rodgers, L. "Alignment Revisited." *CIO,* **10**(15), 44–47 (1997).

Vitale, M. R., Ives, B., and Beath, C. M. "Linking Information Technology and Corporate Strategy: An Organizational View," in *Proceedings of the 7th International Conference on Information Systems,* San Diego, CA, 1986, pp. 265–276.

Woolfe, R. "The Path to Strategic Alignment." *Inform. Strat.,* 13–23 (winter 1993).

Yetton, P. W., Johnston, K. D., and Craig, J. F. "Computer-Aided Architects: A Case Study of IT and Strategic Change." *Sloan Mgt. Rev.,* **35**(4), 57–67 (1994).

Zawrothy, S. B. "Key to IS Success: Alignment with Corporate Goals." *Inform. Res. Mgt. J.,* **2**(4), 32–38 (1989).

THOMPSON SIAN HIN TEO

KNOWLEDGE-BASED CLASSIFICATION TECHNIQUES FOR SOFTWARE QUALITY MANAGEMENT

Introduction

> *As far as I can tell Engineering Judgement just means*
> *they are going to make up numbers.*
> —Richard Feynman

In order to achieve an early indication of software quality, software is subjected to measurement. It would be of great benefit to predict early in the development process those components of a software system that are likely to have a high error rate or that need high development effort. Though the search for underlying structures and rules in a set of observations is performed in many scientific fields and effective solutions to refine forecasting methods based on past data have been suggested, their applicability to software development has been restricted (*1, 2*). Few references give insight that attention has been paid to a systematic analysis of empirical data (e.g., *3–6*).

This article compares different classification techniques as a basis for constructing quality models that can identify outlying software components that might cause potential quality problems. For example, when distinguishing modules that are more error-prone than others, a metric vector consisting of few metrics such as module size, cohesiveness, and data fan-in can be determined during the design phase. Now the goal is to determine those modules that belong to the rather small group of modules that potentially cause most of the errors, costs, and rework. Obviously, the best

---

Note: An earlier version of this article appeared as: "Classification Techniques for Metric-Based Software Development. "*Software Quality Journal,* vol. 5, pp. 255–272 (1996).

solution would be to filter out exactly the specific high-risk components in order to improve their design or start again from scratch.

Unfortunately, the metric vector usually provides rather continuous data, hence preventing clear frontiers between good and bad. Experts' knowledge in such cases covers this problem with linguistic uncertainty and fuzziness ("If length is medium and cohesion is low the module is likely to cause trouble"). We will discuss techniques that allow the differentiation even between such linguistic attributes and come to an exact and reproducible decision.

Such classification models are based on the experience that typically a rather small number of components has a high failure rate and is most difficult to test and maintain. Our own project experiences, for instance, just recently showed that 20 percent of all modules in large telecommunication projects were the origin of over 40 percent of all field failures with high priority (Fig. 1). Even worse is the fact that we could also show that it is not so difficult to identify these modules in advance—either by asking designers and testers and grouping their subjective ratings or by applying classification rules based on simple structural software metrics (7). The article investigates whether or not fuzzy classification applied to criticality prediction provides better results than other classification techniques that have been introduced in this area.

In this context the article addresses typical questions often asked in software engineering projects.

- How can I early identify the relatively small number of critical components that make significant contribution to faults identified later in the life cycle?
- Which modules should be redesigned because their maintainability is bad and their overall criticality to the project's success is high?
- Are there structural properties that can be measured early in the code to predict quality attributes?
- If so, what is the benefit of introducing a metrics program that investigates structural properties of software?
- Can I use the—often heuristic—design and test know-how on trouble identification and risk assessment to build up a knowledge base to identify critical components early in the development process?

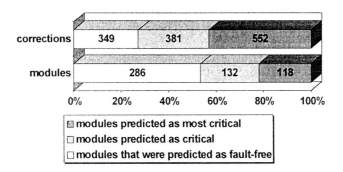

FIGURE 1. *Benefits of using early criticality prediction in a telecommunication project.*

Beyond addressing such questions the article compares different approaches for identifying critical components and provides insight into the most common techniques for complexity-based classification of software modules. Quantitative data both from the literature (in order to provide easy access to some quality data and thus to do one's own experiments and validate results) and from telecommunication software development supports the underlying hypothesis that fault-prone modules can be identified best with fuzzy classification techniques based on their structure and contents.

The effects of applying complexity-based criticality prediction to a new project can be summarized based on results from telecommunication projects (Fig. 1).

- Twenty percent of all modules in the project were predicted as most critical (after coding).
- These modules contained over 40 percent of all faults (up to release time).

We know from these and many other projects that (8, 9)

- Sixty percent of all faults can theoretically be detected until the end of module test
- Fault correction during module test and code reading costs less than 10 percent compared to fault correction during system test.

It can thus be calculated that 24 percent of all faults can be detected early by investigating 20 percent of all modules more intensively with 10 percent of effort compared to fault correction during the system test, therefore yielding a 20 percent total cost reduction for fault correction. Additional costs for providing the statistical analysis are in the range of two person days per project. Necessary tools are off the shelf and account for even less per project.

The article is organized as follows. The introductory section presents a brief overview of background and problems associated with metric-based decision modules. The next section introduces common classification methodologies and their applicability to software quality models, covering Pareto classification, crisp classification trees, factor-based discriminant analysis, neural network approaches, and fuzzy classification. Due to space constraints we will concentrate on brief qualitative introductions with references on archive materials. Only fuzzy classification is given more space, because it has not been adequately covered before. The next section describes the construction of a classification system for software quality management. The next section provides the experimental setup to investigate classification for error and change prediction.

Two projects from the area of real-time systems are introduced for comparing classification results. Project A is based on already published metric data that permit easy access for further (third-party) studies. Project B is a collection of 451 modules from a large telecommunication switching system. The next section provides the results of these experiments, and the subsequent section discusses these results in the context of applicability to other projects from a pragmatic viewpoint. The final section gives an outlook on future research.

Metric-Based Quality Models

Although striving to reach high-quality standards, only a few organizations apply true quality management. Quality management consists of proactively comparing observed quality with expected quality, hence minimizing the effort expended on correcting the sources of defect. In order to achieve software quality, it must be developed in an organized form by using defined methods and techniques and applying them consistently. In order to achieve an indication of software quality, software must be subjected to measurement. This is accomplished through the use of metrics and statistical evaluation techniques that relate specific quantified product requirements to some attributes of quality.

The approach of integrating software metrics and statistical techniques is shown in Fig. 2. The CASE environment provides defined methods and process, and holds descriptions of different products developed during the software lifecycle. Multivariate statistical techniques provide feedback about relationships between components (e.g., factor analysis, *10*; principal component analysis, *4*). Classification techniques help in determining outliers (e.g., error-prone components, *2, 11*). Finally, detailed diagrams and tables provide insight into the reasons why distinct components are potential outliers and how to improve them (*12*).

Quality or productivity factors to be predicted during the development of a software system are affected by many product and process attributes (e.g., software design characteristics or the underlying development process and its environment).

In order to achieve a distinct quality goal that is often only measurable at delivery time, quality criteria are derived that allow *in-process quality checks.* If measured, such quality criteria are indirect quality metrics because they do not directly measure the related quality factor (Fig. 3), however, being available early in the development process they can be used to set up immediate targets for project tracking. Quality criteria are measurable during the development process. (An example is given in Fig. 3.) The quality factor reliability that is contracted based on the failure rate of ten failures per month can only be measured after the product is deployed to the field.

The associated quality criteria, for instance test coverage, can be measured early and they can be kept within a distinct range if experience suggests the need to do so. These quality criteria are part of the development quality plan and can rather easily be checked at appropriate milestones. A comprehensive picture of how quality goals relate to each other and to quality criteria is given in ISO 9126.

Quality prediction models try to give an early indication on achieving quality goals in terms of quality factors. They are based upon former project experiences and combine quantitative quality criteria with a framework of rules (e.g., limits for metrics and appropriate ranges). Figure 4 shows the typical approach of metric-based classification in a project environment. They are generated by combination and statistical analysis of product metrics (e.g., complexity metrics) and product or process attributes (e.g., quality characteristics and effort; *3, 5, 6, 8*).

These models are evaluated by applying and comparing exactly those invariant figures they are intended to predict—the quality factors (e.g., error rate). Iterative repetition of this process can refine the quality models, hence allowing the use of them as predictors for similar environments and projects. Typical problems connected

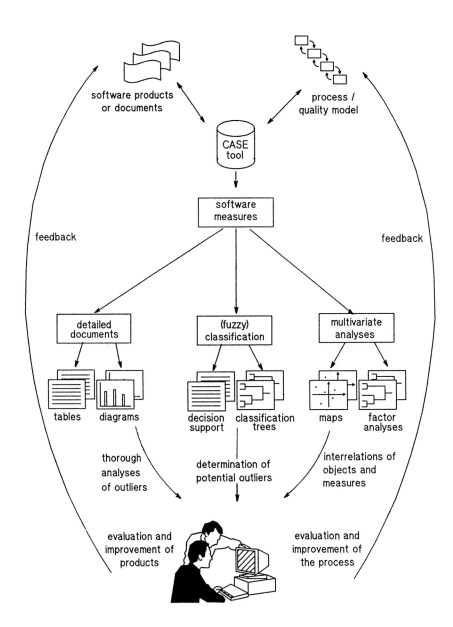

FIGURE 2. *Measures and statistical techniques in software engineering.*

to data collection, analysis, and quality modeling are addressed and discussed comprehensively in Refs. *1, 8,* and *9.*

One of the few examples for a metric-based decision environment with expert rules has been suggested by Behrendt et al. (*13*). This tool is based on a factorial quality taxonomy that classifies the above-mentioned quality factors (e.g., reusability) and

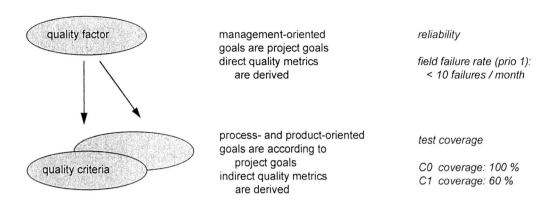

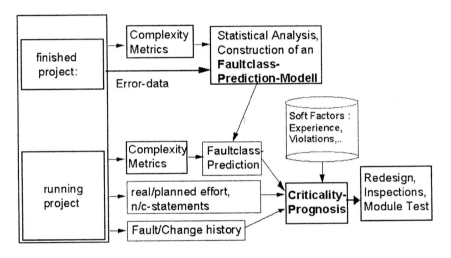

management-oriented goals are project goals direct quality metrics are derived	*reliability* *field failure rate (prio 1):* *< 10 failures / month*	

process- and product-oriented goals are according to project goals indirect quality metrics are derived

test coverage

C0 coverage: 100 %
C1 coverage: 60 %

FIGURE 3. *Quality factors, quality criteria, and metrics.*

FIGURE 4. *Criticality classification during software development.*

related subfactors (e.g., modularity) into linguistic categories (e.g., "not acceptable"). The proposed classification system takes measurable and nonmesurable attributes as an input, such as design of control structures or number of system parameters. Another tool system for assessing risk factors of software components has been developed by Porter and Selby (2, 11). The proposed method generates metric-based models of high-risk components automatically, based on metrics from previous releases or projects.

These models are built according to a classification tree with binary and multivalue decision nodes. While the first approach permits the use of linguistic descriptions and qualitative reasoning without describing how the classes had been created, the latter is based on history-based crisp decisions that do not indicate any intuition. Both approaches thus try to solve the problem of metric-based decision support; however, it is often not clear how to justify the decisions. The most serious constraint imposed by classification trees and other crisp clustering techniques is their goal to identify *mutually exclusive subsets*, thus not allowing fuzzy memberships to several classes.

Classification Techniques

Classification or clustering algorithms are mathematical tools for detecting similarities between members of a collection of objects. Metric vectors assigned to the same cluster are in some sense similar to each other, more so than they are to other metric vectors not assigned to that cluster. Instead of predicting the number of errors or changes (i.e., algorithmic relationships) we are considering assignments to groups (e.g. "change-prone"). While the first goal has been achieved more or less with regression models or neural networks predominantly for finished projects, the latter goal seems to be adequate for predicting potential outliers in running projects, where precision is too expensive and is unnecessary for decision support.

Of course, the primary concern with the use of a classification algorithm is how well it has actually identified underlying structures that are present in the data (cluster validity). Classification algorithms may be constructed manually or automatically. Manual construction reflects intuitive knowledge about underlying structures and relations or influences of metrics on distinct factors to be predicted; automatic construction is applied to large data sets where unknown structures and a variety of interdependencies are to be considered. Because it is a difficult task to try all combinations of ranges of (input) metrics and determine their individual influence on the classification algorithm to predict quality factors, such automated techniques have been developed that solve this problem (*11, 14, 15*).

PARETO CLASSIFICATION

Pareto analysis is included as a classification technique that is common for quick quality analyses. The goal of a Pareto analysis is to identify that 20 percent of all components that contribute heavily to all troubles. The principle is nicknamed the *80:20 rule* because it assumes that the 20 percent share is responsible for 80 percent of the problems. It is amazing that this simple approach holds in most application domains. Software quality management methods, such as root cause analysis, typically also start by applying a Pareto analysis and identifying the small amount of problems (20%) that provide the biggest return on effort when resolved.

We consider Pareto analysis based on the software size (i.e., the top 20% of all modules ranked according to module size are selected). In our comparison this type of analysis clearly performed well with volume as the only input metric for selecting the top 20 percent. It is thus suggested that this be applied as a quick rule of thumb to decide on further activities. The difference to crisp classification trees that could easily provide similar results is that the classification rule is not connected to static boundaries, but to a static rule of thumb with dynamic boundaries in terms of values.

CRISP CLASSIFICATION TREES

Classification trees have been widely used in many areas; for example, in image recognition, taxonomy, or decision table programming. The trees are based on a set of metrics that are used to classify components according to how likely they are to have certain high-risk properties. They consist of several leaf nodes that contain binary or multivalue decisions to indicate whether or not a component is likely to be in a certain class based on historical data. Because each leaf describes values of a distinct metric such trees might be composed from a set of production rules.

Several methods for automatic tree generation have been described and used for real projects (*11*). Each rule imposes crisp boundaries with the result being exclusively allocated to one set based on the values of the input metrics. They are all based on automatic learning from examples with distinct approaches for optimizing, controlling, and supervising the learning process (e.g., pattern recognition). Features with more values can lead to decision trees that are unintelligible to human experts and require a larger increase in computation.

FACTOR-BASED DISCRIMINANT ANALYSIS

Factor-based discriminant analysis is an instrument to identify structures and suggest possible organizations of the data into meaningful groups (*16, 10*). Any given metric vector can be considered as a multidimensional space in which each software component (e.g., a module) is represented as a point with distinct coordinates. We identify as a cluster any subset of the points that is internally well connected and externally poorly connected (i.e., the components of a cluster are closely related to each other based on some similarities within the related input metrics). The underlying assumption is that objects under investigation may be grouped so that elements residing in a particular group or cluster are in some sense more similar to each other than to elements belonging to other groups.

Typically the classification consists of two steps. First, factor analysis or a principal-components procedure is used for reducing the dimensionality of the metric vector to fewer metrics with orthogonal complexity domains. Discriminant analysis is then used to separate groups of software components according to one selected quality attribute (e.g., changes, error rate).

NEURAL NETWORK CLASSIFICATION

To avoid unnecessary crispness while dealing with approximate knowledge, some recent research has focused on employing *artificial neural networks* for metric-based decision support (*17*). The multilayer perceptron is the most widely applied neural network architecture today. Neural network theory showed that only three layers of neurons are sufficient for learning any (non-) linear function combining input data to output data. The input layer consists of one neuron for each complexity metric, while the output layer has one neuron for each quality metric to be predicted.

Because neural network-based approaches are predominantly result-driven, not dealing with design heuristics and intuitive rules for modeling the development process and its products, and because their trained information is not accessible from the outside, they are even less suitable for providing reasons for any result. To our point of view, any decision support system should contain the maximum amount of expert knowledge that is available. Neural networks can be applied when there are only input vectors (software metric data) and results (quality or productivity data), while no intuitive connections are known between the two sets (e.g., pattern recognition approaches in complicated decision situations), however, neural networks can currently not provide any insight into *why* they arrived at a certain decision besides providing result-driven connection weights. It is interesting to note that feedforward neural nets can be approximated to any degree of accuracy by fuzzy expert systems (*18*), hence offering a new approach for classification based on neural fuzzy hybrids that can be trained and prepopulated with expert rules.

FUZZY CLASSIFICATION

In the above-mentioned classification techniques, expert rules are either completely ignored or not adequately covered because neither predicate logic nor probability-based methods provide a systematic basis for dealing with them (*5, 2, 6*). Only recently, have fuzzy classification techniques been introduced to software quality management (*19, 20*).

As a consequence, fuzzy facts and rules are generally manipulated as if they are nonfuzzy, leading to conclusions whose validity is open to question. As a simple illustration of this point, consider the fact (*2*): "If data bindings are between 6 and 10 and cyclomatic complexity is greater than 18 the software component is likely to have errors of a distinct type." Obviously the meaning of this automatically generated fact is less precise than stated and might be provided by a maintenance expert as a fuzzy fact: "If data bindings are medium and cyclomatic complexity is large then the software component is likely to have errors of a distinct type." Of course, the latter fact requires the determination of the fuzzy attributes "medium" or "large" in the context of the linguistic variables they are associated with (i.e., data bindings and cyclomatic complexity).

Fuzzy Sets and Fuzzy Logic

Fuzzy logic provides a method for representing the meaning of both fuzzy and nonfuzzy predicate modifiers or hedges (e.g., *not, very, much, slightly, extremely*), which permits a system for computing with linguistic variables; that is, variables whose values are words in a natural language (*21*). For example, cyclomatic complexity is a linguistic variable when its values are assumed to be: *high, small, medium, very high, rather small*, and so on, where each value can be interpreted as a possibility distribution over all integers. In order to permit rule-based approximate reasoning based on external input data from software products or documents and vague knowledge about the underlying process that produced the software components to be classified, it is necessary to permit the formulation of fuzzy (expert) rules. Fuzzy classification has been introduced to complexity-based criticality prediction in Ref. *20*.

While in two-valued logic systems a proposition may be qualified by associating it with a truth value (i.e., true or false) or a modal value (e.g., impossible), in fuzzy logic these qualifications are either truth (possibility) qualifications expressed as a real value $\tau \in [0,1]$ or probability qualifications with a qualifier $\lambda \in [0,1]$. A fuzzy set A of a given universe of discourse U which is associated with its base variable y is described by its membership function $\mu_A: U \to [0,1]$ which represents each element y of discourse U as a number μ_A in the interval $[0,1]$ that represents the grade of membership of y in A. In other words, the value of the membership function indicates the possibility or certainty with which y belongs to the fuzzy set A. Because both possibility distributions and probability distributions may be associated with y, it is necessary to distinguish exactly between the two interpretations.

As an example, let A be a linguistic variable with the label "cyclomatic complexity" with $y \in U = [1,100]$. The terms of this linguistic variable, which are fuzzy sets, are labeled "high," "small," and so on. The base variable y of A is the number of decisions in a software component plus one. $\mu_A: U \to [0,1]$ is the representation rule that assigns a meaning—that is, a fuzzy set—to the terms. Though different shapes of membership functions have been described, practical applications usually describe fuzzy numbers with a triangular membership function (i.e., the degree of membership of a distinct value to a fuzzy set is of triangular shape starting with 0, indicating nonmembership, to 1, indicating full membership, and back to 0, hence allowing various degrees of membership for the elements of the given set).

Fuzzy Decision Support

In order to permit rule-based approximate reasoning based on external input data from software products or documents and vague knowledge about the underlying process that produced the software components to be classified, it is necessary to permit the formulation of fuzzy (expert) rules. The combination of interacting fuzzy rules derived from expert knowledge is called a fuzzy expert system, because it is supposed to model an expert and make his or her knowledge available for nonexperts for purposes of diagnosis or decision making. The declarative knowledge of fuzzy expert systems is represented as fuzzy sets and data.

Let $M = \{M_1, \ldots, M_m\}$ be a set of m metric vectors in R^n, representing n measures applied on m software components. Fuzzy clustering of the m software components M_i into c clusters results in functions $\mu_1, \ldots, \mu_c$ where $\mu_i: M \to [0,1]$ and $\sum_i \mu_i (M_j) = 1, \forall M_j \in M$, which corresponds to the full membership of each component in M. As already described, these functions are called membership functions that can have as values any real number between 0 and 1. Zadeh proposed that rather than describe a set by its membership, we should describe it by a membership function and allow the function to have values between 0 and 1 to represent ambiguity that might be present in the set. A cyclomatic complexity of 20 might be assigned a membership of 0.8 in the set labeled "medium" and a membership of 0.2 in the set labeled "high," while a cyclomatic complexity of 30 has a membership degree of 0.3 in the set labeled medium and a membership of 0.7 in the set labeled high. The clusters of a fuzzy classification are hence the membership functions themselves. They indicate structure

Membership Functions:

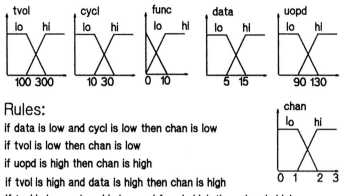

Rules:

If data is low and cycl is low then chan is low

if tvol is low then chan is low

if uopd is high then chan is high

if tvol is high and data is high then chan is high

'f tvol is low and cycl is low and func is high then chan is high

FIGURE 5. *Fuzzy membership functions and inference rules for module design.*

of the input data in a way that two components M_i and M_j with membership functions close to one for the same label can be considered equal to each other. If several components have their individual maximum membership for the same membership function, that component with the highest membership is classified best by the clustering.

Most fuzzy expert systems are using production rules (as opposed to semantic nets or frames) that represent procedural knowledge. Such production rules are used to capture both heuristic rules of thumb and formally known relations among the facts in the domain (Fig. 5). These rules are represented as if-then rules that associate conclusions to given antecedents. An example for a production rule that we use is "if cyclomatic complexity is medium and statement count is medium then the component is error-prone." The advantage of production rules obviously lies in the fact that they are a convenient way to represent one's domain knowledge and that they can be augmented easily by adding further rules. The inference engine that controls the application of fitting rules to given data is based on an extension of set-theoretic operators (e.g., and, or, then). Originally the following three operators were proposed by Zadeh for intersection, union, and complement:

$$\mu_{A \cap B}(y) = \min(\mu_A(y), \mu_B(y)), y \in U;$$
$$\mu_{A \cap B}(y) = \max(\mu_A(y), \mu_B(y)), y \in U;$$
$$\mu_{\neg A}(y) = 1 - \mu_A(y), y \in U.$$

Although other operators have been introduced, we will stick to these definitions since they are most common and simple to deal with.

One of the most important inference rules in traditional logic is the *modus ponens* that has also been generalized to be applicable to fuzzy sets. Let A, A', B, B' be fuzzy sets, then the generalized modus ponens states

Premise: x is A'

Implication: If x is A then y is B

Conclusion: y is B'

Of course, it is possible that different conclusions can be arrived at by using the same implication if the premises vary. Fuzzy inference finally is based on the concepts of fuzzy implication and a compositional rule of inference. Fuzzy implication is represented as $A \rightarrow B$, where A and B are fuzzy sets. The most common implications have already been introduced [e.g., fuzzy union $\mu_{A \cup B}(y)$].

To arrive at a conclusion, the fuzzy implication and the underlying premise have to be interpreted by a compositional rule of inference. If there are many fuzzy production rules their individual results can be superimposed. The conclusion of all rules may be derived by using the centroid of the area under the resulting fuzzy membership curve. This process of ending with a crisp value, called defuzzification, is of course not necessary when the curves can be associated with fuzzy sets of results variables on nominal scales and thus provide qualitative decision support.

Developing a Metric-Based Classification System

The development of a classification system for software quality management consists of the following steps:

1. Describe an exactly defined development process environment from which the software products under investigation are selected.
2. Select a group of expert development staff members who will be asked to develop a consensus concerning distinct quality factors. Of course, this jury should consist of people with respected knowledge in the areas that influence those projects being ranked (e.g., database or real-time experts for projects determined by such problem domains). If the selected quality factors include maintainability or testing effort, staff members assigned to such areas must be considered in the jury.
3. Select a random, however representative, sample of software components of past projects from the environment (e.g., modules, procedures, classes) which is used as training and validating data.
4. Measure these components with respect to a metric vector $M = \{ml, \ldots, mn\}$ based on n selected direct software product metrics that are available during the development process (e.g., cyclomatic complexity or number of input data to a module).
5. Measure or have the jury cluster these software components with respect to quality or productivity factors in a quality vector F by comparing and evaluating them. Typically F considers aspects such as reliability, error count, maintainability, or effort. It can have values such as number of errors or mean time to failure (MTTF) of a given group of software components. Usually F is unknown during project development, and therefore highest interest lies in its early and accurate prediction. To support accurate prediction is actually the task of the classification system. Because F is used for training and validation purposes, an associated metric vector M from the same past projects is

required. The result of this step is a data set {M;F} for each software module or component. If construction and validation of the prediction model is required, the associated data sets M and F need to be divided into two mutually exclusive sets {M';F'} and {M";F"} before the classification process takes place. One is the set used for training or construction of a distinct classification scheme, while the other one will be used to validate the scheme (5).

6. Assign the elements of the set {M;F} to appropriate linguistic variables. Usually one linguistic variable is assigned to each metric and quality element of the vectors.

7. Define values for each linguistic variable. Place membership functions for mapping the scale and (usually numeric) range of metrics or quality factors to membership degrees of these values.

8. For construction of a rule-based system (e.g., prepopulated classification trees, neural-fuzzy hybrids, fuzzy classification) let the experts condense their design knowledge to a set of recursively refined predictive expert rules. The rules are usually dominated by fuzzy linguistic and qualitative descriptions in opposition to quantitative selection formulas that might be preferable on the first sight. Each rule must be explained exactly in order to permit a repeatable classification. When expert knowledge is not available or is too expensive algorithmic fuzzy classification approaches may be used for the training data sets. Integrate this set of rules to a classification scheme that can be applied automatically to analyze other software components. Test the resulting set of production rules in terms of completeness (boundaries of ranges) and inconsistencies (several rules with similar antecedents, or similar consequences with contradictive antecedents, etc.).

9. Validate the classification system by classifying the test data sets {M";F"}.

10. The final step is to improve the model by adjusting its properties to optimization goals (e.g., adjusting weights in neural networks, shifting membership functions in fuzzy classification systems, condensing classification trees). Such goals include reducing chi-square values, which is equal to reducing misclassification errors. (See the next section.) Parameter tuning is measured by separating misclassification errors, either type I errors ("change-prone components" classified as "uncritical components") or type II errors ("uncritical components" classified as "change-prone components"; also called false positives). The goal must be to reduce type I errors at the cost of type II errors because it is less expensive to investigate some components despite the fact that they are not critical compared to labeling critical components as harmless without probing further.

Practical Application: Predicting Changes Based on Complexity Data

It is relatively easy to construct metric-based quality models that happen to classify data of past projects well, because all such models can be calibrated according to quality of fit. The difficulty lies in improving and stabilizing models based on historic data that are of value for use in anticipating future outcomes. While working on software for large real-time systems, we had the task of developing a quality model with predictive accuracy. The main interest of these quality models for metric-based software development was in detecting change-prone modules during the design. Changes include both corrective and additive maintenance; in any case they indicate components requiring more effort than others. The following two subsections introduce three experiments that had been conducted to investigate two hypotheses.

- Fuzzy classification applied to criticality prediction provides better results than other classification techniques that have been used in this area in the past.
- Fuzzy classification as introduced here does not necessarily need training (i.e., it could start

completely untrained based on design heuristics), thus being more portable to other systems and easier to understand than other classification techniques.

While the first part investigates already published data (thus providing access for further studies and validations), by applying the classification techniques already introduced, the second part shows how to use metric-based classification in an ongoing industrial project.

Both hypotheses have been tested with the chi-square test. Based on this test a hypothesis is rejected if the calculated χ^2 is bigger than the respective value of $\chi^2_{1;a}$ from χ^2-tables (22). The population size was in both experiments sufficiently high to employ this test. An additional experiment for the investigation of the different classification techniques was performed based on a random selection of test sets that were then classified. Numbers of type I errors and type II errors are also used for evaluation. The success criteria are in all cases oriented toward low overall misclassification, sufficiently high χ^2-value, and a low number of type I errors. Due to outliers it is intrinsically impossible to optimize one classification method for both types of misclassification errors. Residual analysis was not performed because our goal was to predict change-prone modules and not the number of changes. A sound statistical analysis of change or fault numbers would require a much larger data set with more modules and is usually not requested in practice.

PROJECT A

To investigate the effectiveness of fuzzy classification we applied the classification techniques to data originally published by Kitchenham and Pickard (1). Given two sets of metrics from modules of the ICL general-purpose operating system VME, complexity-based classification was performed to estimate change-proneness of the modules. Both sets of data came from two different implementations of the same subsystem with identical functional requirements. As each program was coded, it was placed under formal configuration control and subsequent changes to modules were recorded. It was not distinguished between corrective and additive changes' intentions. Ten different software complexity metrics are provided, together with change rates for sixty-seven modules altogether. The complexity metrics' set includes machine code instructions, lines of code (executable), modules called (calls to external modules), data items (access to static data items by a program module), parameters, Halstead's unique operator count, Halstead's unique operand count, total operators in a module, total operands in a module, and McCabe's cyclomatic complexity.

Since these data sets had been investigated and used for other studies (4), we will only summarize some explorative outcomes. The given software complexity metrics are highly correlated; most Spearman rank correlation coefficients are above 0.5. For example, the volume of the code in executable lines of code (without comments and without empty lines) is correlated with the cyclomatic complexity (0.90), and with unique operands (0.93) for all modules. Such relations between metrics are typical and were studied extensively (8). Factor analysis was performed for reducing dimensions of the metric space, resulting in three almost orthogonal factors: volume, control, and parameterization. Based on these results we selected five complexity metrics as input values for the prediction models that are most common in complexity metrics application, namely lines of code (tvol), modules called (func), data items (data), unique operands (uopd), and cyclomatic complexity (cycl).

Two VME subsystems had been described within the Kitchenham study, with subsystem 1 containing twenty-seven modules and subsystem 2 containing forty modules. Since all changes to each module had been provided together with several complexity metrics, we first divided both subsystems in two classes for each subsystem containing around 80 percent of modules with few changes and the remaining 20 percent with many changes. Then one subsystem was treated as the data set for training, while the other one was tested for validation purposes after having trained the classification system. For testing the robustness of different classification methods we treated the sets equally despite knowing about the presence of outliers. Compared to other studies (4) we did not eliminate outliers because no common agreement for such filtering exists (8).

Factor-based discriminant analysis could be performed rather easily because it only requires factor analysis for reducing metrics' dimensionality and afterwards discriminant analysis, which needs just one learning cycle. This approach is hence the fastest way for classification. Both classification tree and neural network predictions need several thousand training cycles for optimization that are performed automatically on workstations or PCs. It was interesting to realize that classification tree results were similar to results from crisp cluster analysis with ten classes, although the latter approach takes almost no computational effort. For neural network classification a three-layer perceptron (5, 12, 1 nodes) with backpropagation learning (100,000 training cycles; learning rate: 0.5; momentum between 0 and 0.5) showed the best results. Fuzzy classification was short-cut to only one given rule system without further optimization (as presented in Fig. 5), therefore the rules (weights = 1) and membership functions (trapezoid and symmetrical) provide good comprehension and portability. Optimizing the fuzzy classification resulted in reduction of misclassification errors by one or two (not presented here); however, rules and membership functions looked very strange (i.e., asymmetric membership functions with overly precise boundaries, increasing the number of rules with individual weight factors). We hence discarded those results.

PROJECT B

The second experiment was for portability of the classification methods to bigger projects. Training data were taken from several real-time telecommunication projects that had been developed according to a similar design approach. We will describe classification results for one telecommunication project in the area of switching systems called project B that was used for testing purposes. We investigated a selection of 451 modules that had been placed under configuration control since the start of coding. The overall size of these modules is in the area of 1 million lines of executable code. The specific project had been in field use for over a year, thus showing stability in terms of features and failures. Software changes (comparative to those in project A) are given for each module, together with several complexity metrics based on the *COSMOS* (*ESPRIT*-funded) project (23).

Complexity metrics used in this project include number of (executable) statements, statement complexity, expression complexity, data complexity, depth of nesting (control flow), and database access (number and complexity of database accesses). Statement complexity, expression complexity, and data complexity are simple metrics that count the use of distinct statements (e.g., different data types and their use is considered data complexity) according to given hierarchies of individual complexity assignments. Again, Spearman rank correlations among different complexity metrics were considerably high. For all selected metrics they were above 0.8. Complexity metrics also correlated with the number of changes (average over 0.4).

The second hypothesis being tested is that using fuzzy classification as introduced here does *not necessarily* need training (i.e., it could start completely untrained based on design heuristics), thus being more portable to other systems and easier to understand than the other methods. We tested this hypothesis in a third experiment for project B in order to achieve insight into the portability of classification techniques without further training. Based on an earlier project that had been designed similarly we provided few expert rules for the fuzzy classification. The rules were as follows:

- If statement count is high then changes are high.
- If data complexity is high then changes are high.
- If expression complexity is high then changes are high.
- If database access is high then changes are high.
- If depth of nesting is high then changes are high.
- If data complexity is low then changes are low.
- If statement count is low then changes are low.

Membership functions remained unchanged from the former project, which allows application of these expert rules as design heuristics or vice versa.

Results and Discussion

Table 1 shows a portfolio of predictions versus reality for both subsystems of *project A*. Notions in quotation marks (in the first column) are the predictions. The upper half of the table investigates subsystem I, while the lower half analyzes subsystem II. Instead of common portfolio tables the four values for predictions versus reality are put into single-line entries. For example, subsystem I consists of twenty-seven modules. Twenty-one of these modules (77%) contain five or fewer changes, while six modules (23%) contain more than five changes. This share reflects approximately the 80:20 ratio that is useful for predictions that require rework in terms of redesign or other approaches to improve maintainability. Applying the Pareto classification (second column) results in a selection of six modules that have the biggest volume (i.e., the top 20%). The remaining twenty-one modules are predicted as having "few changes". Now these two groups are compared with reality. Nineteen modules with few changes and four change-prone modules were classified correctly. Two modules were misclassified as having few changes (type I error), and two modules were predicted as change-prone, while belonging to the class of modules with few changes (type II error). Taking these values gives the chi-square result of 8.82.

TABLE 1

Classification Results for Project A with Five Classification Methods

Project A: Two subsystems with 67 modules	Pareto classification by volume (top 20%)	Crisp classification tree	Factor-based discriminant analysis	Neural network classification	Non optimized fuzzy classification
VME subsystem 1 (27 modules) used for testing (subsystem 2 for training)					
reality: ≤ 5 changes: 21 modules (77%)					
Prediction: "few changes"	19	19	20	19	20
Prediction: "change-prone" (type II)	2	2	1	2	1
reality: > 5 changes: 6 modules (23%)					
Prediction: "few changes" (type I)	2	2	5	3	0
Prediction: "change-prone"	4	4	1	3	6
χ^2	8.82	8.82	0.96	5.06	22.0
VME subsystem 2 (40 modules) used for testing (subsystem 1 for training)					
reality: ≤ 4 changes: 31 modules (78%)					
Prediction: "few changes"	28	30	28	30	30
Prediction: "change-prone" (type II)	3	1	3	1	1
reality: > 4 changes: 9 mod. (22%)					
Prediction: "few changes" (type I)	3	4	1	4	3
Prediction: "change-prone"	6	5	8	5	6
χ^2	13.0	15.0	15.5	15.0	19.4
Random selection of test sets (percentage of overall correct classification)	83.0%	78.3%	73.2%	80.7%	92.5%

The last line of Table 1 provides the average percentage of correct classifications for several runs when all data sets (both subsystems) were mixed and then half of them were randomly selected for training or testing, respectively.

Classification seems to be more difficult for subsystem 1, which contains more outlying data sets (i.e., the complexity metrics and the number of changes do not fit together). Fuzzy classification performed best in terms of χ^2, and overall misclassifications were altogether at a minimum. Figure 6 shows a scatterplot of the complete

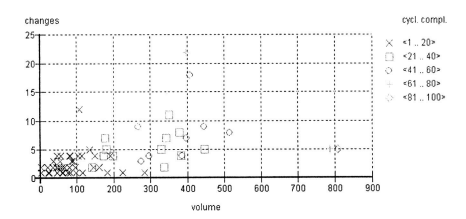

FIGURE 6. *Scatterplot of number of changes with volume and cyclomatic complexity for project A (both subsystems).*

TABLE 2

Classification Results for Project B with Five Classification Methods

Project B: 200 modules used for testing (163 modules with zero or one faults; 37 modules with more than one fault)	Pareto classification by volume (top 20%)	Crisp classification tree	Factor-based discriminant analysis	Neural network classification	Non optimized fuzzy classification
reality: ≤ 1 fault: 163 modules (81.5%)					
Prediction: "few changes"	146	149	137	149	133
Prediction: "change-prone" (type II)	17	14	26	14	30
reality: > 1 faults: 37 modules (18.5%)					
Prediction: "few changes" (type I)	17	16	12	21	8
Prediction: "change-prone"	20	21	25	16	29
χ^2	38.1	48.9	42.3	28.4	52.2

Kitchenham data set (both subsystems) with changes (horizontal axis), lines of code (vertical axis), and cyclomatic complexity (shape). Outliers with small complexity and a high change rate can be clearly identified. It is obviously impossible to strive for zero misclassifications because several data sets are overlapping in the sense that they belong to the—intuitively—wrong group according to the delivered error count.

Applying the five different classification techniques to the switching system data of *project B* showed almost identical results in terms of overall correct classification of the modules (Table 2). The results showed the highest overall correct classification for

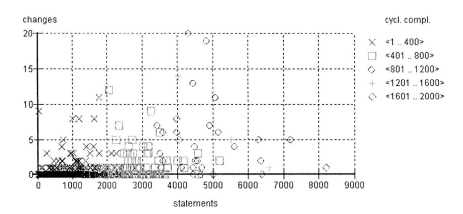

FIGURE 7. *Scatterplot of number of changes with volume and cyclomatic complexity for project B.*

crisp classification trees (85% of all modules). Pareto classification (83% of all modules) and neural network classification (82.5%) performed slightly worse. Factor-based discriminant analysis and nonoptimized fuzzy classification finally achieved 81 percent correct classifications. Obviously there is no clear winner, given this ranking, which is due to a number of outliers that either increase type I or type II misclassifications when optimization of the other area is achieved (Fig. 7).

A better indicator for comparing classification techniques is the number of type I misclassifications. The shaded area of Table 2 provides these results. Fuzzy classification shows lowest misclassification results with only eight modules indicated as having few changes while they actually were change-prone. Chi-square analysis also indicates that fuzzy classification is performing better than the other techniques ($\chi^2 = 52.2$). Automatic optimization of rules (e.g., more than two input values in one rule) and membership functions improved these results; however, due to desired intuitiveness of rules we won't discuss such techniques.

The results of the third experiment on the portability of classification techniques without further training are as follows. Fuzzy classification with data from a follow-on project provided $\chi^2 = 46.1$ for 200 modules. Pareto classification performed slightly worse ($\chi^2 = 35.7$), while the three remaining classification techniques had a χ^2 below 30.

A comparison of different classification approaches suitable for metric-based decision support is presented in Table 3. Results as presented in this table are based on various applications of the four classification techniques to data sets from switching systems. Pareto classification is left out because this mere analytical technique needs neither training nor does it provide any constructive guidelines during design and coding. The upper part of this table presents a summary on learning and knowledge representation. The lower part gives the effects of using manipulated data values (i.e., two metrics are highly correlated; one metric is almost random; several data sets

TABLE 3

Comparison of Different Classification Methods (Without Pareto Classification)

	Crisp classification tree	Factor-based discriminant analysis	Neural network classification	Fuzzy classification
Crisp data values as metric data values	x	x	x	x
Fuzzy, vague, linguistic data values				x
Algorithmic knowledge representation	(x)	x	(x)	(x)
Rule-based knowledge representation	x			x
Information represented by *intuitive* rules				x
Learning is result-driven (as opposed to design heuristics)	x		x	(x)*
Learning can be performed automatically (0,+,++)	++	0	++	+
Reasons for decisions are given (0,+,++)	++	0	0	++
Effects of highly correlated metrics in input training data (0,+,++)	++	++	+	++
Effects of uncorrelated metrics in input training data (0,+,++)	+	+	0	++
Robustness to outlying data sets during training (0,+,++)	++*	+	0	++*
Portability to data sets from other projects with same design methodology (0,+,++)	+	+	0	++
Bibliography for applications and theory	(2, 11, 14, 9)	(4, 16)	(17)	(19, 21, 20, 18)

Note: * dependent on learning approach or classification algorithm; 0 bad results; + medium results; ++ good results.

contain random values). The remaining two parts of Table 3 provide portability results and—again—a short bibliography for improved orientation.

Based on the described experiments, fuzzy classification clearly performed best. Since there are some guiding principles for decision support available, we emphasize utilizing expert-derived, however vague, knowledge that we included in a fuzzy expert system-type classification scheme. For the same reason (i.e., software engineering expert knowledge is available), we strongly oppose using learning strategies that are only result-driven (e.g., classification trees or mere neural network approaches), however, we see the necessity of such approaches when only a few guiding principles are available and sufficient project data can be utilized for supervised learning.

Conclusions

The choice of the proper approach to automatic decision support depends on the problem. To software classification problems, multibranching fuzzy classification provides a more comprehensive solution than crisp decision trees. Such multibranching decision support is based on structures that are not necessarily trees but also networks that resemble expert systems' structures. When these classification schemes are applied to new data sets, the best solution is to provide not only a binary result, but fuzzy attributes that consider those results that lie in between a clear "yes" or "no." We emphasize the necessity of applying fuzzy concepts to the areas of metric-based software project and quality management because subjective and qualitative judgment plays an important role in this area.

The clear benefits of using the described fuzzy classification methodology are

- Compared with other classification methods fuzzy classification shows best results in terms of both chi-square and the reduction of type I misclassification errors.
- Expert rules that are already available (e.g., design heuristics, coding guidelines) can be directly included in the classification scheme.
- Rules can be used independent of the projects because membership functions may be tuned according to project environments without violating the rules.
- Derived classification schemes can be combined with CASE tools and automatic metrics generation for integrated design support.

The impacts of this study for other applications in software development projects are as follows:

- Complexity metrics, together with history data sets of past projects, must be utilized for criticality prediction of modules. They help in identifying those few critical components that later are responsible for most of the faults that show up in integration and in the field.
- Criticality predictions are most effective before the start of system integration.
- For a quick overview, for instance in a project review, Pareto analysis should be applied to identify few highly critical modules.
- The best classification technique among five techniques that are currently applicable for complexity-based criticality prediction is fuzzy classification. This technique can easily be applied because tool environments are available off the shelf.
- The advantage of fuzzy classification in development projects is that available design heuristics can be reused. The technique thus is more intelligible for practitioners than other techniques.
- The outcome of each criticality prediction must be an intensive investigation of the identified modules in order to find out whether or not they indeed contain not yet detected errors.

Summary and Further Research

We have evaluated several classification techniques as an approach for predicting faults based on code complexity metrics. Given complexity metrics and quality data (fault rates) of several different real-time systems, the best results were achieved with fuzzy classification. Pareto analysis (80:20 rule) generally showed good results which clearly underlie its importance as a rule of thumb for easy identification of the top 20 percent of critical modules. Complexity-based classification has been applied to the design and testing of telecommunication systems. Its practical use was showed for detecting fault-prone components and assigning additional fault-detection effort.

As such the technique proves to be effective in early identification of critical components. It must be emphasized that criticality prediction techniques being used do not attempt to detect all faults. Instead they belong to the set of managerial instruments that try to optimize resource allocation by focusing them on areas with many faults that would affect the utility of the delivered product.

The trade-off of applying complexity-based predictive quality models is estimated based on the following:

- Limited resources are assigned to high-risk jobs or components.
- Impact analysis and risk assessment of changes is feasible based on affected or changed complexity.
- Grey-box testing strategies are applied to identified high-risk components.
- Less customer reported failures.

Especially the mentioned levels for reaction and the appropriate measures of how to react most effectively must be subject to continuous evaluation. They will improve over time with more projects being applied. Further research in the area of predictive quality models should focus on the following areas:

- Investigating more projects from different application areas in order to provide fundamental insight into the development of quality models and their influence on different project types. This should include analyses of different approaches for constructing classification schemes (e.g., decision trees) and optimizing their accuracy, intelligibility, and reproducibility.
- Modeling the processes contributing to fault injection, detection, and correction. (Look for examples on staffing, late feature changes, corrections affecting complex components, testing strategies and their coverage, and distribution over the whole system.)
- Coping with noisy data sets for constructing predictive classification systems. Solutions to this problem include robust feature selection and error estimation during the induction of classification schemes.
- Applying practical software project management based on predictive and dynamic classification models. Derived classification schemes must be combined with computer assisted software engineering environments and configuration management tools, thus providing automatic metric generation for integrated design and test management support.

REFERENCES

1. B. A. Kitchenham and L. Pickard, "Towards a Constructive Quality Model." *Software Eng. J.*, **2** (7), 114–126 (July 1987).

2. A. A. Porter and R. W. Selby, "Empirically Guided Software Development Using Metric-Based Classification Trees." *IEEE Software,* **7** (3), 46–54 (March 1990).

3. G. Stark, R. C. Durst, and C. W. Vowell, "Using Metrics in Management Decision Making." *IEEE Computer,* **27** (9), 42–48 (1994).

4. J. C. Munson and T. M. Khoshgoftaar, "Regression Modelling of Software Quality: Empirical Investigation." *Inform. Software Tech.*, **32** (2) 106–114 (1990).

5. N. F. Schneidewind, "Validating Metrics for Ensuring Space Shuttle Flight Software Quality." *IEEE Computer*, **27** (8) 50–57 (1994).

6. R. W. Selby and V. R. Basili, "Analyzing Error-Prone System Structure." *IEEE Trans. Software Egr.,* **17** (2) 141–152 (1991).

7. C. Ebert and T. Liedtke, "An Integrated Approach for Criticality Prediction," Proc. 6. Int. Symp. on Software Reliability Engineering ISSRE'95, IEEE Computer Soc. Press, Los Alamitos, CA, 1995.

8. N. E. Fenton and S. L. Pfleeger, *Software Metrics: A Practical and Rigorous Approach,* Chapman & Hall, London, 1997.

9. R. B. Grady, *Practical Software Metrics for Project Management and Process Improvement,* Prentice-Hall, Englewood Cliffs, NJ, 1992.

10. C. Ebert, "Visualization Techniques for Analyzing and Evaluating Software Measures." *IEEE Trans. Software Egr.,* **18** (11) 1029–1034 (Nov. 1992).

11. R. W. Selby and A. A. Porter, "Learning from Examples: Generation and Evaluation of Decision Trees for Software Resource Analysis." *IEEE Trans. Software Egr.,* **14** (12), 1743–1757 (1988).

12. D. N. Card and R. L. Glass, *Measuring Software Design Quality,* Prentice–Hall, Englewood Cliffs, NJ, 1990.

13. W. Behrendt et al., "A Metrication Framework for Knowledge-Based Systems," in Proc. Eurometrics '92, Comm. of the E.C.: EUREKA, Brussels, April 1992, pp. 197–210.

14. L. Breiman, J. H. Friedman, R. A. Olshen, and C. J. Stone, *Classification and Regression Trees,* Wadsworth, Belmont, CA, 1984.

15. J. J. Shann and H. C. Fu, "A Fuzzy Neural Network for Rule Acquiring on Fuzzy Control Systems." *Fuzzy Sets Syst.,* **71**, 345–357 (1995).

16. W. R. Dillon and M. Goldstein, *Multivariate Analysis-Methods and Applications,* Wiley, New York, 1984.

17. T. Khoshgoftaar and D. L. Lanning, "A Neural Network Approach for Early Detection of Program Modules Having High Risk in the Maintenance Phase." *J. Syst. Software,* **29**, 85–91 (1995).

18. J. J. Buckley and Y. Hayashi, "Neural Nets for Fuzzy Systems." *Fuzzy Sets Syst.,* **71**, 265–276 (1995).

19. W. Pedrycz, and J. Waletzky, "Fuzzy Clustering in Software Reusability." *Software—Practice and Experience.* **27** (3), 245–270 (March 1997).

20. C. Ebert, "Rule-Based Fuzzy Classification for Software Quality Control." *Fuzzy Sets Syst.,* **63**, 349–358 (1994).

21. H.-J. Zimmermann, *Fuzzy Set Theory and Its Applications*, 2nd ed., Kluwer, Boston, 1991.

22. M. G. Kendall and A. Stuart, *The Advanced Theory of Statistics,* vol. II, Griffin, London, 1961.

23. C. Debou, N. Fuchs, and H. Saria, "Selling Believable Technology." *IEEE Software* (Nov. 1993).

BASIC READINGS

Fenton, N. E. and S. L. Pfleeger, *Software Metrics: A Practical and Rigorous Approach,* Chapman & Hall, London, 1997. Good introduction and thorough overview on software metrics theory and application.

Zimmermann, H.-J., *Fuzzy Set Theory and Its Applications,* 2nd ed., Kluwer, Boston, 1991. Introduction and overview on fuzzy set theory. The history, theoretical basis and—most relevant—applications are given.

Ebert, C., "Rule-Based Fuzzy Classification for Software Quality Control." *Fuzzy Sets Syst.,* **63**, 349–358 (1994). The classic introductory article on fuzzy classification in software metrics. Although it provides an earlier stage than the material given above, this article outlines the whole field and contrasts its advantages toward other approaches.

CHRISTOF EBERT
EKKEHARD BAISCH

LIBRARY AND INFORMATION CONSULTANCY IN THE UNITED KINGDOM

Introduction

At long last it can be said that consultancy in the library and information sector (LIS) is regarded in the United Kingdom as an occupation that is legitimate, professional, and almost respectable. Aslib (the former Association of Special Libraries and Information Bureaux, now renamed the Association for Information Management) was an early pioneer, having established a consultancy service in the mid-1960s, and possibly because Aslib membership was predominantly industrial and commercial, the service was soon accepted, growing in size and range into the late 1970s and early 1980s before declining toward its (possibly temporary) demise in 1997. The somewhat more conservative and public service-oriented members of the Library Association were perhaps slower to accept consultants within their ranks; as evidenced by the occasional letter to its journal, the *Library Association Record,* decrying some activity such as total quality management as the latest "management fad" dreamed up by consultants in their search for income. Indeed, Nicholas (*1*), in a short article comparing research and consultancy, gives a somewhat slanted (but tongue in cheek?) view of the objective research worker toiling at his desk and the fast moving consultant skipping from client to client, lining his pockets on the way. Whereas it may be possible to make a reasonable living from LIS consultancy, and perhaps for a few a handsome income, many people overlook the costs which must be borne, including perhaps, although not necessarily, office accommodation, support staff, and consumables. In addition, the consultant may need to purchase indemnity in an increasingly litigious environment, and as a small business must face the overhead of accounting and paying for income tax, Value Added Tax (VAT), and pensions. Furthermore, although the consultant may work long hours and under greater pressure than his employed counterparts, it has been estimated that the time actually spent on fee-earning work is usually of the order of 60 percent of total work time—the remainder being spent on administration, hunting for contracts and writing proposals, and on professional development.

Consultancy is also, of course, highly competitive and increasingly so, and many will be experiencing the new pressures occasioned by the turmoil of what is somewhat prematurely dubbed the "information society". Two particular and related pressures may be noted: one as it were from the bottom up, the other from the top down. In the first it is self-evident that the information industry is now targeting the end user. Suppliers of hardware and software and information providers now have the increased potential to bypass the information professional—a process with the ugly name of *disintermediation.* This process directly affects librarians, information scientists, and publishers, and at least shifts the focus for LIS consultants. For example, the Internet not only connects end users to sources and suppliers but to each other so that, for example, consensus opinions can be formed about new products before reviews appear in printed publications (*2*). The top-down pressure is effected by the far larger firms of management consultants who have discovered "information" as the fourth resource and have entered the fray carrying banners emblazoned with such phrases as *Knowledge Management, the learning organization,* and *intellectual capital.* Such proponents also tend to strengthen disintermediation and will have a direct impact on LIS consultants, particularly those who fail to understand these developments.

The Consultancy Market

Management consultancy is big business, but the LIS consultancy that aspires to be regarded as management consultancy earns only a tiny proportion of the total consultancy income. What is becoming increasingly fuzzy is the definition of, and income generated by, information consultancy as opposed to library consultancy (and pure management consultancy applied to the larger libraries). It is clear that some large management consultancy contracts contain an element of LIS work (which is occasionally subcontracted to LIS consultants when the main contractor recognizes that it does not have the necessary expertise in-house).

As implied above, information management, whether that may be defined as information resource management (largely IT-focused) or as the more abstract management of information *per se,* constitutes a far larger area than that covered by the traditional LIS profession. A recent publication from the *Financial Times* (*3*) identified the following key factors affecting the consultancy market:

- Innovation and information sharing
- Specialization vs. generalization
- Increasing regulation
- Outsourcing
- Globalization

The first is the most indicative of the overlap between management consultancy and LIS consultancy discussed above, although all five have a direct bearing on the changing nature of the consultancy environment.

Just how big a business management consultancy is can be seen from the figures that follow. Table 1 (*4*) shows the fee income for the top twenty consultancy firms in 1996 (in £ sterling), which represents nearly 80 percent of the total earnings of £2.1 billion. These figures have been split for the first time to separate consultancy fee income from nonconsultancy fee income (software development, systems integration, and outsourcing).

The only breakdown of these global figures by activity and by sector that throws some light on LIS activity is that shown for IT consultancy, shown in Table 2 (*4*). Here it can be seen that the top twenty firms in this area earned £343.1 million, or 20 percent of the total income of the top twenty firms in Table 1.

Management consultancy is dominated by the "big six", consisting of Andersen, Coopers & Lybrand, Deloitte Touche, Ernst & Young, KPMG, and Price Waterhouse. In recent moves that have startled the industry, Coopers & Lybrand and Price Waterhouse announced that they are preparing to merge. Rapidly following this news, KPMG and Ernst Young published announcement of their own proposed merger, and

TABLE 1

The 20 Largest Firms, Ranked by Consultancy Fee Income (Excluding Software, Systems Integration, and Outsourcing)

Firm	1996 consultancy fee income (£m)	1996 Fees nonconsultancy fee income (£m)	1995 total fees (£m)	1994 total fees (£m)
Coopers & Lybrand	176.1	35.8	157.6	136.0
Andersen Consulting	129.5e	220.5e	320.0	280.5e
KPMG Management Consultancy	115.0	0.0	109.3	79.1
CAP Gemini (U.K.)	113.5e	160.0e	105.0e	95.0e
Gemini Consultancy	96.0e	Included	88.3	77.7
Deloitte & Touche	95.0e	Included	88.3	77.7
Price Waterhouse	90.0	34.0	79.0	—
McKinsey	86.0e	0.0	76.0e	64.8
Ernst & Young	77.4	Included	55.2	n/a
Sema Group (U.K.) est	72.0e	Not known	51.0	28.0
PA Consulting Group	70.3	7.4	86.4	n/a
ICL Group	67.1	Not known	59.8e	n/a
Logica	67.0e	101.67e	152.8	135.7
Capita Group (est)	63.0e	Not known	56.0	50.8
CSC Computer Sciences	59.8	n/a	47.0	—
Arthur D. Little	54.5	0.0	47.6	32.2
TowersPerrin/Tillinghast	48.2	0.0	40.7	36.1
AT Kearney/EDS	34.0e	Not known	28.0e	9.9
Arthur Andersen	30.0	0.0	19.0	11.0

Note: e = estimate.

Price Waterhouse moved to strengthen its alliance with Dutch IT services giant Origin. These moves will reduce the big six to four. Table 3 (5) shows what the effect might be in terms of revenue. (N.B.: The figures are in U.S. dollars.) Table 3 is also interesting for the tabulation of the numbers of consultants.

Not surprisingly, there are no figures available for the number of LIS consultants in the United Kingdom, let alone their fee income. It is possible, however, to arrive at a rough estimate by talking to colleagues and consulting the few directories that are available. Disregarding information brokers, it would appear that there are about 100 persons earning a living by full-time consultancy in the United Kingdom. The great majority of these will be sole traders with a few partnerships and companies employing fewer, but probably not more, than ten people.

The annual survey of fee rates produced by the Institute of Management Consultants and distributed internally to its members quotes a median figure of £450 per day. If it is assumed (as mentioned in the introduction) that a consultant can expect to spend 60 percent of his time on fee-earning work then we arrive at a total annual

TABLE 2

IT Consultancy in 1996

Firm	1996 Fees (£m)
Andersen Consulting	91.0e
ICL	53.3
CSC Computer Sciences	33.3
Price Waterhouse	30.0
KPMG Management Consulting	29.4
Gemini	25.0e
PA Consulting Group	17.1
Druid	12.3
Cap Gemini	12.0
121 Consulting	7.5
Arthur Andersen	6.0
Coopers & Lybrand	4.4
WS Atkins	4.0
Mason Communications	3.0
Braxxon Technology	3.0
OSI/Duhig Berry	2.8
Methods Application	2.5
French Thornton Partnership	2.2
National Computing Centre	2.2
DMW Group	2.1

Source: Reproduced with the permission of the publishers: VNU Business Publications, VNU House, 32–34 Broadwick Street, London W1A 2HG.

TABLE 3

The World's Largest Consultancies Ranked by Revenues (1996)

Firm	1996 revenue	Growth rate	Number of consultants	Number of partners[1]	Total staff
Andersen Consulting	5,302.0	25.5	37,389	1,036	44,801
Coopers-PW	2,622.0	20.0	17,411	1,034	20,598
Ernst & Young	2,010.4	32.0	10,657	n/a	n/a
McKinsey & Co.	2,000.0	11.1	3,994	587	7,527
KPMG International	1,8365.0[2]	18.9	10,763	888	11,888
Deloitte & Touche Consulting Group/DTTI	1,550.0	29.2	n/a	n/a	10,000
Arthur Andersen	1,379.6	18.0	n/a	n/a	n/a
Mercer Consulting Group	1,159.2	9.7	n/a	n/a	9.241

[1]Or partner equivalent; [2] Gross fee income; n/a = not available. Source: *Management Consultant International*.
Source: Reproduced with the permission of the publishers: Lafferty Publications Ltd., IDA Tower, Pearse Street, Dublin 2, Ireland.

income of about £6 million, or .28% of the total earned by management consultants. If this figure is compared to the occasional remuneration survey conducted internally by the U.K. Institute of Information Scientists it would seem to be rather generous, thus, equating it with the grade for fellows on the assumption that LIS consultants are senior professionals suggests that either the figure of 100 LIS consultants is too low or that their average fee rate is lower than £450 per day.

The Work of LIS Consultants

Consultancy is not just about giving advice; rather, it may comprise a hierarchy of increasingly complex activities as is shown in Fig. 1, taken from an article by Turner (*10*).

What is clear from Fig. 1 and increasingly evident in practice is that the client demands more from the consultant than was the case twenty or even ten years ago, thus the consultant now will often be asked to become involved in the implementation and follow-through process. This may include such activities as software procurement, training, and change management. Where all that is required is a report, it may range from what could be called research to what one writer has described as follows: "I do not want a piece of research that is academically rigorous, analytically comprehensive, methodologically impeccable, unreadable, 200 pages too long and two years too late. What I want is an OK investigation which is analytically and methodologically maybe 80% satisfactory, brief, of practical utility and timely" (*8*).

The implication behind all these observations is that there is now a far greater degree of interaction between the consultant and the client, and often between the

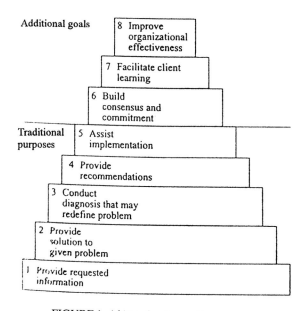

FIGURE 1. *A hierarchy of consulting purposes.*

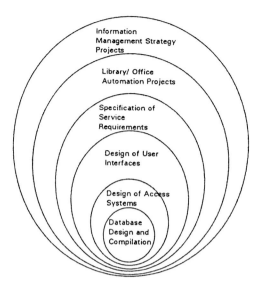

FIGURE 2. *Description of the consultant's role on a directive and nondirective continuum.*

consultant and the suppliers. The client/consultant complementarity is shown in Fig. 2, taken from a useful guide issued by the International Labour Office in Geneva (*9*).

A corollary of this is that the effectiveness of the consultant is likely to increase the higher and more appropriate the level at which he or she can establish a dialogue. As LIS consultancy in the United Kingdom has matured it is evident that its practitioners enjoy such access to a greater extent.

The author of this article has commented elsewhere on the invisible aspect of consultancy, particularly when compared to research (*9*). Whereas research workers must publish or perish, consultants are usually bound by a confidentiality clause in their contracts, even when working in the public sector. Consequently, very few consultancy reports become public, and with the relatively small community of LIS consultants surmised above, little is written about their work at the general level. One exception is a report prepared by Vickers, commissioned and published by the British Library (*10*), but now seven years old. In this report, Vickers proposed a model of information consultancy, shown at Fig. 3.

Though this model, which progresses from the most general to the most specific inner circle, is information oriented (the word library is mentioned once and in conjunction with the word *office*), it retains some validity. What has changed in the past seven years is the even greater emphasis on information technology and on the economics of library and information services. Thus, the major drivers on the U.K. scene (and to a greater or lesser extent in most countries) are

- Digitization (electronic libraries, electronic publishing)
- Impact of the Internet (and intranets)
- Integration of external and internal information
- Economics (cost justification, value for money, rationalization)

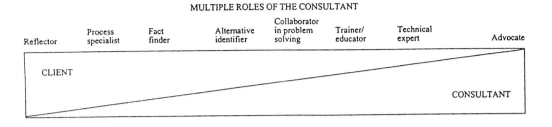

MULTIPLE ROLES OF THE CONSULTANT

Reflector	Process specialist	Fact finder	Alternative identifier	Collaborator in problem solving	Trainer/ educator	Technical expert	Advocate

CLIENT

CONSULTANT

LEVEL OF CONSULTANT ACTIVITY IN PROBLEM SOLVING

Non-directive   Directive

Raises questions for reflection	Observes problem-solving processes and raises issues mirroring feedback	Gathers data and stimulates thinking	Identifies alternatives and resources for client and helps assess consequences	Offers alternatives and partici-pates in decisions	Trains the client and designs learning experiences	Provides information and suggestions for policy or practice decisions	Proposes guidelines, persuades, or directs in the problem-solving process

FIGURE 3. *Model of information consultancy.*

These in turn lead to the inclusion of records management and document management in the information consultants' portfolio as well as such more traditional activities as market research and business requirements analysis, information audit, systems specification and database design, and thesaurus construction.

Most recently, and often following in the slipstream of the influence and activities of the larger management consultants, their LIS counterparts are turning their attention to, and becoming involved in, projects involving strategic planning and business process reengineering, total quality management and the pursuit of business excellence, and knowledge management, the learning organization, and the exploitation of intellectual capital.

Referring back to an earlier statement, the word 'involved' in the previous paragraph is pertinent. The stakes have been raised in the information society and the opportunity for LIS consultants to control organizationwide projects in blue chip companies and government departments is rare.

The LIS Consultant Community

It was estimated earlier that the core community of LIS consultants is probably on the order of 100. If this is true, then it is not surprising that they have not created a formal society. (The figure of 100 was often quoted as the size at which an "invisible college" began to feel the need to form a society, publish a journal, etc.) Some attempts have been made to create special interest groups within the professional institutions, while others have formed information consortia, mainly for the purposes of marketing and contract hunting. Some of these have been created on a wider geographical basis within the European Union, particularly when bidding for contract work required by the Commission that stipulates the need for multinational, multilingual tenders.

A small number of LIS consultants, perhaps around ten, belongs to the Institute of Management Consultants and with five years experience can describe themselves as chartered management consultants. As such, the consultant has an obligation to abide by the code of conduct and to participate actively in professional development.

REFERENCES

1. D. Nicholas, "But Is It Research?" *Assignation,* **13**(10), 1–3 (Jan. 1996).

2. See, for example, WOT (22), Oct. 29, 1997 at http://www.wot.co.uk.

3. "Management Consultancy in Europe." *Datamonitor,* FT Financial publishing, London, 1996.

4. P. Abott, "Top 100 Firms See Steady Rise in Fee Income." *Mgt. Consult.,* 22–3, 25–26, 28, 30, 32–3 (July/Aug. 1996).

5. C. Hancock, "The Mega Merger Makes Sense." *Mgt. Consult. Internat.,* (95), 7 (Sept. 1997).

6. P. Vickers, *Information and Consultancy,* Library and Information Briefings no. 21, M. Feeney and J. Martyn, series eds. British Library, London, 1990.

7. J. Pluse, "Research in Public Libraries: A Project to Find a Way Forward." *Pub. Libr. J.,* **11**(1), 20–21 (1996).

8. M. Kubr, *Management Consulting: A Guide to the Profession,* International Labour Office, Geneva, 1976.

9. A. Gilchrist, "Research and Consultancy," in *Library and Information Work Worldwide,* 1995/6, A. G. Mackenzie et al., eds. Bowker Saur, East Grinstead, U.K. (1998).

10. A. N. Turner, "Consulting Is More Than Giving Advice," *Harvard Bos. Rev.,* (Sept./Oct. 1982).

ALAN GILCHRIST

SEARCH ENGINES

Definition

A *search engine* is computer software that searches a collection of electronic materials to retrieve citations, documents, or information that match or answer a user's query. The retrieved materials may be text documents, facts that have been extracted from text, images, or sounds. A *query* is a question phrased so that it can be interpreted properly by a search engine. Depending on the type of software, it may be a collection of commands, a statement in either full or partial sentences, one or more keywords, or in the case of nontext searching, an image or sequence of sounds to be matched.

Types of Materials Searched

TEXT

Search engines are most commonly associated with searching text and data. This is not surprising, since collections of electronic text predate image or sound collections in digital form. These collections of text are commonly referred to as databases. A *database* is a collection of either citations or full-text articles. Each article or citation is called a *record*. Each record in a database contains the same elements, referred to as *fields*. Commonly occurring fields include title, author, publisher, date, journal title, keywords, and abstracts, as well as the full text of the article.

The search engines with which this article is concerned are the foundation of text information retrieval systems. They are designed to manipulate large amounts of text. New techniques in searching nontext materials, however, are becoming increasingly feasible for widespread use in large collections.

IMAGES

Image collections, whether of moving or still images, are most commonly searched through textual descriptions that have been attached to the images. Such descriptions are often divided into searchable fields such as name of artist, type of medium, subject of work, and date. Direct image searching is increasingly common, however. Software exists at this time for automatically identifying the contents of an image by color, shape, and texture. Some image-searching systems allow the user to submit a picture or drawing that they attempt to match, and some commercial applications have been released. Face recognition is also an active research area. Color recognition software asks the user to specify predominant colors and their position in the image to be retrieved; thus, a search for all pictures of sunsets might specify dark colors at the bottom of a picture and pinks and reds at the top. Output from any image search is generally in the form of a set of "thumbnail images," or small images from which the user chooses the best matches to examine in larger format.

SOUNDS AND MUSIC

This area is largely experimental. Matching musical passages has lagged behind both text and image searching, though there are now some systems which match typed-in musical themes.

History

Large unorganized collections of information are of minimal use to anyone until they have been sorted into a discernible pattern. For that reason, methods for creating access to printed materials were developed as early as the Babylonian era. These methods are commonly referred to as indexing, cataloging, and classification. Their purpose is to help users find materials within a collection.

Libraries create order by sorting information by subject, by author, or even by color of cover. However, the need to physically place a work somewhere on a shelf has limited the ability of a library to create subject groupings that merge two or more disciplines. The object to be cataloged can be shelved in only one location. Works that are on more than one topic must be placed in a single spot. To solve this problem, libraries created card catalogs. The card catalog enabled users to find the same book under multiple entry points, such as author, subject, title, or series name. The card catalog or the online catalog acts as a surrogate to the collection. Unlike the unchanging physical collection to which they point, they can view the collection as if it were in author, title, or subject order by changing how the cards or citations are sorted. Since library cards are easier to duplicate than books, librarians often create multiple access points for each subject within a book as well, thus increasing access to its contents. Standard library access points allow the user to find a work by title, author, or subject.

Library subject heading are standardized in controlled vocabularies so that, for example, works about "skin diving" are not scattered throughout the catalog under alternate terms, such as "scuba diving," according to the whim of the indexer. These standardized subject headings were established centrally in a controlled vocabulary or in a thesaurus such as the *Library of Congress Subject headings,* or the *Sears List of Subject Headings.* Both these traditional thesauri are examples of *precoordinate indexing*; that is, indexing that permanently establishes relationships between two or more subjects in a single heading. Precoordinate indexing allows the user to find precise subtopics within a broader category such as "Cooking." These relationships are fixed so that no matter what library is used, materials will be located under the same predictable heading. Thus the Library of Congress mandates that Provencal cooking will be forever found under "Cookery, French—Provencal style," not under "Provencal cooking." Once offically established, these subject headings are rarely altered. Since new terms must be officially established before they can be used—a lengthy process—appropriate subject headings for new or current topics are often nonexistent long after they have entered into common parlance, thus computers are still found under "electronic data processing" in many libraries.

Outside the traditional library sphere but simultaneously, we find experimentation with a different information retrieval approach. Postcoordinate systems were developed in the 1940s and 1950s to answer the need for quick access to current and precise topics. *Postcoordinate indexing* assigns *single* terms to documents. They are not precoordinated as they are in a library thesaurus or controlled vocabulary. The purpose of postcoordinate indexing is to permit any combination of two or more terms. Cross-discipline searching is facilitated, and the searcher need not know the established terminology or format in order to locate pertinent materials. In other words, Provencal and cooking are assigned separately, to be combined only at the time of the search. Postcoordinate indexing does not preclude using a controlled vocabulary, but in general, systems that developed from this tradition were more apt to include new terms as they arose.

Postcoordinate indexing provided "multidimensional access to multidimensional subject matter (*1*). It permitted the free combination of all or any terms that were assigned to a document. Postcoordinate indexing requires some means for combining terms. Originally this was accomplished either by printing a single term at the top of a sheet of paper, followed by columns of numbers representing the documents that contained that term, or with a fairly cumbersome arrangement of punched cards that had holes cut in them, one hole representing each subject covered by a document. Mortimer Taube's Uniterm system is an example of this type of index. Edge-notched cards that are punched for subject terms are another example. The distinction between post- and precoordinate indexing is that postcoordinate indexing allows any term to be searched for in combination with any other term. In addition, it does not rely on elaborate thesauri. Indexing terms are often chosen from the document itself. While these implementations, when manual, were awkward, they might be considered the precursors to online information retrieval systems. Once computers could take over the process, erasing the manual awkwardness of the system, the virtues of postcoordinate searching became clear. While the distinction between pre- and postcoordinate indexing is important, in practice many systems are hybrids and contain both kinds of terms.

Both precoordinate and postcoordinate indexing led the user to the physical location of the actual document. With the advent of the computer, however, physical location became moot. A document could simultaneously appear to exist at any entry point, and any of its words could serve as that entry point; thus the possibilities for retrieving a work were suddenly expanded. Theoretically, any work could be retrieved by simply matching the words it contained to any question.

In practice, however, it was not so simple to search through large collections of electronic text. Computers were slow and couldn't respond quickly enough to a query if they had to search through full text. Representations of the full text were therefore created, heavily influenced by the library experience with creating access tools for hard-copy collections. Early text databases often looked similar to library card catalogs, containing standard cataloging information such as the author, title, and subjects covered. One notable addition, though, was the abstract, which gave users much more information about the contents of each document. Searching the abstract plus the standard fields gave searchers increased opportunities to locate materials that covered a fairly narrow topic defined by several terms.

Early searches were done as batch processes, permitting only the most minimal interaction between user and computer. Delays of a day between interactions were common. By the 1960s, however, computer capacity had increased enough so that information retrieval systems became interactive. In fact, the 1960s were the fertile decade that spawned both the Boolean-based and the statistical and probabilistic retrieval systems described below.

In the 1960s, several factors combined to speed the development of text-retrieval systems. The first was the impetus provided by NASA, the Atomic Energy Commission, the National Library of Medicine, the Defense Department, and other U.S. government agencies that had begun to accumulate large files of electronic information. They realized that these files contained untapped information potential. The second was the development of mainframe computers and storage media such as disks, which had both the speed and the capacity to handle large text databases. Such projects as NASA RECON were funded by these government agencies, and they provided the foundation for early online information systems such as DIALOG, ORBIT, LEXIS, and BRS. These commercial services were publicly available by the 1970s. Searching them interactively from remote locations required new equipment: a modem and a terminal, as well as a telephone line. When personal computers appeared in the early 1980s, these services were adapted to interact with a computer on the desktop instead of a terminal.

Since the 1960s, research and development of text-retrieval systems has followed two paths simultaneously. The first path continued the development of the commercial Boolean-based systems that still exist today (DIALOG or LEXIS/NEXIS). Improvements were made in speed, in the size of the database searched, and in searching options, which were expanded to include such features as adjacency or the ability to search across several databases at once. These systems emphasized acquisition of new content or databases that covered additional subjects. Databases usually contained bibliographic information plus an abstract of a full-text document. Users could not retrieve a full-text document from these systems. Instead, they were given descriptions of documents so that they could retrieve the printed source in hard copy.

By the 1990s, the ubiquity of personal computers and the Internet changed information-seeking behavior. Users began to expect instant electronic delivery of full text. Consequently, many database providers began to incorporate full text into their products.

Simultaneously, the information retrieval research community was experimenting with statistical probabilistic and natural language processing (NLP) systems. By the late 1960s, the SMART system had been developed by Gerard Salton at Cornell University. This early statistical system proved the utility of applying statistical techniques to text in order to retrieve pertinent documents grouped in relevance-ranked order. These techniques, or algorithms, have been refined until they currently provide the basis for the search engines on the World Wide Web, such as Excite, InfoSeek, Alta Vista, or HotBot.

Natural language processing is the third and newest information retrieval technique. It adds lexical, syntactic, and semantic analysis to document and query processing. Researchers such as Elizabeth Liddy, Bruce Croft, and Chris Buckley are responsible for developing this approach. All three information retrieval methods will be described more fully below.

Both statistical and NLP search systems differ from the traditional Boolean systems in the assumptions they make about the user's ability to frame an appropriate question or query. From the system designer's point of view, this is the crux of the information-seeking dilemma: Is the user asking for precisely what she wants, or is she asking for only an approximation of the subject? Boolean systems match the terms of the query precisely. If the question is accurate, the documents that are retrieved will be good answers. Since users rarely know enough to state every relevant term precisely, however, statistical and NLP systems present almost-matches as well as perfect matches to the query.

The Search Process

Hunting for information is an iterative process. It begins as an initial question or query, usually a broad one. Based on the first retrieved set of information, the user may modify or completely change the initial search strategy, refining it in successive

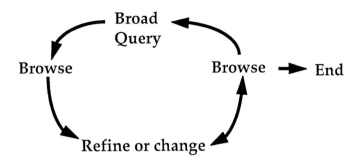

FIGURE 1. *The search process. Susan Feldman, Datasearch © 1997.*

iterations until it brings him what he needs. In the best embodiment of this process, the user is able to interact with someone or something with enough intelligence to give him guidance on where to look and how to describe his information need effectively. Search engines are effective to the extent to which they can ease and emulate the search process.

The Perfect Search Engine

- Finds good answers to questions
- Finds answers quickly
- Interprets a question well enough to search on the ideas and concepts expressed, not just on the terms used in the query
- Is easy to interact with; requires no special formats or commands
- Lets the user know what is happening, and prompts him when the system is in doubt
- Presents the retrieved information in perfect relevance ranked order, with the most relevant information at the top
- Provides full text with illustrations through the same search interface when requested
- Returns no irrelevant information, but includes partially relevant material

Issues in Text Retrieval Performance

While a human has no trouble determining whether or not a document is about the subject he is interested in, computers must have some means for translating the effectiveness of retrieval (whether a document is "about" a subject) into more precise terms. *Precision* and *recall* measure the effectiveness of search engines. Precision measures the ability of the search engine to match a query exactly, without retrieving irrelevant materials. Recall measures the percentage of relevant documents in a database that are retrieved by the query. In general, the greater the precision, the lower the recall. Similarly, the greater the recall, the lower the precision. In designing a search engine, each of the following factors must be considered, and each decision affects the precision and recall of a system. A third measure, which has yet to be quantified, is the usability of a system. In other words, how easy it is to get answers from it without prior training or without expertise in the subject matter contained in the database. Speed, interface design, opportunities for interaction with the system, and the ability to interpret a query in plain language all influence the usability of a system. The annual Text Retrieval Conferences (TREC) sponsored by DARPA (Defense Advanced Research Projects Agency) and the National Institute of Standards and Technology (NIST) provide a standard set of documents and queries to participating retrieval system researchers. The systems run standardized queries against these databases in order to evaluate their performance.

While the succeeding years have whittled away at the problems posed by information retrieval, no one system has solved them all. These issues include the following:

DATA OR FILE STRUCTURE

The data structure of a database determines to some degree which search techniques can be implemented effectively. The typical text retrieval system consists of three separate files: the file of full records or full-text documents, including all bibliographic and indexing information; the dictionary, which is an alphabetical list of all the unique words in the database; and an inversion list, which stores all of the locations of occurrences for each word in the dictionary. This structure is called an *inverted file*. Searching very large databases is efficient with this file structure, since each word in the dictionary is an entry point for beginning a search. Just as a card catalog provides *random access* to a library, with each card acting as a starting point, the dictionary of the inverted file structure enables the system to begin looking at the right place in the alphabet immediately, whether that is *A* or *X*, without having to start at *A* each time. In contrast, a microfilm catalog of a collection provides *linear access* to the collection, with each search beginning at one end of the film examining all records in a collection until the appropriate one is found.

When new records are added to an inverted file structure, the dictionary and the inversion list must be rebuilt with the new records interfiled. Thus an inverted file structure requires more maintenance than if each new record were simply appended at the end of the file.

Signature file structure is a common structure for text databases with a relatively small number of records. The signature file occupies considerably less space than an inverted file, since it consists only of the first of the inverted index files—the full record of each document. Since there is no index to the file, signature file searching is linear. To answer a query, the program starts at record 1 and proceeds through each record consecutively, searching for matches to the query terms. The trade-off is that signature file searching slows as more records are added to the database. New records are appended to the end of the file. As records are added, the search process gets longer.

In contrast *relational databases* build tables that are linked to each other. They are designed to answer predictable queries in a predefined format with a limited set of query variations. They are very efficient at answering such questions as the number of customers who are located in Massachusetts, or listing the addresses of those customers in a report. Each table contains a different attribute of whatever entities are described in the database. Relational database search algorithms are likely to be based on which type of table is the most frequently used, so that it can be brought into memory the most quickly. This format is not suitable for searching large amounts of full text, which is not usually structured as identical sets of related attributes. Searching relational text databases is consequently slow for full text, although it is fast for compiling lists of addresses or part numbers because the information can be retrieved from a single table.

SPEED

Users demand a fast response from interactive systems. Searching through giga-bytes (and now terabytes) of information requires algorithms that can sort efficiently. Some of the factors that affect retrieval speed—aside from the capabilities of the hardware itself—are the size of the database, the size of each individual record, the file format, the type of query processing, and the type of retrieval method.

WHAT IS SEARCHED

Should a search engine search every word in each document for every search, or can some shortcuts increase the speed of retrieval? A text record often contains some predefinable elements. For instance, documents typically contain a title, an author, a date, the name of the publication, and the publisher, as well as indexing words, an abstract, and the full text. Each of these elements can be considered a separate text field. Searching on a single defined field speeds up retrieval time, so that seeking an author's name only in the author field should be very fast. However, searching by field reduces the chances that a relevant document will be found if the search term does not occur in that field, but occurs somewhere else in the document. It is more likely that a query term will appear in the full text of a document than in only its title or its indexing terms, simply because full text contains more words. In addition, many searchers assume that every field is being searched, and create queries based on this assumption. Yet even most full-text retrieval systems do not search some words contained in a document. In particular, stop words and simple string matching limit what a system can retrieve:

- *Stop words.* Very common words are usually eliminated from the default search of most retrieval systems. These words typically include articles, prepositions, or conjunctions, such as *a, the, an, to, and, or,* or *but.* Boolean systems also eliminate those words that function as Boolean commands, (AND, OR, NOT) unless specifically directed to search for them. These stop words form the basis of what may be a very long list of words in non-Boolean systems, particularly in statistical or probabilistic search engines. The stop word list in these latter engines may include any word that occurs so often in the database that it has little ability to discriminate between the relevance of one document and another.
- *String matching vs. more complex types of retrieval.* Retrieval software must also determine what text elements can be retrieved. Matching short strings of letters is much faster than matching phrases or sentences or noting the relative position of terms in order to retrieve adjacent words or words in the same paragraph. Is the search unit the word, or can phrases or sentences be retrieved as well? Every step to a larger unit increases the possibility of retrieving documents that match the user's query more precisely. However, the search

algorithms must be able to determine the relative positions of the words within each document, as well as the fact that they occur at all.

EASE OF USE OR USABILITY

Several aspects of system design either improve or hinder the ability of the user to understand and use a retrieval system effectively. These include the following:

- *How the query is entered.* Ease of use is tangentially related to the search engine itself, since the design of the search engine limits how the user can interact with the system. For instance, a command-driven Boolean system cannot interpret a question that is entered as a full sentence. Intuitive interaction is critical if the user is to find the information he needs. In order to retrieve information effectively, the user must be able to phrase his question so that it reflects his information need accurately. Tools that help the user to frame a query and to modify it as he gains more knowledge about his subject improve the usability of the system and consequently make information finding more effective.

  Users seek information because they don't have it. While this statement may seem simplistic, in fact it is the crux of the information retrieval problem. How can a person who doesn't know very much about a subject ask a question that will retrieve what he doesn't know? While a trained intermediary who is both knowledgeable and skilled at finding information can often steer the user in the right direction, any librarian knows that the process is a lengthy one, requiring numerous questions and answers as well as several false starts that present the wrong information to the user. In addition to knowing how to help the user frame his query so that a retrieval system can interpret it properly, a trained intermediary knows how to interpret the body language and inflections of the user in order to help him find the information he needs. So far, no machine in existence has the wide knowledge and sensitivity to perform as well.

  The typical subject search begins with a user having limited knowledge of the subject being sought. Several iterations are necessary for the user to find out progressively more about the subject altering the query so that it matches his interests more precisely.

- *Feedback.* Feedback is also an issue in text retrieval system design. Users need to understand what the system is doing: how it is interpreting their request and how it arrives at the set of answers it retrieves. If they understand how a system arrives at its set of retrieved documents, they are able to correct wrong system interpretations or to enlarge or narrow the scope of a search. The genius of the first commercial online information retrieval systems was that they were interactive and recursive; that is, they kept a record of all previous steps so that the user could return to any point in a search. They also told the user how many documents matched each term in a query. This information helped the searcher decide how to proceed: to narrow or broaden a search or to take a completely different tack.

  Recent improvements to feedback mechanisms by LEXIS/NEXIS also indicate which documents contain each term, so that searchers can see co-occurrence of terms at a glance. DR-LINK, an NLP system, displays the search terms as they are interpreted by the search engine, and gives the user an opportunity to further disambiguate or correct interpretations, as well as to add or subtract terms and indicate time (past, present, future), and type of information.

POLYSEMY

Polysemy refers to the multiple meanings each word has. For instance, *bank* might be the land next to a river, or it might be a savings and loan institution. As a verb, it might discuss the angle at which a pilot turns an airplane, or it might be a gardening term for piling soil against a plant, or the action of preparing a fire to burn slowly during the night. While humans have no trouble distinguishing these meanings based on their context, computers must be given elaborate sets of rules in order to distinguish one meaning from another. This ability to distinguish among the senses of a word is called *disambiguation.* Most non-natural language processing search engines can not disambiguate words.

SYNONYMY

Synonymy is the antithesis of polysemy. Synonyms are two or more words that mean roughly the same thing. Search engines that search for words rather than for ideas will miss relevant documents that use other synonymous alternatives. The user's imperfect knowledge of a subject often prevents a full list of synonyms from being incorporated into a query. A search engine that adds synonymous terms accurately can improve the recall of a search.

INDEXING CONSISTENCY

Indexing is the process of applying terms from an established specialized vocabulary to each document in a database. Each term in the thesaurus, or controlled vocabulary, has been chosen as the single representative of an idea or concept, thus avoiding problems of synonymy or polysemy. Databases frequently rely on indexing in order to increase the precision of retrieval. In theory, indexing should employ no more than one standard term for each idea. Thus any document about that subject will be tagged with the same word, and problems of too many senses or too many similar terms will be avoided. In practice, studies have shown that indexers do not apply terms consistently. A study at the National Library of Medicine estimated that agreement between indexers in applying the same terms averages about 50 percent. Thus while indexing may enhance the quality of search results in any database (2), it can not be relied upon as a sole source of subject content information.

SPELLING CONSISTENCY AND TYPOGRAPHICAL ERRORS

Variations in spelling, particularly between British and American spellings, as well as typographical errors can reject an otherwise relevant document. Examples are *labor* and *labour,* or *aluminum* and *aluminium.* Today, as paper documents are scanned into electronic format, the potential for spelling errors is increasing dramatically, since today's OCR (optical character recognition) programs perform on average at 95 percent to 98 percent accuracy. Search engines that perform a "fuzzy search," which retrieves almost-matches such as misspellings, are necessary for accurate searching of optically scanned text files.

RETRIEVING ONLY USEFUL INFORMATION

Culling the set of retrieved information so that it contains everything we would like to know and nothing we aren't interested in is a major problem, given that most users do not ask for precisely what they need. Too much precision eliminates the possibility that the user will find a partially relevant document to be extremely useful. Not enough precision returns too many irrelevant documents and obscures the useful ones within an overwhelming pile. In other words, how do we avoid information overload while still finding out everything that is important about the subject?

FALSE DROPS

False drops occur because either a word is used in a different sense in an article or the query terms all appear in an article but are not related to each other. A good example of this would be a search for American foreign policy for Japan which retrieves a news digest containing brief paragraphs on American foreign policy for China and news of a tsunami in Japan. This false drop contains all the query terms, but not in the right context. Any text retrieval system that searches solely by matching terms is likely to retrieve false drops under these circumstances. Another cause of false drops is misinterpretation of a term. In other words, in a query asking for the effects of pollution on plants, retrieving "industrial plants" when we really meant "green plants."

The ultimate search engine requires a certain degree of intelligence in order to interpret a user's question correctly. This is because users are seeking information about which they know relatively little or about which they have incomplete or inaccurate information. The best search engine would be able to act like a knowledgeable human to help the user enlarge the scope of the question or change its focus. Artificial intelligence is only beginning to emulate that capability.

Types of Text Retrieval Systems

We can divide text retrieval search engines into three broad categories: Boolean, probabilistic or statistical, and natural language processing. Each has its particular advantages and faults. At this time no commercially available search engine finds every relevant item within a database. This is partially due to the vagaries of the English language, which is rich in synonyms and homonyms, and partially due to the difficulty most users have in framing their information need precisely. Most users, however, are interested in finding *an* answer to their question, not in finding everything on a subject. In fact, if they were given everything on a topic, they might be overwhelmed with too much information. Therefore, if they retrieve enough information of value to fill their information need, they are satisfied with the results. New artificial intelligence and linguistic capabilities promise to improve the performance of search engines both in terms of usability and precision/recall.

The choice of a search engine partially depends on the type of database to be searched and who will be searching it. Boolean systems work well with trained users and with well-indexed contents. They are useful for document records that do not contain full text and for finding precise answers such as known authors or titles. Statistical and natural language processing require full text (or at least abstracts) in order to function to their full potential. They excel in finding information about subjects or poorly defined questions. Both, however, benefit from well-designed and carefully executed indexing.

BOOLEAN SYSTEMS

Boolean searching is the foundation of today's traditional online information retrieval services such as DIALOG, MEDLINE, LEXIS/NEXIS, or Westlaw. A Boolean search matches the terms in a document with the terms in a user's query. Boolean searching is based on Boolean logic. The searcher is trained to make semi-mathematical statements in order to enter a search request or query. The basic Boolean operators join two or more terms in a query, and are as follows:

> *AND*—indicates that the two words connected by the AND operator must both appear in a document in order for that document to be retrieved (e.g., "A and B": both A and B must appear in order to retrieve the document).
> *OR*—indicates that either of two (or more) terms must appear. (e.g., "A or B": either A or B must be present to retrieve a document, but only one is necessary).
> *NOT*—directs the system to reject any document that contains the term following the NOT operator (e.g., "A not B": A must be present, but B must not be present in a document in order for the document to be retrieved).
> ( )—parentheses are used to group words that should be acted upon by whatever operator precedes them [e.g., "A and (B or C)" means that we will retrieve any occurrence of A as long as the document also contains either B or C. "(A and B) or C," in contrast, directs the software to retrieve all documents that contain either *both* A and B *or* that contain C, even if they don't contain either A or B].

Additional commands commonly include some sort of "wild card," such as a * or a $ or a ?. The wild card indicates a missing letter or letters, and is used to retrieve both plural or singular forms ("cat*" retrieves *cat, cats,* or *catalogue*) or spelling variations. Most Boolean systems also use several adjacency commands to indicate that words must or may not be in a specified order, or that they must be within one or more words of each other.

These commands are combined with query terms to create mathematically logical statements that group words using parentheses.

For example, in order to find articles on child labor laws in the United States and the United Kingdom, a Boolean system would require a query such as the following:

> (child () labo*r () law*) and (U.S. or (United () States) or American or British or UK or (United()Kingdom))

This Boolean statement tells the system that a phrase consisting of *child* (preceding and next to) *labor* (in which any number of extra letters may come between the "o" and the "r"), and *law* (which immediately follows labo*r, and which may end in anything after law such as *laws, lawless,* or *lawsuit*) must appear in any document retrieved, as long as it is accompanied by any of the following: U.S. or United (next to and preceding) States or American or British or UK or United (next to and preceding) Kingdom.

Most of the large commercial online information systems, such as DIALOG,

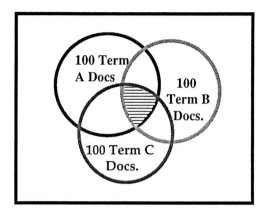

FIGURE 2. *Boolean AND search. Susan Feldman, Datasearch © 1997.*

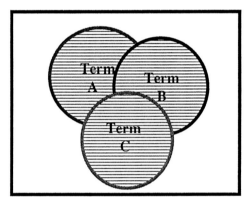

FIGURE 3. *Boolean OR search. Susan Feldman, Datasearch © 1997.*

LEXIS/NEXIS, or Westlaw, rely on command-driven interfaces and Boolean operators, as well as a long list of other commands, although there has been some movement
away from these systems toward statistical systems. Boolean systems require extensive
training on the part of the user and have other shortcomings as well. Boolean systems
are exact match systems; they only give the user the exact words that are requested.
This means that a well-trained, clever searcher can find precise matches to a query, as
long as the searcher, the indexer, and the author all select the same terms to use in
describing an idea. The problem is that most languages, and English in particular,
offer numerous variations in how to state an idea. They are full of synonyms. If the
indexer or author chooses a different synonym from the searcher's, a document will
not be found in a Boolean-based system. Variant spellings such as "labor" and
"labour" will also not show up automatically. In order to get around these obstacles,
command languages have become quite complex. Despite this complexity, Boolean
systems remain relatively inflexible and unforgiving. The above example would not

have found "labor laws for minors," first, because we specified the phrase "*child* labor law(s)" and second because we never asked for "minors" or "children." Only the exact phrase or words as specified will be retrieved, thus a query that does not precisely reflect the user's need will return precise matches to the wrong question.

Venn diagrams are visual portrayal of how a search system matches query terms to retrieve documents from its database. Each circle represents the set of documents that contain one query term. Overlapping areas among the circles represent those documents that contain both terms, or even all three. The following diagrams show a Boolean AND and OR search on three terms.

Boolean systems are exact match systems. Their goal is precision, not recall. They rely on the training, cleverness, and experience of the searcher to use complex commands.

The striped central overlapping area in this Boolean AND search shows the documents that are retrieved. Each document must contain all three of the search terms. Note that the search precisely matches the user's knowledge of the subject, because the terms retrieved match the ones he asked for. For precise searches by knowledgeable subject experts, this is a successful strategy. It is unsuccessful for finding information about a subject only vaguely known or defined because it leaves no latitude for error.

The Boolean OR search retrieves any document that contains one or more of the query terms. This broadens the scope of the search, but it may return more documents than the user can scan, many of which are entirely irrelevant to his interests. Given a small number of documents, however, the Boolean OR search is successful in locating documents of interest that contain at least one but not necessarily more of the user's search terms.

STATISTICAL AND PROBABILISTIC RETRIEVAL SYSTEMS

At the same time that Boolean search systems were being developed, such researchers as Gerard Salton and R. J. Tritschler were experimenting with statistical search engines. These search engines use statistics and probability to predict the similarity of any document in a database to a query. This methodology can be quite complex, and the algorithm for computing the degree of relevance of any document in a database to a query differs from one search engine to another. The underlying assumption, though, is that the more times a term appears in a document, the more likely it is that the document will be about that subject. This is known as *term frequency* (TF). The second assumption on which these systems is based is that terms that appear more frequently in a document than they do in the database as a whole further indicate that the term or word in question is a major topic of that document. If the term appears *frequently* in the document, but *infrequently* in the database as a whole, the chances are that the document is about that subject. This measure is known as *inverse document frequency* (IDF).

Since many documents can be said to be somewhat related to a subject, as they are in Boolean OR search, statistical systems often retrieve large sets of documents to answer a query. Unlike the Boolean OR search, however, they use statistical methods for computing the degree of relevance to a query for each document based on TF/IDF and display the documents retrieved in ranked order, with the most relevant first. In other words, documents that contain more occurrences of a query term will be ranked higher than those with fewer occurrences of that term.

Relevance ranking is based on weights assigned to each term within each document, and it is in the assignment of weights that the statistical search engines diverge from each other. In general, more occurrences of a query term give the document a higher relevance ranking. In addition, documents that contain more than one of the query terms and several instances of those terms are ranked more highly. Thus, the *co-occurrence* of query terms, in addition to the frequency of occurrence of those terms, determines the relative ranking of that document within a retrieved set of documents.

Statistical methods are also useful in information retrieval systems for

- Clustering documents on a broad topic together to create a browsable collection on a topic.
- Expanding a search statement or query by suggesting terms in the database that co-occur with the query terms. These are known as associated terms.

Statistical search engines present two advantages to the user. The first is that relevance ranking is a useful approach for retrieving a fairly large set of documents without confusing or overwhelming the user. The most relevant documents should be in the top group of documents; a user need not wade through all the documents in order to find the ones that are most useful. In addition, statistical systems are not exact match systems. While they do return exact matches to the user's query, they also return approximate, or *fuzzy* matches: if a document has two out of the three query terms, and those terms occur frequently, the document may appear near the top of the retrieved set, even though it lacks the third term. This is extremely useful for the user, whose imperfect grasp of a subject may have influenced him to choose a term that is tangential to the heart of that subject.

These systems are more computationally complex than the straightforward matching of the Boolean system, and numerous factors are adjusted differently for each search engine, so that statistical search engines rarely retrieve exactly equivalent sets from the same database, since their algorithms differ. Search algorithms for statistical systems may include the following:

- Normalization: adjusting the algorithm to take the length of the document into account. Longer documents are more likely to have more occurrences of any term. To prevent long documents from receiving higher relevance rankings, the length of the document is factored into determining the weight to assign to a term.
- Proximity and adjacency. If query terms appear close to or adjacent to each other, they give the document a higher ranking. This reduces the problem of false drops.
- Position of query term. Terms that appear at the beginning of a document often receive a higher weight. Terms that appear in the title field or in the descriptor field may also be weighted more heavily.
- Stemming. Many statistical systems automatically search for both plural and singular forms of the word. They may also extract the stem of a word and search for variations on the stem. In other words, if I ask for *law,* the system may also retrieve *laws, lawless, lawsuit,* and *in-laws.* This may serve to improve or degrade the output of a search, depending on the degree to which stemming is applied. Most systems perform only plural/singular stemming, since too much extraneous information can be retrieved by rampant stemming.
- Stop words. Most statistical systems ignore the same stop words that Boolean systems

ignore. They also eliminate very common and very rare terms as well when calculating relevance. Terms that appear too frequently cannot be used to distinguish the value of one document from another. Similarly, very rare terms do not enhance relevance ranking. For instance, misspellings may be interpreted as rare terms. Relevance-ranking algorithms seem to work best when they are applied to the middle range of words in the database. For that reason, many statistical systems eliminate 400 or 500 words, including the usual stop words.

Statistical systems usually allow the user to enter queries in plain English without commands. They substitute smart programming for some of the knowledge that professional searchers have been required to learn.

Recognizing that one of the major shortcomings of Boolean searching is the inability to match the *idea* or *concept* of a query to documents in the database, some statistically based systems use either of two methods to match query concepts. The first is to match concepts by co-occurrence of terms. In other words, terms that occur in the same documents are expected to be about the same topic. While this is often useful, the entire list of terms that co-occur frequently with the query term is unpredictable in its accuracy because it is based on the statistics of occurrence rather than on the meaning of the word. A second approach is to add a lexicon to the software that is consulted by the system to provide additional pertinent document matches. This process gives better results, but is not adequate for deducing the meaning of new terms in the language. They must be added to the lexicon manually.

Statistical systems have their own shortcomings. The foremost is that they are not designed to work well on document records that do not contain enough text. Bibliographic records such as those that appear in a typical library catalog are thus not good candidates for statistical systems. In addition, statistical retrieval systems tend to return large sets, which may overwhelm the user. Also, since statistical search engines are based on frequency of words within a document, unless some sort of normalizing algorithm is applied, short documents can get short shrift. If they are compared to long documents the word frequency won't be as high, since there are fewer words to begin with. Authors who use many synonyms for an idea will have lower frequency counts for their writing, even if a document is highly pertinent to a searcher's query.

The big advantage to these systems is that they add a degree of flexibility and fuzziness to the search process. Since they return partial matches, they enlarge a search beyond the boundaries that the query originally defined. Since initial queries rarely describe an information need well, the partially relevant materials can broaden the scope of a search in order to find materials that are ultimately of greater use to the user than a Boolean AND operation would be. In addition, elimination of command language and Boolean logic means that a user can search and interact with a database without the intervention of a trained intermediary. Statistical systems often enable the user to ask for "more like this one"—using a "perfect" document from an initial list of retrieved results to act as an enriched query for the next search iteration. More like this has been demonstrated to be an effective method for finding the information that the user needs, but that he perhaps did not specify precisely in his initial query.

The statistical system finds all the documents located by a Boolean OR search, as well as some that contained misspellings or alternate forms of the query term. The ranked retrieval set allows the user to find the most relevant documents first. This is an

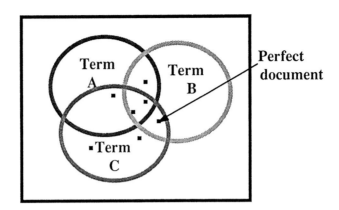

FIGURE 4. *Statistically based search. Susan Feldman, Datasearch © 1997.*

effective method for giving the user precise matches but also approximate matches so that he can enlarge the scope of his query. The technique solves the problem of handling large retrieved sets. The dots on Fig. 4 indicate most relevant documents. Note that the perfect document was located outside the Boolean AND set. It contained only two of the three query terms specified.

NATURAL LANGUAGE PROCESSING (NLP) SYSTEMS

Natural language processing is linguistically based. It extracts meaning from text as a human would, from the multiple levels of language that add layers of understanding to the words. Humans derive their understanding from contextual meaning based on both the structure of the text and the words themselves, as well as from their knowledge of the world. Similarly, NLP systems have attempted to determine meaning based on two approaches: by building knowledge about a subject domain into an information system, or by interpreting the words in a text from the structure and context of that document. While statistical and Boolean information retrieval systems use a simple matching technique and therefore miss some relevant items that are described with different terms or include items that are false drops, NLP systems incorporate contextual knowledge in order to interpret questions appropriately. Therefore, to return to our example of "child labor laws," and NLP system should be able to "know" that *children* and *minors* are both germane to our search. It should be able to retrieve articles about sweatshops in the early 1900s, and find *legislation* as well as laws.

Natural language processing systems based on domain knowledge analyze the language usage and terminology of one subject domain to create a knowledge base for each system, thus a system designed for one subject domain must be redesigned for each new subject area. In addition, new terminology must be added to the system as it arises.

Natural language processing systems that are based on text structure examine the structure of various types of text, and use that knowledge to interpret the meaning of document contents. While they can search across many subject domains, they must be adapted to each new text type, such as newspaper articles, instructional texts, or technical reports. These systems seek meaning as a person would. Meaning is conveyed to humans on several layers, which include the morphological, lexical, syntactic, semantic, discourse, and pragmatic levels of understanding. Morphology refers to the pieces of words that carry meaning—such prefixes as *un-* which mean "not" when added to a word, or word stems such as *affect,* which forms the basis for *affected, affecting, unaffected,* or *affection.* Lexical meaning refers to the dictionary definitions of a word. Syntactic meaning concerns a word's grammatical role in a sentence. Semantic meaning refers to meaning in the dictionary sense also, but is in addition the sum of meaning based on the collection of words and grammatical structure within a sentence. These are all important considerations in interpreting text. We need to know, for example, if a person is the cause or the recipient of an action. Changing a person's role from initiator to recipient of an action changes the meaning of a sentence profoundly. ("John hit Jack" as opposed to "Jack hit John.") The discourse level refers to the meaning conveyed by the text as a whole—the sum of its sentences. Pragmatic meaning relies on knowledge of the real world to supply extra understanding to a text. For instance, "He went out" means that he left where he was, and that he was inside some sort of structure, and went outside it, yet without pragmatic understanding, that sentence would be hard to interpret.

While some statistical systems have been referred to as NLP because they can accept queries without commands, true NLP requires linguistic analysis of both queries and documents. An NLP system should be able to distinguish between the different senses of *leaves* in the two statements "The leaves turn brown" and "The train leaves for New York in ten minutes." In contrast, both statistical and Boolean systems match words in a document to the words in a query, regardless of meaning, so they would retrieve either sense of leaves, resulting in false drops.

Natural language processing relies on some elements of both the Boolean and statistical approaches. It uses statistical methods to create a relevance-ranked set and translates queries into logical statements. However, it attempts to correct the shortcomings of both by adding some "understanding" of the meanings of words to the system. In other words, it incorporates linguistic knowledge of the structure of language into its interpretation of both documents and queries. This kind of system should never return "green plants" for "industrial plants," because it "understands" that the two concepts occupy different subject areas even though they are spelled alike. Natural language processing systems should also be able to "figure out" that a query asking for *EEC* should also find *Common Market* or *European Community* pertinent. Some of these systems go farther, and allow the user to search for vague concepts such as "future of," "impact of," and "effect of." They automatically truncate and stem query words, and find synonyms for query concepts. They identify noun phrases such as *trade bans* automatically. Words within the database are still given weights, and the statistical co-occurrence of words may be relied on for computing relevance as well as for finding synonyms. As in the statistical systems, results can be returned to the user in a single list ranked in descending order of relevance. The user may also be given other choices of how results are returned,

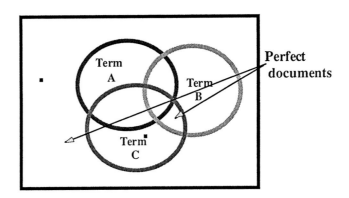

FIGURE 5. *Search with concept matching. Susan Feldman, Datasearch © 1997.*

however—for instance, by broad subject category. Natural language processing systems often enable the user to ask for "more like this one"—using a "perfect" document from an initial list of retrieved results to act as an enriched query for the next search iteration. More like this enriches a query with sufficient text to improve the ability of the system to interpret the intent of the user correctly.

Queries to NLP systems can be sentences or whole paragraphs describing an information need fully. Our example of child labor laws, stated as a NLP query would be as follows:

I would like to know about child labor laws in either the U.S. or Great Britain.

Although NLP is designed for searching, it also may become a solution to the need for automatic indexing systems.

Using the same three query terms, Fig. 5 demonstrates the value of matching ideas as well as terms from a query. Two perfect documents were located. One contained only two of the original query terms. The other contained none of them. Since users have an imperfect understanding of the subject they seek, they may not know the most appropriate terms to use. The NLP search can find equivalent terms and include documents containing them in the search output. Dots indicate the most relevant documents returned by the search using a NLP system.

Pressures for Change

It seems clear that information retrieval systems are poised for change in the next decade. Pressures for change come from several directions.

END USER SEARCHING

Prior to the development of end-user retrieval interfaces to traditional retrieval services, as well as the World Wide Web, searching was a professional activity largely confined to a trained information professional population. Extensive training was required to use the traditional online systems, and mistakes were costly because of the high price of connect time and contents. The World Wide Web developed simultaneously with the first serious forays by traditional online systems into end-user products. Lotus Notes, as well as such simplified online systems as EyeQ, Physicians Online, Knowledge Finder, and Profound, were aimed at the business or medical professional rather than the information professional. They required little or no training. This spate of new products would have changed the face of online searching in itself, but it was soon overwhelmed by the emergence of the World Wide Web as the dominant carrier of information.

The entry of the end-user into the information-seeking process created pressure to design systems that were easy to use without training. Researchers in information retrieval and computer science answered this need with the statistical search engines now prevalent on the World Wide Web. Traditional online vendors did not acknowledge the need for a new kind of search product until the statistical systems were well established. This has left the major online services with their original but shrinking market of professional search intermediaries who understand the value of the content these services represent. Difficult interfaces and high prices, however, have prevented end-users, a growing market, from becoming acquainted with these established online services.

DEMAND FOR INSTANT ACCESS TO INFORMATION

Researchers are no longer satisfied with the traditional two-step process of finding information. Before the advent of full-text information online, the researcher first consulted a library catalog or index, and then retrieved the full article in paper from the shelves of a library. Once it became possible to gain immediate access to the full text in one step without the need for going to a library or asking for an interlibrary loan of an article, researchers began demanding the same access to all resources. In fact, since it is possible to search the full text of a document, researchers who are eager for the newest information in their fields prefer quick access to waiting for indexing and abstracting services to process materials.

GROWTH OF UNINDEXED FULL-TEXT SOURCES

Traditional databases have been carefully structured and well-indexed and -edited guides to full text. New electronic information sources, both on the Internet and off are now often unindexed and unstructured full text. These may include internal documents that have been scanned to create internal databases available to an organization on an intranet or outside sources containing the full text of documents. Boolean systems rely on well-indexed and structured text; they do not perform as well with unindexed unstructured text. On the other hand, both statistical and NLP systems perform best with full-text sources. Thus it seems clear that a shift will occur away from traditional Boolean search engines.

DEVELOPMENT OF READILY AVAILABLE POWERFUL COMPUTERS WITH LARGE COMPUTATIONAL AND STORAGE CAPACITIES

Speed has been a barrier to elegant data handling because complex operations are computationally expensive and slow down response time of an interactive system. Newer computers make complex massaging of data feasible.

INCREASING COSTS OF CREATING TRADITIONAL DATABASES

Human indexers and abstracting is expensive and time-intensive. Non-automated systems can't keep pace with the increased outpouring of searchable text in both formal and informal publications. Labor costs for indexing, abstracting, and editing are among the largest continuing costs incurred in creating traditional structured databases. Database producers hope that new retrieval methods will eliminate or at least diminish these costs through machine-aided indexing.

INTELLECTUAL PROPERTY RIGHTS QUESTIONS

Questions of copyright and other intellectual property rights are at this time both a barrier and an impetus for change to quick development of advanced publicly available information systems. These questions are fueling the development of instant electronic commerce transactions, and may also speed the development of centralized resolution of copyright payments. They are a barrier to the legal exchange of information between scholars as well as among others who need to exchange information. The technology exists to instantly send a copy of a document to anyone who is connected to the Internet. The illegality of this act hinders the free exchange of information.

Trends

The original goal of information retrieval systems was to retrieve everything the user wanted and nothing he did not. That goal remains. Current information retrieval research concentrates on adding more intelligence to information systems for the following reasons.

REDUCE THE TIME INFORMATION USERS DEVOTE TO PROCESSING INFORMATION

This includes reducing information hunting time, organizing and filing time, and reading time. Several fertile areas of research have developed to address these problems.

- Automatic summarization. Brief, accurate summaries of materials reduce reading time. Human-produced summaries delay the arrival of information on the end user's desk. If summaries can be produced automatically, their usefulness will not be decreased by lack of timeliness.
- Intelligent agents. Intelligent agents based on machine learning theory obey an initial set of information-finding commands, but then through feedback adapt to changes in the user's profile of interests.
- Automatic alerting. Most information consumers have continuing information needs that can be categorized by broad subject or type. Alerting services run the same profile against all new materials as they are published to retrieve those that match.
- Automatic filtering. Simple programs that can identify materials by category and automatically file them reduce the information-handling workload.
- Question-answering systems. These systems answer who-what-where-when-why questions. They extract information from a database and return answers rather than collections of documents. The user need not sift through the documents to extract the answers himself.
- Improved relevance ranking and concept identification techniques.
- Faster retrieval from large and distributed databases. Distributed databases are databases that are located on multiple machines, perhaps in many geographic locations, but they are searched as if they are one virtual database. To improve speed, retrieval algorithms must be streamlined, and research is also exploring parallel processing of queries as well as parallel searching across distributed databases.
- Improved concept retrieval techniques, based on the subject discipline of the database being searched.
- Automated indexing. Also called machine-aided indexing, this capability would speed the preparation of databases and add indexing to full text for improved retrieval, but lower preparation costs at the same time.

IMPROVE HUMAN–COMPUTER INTERACTION

Lack of ease of use is still cited as one of the greatest barriers to increased use of information retrieval systems. Users are unsure of how to communicate with a machine. They hesitate to use real language, and find typing awkward. Their discriptions of information needs are hence incomplete. Developers of information retrieval systems need to create methods that ease interaction, and that allow the user to intercede at many points in the process, as they would in a conversation with an information professional. Active areas of research include the following:

- Visual information navigation tools. Humans absorb some types of information more readily if it is presented visually. They can react quickly to color or graphics, while it takes longer for the brain to process text, yet most retrieval systems rely on abstract thinking—reading of text—as a tool for finding information. Visual information navigation tools give people the cues they need, such as color or location or visual pathways so that the contents of a database are easy to understand. People who use online information systems must find information that is invisible. They lack such cues as color of cover or location next to other items of interest, yet we know from decades of library use that information seekers rely on precisely these cues to help them find the information they seek. Here again, the inability to ask a question that will elicit the precise answer needed is a significant barrier to information finding. This is an active research area. Shneiderman (3) and Marchionini (4) at the University of Maryland's human–computer interaction laboratory have developed a number of new approaches to information navigation. TOPIX from Verity Northern Light's custom folders, and AltaVista's graphical representations of related terms are new visual tools that explain the contents of the database to the user or suggest related terms in order to improve a query.

TABLE 1

Comparing Search Engines

	Boolean	Statistical	Intelligent text retrieval
How they work	Matches query terms exactly. Best used with a suite of commands. Good for precise searching, finding known items.	Assigns statistical weights to each term in document based on frequency of term in document in inverse proportion to frequency of term in database. Terms that are more frequent in document and infrequent in database get higher weight. Some systems also count proximity of words, position of word in document, length of documents in assigning weights.	Based on linguistic analysis of text plus statistical weighting algorithms. Maps terms to synonyms. Interprets titles such as "Secretary of State" to person's name; expands geographic regions to include all sublocalities (e.g., U.S. includes names of states, cities, and counties). Interprets meaning from context instead of just string matching. Some systems find trends/predictions/opinions.
Matching	Exact matches only.	Exact and partial matches.	Exact, partial, and concept matches. Meaning matches based on position in sentence/paragraph/document.
Queries	Commands needed for good searching.	Keywords. Commands not necessary, but sometimes useful.	No commands necessary. Natural language input interprets full sentences/paragraphs.
Variant spelling/spelling errors	No results.	Fuzzy matching corrects some errors, British spellings in some systems. Important for searching full text from OCR output.	Fuzzy matching finds many errors, British spellings. Important for searching full text from OCR output.
Disambiguation	None. Get false drops.	False drops, but fewer because of lower co-occurrence of query terms. False drops usually receive less weight.	Disambiguation based on context. Feedback to user in some systems for clarification and chance to override the system.
Notes	Precise controlled vocabulary used by searcher and indexer important. Good query is imperative.	Retrieves citations or short entries, but full text or abstract is important to use features of system.	Retrieves citations and short entries, but full text or abstract is important to use features of system.

• Aids for distinguishing among types of information needs. The type of answer required should determine the information-finding process. Some questions require a quick factual answer. Others seek broad background information and expect large amounts of data to be returned. Decision support requires an analysis of retrieved data to determine patterns and recommendations. At present, each information-finding system offers a single standard response to every question. Flexibility in what kind of answer is returned would improve the utility of information retrieval systems.

ANSWER QUESTIONS RATHER THAN RETRIEVE WHOLE DOCUMENTS

Data mining and question-answering systems extract facts that are contained in a database and return them to the user in answer to a question. This differs from document retrieval by finding and extracting the actual information rather than retrieving an entire document that might contain that information. Particularly for answering direct questions, data mining saves the user time. In addition, data-mining systems seek to develop enough understanding of how the mind processes data to be able to duplicate some of its analytical abilities. While information retrieval systems have existed for some time, they simply dump retrieved data or documents in the user's lap. What the human mind adds to this compilation is organization and understanding. People are able to observe data and discern patterns. They use this talent in order to make informed decisions or to understand the nature of the world. Data-mining techniques that can find patterns as a human would are the subject at present of intensive research. This technology would be used for decision support and crisis management, both activities that require fast finding and processing of large amounts of data in order to make quick but reliable decisions.

DATA FUSION

As more and more information is organized into electronic libraries, we must develop tools that retrieve information from several sources at once and then merge those diverse materials into a single collection of results for the user. In addition, we find that each kind of search engine, particularly those that depend on different statistical algorithms, returns different results. Each appears to be more effective in answering some kinds of queries than others. The ability to discriminate among query types, to merge results, and to present results to the user in an easy-to-navigate merged set will improve the information-seeking process immeasurably.

We must improve our understanding of human intelligence and thought processes if this research is to be successful. The degree to which this knowledge can be translated into computer mimicry is unknown. However, the need for better aids to information finding and processing is acute. For that reason, research on information retrieval systems is a fertile field.

REFERENCES

1. F. W. Lancaster, *Information Retrieval Systems: Characteristics, Testing and Evaluation,* Wiley, NY, 1979.
2. T. Pritchard-Schoch, "Natural Language Comes of Age." *Online,* **17**(3), 33–43 (May 1994).
3. B. Shneiderman, *Designing the User Interface,* 3rd ed., Addison–Wesley, Reading, MA, 1997.
4. G. Marchionini, *Information Seeking in Electronic Environments,* Cambridge University Press, Cambridge, UK, 1995.

BIBLIOGRAPHY

Appraisal and Evaluation Library: Text-based Information Management Systems, CCTA, the Government Centre for Information Systems, Her Majesty's Stationer's Office, London, UK, 1991.

Barfield, L. *The User Interface: Concepts and Design,* Addison–Wesley, Reading, MA, 1994.

Bates, M. J. "Design for a Subject Search Interface and Online Thesaurus for a Very Large Records Management Database," *ASIS 90: Proceedings of the 53rd ASIS Annual Meeting,* Silver Springs, MD, 1990, pp. 20–28.

Bates, M. J. "Where Should the Person Stop and the Information Search Interface Start?" *Inform. Proc. Mgt.,* **26**(5), 575–591 (1990).

Benbasat, I. and Todd, P. "An Experimental Investigation of Interface Design Alternatives: Icon vs. Text and Direct Manipulation vs. Menus." *Internat. J. Man–Machine Stud.,* **38**, 369–402 (1993).

Blair, D. C. and Maron, M. E. "An Evaluation of Retrieval Effectiveness of a Full-Text Document Retrieval System." *Commun. ACM,* **28**(3), 289–299 (March 1985).

Borgman, C. "All Users of Information Retrieval Systems Are Not Created Equal: An Exploration into Individual Differences." *Inform. Proc. Mgt.,* **25**(3), 237–251 (1989).

Brenner, E. "Beyond Boolean—New Approaches to Information Retrieval," National Federation of Abstracting and Information Services, Philadelphia, 1996.

Brown, M. E. "Design for a Bibliographic Database for Non-Professional Users," in *ASIS '91: Proceedings of the 54th ASIS Annual Meeting,* J. M. Griffiths, ed. 1991, pp. 276–282.

Buchan, R. L. "Computer-Aided Indexing at NASA." *Ref. Librar.,* **18,** 269–277 (1987).

Crane, J. "Selection of a Text Retrieval System in Two User Environments." *J. Inform. Sci.,* **17**(2), 93–104 (1991).

Croft, W. B. "Approaches to Intelligent Information Retrieval." *Inform. Proc. Mgt.,* **23**(4), 249–254 (1987).

Dimitroff, A. and Wolfram, D. "Design Issues in a Hypertext-Based Information System for Bibliographic Retrieval," in *ASIS '93: Proceedings of the 56th ASIS Annual Meeting,* 1993, pp. 191–198.

Feldman, S. E. "Searching Natural Language Search Systems." *Searcher,* 34–39 (Oct. 1994).

Harman, D. K., ed. *The First Text Retrieval Conference (TREC-1),* National Institute of Standards and Technology, Bethesda, MD, March 1993 (available from NTIS: PB93–191641).

Hayes, P. J. and Koerner, G. "Intelligent Text Technologies and Their Successful Use by the Information Industry," in *Proceedings of the Fourteenth National Online Meeting, 1993,* Information Today, Medford, NJ, pp. 189–196.

Humphrey, S. M. and Chien, D.-C. *The MedIndEx System: Research on Interactive Knowledge-Based Indexing and Knowledge Base Management,* National Library of Medicine, Lister Hill Center for Biomedical Communication, Bethesda, MD, July 1990 (NLM–LHC–90–03; PB90–234964/AS).

Jacobs, P. S., ed. *Text-Based Intelligent Systems: Current Research and Practice in Information Extraction and Retrieval,* Lawrence Erlbaum, Hillsdale, NJ, 1992.

Jacobson, T. L. "Sense-making in a Database Environment," *Inform. Proc. Mgt.,* **27**(6), 647–657 (1991).

Kowalski, G. *Information Retrieval Systems: Theory and Implementation,* Kluwer, Boston, 1997.

Laurel, B., ed. *The Art of Human Computer Interface Design,* Addison–Wesley, Reading, MA, 1990.

Lenat, D. B. and Guha, R. V. *Building Large Knowledge-Based Systems: Representation and Inference in the Cyc Project,* Addison–Wesley, Reading, MA, 1990.

Lesk, M. *Practical Digital Libraries: Books, Bytes and Bucks,* Morgan Kaufmann, San Francisco, 1997.

Liddy, E. D., Paik, W., Yu, E. S., and McKenna, M. *Document Retrieval Using Linguistic Knowledge,* RIAO Proceedings, 1994.

Liddy, E. *Information Retrieval via Natural Language Processing or an Intelligent Digital Librarian,* paper presented at ASIS Midyear Conference, May 24, 1994.

Lundeen, G. W. and Tenopir, C. "Text Retrieval Software for Microcomputers and Beyond: An Overview and a Review of Four Packages." *Database,* **15**(4), 51–63 (Aug. 1992).

Lynch, C. A. "The Next Generation of Public Access Information Retrieval Systems for Research Libraries: Lessons from Ten Years of the MELVYL System," *Inform. Tech. Libr.,* **11**(4), 405–415 (Dec. 1992).

Marchionini, G., Dwiggins, S., Katz, A., and Lin, X. "Information Seeking in Full-Text End-User Oriented Search Systems: The Roles of Domain and Search Expertise." *Libr. Inform. Sci. Res.,* **15**, 35–69 (1993).

Martinez, C., Lucey, J., and Linder, E. "An Expert System for Machine-Aided Indexing." *J. Chem. Inform. Computer Sci.,* **27**, 158–162 (1987).

Meadow, C. T. *Text Information Retrieval Systems,* Academic Press, San Diego, CA, 1992.

Milstead, J. *Methodologies for Subject Analysis in Bibliographic Databases,* background paper, International Atomic Energy Agency and Energy Technology Data Exchange, EDTE, Oak Ridge, Tennessee, Sept. 24–26, 1990.

Rasmussen, E. M. *An Evaluation of Free Text and Controlled Vocabulary Searching for the Research in Progress Database,* OSTI, Report to U.S. Dept. of Energy, 1993.

Salton, G. *Automatic Text Processing: The Transformation, Analysis, and Retrieval of Information by Computer,* Addison–Wesley, Reading, MA, 1989.

Saracevic, T. "Individual Differences in Organizing, Searching, and Retrieving Information," in *ASIS '91: Proceedings of the 54th ASIS Annual Meeting,* 1991, Silver Springs, pp. 82–86.

Spink, A. and Greisdorf, H. "Partial Relevance Judgments and Changes in Users' Information Problems During Online Searching," Proceedings of 18th National Online Meeting, Information Today, Medford, NJ, 1997, pp. 323–334.

Tritschler, R. J. "Effective Information-Searching Without 'Perfect' Indexing." *Amer. Doc.* (July 1964).

Tufte, E. R. *Envisioning Information,* Graphics Press, Cheshire, CT, 1990.

SUSAN FELDMAN

SENSITIVITY ASPECTS OF INEQUALITY MEASURES

Introduction

It is intuitively easy to understand what is meant by inequality measures, because applications occur in very sensitive situations: rich versus poor persons or countries, or high productivity versus low productivity (in various aspects: economic, scientific, biological, etc.). Inequality applies to virtually every aspect of human and nonhuman life. It is therefore not surprising that one wishes to measure "degrees" of inequality. Such inequality measures (also called concentration measures) have the property that the larger the value, the more unequal (uneven, concentrated) the situation is. Usually these measures are "normalized" so that they range between 0 and 1, but this is not necessary.

Sometimes one is not interested in the degree of inequality but in the opposite aspect: how even a situation is (e.g., in biology when one is interested in the diversity of species that are available). Large concentrations of some species imply the rare (or non-) occurrence of other species and this is considered as an impoverishment of the situation. However, a special theory on evenness measures or diversity measures is only needed if one wants to study specific problems in specific domains of the sciences (e.g., in biodiversity studies). General aspects of these evenness measures indeed follow immediately from the analog ones of concentration measures. Indeed, let f be a concentration measure bounded by, for example, 0 and 1. Then it is intuitively clear that

$$g = 1 - f \tag{1}$$

is an evenness measure (e.g., the most concentrated situation gives $f = 1$ and hence $g = 0$, and the most even situation gives $f = 0$ and hence $g = 1$).

Therefore, we will limit ourselves mainly to the study of concentration measures, also because in computer science and technology and in information theory it is far more important to study inequality than to study equality. The intuitive reason for this is clear: the more unequal a situation is, the better we can exploit this in order to optimize certain situations. Let us give an example. The more unequal symbols or words occur in a "text," the better this text can be compressed by giving the shorter codes (e.g., binary codes) to these symbols or words that occur most. An example of application is the Huffman compression technique, which we will discuss briefly in the context of entropy.

Unequal situations are often encountered in the information sciences. Only a few scientists are prolific (publish a lot), but many publish little; a scientific discipline has only a few "top journals," whereas many journals occasionally publish in this area. In linguistics, computer sciences, and information sciences, one has the law of Zipf stating that the occurrence of words in a text (the tokens, as one says in linguistics) is inversely proportional to the rank of this word ("type" in linguistics; rank according to the occurrence of this word in the text).

Unequal situations can be explained by studying probabilistic properties such as the so-called success breeds success principle that states (simplifying) that prolific sources have a higher probability to produce a new item than less prolific ones. In this article, we do not go into these probabilistic aspects; we limit our attention to the problem of "how to measure inequality."

For more on these probabilistic aspects of inequality, we refer the reader to Refs. *1* and *2,* and references therein.

Principles of Inequality

BASIC PRINCIPLES

In the sequel, we will use the terminology of sources that produce items (e.g., words and their uses in texts, authors producing publications). We want to measure the degree of inequality (i.e., the degree of the differences in production quantities of these sources). Related to this, one could mention the so-called 80/20 rule which states that 20 percent of the most prolific sources produce 80 percent of all items. Of course, in general other numbers might occur. It is clear that a 90/10 result gives a more concentrated situation than a 80/20 result, whereas a 70/25 result is more even. Not directly comparable with 80/20 is, for example, a 90/30 result. We will go into this later.

These "generalized" 80/20 rules will be encountered in the sequel as an application of our more general framework in which we want to produce a single number that measures concentration (rather than two as above).

Let us define some notation. Let N be the total number of sources. For source $i \in \{1, \dots, N\}$, denote by x_i, its production $(x_i \in \mathrm{R}^+)$. It is clear that a concentration measure must be a function of the N-tuple $(x_1, \dots, x_N)$, preferably with positive values:

$$f: (x_1, \dots, x_N) \to f(x_1, \dots, x_N) \in \mathrm{R}^+.$$

We will assume (although it is not strictly necessary) that the values of f are bounded (i.e., $\min f$ and $\max f$ exist in R). Most commonly these are 0 and 1 and it will be clear from the sequel that any good bounded concentration measures can be transformed into one in which $\min f = 0$ and $\max f = 1$. These situations must occur in the following cases. Let $X = (x, 0, \dots, 0)$ [i.e., one source (here the first one) produces everything $(x \in \mathrm{R}^+)$], then $f(X) = 1$. In the other extreme, if $Y = (y, y, \dots , y)$ $(y \in \mathrm{R}^+)$ (i.e., all sources produce the same quantity y), then $f(Y) = 0$. We will call this principle (Z), if $x > 0$, then:

$$f(x, \dots, 0) = 1 \tag{2}$$

[or, more generally, $\max f(X)$, where the maximum is taken over all $X = (x_1, \dots, x_N)$ such that $\sum_{i=1}^{N} x_i = x$] and

$$f(y, y, \dots, y) = 0 \tag{3}$$

[or, more generally, $\min f(X)$, where the minimum is taken over all $X = (x_1, \dots, x_N)$ for which $\sum_{i=1}^{N} x_i = Ny$, hence $\overline{X} = y$, where $\overline{X}$ denotes the average of the values $x_1, \dots, x_N$].

The next principle is called "permutation invariance" and is denoted by (P). It states that concentration is not a labeled property; that is, the concentration value is not changed if, for example, names of persons are interchanged. Formulated exactly, we state that for every $(x_1, \dots, x_N)$ and every permutation π

$$\pi: \{1, 2, \dots, N\} \to \{1, 2, \dots, N\}$$

of the numbers $1, \dots, N$, we have that

$$f(x_1, \dots, x_N) = f(x_{\pi(1)}, \dots, x_{\pi(N)}). \tag{4}$$

Concentration measures should be "normalized" w.r.t. (with respect to) the total production $\sum_{i=1}^{N} x_i$. Indeed, we need, for example, to compare the concentration of words in texts, and this comparison may not be dependent on the size of the text;

independent of the size of the database, one should indeed be able to determine the optimal compression technique. It is even so that the size of a database is not always known or at least cannot be predicted (e.g., when considering the growth of such databases). An example from econometrics also illustrates this principle very clearly. Concentration must be independent of the units; for example, when measuring wealth, the value of f must be independent of the currency used (U.S. dollars, yen, pound, Euro, etc.). This principle is called "scale invariance" (S): For every $(x_1, \ldots, x_N)$ and every $c > 0$,

$$f(cx_1, \ldots, cx_N) = f(x_1, \ldots, x_N). \tag{5}$$

Last but not least, at the real heart of concentration theory it should be obvious that "if one takes away from the poor and gives it to the rich, inequality concentration must increase." Obviously, this principle is called the "transfer principle" (T); for every $(x_1, \ldots, x_N)$ and if $i, j \in \{1, \ldots, N\}$ are such that $x_i \leq x_j$, and if $0 < h \leq x_i$, then

$$f(x_1, \ldots, x_i - h, \ldots, x_j + h, \ldots, x_N) > f(x_1, \ldots, x_i, \ldots, x_j, \ldots, x_N) \tag{6}$$

(h is the amount that is taken away from the "poorer" source i and given to the "richer" source j). This is a very natural principle. It also includes several other principles:

Principle (R): If the richest gets richer, inequality increases: For every $(x_1, \ldots, x_N)$, if $x_i = \max\{x_1, \ldots, x_N\}$ and if there exists a $k \neq i$ such that $x_k \neq 0$, then, for every $h > 0$.

$$f(x_1, \ldots, x_i + h, \ldots, x_N) > f(x_1, \ldots, x_i, \ldots, x_N) \tag{7}$$

Principle (N): The principle of the nominal increase: For every $(x_1, \ldots, x_N)$ where not all x_i are equal, and every $h > 0$,

$$f(x_1 + h, \ldots, x_N + h) < f(x_1, \ldots, x_N). \tag{8}$$

All these principles are in accordance with our intuitive feeling about inequality. Of course, independent of all these principles, one is not yet sure that such functions f exist. That they exist (abundantly) will be clear in the sequel. As stated, (T) $\Rightarrow$ (R) and (T) $\Rightarrow$ (N), therefore, we only consider the set of principles

$$(B) = \{(Z), (P), (S), (T)\} \tag{9}$$

and consider (B) as a minimum requirement for a good concentration measure. Further refinements of principle (T) will lead to finer requirements for concentration measures and hence to a reduction of their quantity. This will be the main purpose of this survey article: feeling the sensitivity of concentration measures with respect to diverse transfer principles such as (T).

THE LORENZ CURVE AND LORENZ ORDER

The Lorenz curve and order are two of the most important findings in contemporary mathematics with basic applications in concentration theory. The concept is simple and beautiful. Let us consider one situation $X = (x_1, \ldots, x_N)$; N sources where source i has a production of x_i items. Consider the "normalized" vector

$$A_x = (a_1, \ldots, a_N),$$

where, for every $i = 1, \ldots, N$,

$$a_i = \frac{x_i}{\displaystyle\sum_{k=1}^{N} x_k}. \tag{10}$$

Then consider the set of points

$$\left(\frac{i}{N}, \sum_{j=1}^{i} a_j \right) \tag{11}$$

(i.e., the cumulative fraction of the items in the first i sources). Let us suppose that X is decreasing (if it is not, a rearrangement of the coordinates in X will yield a decreasing vector, still called X). In this case, by interconnecting the points in the term Eq. (*11*), and linking the first point with $(0, 0)$ yields a concavely increasing polygonal curve. For example, Fig. 1 shows the Lorenz curve for the vector $X = (1, 4, 3, 10)$, rearranged to yield a decreasing vector $(10, 4, 3, 1)$. We could, of course, also consider increasing vectors. In this case, our Lorenz curve is convexly increasing, being the mirror image of the first one over the diagonal [connecting $(0, 0)$ and $(1, 1)$] of the unit square.

That the Lorenz curve has something to offer to concentration theory is already clear from its very definition. It contains all applicable forms of the so-called 80/20 rule. Indeed, every vertical line indicates an abscissa x which corresponds with an ordinate y given by the Lorenz curve. Hence, a $100y/100x$ rule is obtained and this for every value of $x \in [0, 1]$.

In informetrics, one has the so-called Bradford curves. (See Ref. *1.*) They are nothing else than the Lorenz curves, but where the fractions are replaced by their counts (i.e., i versus $\sum_{j=1}^{i} x_j$) and where the ordinates are given in a logarithmic scale. The use of these so-called semilogarithmic scales yielded additional information on the type of bibliography (here sources are journals and items are the articles in these journals) under study. For more on this, we refer the reader to Ref. *1.*

We are now in a position to introduce the Lorenz order between two vectors $X = (x_1, \ldots, x_N)$ and $X' = (x'_1, \ldots, x'_N)$. We suppose that both X and X' are decreasing and that

$$\sum_{i=1}^{N} x_i = \sum_{i=1}^{N} x'_i.$$

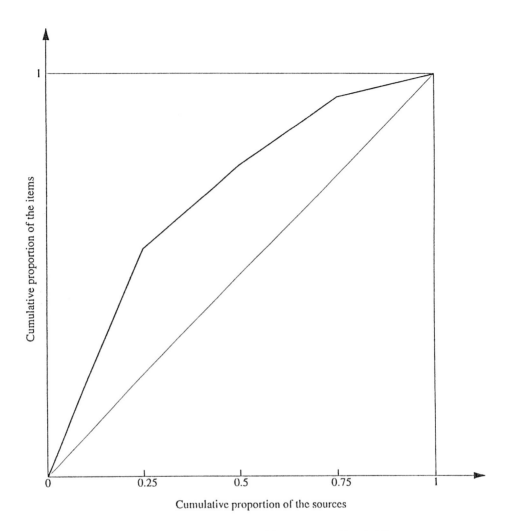

FIGURE 1. *The Lorenze curve of the vector* X = *(1, 4, 3, 10).*

Then we say that X' dominates X (in notation $X \prec X'$ or $X' \succ X$) if

$$\sum_{i=1}^{j} x_i \leq \sum_{i=1}^{j} x_i'. \tag{12}$$

for every $j = 1, \ldots, N - 1$. Because

$$\sum_{i=1}^{N} x_i = \sum_{i=1}^{N} x_i'.$$

inequality (12) is also valid for $j = N$. Because of this equality and by Eq. (10), we have now that $X \prec X'$ if and only if the Lorenz curve of X is always below the one of X'

(i.e., the Lorenz curve of X never intersects the one of X'). The order expressed by $\prec$ (a partial order) is called the Lorenz order.

The Lorenz order is very important in mathematics (e.g., in the study of convex function inequalities, geometric inequalities, combinatorial analysis, and matrix theory; for more on this, see Ref. *3*). The importance for the topic discussed in this article will become apparent from the next definition and theorem.

Let f be a function as above. We say that f satisfies principle (L) if it satisfies principles (Z), (P), and (S) and whenever $X = (x_1, \ldots, x_N) \prec X' = (x_1', \ldots, x_N')$ and $X \neq X'$, we have

$$f(X) < f(X').\tag{13}$$

Functions for which $X \prec X'$ implies $f(X) \leq f(X')$ are sometimes called Schur convex functions.

Theorem: (L) *is equivalent to* (B).

In other words, the preservation by f of the Lorenz dominance order is equivalent to the transfer principle. The Transfer principle was hinted at by Pigou (*4*) in 1912, but was first exactly described by Dalton in 1920 (*5*). The Lorenz curve was introduced in Ref. *6* in 1905. The Lorenz order was introduced (as notation and terminology) by Hardy et al. (*7*). It is therefore a bit surprising to state that the above theorem was essentially known (of course, in other terminology) by Muirhead in 1903; see Ref. *8* and also Ref. *9*.

The above theorem offers a geometric "visualization" of what is required of a good concentration measure. It summarizes in one graph and one notation ($\prec$) of what, more or less, concentration is all about.

Of course, all the definitions and results mentioned so far are empty if we cannot give concrete examples of good inequality measures.

Concentration Measures

Let $X = (x_1, \ldots, x_N)$ be an arbitrary vector.

THE COEFFICIENT OF VARIATION V

This is the most well-known concentration measure. This measure V is defined as the quotient of the standard deviation σ of X and of the average (mean) μ of X:

$$V = \frac{\sigma}{\mu}.\tag{14}$$

Recall that

$$\mu = \frac{1}{N} \sum_{i=1}^{N} x_i$$

and that

$$\sigma^2 = \frac{1}{N} \sum_{i=1}^{N} (x_i - \mu)^2 = \frac{1}{N} \sum_{i=1}^{N} x_i^2 - \mu^2.$$

THE YULE CHARACTERISTIC K

This measure is derived from V:

$$K = \frac{V^2}{N}. \tag{15}$$

The measure is used in linguistics.

PRATT'S MEASURE AND THE GINI INDEX

We suppose here that X is decreasing.
Denote

$$q = \sum_{i=1}^{N} ia_i$$

with a_i as in Eq. (10). Then Pratt's measure C is defined as

$$C = \frac{2[((N + 1)/2 - q)]}{N - 1} \tag{16}$$

and Gini's index by

$$G = \frac{N - 1}{N} C. \tag{17}$$

It must, however, be remarked that Gini's index was introduced in 1909 in econometrics (see Ref. *10*), long before Pratt's measure was, namely in 1977 (see Ref. *11*), the latter one in informetrics. Originally, the Gini index G was defined as twice the area between the Lorenz curve and the straight line joining (0, 0) and (1, 1); (i.e., the Lorenz curve of a uniform distribution). That they are essentially the same [see Eq. (17) with N usually very high] was only seen in 1979. (See Ref. *12.*) This is a typical example of "reinventing the wheel," not so surprising with this highly interdisciplinary subject!

The measures V, C, and G are generalized as follows. Define, for $r \geq 1$,

$$P(r) = \frac{\left\{ [1/2N(N - 1)] \sum_{i,j=1}^{N} |x_i - x_j|^r \right\}^{1/r}}{\mu}, \tag{18}$$

the so-called generalized Pratt measure, essentially introduced in Ref. *13*. It can be shown (see Ref. *14*) that

$$P(1) = C \text{ and } P(2) = \sqrt{\frac{N}{N-1}} V.$$

THEIL'S MEASURES Th AND L

These measures were introduced in 1967 in Ref. *15* as follows:

$$Th = \frac{1}{N} \sum_{i=1}^{N} \left(\frac{x_i}{\mu}\right) \ell n \left(\frac{x_i}{\mu}\right) \tag{19}$$

and

$$L = -\left(\ell n(N) + \frac{1}{N} \sum_{i=1}^{N} \ell n(a_i)\right), \tag{19'}$$

again with a_i as in Eq. (10).

We close this nonexhaustive list with the Atkinson indices.

THE ATKINSON INDICES $A(e)$

For $0 < e < 1$, define

$$A(e) = 1 - \left[\frac{1}{N} \sum_{i=1}^{N} \left(\frac{x_i}{\mu}\right)^{1-e}\right]^{1/(1-e)} \tag{20}$$

and for $e = 1$

$$A(1) = 1 - \frac{(x_1 \cdots x_N)^{1/N}}{\mu}; \tag{21}$$

see Ref. *16*. As is clear from the above, most of these measures originate from econometrics or sociometrics.

We refer to Ref. *14* for the proofs that all these measures satisfy principle (L) and hence are to be considered good concentration measures.

Note 1: The Theil measures are also called Theil's entropy measures. Indeed, they resemble the well-known average entropy formula (known in information theory)

$$\overline{H} = -\sum_{i=1}^{N} a_i \log_2 a_i. \tag{22}$$

Stated in this form, $\overline{H}$ is a valuable measure but is not a concentration measure; it is a measure of evenness. Of course, upon normalization and the application of the tranformation (Eq. 1), we obtain a concentration measure. Do not be mistaken; the measures Th and L *are* concentration measures.

Note 2: So far we have always supposed that N is fixed. This, of course, excludes dynamic studies of concentration (or evenness or diversity) because if time is variable, N is variable too, in most cases. Especially in biology, the variability of N has an implication on possibilities of studying diversity of species. We assume that the N variability is less important in computer science and technology as well as in informetrics; there one can still compare concentration values of, for example, databases of different sizes and draw professional conclusions based on these comparisons. An example of this is given in the next section.

N-dependent theories can be developed as follows. It is clear that it is possible to draw a Lorenz curve for any vector $X = (x_1, \ldots, x_N)$ and any N. Now we generalize the Lorenz order, introduced earlier (see Ref. *12*) by stating that the N vector X dominates the N' vector X' if the Lorenze curve of X' never lies above the Lorenz curve of X. This will be denoted as $X' \prec\!\!< X$. This requirement generalizes the partial order introduced for fixed N.

A good concentration measure should respect this generalized Lorenz order. This means that such a concentration measure f should satisfy the following relation:

$$X' \neq X \text{ and } X' \prec\!\!< X \Rightarrow f(X') < f(X). \tag{23}$$

Related to this, we introduce the cell-replication axiom (introduced by Dalton, Ref. *5*). First, we define the mathematical operator REPEAT$_c$, with c a nonzero natural number, as

$$\text{REPEAT}_c(x_1, \ldots, x_N) = (x_1, \ldots, x_1, x_2, \ldots, x_2, x_N, \ldots, x_N), \tag{24}$$

where every x_i is repeated c times. Then, a function f satisfies the cell-replication axiom if

$$f(\text{REPEAT}_c(X)) = f(X). \tag{25}$$

Note that the Lorenz curve of X and of REPEAT$_c(X)$ coincide, so that this is a very natural requirement.

It can be shown in Ref. *17* that if a function is a good concentration measure for fixed N and moreover satisfies the cell-replication axiom, then it satisfies relation (23).

Now, the coefficient of variation V, the Gini index G, Theil's measures Th and L, and all Atkinson indices $A(e)$ satisfy this additional requirement, hence they can be used to compare situations in which the number of sources is different. The Yule characteristic K and Pratt's measure C on the other hand, do not satisfy this additional axiom.

Finally, we note that it is possible to introduce other requirements to compare situations with a different number of sources. These requirements take the number of sources explicitly into account (*17*).

Some Applications in Computer Science, Information Science, and Linguistics

HUFFMAN COMPRESSION OF CODES

It is obvious that the occurrence of words in texts is very dependent on the words; some words occur very often (e.g., the, a, of, for) for grammatical reasons and some only occur a few times. It is then logical (and it is so in most cases) that the words that occur more often should be the shortest ones. This is often the case in natural language, although not in an optimal way. It is for this reason that one often uses abbreviations, acronyms, and so forth.

In the same way, codes for symbols should be shorter if the symbols occur more often than others. Let us give an example with an alphabet of only eight symbols (A, B, C, D, E, F, G, H). As is always the case in practice, we will suppose that these symbols do not occur the same number of times. Suppose we have already ordered the symbols in decreasing order of occurrence. Suppose their fraction (probability) of occurrence is as follows: A, 0.338; B, 0.203; C, 0.135; D, 0.088; E, 0.081; F, 0.061; G. 0.054; H, 0.040.

For the sake of simplicity we only look at binary coding of these eight symbols, but any n-ary coding can be studied in the same way. It is clear that binary codes of length 3 suffice, as $2^3 = 8$. We could then code these eight symbols as follows: A = $\phi\phi\phi$, B = $\phi\phi1$, C = $\phi1\phi$, D = $\phi11$, E = $1\phi\phi$, F = $1\phi1$, G = 11ϕ, and H = 111, hence the average length per symbol is 3. There is, however, the following theorem, which can be used to decrease the average length required to code this alphabet.

Theorem (Huffman, Ref. *18*). *There exists a non-fixed-length decodable coding which is optimal in the sense that no shorter average length per symbol is possible. The average length per symbol of this coding is $\overline{H}$ as given by formula* (22).

This coding is called the Huffman coding. In the above example, one can calculate (using $a_1 = 0.338$, $a_2 = 0.203$, and so on, and $N = 8$, of course) that $\overline{H} = 2.65 < 3$. One cannot give the "shortest" binary coding A = ϕ, B = 1, C = $\phi\phi$, D = $\phi1$, E = 1ϕ, F = 11, G = $1\phi\phi$, and H = $1\phi1$ because this coding is not decodable. The (up to a permutation of ϕ and 1) unique solution is A = $\phi\phi$, B = 1ϕ, C = $\phi11$, D = 111, E = $\phi1\phi\phi$, F = $\phi1\phi1$, G = $11\phi\phi$, and H = $11\phi1$, with the average length per symbol equal to 2.7, very close to 2.65 and a serious improvement (i.e., compression) w.r.t. the fixed-length coding with length 3. There is a simple algorithm to find this solution. The reader is referred to Ref. *19* for this as well as for much more on the compression of texts. Note that the Huffman coding is decodable, as no code is the beginning of a larger code, so it is clear that the text $\phi11111111\phi11\phi\phi\phi11\phi111\phi\phi$ is uniquely decodable as CDDCAAHG.

ZIPF'S LAW AND MANDELBROT'S LAW

One can ask the question: How do we obtain the probabilities (fractions) for the occurrence of the symbols as in the above example? More generally, how can we know the fraction of occurrence of the different words or letters in a text? The general answer is that this can be done statistically by sampling and then calculating confidence intervals for these sampled fractions. We must warn the reader that calculating confidence intervals for a large number of fractions requires very high sample sizes. (See Ref. 20.) If this cannot be executed, we can put all our hopes to known distributions of these multinomial fractions. They will give a good approximation of the concrete situations of the text and hence (also because the Huffman technique is very stable w.r.t. the initial input parameters; i.e., the fractions of occurrence) will yield an optimal or at least a quasi-optimal compression of the text. We will discuss two "classical" distributions.

The Law of Zipf

The law of Zipf (*21, 22*) is a distribution that is encountered in linguistics. It states that if one orders the words in a text in decreasing order of their occurrence in this text, then the number of occurrences is inversely proportional to its rank. In mathematical notation, if r denotes the rank of the word and $y(r)$ the fraction of the number of times this word occurs in the text, then

$$y(r) = \frac{C}{r}, \tag{26}$$

where C is a constant for the text. It is clear that formula (26) expresses the unequal occurrence of words in the text. In Ref. *23*, I calculated the measure of Pratt, expressing the degree of concentration and found, for example, for a text of 10,000 words, a value of $C = 0.80$.

The Law of Mandelbrot

Even in linguistics, it is clear that the law of Zipf is not always valid. Often one finds better approximations (of the data derived from the text) by using an extra parameter [e.g., r^a instead of r in formula (26)]. Of a different nature is the law of Mandelbrot (*24, 25*). Stated more generally in terms of sources and items, it can be formulated as follows: if we rank the sources in decreasing order of the number of items they produce and if r denotes the rank of the source and $y(r)$ its fraction of the total production, then

$$y(r) = \frac{A}{1 + Br}, \tag{27}$$

where A and B are constants. This law is encountered very often in informetrics (e.g., when describing inequality in publication patterns by authors or journals in a certain field). For this law, one finds the value $C = 0.61$ for Pratt's measure of inequality (again for 10,000 sources).

We see that this value is much lower than the one found for Zipf's law, hence Zipf's law expresses a more concentrated situation than Mandelbrot's. This result is somewhat surprising but can be explained—philosophically—as follows. In all situations in which Zipf's or Mandelbrot's law applies, we clearly deal with an unequal situation; few sources produce a lot of items and many sources produce only a few. In cases in which Mandelbrot's law applies, however, the most prolific sources refrain their high production a bit. This is so in the case of author–publication patterns—here the most prolific authors will only publish their best work. This is also the case in the journal–article pattern—the more important a journal develops in a certain discipline the most strict (by applying heavy refereeing procedures) it will be in accepting papers for publication. This is not so in, for example, texts (in which Zipf's law usually applies); the most heavily used words continue to be used in that pace, no matter how long the text is, due to grammatical reasons. This creates the more concentrated situation, which is not a adverse result from the point of view of compression of the text—the use of many small words and possibly of abbreviations (e.g., Prof., Dr.) of heavily used words that are somewhat longer.

In the same way, one also finds the following result on the generalized 80/20 rule: the higher the average number of items per source, the smaller the fraction of the most prolific sources one needs in order to have a fixed cumulative fraction of the items. This has applications in libraries; the higher the average number of circulations per book (say per year) in a library, the smaller the fraction of the most heavily used books needed to cover, say, 95 percent of all circulations. In other words (as is the case in public libraries as compared to scientific libraries), the weeding problem is easier in such libraries, as there a larger fraction (now of the least-used books) can be taken that accounts for a very low fixed percentage of the circulation. In general, one could also say that the higher the average number of items per source, the higher the Lorenz curve situated in the unit square.

In the next section, we will study some refinements of the transfer principle (T), as it is the basis in concentration theory. Most of these refinements go in the direction of the study of sensitivity properties of concentration measures with respect to transfers.

Other Transfer Principles and Sensitivity with Respect to Transfers

The classical transfer principle (T) deals with "taking away from one poor and giving it to one rich." Of course, as is also reflected in the theorem in the subsection "The Lorenz Curve and Lorenz Order," consecutive compositions of bilateral transfers are possible, yielding the same inequality for our concentration measure f, but real life is more complicated! It can be that—to stay within the appealing econometric terminology—many transfers of different types happen (from poor to rich sources but also vice-versa) but with an overall bonus to the richer sources. The next transfer principle, stronger than (T), goes in this direction.

THE TRANSFER PRINCIPLES $E(p)$

It is immediately verified that the change of $X = (x_1, \ldots, x_i, \ldots, x_j, \ldots, x_N)$ into $X' = (x_1, \ldots, x_i - h, \ldots, x_j + h, \ldots, x_N)$, where $x_i \leq x_j$ and where $0 < h \leq x_i$ [as in the definition of the transfer principle (T)], implies that the variance of the vector X' is strictly larger than the variance of the vector X, hence a good generalization of principle (T), possibly affecting all sources, is as follows. (See Ref. 9).

Let f be as always. We say that it satisfies the principle $E(p)$ $(p \geq 1)$ if for every $X = (x_1, \ldots, x_N)$ and $X' = (x_1', \ldots, x_N')$ such that

$$\sum_{i=1}^{N} x_j = \sum_{i=1}^{N} x_j'$$

and such that

$$\sum_{i,j=1}^{N} |x_i - x_j|^p < \sum_{i,j=1}^{N} |x_i' - x_j'|^p, \tag{28}$$

we have that

$$f(x_1, \ldots, x_N) < f(x_1', \ldots, x_N'). \tag{29}$$

Note that

$$\frac{1}{2N^2} \sum_{i,j=1}^{N} |x_i - x_j|^p \tag{30}$$

is the p variance of the vector X and also that it is equal to σ^2 if $p = 2$. The above definition can even be extended by replacing the function $x \to |x|^p$ by any convex function. In Ref. 9, it is shown that $E(p) \Rightarrow (T)$ for every $p \geq 1$; hence we have at our disposal a stronger transfer principle. The concentration measures encountered so far, which also satisfy a principle $E(p)$ $(p \geq 1)$, are thus stronger (better) measures than those that satisfy (T) but not $E(p)$.

Obviously, V and K satisfy $E(2)$, and in Ref. 14 it was shown that C and G satisfy $E(1)$ [in essence because $P(1) = C$, with $P(1)$ as in Eq. (18) with $r = 1$]. Obviously, $P(r)$ satisfies $E(r)$ for every $r \geq 1$. That any $E(p)$ is strictly stronger than (T) follows from the fact that neither Th nor $A(e)$ $(0 < e < 1)$ satisfy any $E(p)$, whereas they all satisfy (T). It is shown in Ref. 26 that the validity of one $E(p)$ $(p \geq 1)$ excludes the validity of any $E(q)$ $(q \geq 1, q \neq p)$ at least if $N \geq 3$, which is always the case in practice. It is also so for $N = 3$ except for $p = 2$, $q = 4$, as here $E(2) = E(4)$. Because $E(2)$ relates to the classical variance, we could consider it to be the most important $E(p)$ principle, and hence we can consider V, K, or other from V-derived measures to be the most important concentration measures. Also, its formulation $V = \sigma\mu$ is very simple. The principle $E(2)$ is equivalent with the following desirable transfer principle. Let $X = (x_1, \ldots, x_N)$ and $X' = (x_1', \ldots, x_N')$ be such that $x_i' = x_i + h_i$ $(i = 1, \ldots, N)$ with

$$\sum_{i=1}^{N} h_i = 0$$

and such that

$$\sum_{i=1}^{N} h_i(x_i + x_i') \geq 0. \tag{31}$$

If $X \neq X'$ then

$$f(x_1, \ldots, x_N) < f(x_1', \ldots, x_N').$$

The proof can be found in Ref. *9.*

SENSITIVITY ASPECTS OF INEQUALITY MEASURES WITH RESPECT TO TRANSFERS

It is very difficult to express what is meant by "sensitivity" of inequality measures. It is a "second-order" aspect, describing how dependent a measure is w.r.t. a transfer (apart from the fact that we have a strict inequality).* Let us go back to the original definition of the transfer principle (T). It states that when $x_i \leq x_j$ and when $0 < h \leq x_i$,

$$f(x_1, \ldots, x_i, \ldots, x_j, \ldots, x_N) < f(x_1, \ldots, x_i - h, \ldots, x_j + h, \ldots, x_N). \tag{32}$$

In this formulation, it is in no way stated how the difference

$$\Delta f = f(x_1, \ldots, x_i - h, \ldots, x_j + h, \ldots, x_N) - f(x_1, \ldots, x_N)$$

is dependent on x_i or i or x_j or j or even $x_j - x_i$ or $j - i$, and so forth (dependence on the indices presupposes, of course, a certain ordering of the x_i's). Discussions around this theme in econometrics can be found in Ref. *16* and for sociometrics in Ref. *13.* In Ref. *27,* Allison pleads for measures that are sensitive for differences (such as $x_j - x_i$). This plea is given in the context of publications and citations, and indeed it is our feeling that sensitivity must be studied within the context of the application.

In Ref. *14,* one found that ΔV^2 is linearly dependent on $x_j - x_i$ but independent of i or j. Dependence of the latter is found for ΔG and ΔC, whereas, not surprisingly, ΔTh is dependent on $\ell n(x_j) - \ell n(x_i)$.

We will now look at (T) in another way. It is an easy consequence of (T) that [by applying inequality (32) $N - 1$ times] (supposing $x_1 = \max\{x_i; i = 1, \ldots, N\}$ and using property (P), this can always be realized)

$$f(x_1, \ldots, x_N) < f\left(x_1 + h, x_2 - \frac{h}{N-1}, \ldots, x_N - \frac{h}{N-1}\right) \tag{33}$$

---

*We do not deal with statistical sensitivity (e.g., the dependence of the sensitivity of statistical methods w.r.t. the sample size).

if $0 < h < \min\{(N - 1)x_i; i = 1, \ldots, N\}$.

This principle is related to moonlighting; one source (here the first one) gets richer (e.g., by not paying taxes), which is detrimental to all other citizens. In scientometrics, we have an example whereby the most important research group in a certain domain is recognized by a subsidizing authority (such as a government), thereby donating an important amount of money to this group, which is then not available any more for all the other groups.

Now it is clear that inequality (33) is rather artificial. What happens if the second largest source grows at the cost of all the others, and so on? It is intuitive that if x_1 is "above average production," then inequality (33) should be valid. What average can we use? This will become clear in the sequel. Let us fix some notation. Let $X = (x_1, x_2, \ldots, x_N)$ be rearranged in such a way that the transfer h occurs at the first source (not necessarily any more the source with maximum production). Denote

$$Y = \left(1, -\frac{1}{N-1}, -\frac{1}{N-1}, \ldots, -\frac{1}{N-1}\right), \tag{34}$$

where there are $N - 1$ coordinates with value $-1/(N - 1)$. Then inequality (33) is equivalent to

$$f(X + hY) - f(X) > 0. \tag{35}$$

This only compares two situations: X (before the transfer) and $X' = X + hY$ (after the transfer). In these cases, a total transfer of $h > 0$ is involved and the inequalities should change if $h < 0$, and furthermore any small $|h|$ can be used. This boils down to calculating (for every "small" h)

$$\frac{f(X + hY) - f(X)}{h} \tag{36}$$

and examining the sign of this number, now irrespective of the sign of h. This leads to the use of the directional derivative.

$$f'(X; Y) = \lim_{h \to 0} \frac{f(X + hY) - f(X)}{h}$$
$$= \sum_{i=1}^{N} \frac{\partial f}{\partial x_i}(X)y_i,$$

where $Y = (y_1, \ldots, y_N)$ as in Eq. (34), hence,

$$f'(X; Y) = \frac{\partial f}{\partial x_1}(X) - \frac{1}{N-1} \sum_{i=2}^{N} \frac{\partial f}{\partial x_i}(X). \tag{37}$$

This leads us to several new transfer principles (which will lead us to the notion of sensitivity). Let $M(X)$ denote any average (arithmetic, geometric, harmonic, median, etc.). We say that f satisfies transfer principle (T_M) if $x_1 > M(X)$ implies

$$f'(X; Y) > 0 \tag{38}$$

This transfer principle has been introduced in Ref. *28*. Also in Ref. *28* it is noted that the value of $f'(X; Y)$ is a measure for the sensitivity of f w.r.t. transfers. Note that the sign of $f'(X; Y)$ changes for evenness measures and hence the value of $f'(X: Y)$ [or rather $|f'(X; Y)|$] can also be used for evenness measures. Here, however, we restrict ourselves to concentration measures.

Let us fix some notations for the different averages of a vector $X = (x_1, \ldots, x_N)$.

$$\mu = \frac{1}{N} \sum_{i=1}^{N} x_i \tag{39}$$

the arithmetic mean,

$$g = (x_1 \cdots x_N)^{1/N} \tag{40}$$

the geometric mean,

$$h = \frac{N}{\sum_{i=1}^{N} \left(\frac{1}{x_i}\right)} \tag{41}$$

the harmonic mean, and by m the median; that is, x_m for which

$$m = \frac{N + 1}{2} \tag{42}$$

(and in case N is even, take the average of the two middle x_i-values).

In these cases, we can talk of the transfer principles (T_μ), (T_g), (T_h), and (T_m).

In Ref. *28*, the following theorem has been proved, based on EQ. (34) and inequality (35).

Theorem

$$(1) \quad V'(X; Y) = \frac{1/(\mu\sqrt{N})}{\sqrt{\sum_{i=1}^{N} (x_i - \mu)^2}} \left((x_1 - \mu) - \sum_{i=2}^{N} \frac{(x_i - \mu)}{N - 1} \right). \tag{43}$$

Hence, V satisfies (T_μ). Hence, also, K satisfies (T_μ).

$$(2) \quad Th'(X; Y) = \frac{1}{N\mu} \left[\left(\ell n\left(\frac{x_1}{\mu}\right) + \mu \right) - \frac{1}{N - 1} \sum_{i=2}^{N} \left(\ell n\left(\frac{x_1}{\mu}\right) + \mu \right) \right]. \tag{44}$$

Hence, Th satisfies (T_g).

$$(3) \quad L'(X;Y) = -\frac{1}{N}\left(\frac{1}{x_1} - \frac{1}{N-1}\sum_{i=2}^{N}\frac{1}{x_i}\right). \tag{45}$$

Hence, L satisfies (T_h). Also, $A(1)$ satisfies (T_h).

$$(4) \quad G'(X;Y) = -\frac{2(N+1-i)}{\mu N^2} + \frac{2}{\mu N^2(N-1)}\sum_{j\neq i}(N+1-j). \tag{46}$$

Hence, G satisfies (T_m). Hence, also, C satisfies (T_m).

The respective values of $f'(X;Y)$ for $f = $ V, Th, L, or G give the sensitivity of these measures w.r.t. transfers. To the best of our knowledge, Ref. *28* is the first time that a connection has been found between these classical measures of concentration and these different averages of a vector $X = (x_1, \ldots, x_N)$. In Ref. *28*, some other concentration measures have been linked with some other (T_M) transfer properties (for generalized averages M).

This theory of sensitivity w.r.t. transfers is exact in the sense that it uses a clear definition $[f'(X;Y) > 0]$ involving a derivative, which is expected for the study of sensitivity, yet it allows for differences in nature of the diverse concentration measures (w.r.t. the used average). The appearance of the four basic averages (arithmetic, geometric, harmonic, and the median) is remarkable. Overall, this sensitivity theory can be considered as a mathematical solution to some problems raised (with partial solutions) in Refs. *13, 16,* and *27*.

Summary and Conclusion

This review dealt with various ways of describing inequality (or concentration) as occurs in virtually every aspect of life. The emphasis here is on computer science, linguistics, and information science. We underline the importance of unequal situations (as opposed to evenness studies as, e.g., in biology) in these domains (e.g., in applications such as compression of databases and texts).

The Lorenz curve gives a visual method of studying concentration. The relation with the so-called 80/20 rule is given. We also give basic principles ("axioms") that good concentration measures should satisfy, among which is the appealing transfer principle. The article then continues by giving examples of good concentration measures such as V (the coefficient of variation), Pratt's measure C, the Gini index G, and their generalizations. Theil's measures Th and L, and, finally, the Atkinson indices $A(e)$ $(0 < e < 1)$. In this connection, the entropy formula from information theory is described and applied to aspects of compression. (See the Huffman compression of codes). Also, the concentration aspects of the laws of Zipf and Mandelbrot are discussed. Some remarks are made about the N dependence of these theories (i.e., the dependence on the number of sources).

The rest of the article dealt with the sensitivity of concentration measures w.r.t. transfers. New transfer principles, stronger than the classical one, are introduced and we indicate which concentration measures satisfy which generalized transfer principles. A nice class of transfer principles can be defined as follows. Let f be a concentration measure and denote by $f'(X; Y)$ the directional derivative in X (in the direction Y). Let

$$Y = \left(1, -\frac{1}{N-1}, \ldots, -\frac{1}{N-1}\right) \in R^N.$$

Then x_1 greater than a certain average of X should lead to $f'(X; Y) > 0$. This is the case for V with the arithmetic average, for Th with the geometric average, for L with the harmonic average, and for G and C for the median of X. The values of $f'(X; Y)$ can be used as a measure of sensitivity of the measure f w.r.t. transfers.

The merit of this sensitivity theory for concentration measures is that it presents a clear and exact definition of what sensitivity means, yet it allows for differences in nature of the diverse concentration measures (as revealed by the use of four different averages of X).

Acknowledgment

The author is indebted to Prof. Dr. R. Rousseau for valuable comments on both the content as well as the style of this article.

REFERENCES

1. L. Egghe and R. Rousseau, *Introduction to Informetrics. Quantitative Methods in Library, Documentation and Information Science,* Elsevier, Amsterdam, 1990.
2. L. Egghe and R. Rousseau, *Math. Computer Model., 23,* 93–104 (1996).
3. A. W. Marshall and I. Olkin, *Inequalities: Theory of Majorization and its Applications,* Academic Press, New York, 1979.
4. L. Pigou, *Wealth and Welfare,* Macmillan, New York, 1912.
5. H. Dalton, *Econ. J., 30,* 348–361 (1920).
6. M. O. Lorenz, *J. Amer. Statist. Assoc., 9,* 209–219 (1905).
7. G. H. Hardy, J. E. Littlewood, and G. Polya, *Inequalities,* 1st ed., Cambridge University Press, Cambridge, U.K., 1934; 2nd ed., 1952.
8. R. F. Muirhead, *Proc. Edinburgh Math. Soc., 21,* 144–157 (1903).
9. L. Egghe and R. Rousseau, *J. Amer. Soc. Inform. Sci., 42,* 479–489 (1991).
10. C. Gini, *Giornale Econom., 11,* 37 (1909).
11. A. D. Pratt, *J. Amer. Soc. Inform. Sci., 28,* 285–292 (1977).
12. M. P. Carpenter, *J. Amer. Soc. Inform. Sci., 30,* 108–110 (1979).
13. P. D. Allison, *Amer. Sociol. Rev., 43,* 865–880 (1978).
14. L. Egghe and R. Rousseau, "Elements of Concentration Theory," in *Informetrics 89/90,* L. Egghe and R. Rousseau, eds. Elsevier, Amsterdam, 1990, pp. 97–137.
15. H. Theil, *Economics and Information Theory,* North-Holland, Amsterdam, 1967.
16. A. B. Atkinson, *J. Econ. Theory, 30,* 244–263 (1970).
17. R. Rousseau, *Belgian J. Oper. Res., Statist. Computer Sci., 32,* 99–126 (1992).

18. D. A. Huffman, *Proc. IRE,* **40***, 1098–1101 (1952).*
19. J. A. Storer, *Data Compression. Methods and Theory,* Computer Science Press, Rockville, MD, 1988.
20. L. Egghe and N. Veraverbeke, *Int. J. Scientometr. Informetr.,* **1**, 183–193 (1995).
21. G. K. Zipf, *Selected Studies of the Principle of Relative Frequency in Language,* Harvard University Press, Cambridge, MA, 1932.
22. G. K. Zipf, *The Psycho-Biology of Language: An Introduction to Dynamic Philology,* Houghton Mifflin, New York, 1935; reprinted by MIT Press, Cambridge, MA, 1965.
23. L. Egghe, *J. Amer. Soc. Inform. Sci.,* **38,** 288–297 (1987).
24. B. Mandelbrot, *Word,* **10**, 1–27 (1954).
25. B. Mandelbrot, *The Fractal Geometry of Nature,* Freeman, New York, 1977.
26. L. Egghe, *Scientometrics,* **25**, 167–191 (1992).
27. P. D. Allison, *Soc. Stud. Sci.,* **10**, 163–179 (1980).
28. L. Egghe and R. Rousseau, *Inform. Proc. Mgt.,* **31**, 511–523, 1995.

BIBLIOGRAPHY

Allison, P. D., "Measures of Inequality." *Amer. Sociol. Rev.,* **43**, 865–880 (1978).

Arnold, B. C., *Majorization and the Lorenz Order: A Brief Introduction,* Springer-Verlag, Berlin, 1987.

Egghe, L. and R. Rousseau, *Introduction to Informetrics. Quantitative Methods in Library, Documentation and Information Science,* Elsevier, Amsterdam, 1990.

Gini, C., *Memorie di Metodologia Statistica, Vol. 1: Variabilità e Concentrazione,* Libreria Eredi Virgilio Veschi, Rome, 1955.

Hardy, G. H., J. E. Littlewood, and G. Polya, *Inequalities,* 1st ed., Cambridge University Press, Cambridge, 1934; 2nd ed., 1952.

Lambert, P. J., *The Distribution and Redistribution of Income: A Mathematical Analysis,* 2nd ed., Manchester University Press, Manchester, UK, 1993.

Magurran, A., *Ecological Diversity and Its Measurement,* Chapman & Hall, London, 1991.

Marshall, A. W., and I. Olkin, *Inequalities: Theory of Majorization and its Applications,* Academic Press, New York, 1979.

Sen, A. K., *On Economic Inequality,* Clarendon Press, Oxford, 1973.

Storer, J. A., *Data Compression. Methods and Theory,* Computer Science Press, Rockville, MD, 1988.

Theil, H., *Economics and Information Theory,* North-Holland, Amsterdam, 1967.

Zipf, G. K., *Human Behavior and the Principle of Least Effort,* Addison-Wesley, Cambridge, MA, 1949; reprinted by Hafner, New York, 1965.

LEO EGGHE

STRATEGY AND IMPACTS OF EXPERT SYSTEMS FOR BANK LENDING

Introduction

Few discussions have surfaced concerning the strategies motivating the development of banking expert systems and of the impacts resulting from their use. The purpose of this paper is to describe the strategy and impacts of expert systems development and use in banking, particularly bank lending. The paper proceeds as follows: the strategy of expert systems development is outlined; a matrix model of expert systems impacts is described and applied to banking expert systems in general; the strategy process related to the Bank of Scotland's lending advisor expert system, COMPASS, is discussed; and the matrix model is used to identify the impacts of COMPASS; finally, conclusions about strategy and impacts of bank expert systems are addressed.

Strategy of Expert Systems for Bank Lending

Expert systems that evaluate business and consumer loan applications have been developed in many countries and in many banks. (See, e.g., Lee, 1988; Radding, 1991; Keyes, 1991; Bridge and Lin, 1992; Kader, 1992; Klein, 1992; Goodall, 1993; Sangster, 1995; Shao et al., 1995.) Banks develop expert systems because they expect these systems to create a comparative advantage (Chorafas and Steinmann, 1991). This ultimately desirable result may be achieved through such intermediate impacts as reduced cost (Shao et al., 1995; Schwartz and Treece, 1992), an improvement in task process (Sviokla, 1986), an increase in decision quality (Leonard-Barton and Sviokla, 1988), and improved human productivity (Brown & Phillips, 1995). With many banking activities, the reduction of risk is also an important goal (Friedman, 1989; *The Economist,* 1993). These impacts and the motivation to use them to alter competitive forces are an important part of an organization's strategy and development (Bakos and Treacy, 1986).

The organizational strategy process can be presented as a six-phase model (Fig. 1). These interrelated and interdependent phases are described as distinct steps for the purpose of discussion (Baldwin-Morgan and Stone, 1995).

1. The state of the organization is assessed according to the organization's overall strategy. For example, a bank will assess its levels of risk, return, and exposure, and determine whether their current levels fit in with the bank's strategy.
2. If the organization is not flawless, then the strategy indicates a desire to change the state of the organization. For example, a bank's management may determine that levels of risk are too high and must be decreased.

Reprinted with permission from Elsevier Science Ltd., The Boulevard, Langford Lane, Kidlington 0X5 1GB, UK.

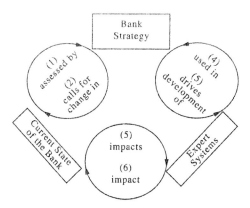

FIGURE 1. *The strategy process.*

3. The organization strategy drives the development of expert systems that will be used to change the organization as desired.
4. The implemented expert systems are used as a part of the organization's strategy for changing itself. For example, a bank may develop an expert system to assist in analyzing loan applications to reduce the risks associated with granting loans.
5. The state of the organization impacts the expert system development. For example, a bank that has a history of technology innovation may be more likely to successfully develop and use an expert system than a bank that has traditionally been a "late-adopter" of useful banking technologies.
6. The development and use of the expert system(s) impact the state of the organization. For example, a bank that successfully develops a credit card authorization system could see reduced costs, leading to higher profit.

Impacts of Expert Systems for Bank Lending

Because the strategy process uses expert systems to create impacts that change the organization, consideration of potential expert systems' impacts may be worthwhile. Baldwin-Morgan and Stone's matrix model (1995) is a visualization tool for organizing and describing impacts of a particular expert system or of a set of expert systems. It comprises a 4×5 matrix of potential types of impacts that may result from the use of expert systems. The horizontal axis comprises levels of impacts: industry, organizational, individual, and task. The vertical axis represents categories of impacts: efficiency, effectiveness, expertise, education, and environment.

Although many have reported on the impacts of expert systems (e.g., Sviokla, 1986; Murphy, 1990; Eining and Dorr, 1991; Fedorowicz et al., 1992; Murphy and Dorr, 1992; Baldwin-Morgan, 1994; Bouwman and Knox-Quinn, 1994; Swinney, 1994; Trewein, 1994), the impacts of expert systems in banking have been largely overlooked. An awareness of the nature of the impact that expert systems are having in this sector would inform future development and research and help pinpoint strengths and

TABLE 1

Reported Impacts of Bank Expert Systems

Categories of impact	Levels of analysis			
	Industry	Organization	Individual	Task
Efficiency	●	● Reduced Costs ● Fewer losses	● Improved individual productivity ● Less individual time needed for decision	● Faster processing ● Reduced test-specific costs
Effectiveness	●	● Improved customer service	● Increased individual productivity ● Increased individual authority	● Fewer errors ● Improved consistency
Expertise	●	● Distribution of expertise	● Enhanced individual expertise	● Preservation of task expertise
Education	●	● ES used for staff training	● ES changed education of individuals	● Changes to task education
Environment	● Balance of competition is changed	● Business risk is reduced	● Employment patterns altered ● More or fewer jobs	● Change in task process ● Reduction of task-specific risk

weakness that may otherwise remain undetected and/or unobserved. Through the Baldwin-Morgan and Stone matrix model, a contextual view of a number of impacts that have been reported by various banks using expert systems may be presented (Table 1).

EFFICIENCY IMPACTS

- *Organizational efficiency* impacts have been indicated by a number of banks. Reduced costs were the result of using Security Pacific National Bank's expert system for controlling debit card fraud and also of Citicorp's CitiExpert system for international funds transfer. Reduced credit card fraud losses resulted from Colonial National Bank's use of the FALCON expert system (Brown and Phillips, 1995) and reduced costs resulted from expert systems use at a U.K. bank (Shao et al., 1995).
- *Individual efficiency* impacts include better productivity at Manufacturers Hanover Trust as a result of using the TARA foreign currency exchange expert system. The Canadian Imperial Bank of Commerce's Lending Advisor has individuals spending less time on administrative tasks. In addition, Kredictbank's personal loan application expert system removed the need for head office involvement in individual loan granting decisions (Brown and Phillips, 1995).
- *Task efficiency* involves such impacts as faster processing, found with Security Pacific Bank's wire transfer system, Union Bank of Zurich's foreign currency trading expert system, and another expert system at Ohio's Star Bank Corp. Bank-Tec's check processing costs were reduced by use of a check processing expert system (Brown and Phillips, 1995).

EFFECTIVENESS IMPACTS

- *Organizational effectiveness* may be evidenced by the reduction in card fraud due to use of

Barclay's credit card fraud expert system. Both the Bank of America's customer service automation expert system and Citicorp's CitiExpert result in improved customer service.
- *Individual effectiveness* involves decision makers. Using Sanwa (Japan) Bank's Personal Portfolio Management System, individual managers have increased productivity and customer service (Bridge and Lin, 1992). Kredictbank's personal loan processing expert system provides increased authority for individuals in local bank branches (Lee, 1988).
- *Task effectiveness* impacts may include fewer data entry errors, as with Citicorp's international funds transfer expert system, eliminated wire transfer errors at Security Pacific Bank and reduced errors in identifying fraudulent accounts with Barclaycard's FraudWatch. Improved consistency is also an important impact evident at Ohio's Star Bank Corp and Swiss Bank as a result of using an expert system (Brown and Phillips, 1995).

EXPERTISE IMPACTS

- *Organizational expertise* may be impacted as knowledge of experienced fraud investigators is made available to all employees, such as those using Security Pacific National Bank's debit card fraud system (Brown and Phillips, 1995).
- *Individual expertise* may be enhanced through the use of an expert system as with Swiss bank's MOCCA system.
- *Task expertise* is preserved for future use by nonexperts by practically every banking expert system.

EDUCATIONAL IMPACTS

- *Organizational education* is impacted when an expert system, such as Swiss Bank's CUBUS, is used for staff training.
- *Individual education* is impacted when CUBUS is used to improve the skills of staff.
- *Task-specific expertise* is improved when an expert system, such as Security Pacific's debit card fraud system, actually educates employees on fraud prevention and detection as it is used (Brown and Phillips, 1995).

ENVIRONMENTAL IMPACTS

- One way the *industry environment* is impacted is by affecting the balance of competition. Shao et al. (1995) report on two U.K. banks whose expert systems provide a competitive advantage. Manufacturers Hanover Trust's TARA expert system is another example of an expert system that is acknowledged as giving the bank that is using it a competitive edge (Brown and Phillips, 1995).
- The *organizational environment* is impacted when an expert system reduces business risk. Some banks build expert systems expressly because they are concerned with lowering risk. Swiss bank's MOCCA has reduced business risk and CUBUS has reduced the risk of loan defaults (Brown and Phillips, 1995).
- The *individual environment* may be impacted as employment patterns are altered. Some expert systems result in the need for less employees; however, one U.K. bank expert system actually created jobs (Shao et al., 1995). The Canadian Imperial Bank of Commerce's Lending Advisor is reported to boost employee confidence.
- The *task environment* may be impacted by changes in the task process. Swiss Bank's MOCCA system resulted in the lending process being decentralized. Expert systems may also be used to reduce task-specific risk. The Canadian Imperial Bank of Commerce's Lending Advisor controls the risk of the commercial loan evaluation task. The Bank of Boston's automated credit application processing system provides better management of credit risk (Brown and Phillips, 1995).

The macro-level impact analysis shown in Table 1 presents an overall view on how expert system technology has been found to impact a range of aspects. As such, it is a guide to the possibilities offered through adopting the technology in the banking environment. However, it has been constructed from published research material on each of the systems and, as such, can only include those impacts considered most significant in each case. In order to obtain a clearer view of the nature of the impacts that may arise through use of expert system technology, it may be more useful to consider the impacts of specific in-depth example of banking expert systems. To this end, the following sections consider the impacts of one specific expert system, COMPASS, developed by the Bank of Scotland in order to control for risk on commercial lending (Sangster, 1995).

Strategy of Compass

This section reviews the strategy process that led to the development of the COMPASS expert system (Table 2); and the following section considers the impact of COMPASS within the context of the Baldwin-Morgan and Stone matrix model.

In the past decade, many banks recorded large commercial loan losses (*The Economist,* 1993). Many financial institutions, including the Bank of Scotland, saw the need to better address risk. The Bank of Scotland perceived a need for a consistent

TABLE 2

The Bank of Scotland's Strategy Process, Following the Six-Phase Model Presented in Fig. 1

Generic strategy process	The COMPASS expert system (Bank of Scotland)
Background	Banks have seen large lending losses since the late 1980s Banks have not been addressing risk effectively.
1. The state of the organization is assessed in light of the organization's strategy.	Bank of Scotland recognizes the importance of risk minimization and the need to address risk effectively.
2. The organizational strategy desires to change the state of the organization.	Bank of Scotland wants to apply a consistent lending policy that includes the use of both quantitative and qualitative methods of expertise to control lending risk and loss.
3. The organizational strategy drives the development of expert system(s).	Bank of Scotland develops COMPASS.
4. Expert systems are used in the organization strategy.	COMPASS is used in corporate branches representing 80% of the bank's corporate portfolio.
5. The state of the organization impacts the expert system(s).	The use of COMPASS was made part of bank policy, although users retain financial decision control.
6. The expert system(s) impacts the state of the organization.	See the "Impacts of COMPASS" section of the paper.

lending policy if it were to reduce effectively. This policy needed to address both qualitative and quantitative methods of evaluating loan applications (Sangster, 1995).

To this end, the Bank of Scotland developed the COMPASS expert system. It was developed in-house using the expertise of the bank's senior loans officer. The system includes customer information, analysis and modeling of accounts, and expertise regarding viability, credentials and safety relevant to the proposed loan. The system contains both qualitative and quantitative information, and both customer-specific and general industry information. Development of COMPASS took about five years (Sangster, 1995).

In 1993 and 1994, COMPASS was released to branches of the Bank of Scotland. As a part of the bank's strategy for controlling risk, COMPASS is now used throughout the corporate branches of the bank, originally for middle range lending, but subsequently for all corporate lending in excess of $15,000.

Some characteristics of the Bank of Scotland impacted the development of the expert system. For example, top management completely supported the expert system. In addition, the developers adopted a philosophy that the expert system should be sensible, flexible, and focused. The developers were also characterized by a strong loyalty to the development project and unusual patience. These factors contributed to the success of the development (Sangster, 1995).

The Bank of Scotland developed COMPASS because of a need to minimize risk. The expert system has had additional specific impacts on the bank, which are discussed in detail in the next section.

Impacts of Compass

COMPASS has resulted in many positive impacts for the Bank of Scotland that can be organized and discussed using the matrix model shown in Table 3. For greater depth of analysis, the matrix model has been extended through the inclusion of an additional impact dimension, technology.

EFFICIENCY IMPACTS

- COMPASS has impacted the *organizational efficiency* of the Bank of Scotland in two principle ways. The head office now has more time to spend on activities other than dealing with individual loan applications; and the costs associated with lending, a principle activity of the bank, have been reduced.
- The *individual efficiency* of those involved in the lending process has also been impacted—loan officers are now able to process loans more efficiently than before COMPASS was introduced. The time needed for loan officers to make decisions has been greatly reduced, freeing significant amounts of time for other activities.
- It has resulted in impressive improvements in *task efficiency*. The response time to customer requests for borrowing, which used to be about a week, is now between 5 and 30 minutes. The consultation process is more dynamic, with changes to lending related information made continuously.
- *Technology* is now more efficiently used with COMPASS acting as the catalyst for links being formed between various databases.

TABLE 3

Impacts of COMPASS

Categories of impact	Levels of analysis				
	Industry	Organization	Individual	Task	Technology
Efficiency		• Head office has more time for other activities. • Reduced costs.	• Increased efficiency in loan processing by loan officers. • Reduced decision time. • Frees significant amount of officer time.	• Faster response to customer requests for borrowing. • consultation process is more dynamic, changes updated continuously. • Reduced task time.	• More efficient use—links built between the various databases where previously there was none.
Effectiveness		• Head office work on individual applications is more focused. • More improvement in bad debts.	• Loan officers now concentrating on significant issues. • Judgments are easier and more likely to be appropriate. • Increased loan facility.	• Task time now 5–30 minutes vs. week or more before COMPASS. • Customer credibility is assessed "objectively." • Task decisions are based on consistent comprehensive methodology. • Changes in lending task policy are automatically encapsulated into lending decisions. • Consistency in decisions.	• More effective use of technology.

TABLE 3 (continued)

Impacts of COMPASS

Categories of impact	Levels of analysis				
	Industry	Organization	Individual	Task	Technology
Expertise		• Consultation results are fed into the organization's knowledge base and database within 24 hours. • Any new info on customer becomes part of sector environment within 24 hours.	• altered loan officer thinking and general approach to lending.	• knowledge of senior loans officer and suggestions of others (later) preserved.	• Updates and amendments being performed as required.
Education		• The organization is now more conscious of the benefits of an efficient and effective approach to bank lending assessment.	• Enhanced awareness of what is relevant.	• The task is now clearer and better understood.	• Feedback from users being utilized to fine tune/amend how technology is being used.
Environment		• Enhanced external reputation. • Leads to a lending portfolio more in line with the bank's policy. • Significant long-term edge over competitors. • Improved loan structuring and pricing in relation to risk.	• No longer any need to personally react to changes that are automatically incorporated into COMPASS. • Change in image from the customer's perspective. • Appearance of sophistication/"modernness."	• COMPASS clarifies the risk situation. • The environmental aspects of the assessment are now automatically incorporated.	• Changes in the environment being reflected in changes in programming languages, operating systems.

EFFECTIVENESS IMPACTS

- *Organizational effectiveness* impacts are evident in the head office and in the bank's overall debt structure. The head office work now done on (fewer) individual applications is much more focused than previously. The bank has also seen improvement in the amount of its bad debts.
- Impacts on *individual effectiveness* are apparent on loan officers and their judgment. Loan officers are now concentrating on more significant issues, and the amount of loans they can approve has been increased. In addition, lending judgments are more likely to be suitable and are easier.
- It is in respect of *task effectiveness* that the most obvious effectiveness impacts of COMPASS are seen. With COMPASS, the impact of loan officer bias is minimized. All task decisions involve extensive methodology, which translates to consistency. Any changes in these methods or bank policies are automatically included in the lending process through COMPASS.
- *Technology* is now being used more effectively, its potential to help improve decision making being maximized where previously it was only being used for traditional tasks.

EXPERTISE IMPACTS

- *Organizational expertise* is most impacted through lending-related expertise now being distributed throughout the bank and its branches in COMPASS. Expertise and knowledge is distributed so comprehensively that the results of lending consultation are automatically filtered to the relevant part of the COMPASS knowledge base. Any new information on an existing customer is updated to the appropriate industry information area.
- *Individual expertise* has been impacted to the extent that loan officers report they have altered their thinking about and approach to lending decisions.
- Task expertise has been preserved in COMPASS, not only the expertise of the senior loan officer but also the suggestions and changes proposed by loan officer users of COMPASS.
- The *technology* adopted in order to embed and distribute the expertise that comprises COMPASS is being continuously updated in response to a growing level of expertise that is, itself, the result of using COMPASS.

EDUCATION IMPACTS

- The *organizational education* has been impacted to the extent that the organization is now more conscious of the benefits of an efficient and effective approach to bank lending assessment. This approach is now universal throughout the organization.
- *Individuals* have a much enhanced awareness of what is really relevant to the lending task, which is more clear and better understood than previously.
- The way in which *technology* is being used has been altered as a result of an increased awareness of the manner in which it may usefully be applied.

ENVIRONMENTAL IMPACTS

- The *organizational environment* is changed due to the Bank of Scotland's enhanced reputation and increased business. In addition, the loan structuring and pricing of the bank have been improved, thus reducing business risk. COMPASS may also give the Bank of Scotland a long-term edge over competitors.
- The *individual environment* has been affected in that loan officers need not react to each new change in the lending process because such changes are automatically incorporated

into COMPASS. From the customer's perspective, the image of the loan officer is altered and increased appearance of sophistication or moderness is apparent.

- COMPASS impacts the *task environment* by changing the lending task. The task now explicitly involves qualitative methods as well as quantitative analyses. COMPASS also clarifies the risk associated with the lending task.
- The *technology environment* of the Bank of Scotland has undergone a major change as a result of the introduction and use of COMPASS.

COMPASS is a catalyst for change. While the impact at the industry level must be small at this time, a number of financial institutions are actively considering adoption of COMPASS and, if it is as effective and durable as it appears, it may have a significant long-term impact upon the industry. However, speculation about such impacts is premature at this time.

Conclusion

Clearly, expert systems in banking, and specifically in lending, can provide a myriad of impacts to the financial institutions that development them. Not all expert systems in banking are successful (Duchessi and O'Keefe, 1992). However, those systems that are developed according to appropriate knowledge elicitation and technological innovation techniques can provide many important and profitable impacts. COMPASS provides an important example of such an expert system. Financial institutions seeking to decrease their exposure to risk should consider expert systems as a possible tool for achieving this objective.

Use of the matrix model provides a focus for deeper analysis of the benefits of adopting expert systems technology. While it has been applied to COMPASS from a purely positive perspective, there is no reason why it could not be utilized to help identify and compare positive and negative impacts; and not just after adoption. It could also be used at the planning and prototyping phases of expert systems development, thereby highlighting aspects worthy of consideration that may otherwise have passed unnoticed.

REFERENCES

Bakos, J. Y. and Treacy, M. E. (1986). Information technology and corporate strategy: A research perspective. *MIS Quarterly,* **June**, 106–119.

Baldwin-Morgan, A. A. (1993). The impact of expert system audit tools on auditing firms in the year 2001: A Delphi investigation. *Journal of Information Systems, 7*.

Baldwin-Morgan, A. A. (1994). The impact of expert systems on auditing firms: Evidence from a cast study. *International Journal of Applied Expert Systems, 2*, 159–174.

Baldwin-Morgan, A. A. & Stone, M. F. (1995). A matrix model of expert systems impacts. *Experts Systems With Applications, 9*, 599–608.

Bouwman, M. J. & Knox-Quinn, C. (1994). Student knowledge engineering in accounting: A case study in learning. Working paper, July.

Bridge, T. & Lin, Y. T. (1992). Expert systems in banking. *Canadian Banker,* **99(4)**, 20–25.

Brown, C. E. & Phillips, M. E. (1995). *Expert systems for management accounting tasks.* Montvale, NJ: Institute of Management Accountants.

Chorafas, D. N. & Steinmann, H. (1991). *Expert systems in banking.* Basingstoke: Macmillan.

Duchessi, P. & O'Keefe, R. M. (1992). Contrasting successful and unsuccessful expert systems. *European Journal of Operations Research,* **61**, 122–134.

The Economist (1993). Banking: New tricks to learn. *The Economist,* 7806. April 19 survey.

Eining, M. & Dorr, P. (1991). The impact of expert systems usage on experiential learning in an auditing setting. *Journal of Information Systems,* **5(2)**, 1–16.

Federowicz, J., Oz, E. & Berger, P. (1992). A learning curve analysis of expert system use. *Decision Sciences,* **23**, 797–818.

Friedman, R. (1989). Credit analysis automation. *United States Banker,* **96(6)**, 58.

Goodall, A. (1993). KBS developments at Swiss Bank. *AI Watch,* **Nov.**, 1–2.

Kader, V. (1992). Use of "Expert systems" spreads, particularly in Europe, and U.S. has technological lead. *Business America,* **113(18)**, 18–20.

Keyes, J. (1991). Artificial financial intelligence. *Financial & Accounting Systems,* **7(3)**, 12–15.

Klein, E. (1992). "Thinking" machines add new expertise to banking functions. *Savings Institutions,* **Feb.**, 37–38.

Lee, A. (1988). An intelligence stirs in the grey zone. *Credit Management,* **Dec.**, 38–40.

Leonard-Barton, D. & Sviokla, J. J. (1988). Putting expert systems to work. *Harvard Business Review,* **66(2)**, 98–99.

Murphy, D. S. (1990). Expert systems use and the development of expertise in auditing: A preliminary Investigation. *Journal of Information Systems,* **4**, 18–35.

Murphy, D. S. & Dorr, P. B. (1992). Potential social effects of expert system use. *Accounting Systems Journal,* **Fall**, 58–73.

O'Keefe, R. M., O'Leary, D., Rebne D. & Chung, Q. B. (1993). The impact of expert systems in accounting: System characteristics, productivity and work unit effects. *International Journal of Intelligent Systems in Accounting, Finance and Management,* **2**, 177–189.

Radding, A. (1991). AI in action. *Computerworld,* **25(30)**, 61.

Sangster, A. (1995). The Bank of Scotland's COMPASS—the future of bank lending? *Expert Systems With Applications,* **9**, 457–468.

Schwartz, E. I. & Treece, J. B. (1992). Smart programs go to work. *Business Week,* **March 2**, 97–100, 105.

Shao, Y. P., Wilson, A. & Oppenheim, C. (1995). Expert systems in UK banking. In *Proceedings of the Eleventh Conference on Artificial Intelligence for Applications,* pp. 18–23, Los Angeles.

Sviokla, J. J. (1986). PlanPower, XCON, and MUDMAN: An in-depth investigation into three commercial expert-systems in use. Unpublished doctoral dissertation, Harvard Business School, Boston, MA.

Swinney, L. (1994). The impact of expert system use on audit judgement. Working paper presented at the *Third Annual Research Workshop on AI/ES in Accounting, Auditing and Tax,* New York, 9 August.

Trewin, J. (1994). The impact of the introduction of an expert systems on a professional accounting organisation. Unpublished working paper.

AMELIA A. BALDWIN
ALAN SANGSTER

THE USE OF DECISION SUPPORT SYSTEMS IN CRISIS NEGOTIATION

Introduction

It is widely contended that negotiations during a crisis differ substantially from more routine negotiations in that such situations are characterized by decision maker's perceptions of a serious threat to basic values, a finite time for response, and a heightened probability of involvement in military hostilities (*1*). Under such circumstances, decision makers are often unable to either access the information necessary to make utility-maximizing decisions or to properly evaluate the information in the amount of time available for decisions. Decisions are thus often made on the basis of previous experience, long-held beliefs, and analogies to seemingly comparable situations rather than with a factual, analytical calculation. As a consequence, suboptimal outcomes are likely to result. While all decision-making environments possess the potential for suboptimality, international crises are particularly dangerous because they can quickly escalate to violence and war. The vast literature of crisis decision making has shown that situations of intense crisis can create a reduced span of attention, cognitive rigidity, and a distorted perspective of time. (See Ref. *2* for an excellent review of the crisis decision-making literature.)

Use of a decision support system (DSS) can help overcome some of the problems that contribute to suboptimality in crisis decision making. Decision support systems facilitate the rapid examination of large amounts of information and the exploration of the interrelatedness of the many factors that can influence the decision. Decision makers supported by a DSS can evaluate multiple positions simultaneously in order to formulate dynamic strategies and evaluate opponents' offers quickly. This article will examine the application of DSSs to negotiation and then discuss how one such DSS, GENIE, has been specially tailored for hostage crisis negotiations.

The Use of Decision Support Systems in Negotiation

A wide variety of DSSs have been applied to negotiation. These negotiation support systems (NSSs) utilize diverse technologies ranging from conflict analysis and mathematical models to artificial intelligence methodology, and are designed to support either the entire negotiation group by facilitating communication or suggesting possible agreements, or individual negotiators in developing appropriate plans of action.

Note: This work was supported by the National Science Foundation under grant #IRI-9423967, and by the United States Institute of Peace under grant #SG-35-95.

This paper originally appeared in Volume 63 of the *Encyclopedia of Library and Information Science* but due to an oversight in the production process, was published without figures and the table. It is presented here in its complete format.

SUPPORT FOR THE ENTIRE NEGOTIATION GROUP

Group NSSs can be very helpful in situations in which a group of decision makers attempts to engage in joint problem solving but is hampered by difficulties resulting from incomplete information, different subgoals, or different perspectives on the problem. These packages, often referred to as group decision support systems (GDSS), allow decision makers to exchange information about goals, assumptions, and evaluation criteria (*3*). Group DSSs generally include features for representing members' positions, discussion agendas to help decision makers order the discussion of issues, and problem definition utilities (*4–6*). In addition to facilitating information exchange, some GDSSs aid decision makers or mediators in the development of arguments and justifications or in locating possible compromises. Examples of NSSs that support the entire group are: PERSUADER, DENEGOT, NEGO, MEDIATOR, MCBARG, ISES, SAM, RAMONA, and DecisionMaker.

PERSUADER can help parties to communicate arguments and justifications and can also suggest suitable arguments. PERSUADER uses multiattribute utility methods from decision theory and case-based reasoning from artificial intelligence to incrementally propose modifications to proposals and to help parties narrow their divergent views. PERSUADER is an intelligent system in that it learns from past negotiation cases and can make use of information from these cases in addition to actors' preferences when searching for compromises (*3*).

Another GDSS, DENEGOT, makes use of a distributed search through potential compromises. These compromises are calculated from information about each individual decision maker's idea of an acceptable solution. DENEGOT provides near-optimal compromises with a minimal amount of computation (*7*).

MEDIATOR (*8*) makes use of a database-centered approach to support consensus seeking. Each individual negotiator is supported by the PREFCALC DSS, which aids them in analyzing their individual utilities. A joint problem representation is then built for the group by a mediator. MEDIATOR was applied to a hostage crisis simulation by Faure (*9*). In hostage crises, the level of hostility makes it difficult for individual players to feel secure enough to share their true utilities. In these cases, the human mediator develops his or her own impression of the parties' utilities and creates the database for the parties.

NEGO (*10*) uses multiobjective linear programming methods. This interactive system establishes proposals from each of the individual participants and then forms a sequence of compromise proposals based on relaxed participant demands. The problem is solved when a compromise proposal is produced that satisfies the revised set of demands.

MCBARG (*11*) allows negotiators to consider a model and select a preferred outcome. It then uses these results to develop a revised model that the parties can examine. In effect, MCBARG acts as a single negotiation text that can be refined by running additional iterations.

ISES and SAM (*12*), developed by the MIT Project on Modeling for Negotiation Management, make use of simulation techniques. Negotiators can use ISES to transfer proposals defined by lists of parameters and then to run simulations to determine what effect each proposal may have. SAM also allows users to identify important norms and then simulate the outcome likely to result from following these norms.

The Resources Allocating Multiple Objective Negotiation Approach (RAMONA) guides users through a series of questions that identify several points on a Pareto optimal frontier. The parties then work out an agreeable solution on this frontier (*13*).

DecisionMaker: The Conflict Analysis Program (*14*) relies upon the conflict analysis approach to identify compromise solutions. In addition to mediation use, it can also be used by an individual negotiator to determine the probable moves of an opponent, given a world state. DecisionMaker determines what moves actors would make to reach one of the conflict equilibria.

SUPPORT FOR INDIVIDUAL NEGOTIATORS

Another approach to negotiation support is to provide individual parties with a stand-alone system that will aid in their determination of a successful strategy or goal. Examples of these systems include NEGOPLAN, NEGOTIATOR, and MATCH.

NEGOPLAN (*15*) allows a user to develop a model of a two-party negotiation using And/Or trees of Prolog-like facts. This expert system shell then uses forward inference to predict opponent reaction to the chosen model. NEGOPLAN supports an individual negotiator by allowing him or her to try out different negotiating positions and see the likely results. NEGOPLAN has been applied to a hostage crisis situation by Michalowski et al. (*16*).

NEGOTIATOR (*17*) uses a fusion of multiple-attribute utility theory and neural network techniques to support individual negotiators. Separate instances of NEGOTIATOR can be connected with a communications package to form a group decision environment. In this way, it is like its predecessor, CO-OP, which made use of MAU methods alone (*18*).

MATCH (*12*) compares past negotiation scenarios with the present situation to identify which strategies have been successful in similar situations.

The subject of this article, GENIE, is an individual NSS. Since GENIE was developed based on a full information model, any of the players in the scenario can be supported by GENIE. Each individual acts alone, however (although participants can use an electronic communications package to communicate their findings). GENIE makes use of mathematical modeling techniques in order to aid the user in visualizing the negotiation situation and in considering what-if scenarios. GENIE shares the use of MAU modeling with NEGOTIATOR and the what-if approach with NEGOPLAN.

GENIE: A DSS for Crisis Negotiation

The GENIE DSS is capable of providing support for negotiators involved in time variant, n-player negotiations with full information. It is based on a strategic model of negotiation (*19*) that focuses on the passage of time during the negotiation and the preferences of the players for different agreements as well as for opting out of the negotiations. (For additional details on this model, see Ref. *20*.) The version of GENIE that has been used in experimental research and that will be discussed here has been customized for a hostage crisis scenario; a more generalized version is currently under development. (See the section "Future Work" below.)

By full information, we mean that all players in a GENIE-supported negotiation have full knowledge of their own objectives as well as those of the other actors. This specification was made in order to simplify the strategic model of negotiation upon which the DSS is based. (A detailed description of the strategic model of negotiation can be found in Ref. *21*.) The model, however, was recently extended to situations of incomplete information (*20, 22*). As will be discussed below, plans for a DSS that supports an incomplete information model are under consideration. It is important to note that while the players have full information about each other's preferences, they do not have full information about the state of the world. Since bilateral messages are private, the Sikhs, for instance, do not have knowledge of secret India/Pakistan agreements for military support and so forth. Players also lack information about their opponents' risk attitude. The assumption of full information about objectives in the hostage crisis simulation is not problematic given that this type of crisis generally occurs between parties that have been involved in a protracted conflict and know each other and each other's objectives well. The hostage crisis scenario supported by GENIE will be discussed below.

THE HOSTAGE CRISIS

GENIE was developed using a crisis scenario as a typical example of multiparty crisis negotiation. The specific scenario is based on a commercial airliner carrying primarily Indian citizens that has been hijacked by Sikh separatists and forced to land in Pakistan. Among the hijackers' demands are the release of up to 800 Sikh security prisoners being held in India. (The model was originally placed in the Middle East with roles for Israel, Egypt, and Palestinian terrorists. The venue was changed to Asia in order to minimize student bias during experiments.) The crisis can end in several different ways. Two different types of negotiated settlements are possible. India and the Sikhs can reach a deal for the release of prisoners in exchange for hostages, or Pakistan and the Sikhs can negotiate a deal in which Pakistan allows the Sikhs safe passage if they release the hostages unharmed. Each player also has the ability to opt out of the negotiations. India or Pakistan can opt out of the negotiations and end the crisis with a military operation. The Sikhs can opt out by blowing up the plane (a suicide bombing). The Sikhs can also end the crisis by surrendering.

In addition to the six possible outcomes, the crisis is defined by several world state parameters. These include: time, logistical information, press access, military support, and the number of hostages killed or released. Each party has control over different aspects of the world state. India can agree to give military support in the event of a Pakistani operation. The Sikhs have the ability to kill or release hostages. Pakistan, as the unwilling host of the crisis, has control over a number of world state parameters. Pakistan can share logistical information (location and type of plane, etc.) with India to increase the probability that an Indian operation will succeed. Pakistan can also increase India's probability of success by agreeing to assist in an Indian operation. Pakistan can increase the utility of the Sikhs' outcomes across the board by granting them direct access to the international press.

During the simulation, players negotiate to improve the world state to their advantage and to reach an outcome that provides them with the highest possible point total. Negotiations continue until a final agreement is reached or a player opts out of the negotiations by undertaking a military action. As indicated earlier, time plays a crucial role in a crisis. In the hostage crisis model, time has an impact upon both the utility of different outcomes for the different actors and upon the probability that risky outcomes will be successful. The passage of time impacts the actors differently. The Sikhs tend to gain over time as publicity about their cause increases. This trend reverses itself when enough time has passed that press coverage focuses on the hostages themselves instead of the larger political picture. For the Indians and the Pakistanis, the passage of time erodes their point totals since the longer the crisis drags on their ability to control the situation is called into question. Time also has an impact upon the probability that military operations will be successful. The Indians and Pakistanis gain probability points over time as their forces receive more focused training. The Sikhs' ability to successfully blow up the plane is slightly eroded over time as the hijackers tire. In addition to cumulative impact over time, there is also an oscillating impact upon India and Pakistan's ability to successfully undertake a military operation as night becomes day and then night again. (For more detail on the hostage crisis simulation, see Ref. *23*.)

The value of each outcome for each player is determined by how well that outcome fulfills the players' objectives given the state of the world. Each player in the hostage crisis has several somewhat competing objectives to achieve. (See Table 1.) GENIE helps the decision makers evaluate these competing goals by calculating utility point totals for any outcome given a specified state of the world using multiattribute utility methodology; that is, GENIE determines the level at which each objective is achieved given the specified state of the world and tallies the totals for each objective to produce a point total for the outcome.

This methodology is frequently used in NSSs and has been used by DecisionMap, ExpertChoice, and Aborist (*24*) as well as the NSS NEGOTIATOR. Despite its popularity, MAU has received some criticism. Spector (*25*) points out that MAU requires criteria to be mutually exclusive and independent, is hampered by difficulties in assessing the preferences of other actors in multicultural situations, and provides a static view of negotiation since preferences are not changed during the course of the negotiation.

Although these are in fact shortcomings of the methodology, they do not present overwhelming problems for the present DSS. Our goal is to support crisis negotiations. As discussed above, crisis decision making is hampered by reduced attention span and cognitive rigidity. Decision makers under these situations are not able to achieve even the simplified representation of the model that MAU provides. This holds true as well for difficulties in determining the objectives of opponents in multicultural situations; as explained earlier, these types of crises tend to take place between historic enemies who have a good sense of the other's objective. As to the static nature of MAU, crises are by definition very short-term situations in which not enough time passes to result in any real changes to the parties' objectives. The MAU methodology does provide the GENIE user with a method of evaluating conflicting goals.

TABLE 1

Objectives

INDIAN OBJECTIVES	
Safe return of the passengers	180 points
Acceptable level of casualties among military	45 points
Maintenance of status quo in relations with Pakistan	50 points
Maintenance of status quo in relations with US	80 points
No concession to terrorists	100 points
No negative effect on Indian public opinion	100 points
Restrict publicity for terrorist cause	80 points
No damage to India's external image	50 points
Credibility of India's deterrence against terrorism is maintained	140 points
India's overall strategic interests are unchanged	140 points
Experience in counterterrorism operations augmented	35 points
TOTAL	**1000 points**
SIKH OBJECTIVES	
Release of prisoners held in India	180 points
Safe passage for terrorists	100 points
Message of Sikhs—publicity	320 points
Damage to India deterrence against terrorism	75 points
Damage to Indian relations with Pakistan	25 points
Damage to U.S.–Indian relations	50 points
Damage to Indian external image	100 points
Damage to Indian internal image	75 points
Enhanced position of terrorist group in Sikh movement	75 points
TOTAL	**1000 points**
PAKISTANI OBJECTIVES	
Pakistani demonstration of control	375 points
Pakistani internal image	100 points
India is not strengthened	50 points
India is not weakened	25 points
No strengthening of terrorists	50 points
Maintenance of status quo with U.S.	50 points
Maintenance of status quo within region	275 points
Maintenance of status quo with India	25 points
Maintenance of status quo with Sikhs	50 points
TOTAL	**1000 points**

COMPONENTS OF GENIE

GENIE was designed to be used by individuals with little experience in using computers for decision support. It is menu-driven and allows users to make choices either by keyboard entries or mouse clicks. Menu-driven systems allow novice users to navigate complex systems in an easy fashion while allowing a more advanced user access to more sophisticated features (26).

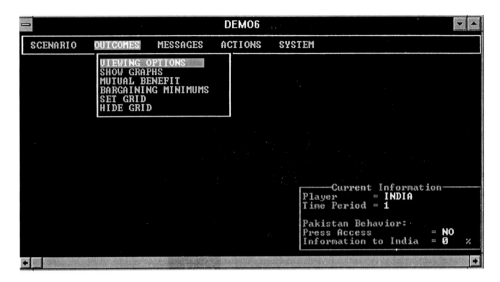

FIGURE 1. *Five choices in the main menu for GENIE.*

Five choices make up the main menu bar: SCENARIO, OUTCOMES, MES-SAGES, ACTIONS, and SYSTEM. (See Fig. 1.) In addition to the main menu bar, the main screen contains a window that displays the current simulation information. Users can pull down the SCENARIO menu to access information about the main simulation scenario as well as information about the objectives of the actors, the simulation rules, strategy guidelines, and information about the DSS's calculation of probabilities and outcome totals. The MESSAGE menu provides a link to the electronic communications package that handles all messages between the parties. A user can click on this menu to send or read messages. When a call is made to the messaging software all information in the DSS is saved so that when the user returns to the DSS the environment is exactly as it was prior to the call to the communications software. This facilitates the rapid evaluation of any threats or offers that may have been made.

The ACTIONS menu provides the user with a reminder of the available actions and how to undertake them. The SYSTEMS menu allows the user to make changes to the current information window as well as to save the current information and end the current DSS session. The user could then run the DSS again later and have all selected information within the DSS remain the same as it was in the last session.

The OUTCOMES menu provides access to the main decision support features of GENIE. It provides links to available graphical displays and analytical tools as well as to the interactive outline that forms the heart of GENIE.

Interactive Outline

The interactive outline (see Fig. 2) represents the heart of the GENIE DSS. The outline provides a full representation of the hostage crisis model. In this manner, it

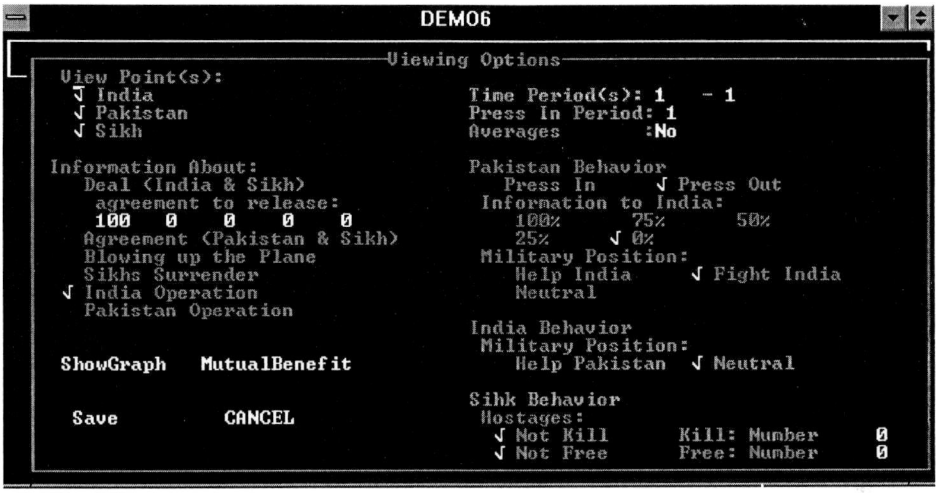

FIGURE 2. *Interactive outline of GENIE for hostage crisis model.*

fulfills Pracht's (27) suggestion that symbolic images are easier for a user to grasp than plain text information. Three main categories, which fully define the model, make up the interactive outline. The first section, "Viewpoints," lists the actors in the crisis. With a click of the mouse, a user can select information from the perspective of one or more of these actors. When the user selects more than one actor, information from each perspective is displayed simultaneously to facilitate comparative analysis of the outcomes.

The second section of the interactive outline is "Information Items," which lists all the possible outcomes to the crisis. These include: a deal for the exchange of prisoners for hostages, a safe passage agreement between Pakistan and the Sikhs, the Sikhs blowing up the plane, the Sikhs surrendering, or India or Pakistan launching military operations. The user can evaluate one or more outcomes. Again, if more than one is selected, information about these outcomes is displayed simultaneously to facilitate comparative analysis.

The third section of the interactive outline lists the world state parameters that have an impact on how the different outcomes are valued. These include whether or not (and when) press access has been granted, the time period(s) of interest, how much information Pakistan has shared with India, India and Pakistan's stance toward a military operation by the other, and how many hostages the Sikhs have killed and/or released. The user makes judgments about the current state of the world and either makes the appropriate selections in order to evaluate a current offer or choose world state parameters in order to see the value of continuing to negotiate to change the state of the world. More than one value of the world state parameter may be selected in order to facilitate this type of analysis.

Display Module

Two types of graphical displays are available in the GENIE system. By specifying only one time period in the world state parameters section, the user requests bar graphs (see Fig. 3) from the display module. The point totals are specific and easy to read; since information for different outcomes and world state parameters and viewpoints are displayed side by side, it is straightforward to conduct a comparative analysis. In addition to displaying the point totals for all of the selected outcomes for each selected viewpoint for every combination of selected world state parameter values, the bar graph also provides information on the probability of success, partial success, and failure for risky actions. An additional tool available on the interactive outline is called averages. Selection of the averages outcome results in the display of the point total that an actor would expect to earn on average by undertaking the risky actions in question rather than a display of the point totals and probabilities for success, partial success, and failure. This expected utility is calculated by multiplying the probability of each level of success by the associated point total and summing these scores.

The user selects the second graphical option by specifying a range of time periods of interest in the world state parameter section. The result is a line graph display (see Fig. 4) that facilitates user evaluation of the role of time in the negotiations.

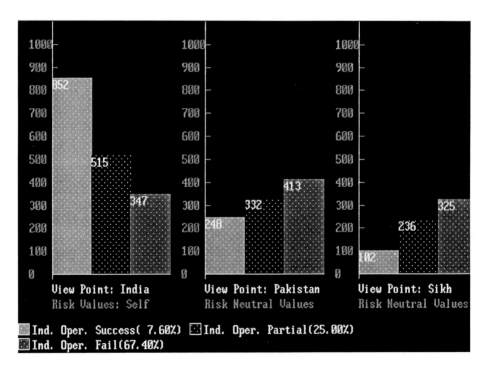

FIGURE 3. *Bar graphs available in GENIE.*

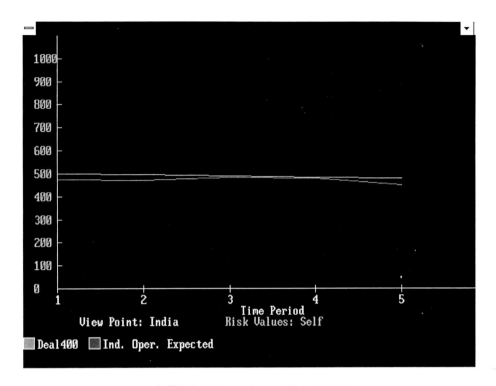

FIGURE 4. *Line graphs available in GENIE.*

Analytical Tools

GENIE provides two analytical tools in addition to the graphical displays. These include a search for mutually beneficial resolutions and bargaining minimums. Mutually beneficial resolutions (MBRs; see Fig. 5) represent outcomes that are acceptable to all parties. Although a negotiator's main goal is to achieve the highest possible point total for him- or herself, it is generally not possible to reach a negotiated solution that does not take the other negotiatiors' interests into account. The MBRs tool takes all outcomes that have been selected by the user, rank orders their values (given the current world state) for each selected point of view, and displays the top three. If any of these top three resolutions are common to more than one player, they are highlighted for easy identification. These highlighted outcomes are mutually beneficial outcomes to the crisis.

The bargaining minimums tool (see Fig. 6) calculates the reservation prices for the players in a given world state. The reservation price is the value that a player can expect to earn through unilateral action in absence of a negotiated agreement. In other words, the reservation price represents the expected value of opting out of the negotiations. In the hostage crisis, players can opt out by launching military operations

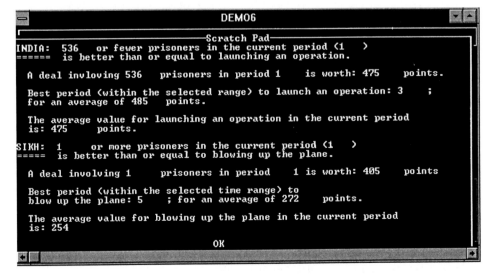

FIGURE 5. *Display of MBRs in GENIE.*

```
┌─────────────────────────────────────────────────────────────────────┐
│ ▼ │                          DEMO6                        ·    ▼ ▲│ ↑│
│I ├──────────┬──────────┬──────────┬──────────┬──────────┤           │
│n │    1     │    2     │    3     │    4     │    5      │           │
│d │          │          │          │          │          │           │
│i │          │          │          │          │          │           │
│a │SPA,845   │SPA,840   │SPA,834   │SPA,829   │SPA,824   │           │
│  │          │          │          │          │          │           │
│  │POE,607   │POE,604   │POE,605   │POE,601   │POE,591   │           │
│  │          │          │          │          │          │           │
│  │SBPE,535  │SBPE,540  │SBPE,546  │SBPE,551  │SBPE,555  │           │
│P ├──────────┼──────────┼──────────┼──────────┼──────────┤           │
│a │    1     │    2     │    3     │    4     │    5      │           │
│k │          │          │          │          │          │           │
│i │          │          │          │          │          │           │
│s │SPA,685   │SPA,681   │SPA,678   │SPA,674   │SPA,671   │           │
│t │          │          │          │          │          │           │
│a │D400,639  │D400,635  │D400,632  │D400,628  │D400,625  │           │
│n │          │          │          │          │          │           │
│  │IOE,363   │IOE,360   │IOE,350   │IOE,346   │SBPE,353  │           │
│S ├──────────┼──────────┼──────────┼──────────┼──────────┤           │
│i │    1     │    2     │    3     │    4     │    5      │           │
│k │          │          │          │          │          │           │
│h │D400,577  │D400,585  │D400,593  │D400,601  │D400,608  │           │
│  │          │          │          │          │          │           │
│  │SPA,269   │SPA,277   │SPA,284   │SPA,292   │SPA,300   │           │
│  │          │          │          │          │          │           │
│  │IOE,264   │IOE,272   │IOE,271   │IOE,279   │IOE,298   │           │
│  └──────────┴──────────┴──────────┴──────────┴──────────┘           │
│KEY:                                                                 │
│Mutually Beneficial India-Pakistan-Sikh Resolution.                  │
│D400: Deal400                           SPA: Sikh-Pak. Agreement     │
│IOE: Ind. Oper. Expected                POE: Pak. Oper. Expected      │
│SBPE: Sikh Blowup Plane Expected                                     │
│ ◄ │                                                              │ ► │
└─────────────────────────────────────────────────────────────────────┘
```

FIGURE 5. *Display of MBRs in GENIE.*

```
┌─────────────────────────────────────────────────────────────────────┐
│ ▼ │                          DEMO6                             ▼ ▲│  │
│ ┌─────────────────────────Scratch Pad───────────────────────────┐   │
│INDIA:  536   or fewer prisoners in the current period (1   )        │
│======  is better than or equal to launching an operation.           │
│                                                                     │
│  A deal involving 536   prisoners in period 1   is worth: 475   points. │
│                                                                     │
│  Best period (within the selected range) to launch an operation: 3   ; │
│  for an average of 485   points.                                    │
│                                                                     │
│  The average value for launching an operation in the current period │
│  is: 475      points.                                               │
│                                                                     │
│SIKH:  1    or more prisoners in the current period (1   )           │
│=====  is better than or equal to blowing up the plane.              │
│                                                                     │
│  A deal involving 1    prisoners in period   1 is worth: 405   points │
│                                                                     │
│  Best period (within the selected time range) to                    │
│  blow up the plane: 5   ; for an average of 272   points.           │
│                                                                     │
│  The average value for blowing up the plane in the current period   │
│  is: 254                                                            │
│                               OK                                    │
│ ◄ │                                                              │ ► │
└─────────────────────────────────────────────────────────────────────┘
```

FIGURE 6. *Bargaining minimums tool provided by GENIE.*

or blowing up the plane. Negotiation theory identifies the concept of a reservation price as important to strategy selection (*28, 29*).

The bargaining minimums feature calculates the reservation price for each selected player given a selected state of the world. It calculates the time period that will yield the highest expected payoff and displays this information. It then identifies the negotiated settlement that provides an equivalent (or slightly higher) payoff. Negotiation theory suggests that negotiators should not accept settlements valued lower than their reservation price (*28, 29*); however, in the hostage crisis scenario all options for opting out of the negotiations are probabilistic, so this choice will be tempered by the negotiator's risk attitude.

Language and Communication

All communications during the negotiation take place through the use of a language editor. (See Fig. 7.) This menu-driven program allows the user to choose a recipient, select from different categories of messages, select a message, and then, if appropriate, add threats or promises to the message. The message sets are different for each of the three roles. Once a messsage is built, it is sent via an electronic mail system. As messages are sent, they are recorded in data files, which facilitates later analysis in conjunction with other features of either training or experimental work.

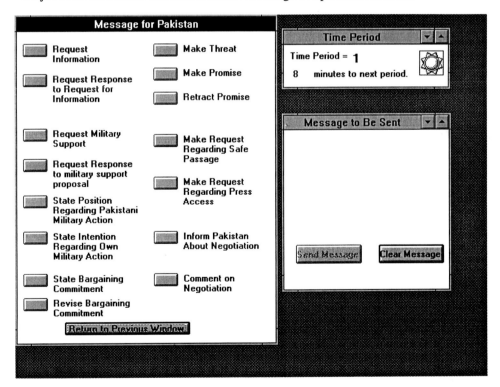

FIGURE 7. *Language editor provided in GENIE.*

Experimental Results

Negotiation support systems have been used to conduct a wide variety of negotiation research, examining factors such as the negotiation context or process and socioeconomic issues. (See Refs. *30* and *31* for excellent analysis of this research.) To date, two research programs have been conducted using GENIE. The first compared the performance of negotiators supported by the DSS in the hostage crisis with those who were not supported. The second and continuing program explores the impact of cognitive complexity (*32*) on the use of the DSS and negotiation behavior and outcomes.

DSS USE AND UTILITY MAXIMIZATION

Our first line of research examined the proposition that the use of GENIE encourages subjects to be utility maximizers, which in turn results in a better negotiation performance than is the case for nonusers (*33*). Subjects were drawn from political science classes at the University of Maryland that included international negotiation components. They were randomly assigned to either DSS or non-DSS treatment groups. The DSS users received training in how to use GENIE's many features. The non-DSS group received printed materials detailing all of the data in GENIE's knowledge base and how to calculate point total, probabilities, expected utilities, and reservation prices from this data. At no time was this group told of the existence of a DSS. At the end of the training sessions, each group took identical quizzes assessing their proficiency with the model and received scores that differed by only 3 percent. A one-tailed t test produced a p value of .355, giving us statistical confidence that the two groups did in fact perform equally well in evaluating the utility of outcomes in the absence of the time pressures associated with crisis negotiation.

Subjects were randomly assigned to DSS and non-DSS simulation groups. The non-DSS control groups all comprised non-DSS subjects. The DSS treatment groups consisted of two non-DSS users and one DSS user. Pakistan was chosen as the DSS user since Pakistan plays the role of a self-interested mediator, which is very different from the other two roles. Both groups were informed that they would receive a cash payment based upon the point totals that they achieved in the simulation. In total, ten treatment groups and nine control groups (a total of 57 subjects) participated in the simulation. At the end of the simulation, each subject filled out a postsimulation questionnaire asking for information on motivation, strategy, and information usage during the simulation.

The major findings can be summarized as follows:

1. DSS users are more likely than non-DSS users to identify utility maximization as their primary objective in a crisis negotiation. While DSS users are able to evaluate alternative outcomes and thus improve their probability of achieving high utility scores, non-DSS users faced with the same mass of information and time constraints are forced to use less objective and less easily quantified tools.
2. DSS users are likely to achieve higher utility scores in the simulation than their non-DSS counterparts; that is, not only will they be more motivated to see utility maximization as a goal, but they will be more successful in actually achieving such outcomes.
3. The presence of a DSS user among the parties in a crisis simulation will lead to the

achievement of higher total utility scores for that group, as compared to simulations in which none of the parties was DSS-supported. The supported party is thus likely to use his or her superior analytic ability to move the negotiation toward mutual benefit.

4. The presence of a DSS-supported user among the parties increases the probability of achieving agreement in the negotiation. This finding is consistent with the earlier finding in which mutual benefit is more easily achieved when DSS-support is available.

COGNITIVE STRUCTURE AND CRISIS DECISION MAKING

The second line of research explores the impact of differing levels of cognitive complexity upon crisis negotiation (34). We expect that the more developed the decision maker's cognitive schema, the more likely it is that utility-maximizing behavior will take place: accurate definition of goals, identification of strategies available for achieving goals, evaluation of the utilities associated with each strategy, and choice of that strategy most likely to maximize expected utility. This line of experiments was based on a measure of cognitive complexity first developed by Harvey, Hunt, and Schroder (35) and Schroder, Driver, and Streufert (36). (For a recent review of the state of this approach, see Ref. 37). While a diverse set of hypotheses has been examined in our work, the following major findings are illustrative:

1. A moderate relationship was found between cognitive complexity and the ability to understand features of the DSS; that is, without the ability to deal with a certain amount of complexity in a crisis, a sophisticated tool such as the GENIE DSS will not be able to overcome the inherent difficulty some individuals have in coping with complex and interdependent phenomena.

2. While no overall relationship was found between the level of cognitive complexity and performance in the hostage crisis simulation, role appears to be an important intervening variable. Subjects randomly assigned to represent India in the simulation showed a significant positive relationship between cognitive complexity and score on the simulation outcome, while negative results were found for the Sikhs and no relationship was found for the Pakistani. We conclude that the ability of the subject to identify with the role being played allows the subject to take advantage of his or her cognitive skills to enhance the probability of achieving a utility-maximizing outcome.

3. Experience in decision making and familiarity with crises' impacts on the individuals' ability to take advantage of superior cognitive development. In particular, this is manifested in the ability to resolve crises through the achievement of agreements among the parties and to avoid the use of violence in the resolution of conflict.

4. The closer the parties to a crisis were in terms of their cognitive complexity scores, the more likely they were to achieve positive outcomes, both individually and as a group. In addition, the more diverse the group, the greater the feeling of frustration, and the longer it took to reach an outcome.

Future Work

The version of GENIE reported upon in this article is fully dedicated to the hostage crisis scenario. A generalized version is currently under development. (See Fig. 8.) This generalized DSS is capable of supporting any $n < = 6$ player time variant negotiations with full information. This new version of the DSS will actually consist of two

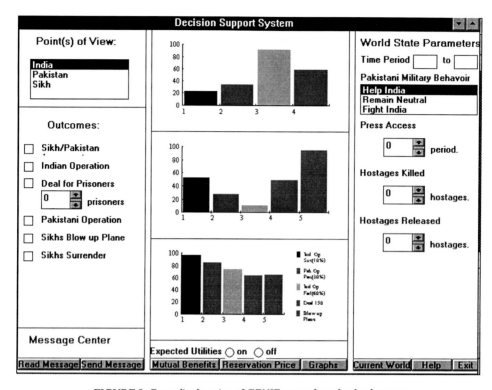

FIGURE 8. *Generalized version of GENIE currently under development.*

different programs. The first is the DSS creation shell, which is intended for the use of the scenario author. The second is the actual DSS, which reads data files created by the shell and displays the appropriate interface and information. Both packages are written in Java and are designed to run on the World Wide Web.

The DSS shell leads the scenario author through the process of entering the viewpoints, outcomes, and world state parameters and then their associated impact upon utility point totals and probabilities associated with each outcome. This information is written into an interface file (which contains all labels and input types) and a database file, which are read by the generalized DSS.

The generalized DSS program consists of one single-screen-sized form that is divided into four sections with a button bar across the bottom. The first three sections correspond to the viewpoints, outcomes, and world state parameters sections of GENIE's interactive outline. Each of these sections contains all possible labels, list boxes, and text boxes, which are assigned values and made visible as needed. When users select graphical displays or analytical tools from the button bar, the display is shown in the middle of the DSS screen so that all of the DSS controls remain visible. These displays can be enlarged to full screen for easy viewing or viewed in their smaller size alongside the model visualization capability of GENIE. This represents an improvement over the current version.

As discussed earlier, the current conceptualization of GENIE is a full information model. The strategic model of negotiation has been extended to include situations of incomplete information. The generalized DSS methodology can easily be extended to support an incomplete information model by providing the actor with information about his or her objectives only and the tools to enter impressions about the other players' objectives as developed through the course of negotiations. Future plans include developing this model, which will result in a DSS that in addition to being useful for research and training purposes in a simulation, can also be useful for actual decision support in a real-world crisis.

REFERENCES

1. I. M. Brecher and J. Wilkenfeld, A Study of Crisis, Ann Arbor, MI, Univ. of Michigan Press, 1997.
2. O. R. Holsti, "Crisis Decision Making," in *Behavior, Society and Nuclear War,* P. E. Tetlock., J. L. Husbands, R. Jervis, P. C. Stern, and C. Tilly, eds. Oxford University Press, England, 1989, pp. 8–84.
3. K. P. Sycara, *Decis. Sup. Syst.,* **10**, 121–126 (1993).
4. M. Poole, M. Holmes, and G. Descantis, *Mgt. Sci.,* **37**(8), 926–953 (1991).
5. P. Gray, D. Vogel, and R. Beaulair, *Eur. J. Op. Res.,* **46**, 162–176 (1990).
6. L. Jessup and D. Tansik, *Decis. Sci.,* **22**, 266–279 (1991).
7. T. Moehlman, V. Lesser, and B. Buteau, *Group Decis. Negot.,* **2**, 161–191 (1992).
8. M. Jarke, M. Jelassi, and M. Shakun, *Eur. J. Op. Res.,* **31**, 314–344 (1987).
9. G. O. Faure and M. F. Shakun, "Negotiating to Free Hostages: A Challenge for Negotiation Support Systems," in *Evolutionary Systems Design: Policy Making under Complexity and Group Decision Support Systems,* Holden Day, 1988, pp. 219–245.
10. G. Kersten, *Inform. Mgt.,* **8**, 237–246 (1985).
11. A. P. Wierzbicki, L. Krus, and M. Makowski, *Theory Dec.,* **34**, 201–214 (1993).
12. D. K. Samarasan, *Theory Dec.,* **34**, 275–291 (1993).
13. J. Teich, W. Wallenius, M. Kuula, and S. Zionts, *Eur. J. Op. Res.,* **81**, 76–87 (1995).
14. N. M. Fraser and K. W. Hipel, *Managerial DSS,* 13–21 (1988).
15. S. Matwin, S. Szpakowics, Z. Koperczak, G. E. Kersten, and W. Michalowski, *IEEE Exp.,* **4**(4), 50–62 (1989).
16. W. Michalowski, G. E. Kersten, Z. Koperczak, S. Matwin, and S. Szpakowicz, "Negotiating with a Terrorist: Can an Expert System Help," in *Managerial Decision Support Systems,* M. G. Singh, K. S. Hindi, and D. Salassa, eds. North-Holland, NY, 1988, pp. 193–200.
17. T. X. Bui, Buikling DSS for Negotiators *IEEE,* 164–173 (1992).
18. T. X. Bui, "Co-op," in *Lecture Notes in Computer Science,* vol. 290, G. Goos and J. Hartmanis, eds. Springer-Verlag, Berlin, 1987.
19. A. Rubinstein, *Econometrica,* **50**, 97–109 (1982).
20. S. Kraus, J. Wilkenfeld, and G. Zlotkin, *AI,* **75**, 297–345 (1995).
21. S. Kraus and J. Wilkenfeld, *IEEE Trans. Syst. Man Cyber.,* **23**, 313–323 (1993).
22. S. Kraus and J. Wilkenfeld, "The Updating of Beliefs in Negotiations Under Time Constraints and Uncertainty," in *Proc. of IJCAI93 Workshop on Artificial Economics,* Paris, France, 1993, pp. 57–68.
23. S. Kraus and J. Wilkenfeld, *Modeling a Hostage Crisis: Formalizing the Negotiation Process,* technical report UMIACS TR 90–19 CS TR 2406, Institute for Advanced Computer Studies, University of Maryland, College Park, 1991.
24. S. J. Andriole, *Handbook of Decision Support Systems,* Tab Books, Blue Ridge Summit, PA, 1989.
25. B. Spector, ed., *Supporting Negotiations: Methods, Techniques, and Practice,* International Institute for Applied Systems Analysis, Luxemburg, Austria, 1993.
26. B. Shneiderman, *Designing the User Interface: Strategies for Effective Human–Computer Interaction,* Addison Wesley, Reading, MA, 1992.
27. W. Pracht, *Dec. Sup. Syst.,* **6**, 13–27 (1990).
28. H. Raiffa, *The Art and Science of Negotiation,* Harvard University Press, Cambridge, MA, 1982.
29. R. Fisher and W. Ury, *Getting to Yes: Negotiating Agreement Without Giving in,* Houghton Mifflin, Boston, 1981.

30.   C. W. Holsapple, L. Hsiangchu, and A. B. Whinston, *J. Computer IS,* 2–8 (1995).
31.   D. Druckman, *Conflict Resol.,* **38,** 507–556 (1994).
32.   P. Suedfeld and P. Tetlock, "Psychological Advice about Foreign Policy Decision Making," in *Psychology and Social Policy,* P. Suedfeld and P. Tetlock, eds. Hemisphere, New York, 1991.
33.   S. Kraus, J. Wilkenfeld, K. M. Holley, and M. Harris, *Decis. Sup. Syst.,* **14,** 369–391 (1995).
34.   J. Wilkenfeld, S. Kraus, T. E. Santmire, K. M. Holley, and T. E. Santmire, *Cognitive Structure and Crisis Decision Making,* International Studies Association, 1996.
35.   O. J. Harvey, D. E. Hunt, and H. M. Schroder, *Conceptual Systems and Personality Organization,* Wiley, New York, 1961.
36.   H. M. Schroder, M. J. Driver, and S. Streufert, *Human Information Processing,* Holt, Rinehart and Winston, New York, 1967.
37.   P. Suedfeld, P. E. Tetlock, and S. Streufert, "Conceptual/Integrative Complexity," in *Motivation and Personality: Handbook of Thematic Content Analysis,* C. P. Smith ed. Cambridge Univ. Press, NY, Cambridge, 1992.

JONATHAN WILKENFELD
SARIT KRAUS
KIM M. HOLLEY

THE USE OF KNOWLEDGE-BASED DECISION SUPPORT SYSTEMS IN FINANCIAL MODELING

Introduction

Financial management includes a wide variety of significant decisions regarding three crucial issues: investment, financing, and dividend policy (*1*). Financial theory constitutes an essential framework, describing in general the effect of financial decisions on the operation of a firm or an institution, or on the wealth of an investor. This general framework is necessary for understanding the nature of financial decisions as well as the operation of financial markets, however, a precise framework is required for supporting financial decision making in a more specific context.

The determination of such a decision support framework is the aim of financial modeling. The term financial modeling has been used by several researchers to describe every quantitative analysis of a financial or economic system. This is a rather ambiguous and general definition that does not comprise the basic goal of financial modeling; that is, supporting financial decision making. Spronk and Hallerback (*2*), on the other hand, propose a more specific definition: "financial modeling is concerned with the development of tools supporting firms, investors, intermediaries, governments, etc. in their financial-economic decision making, including the validation of the premises behind these tools and the measurement of the efficacy of these tools." This definition is clearly decision support-oriented, focusing on a particular financial decision problem, the methodologies that are the most appropriate for solving this problem, and the way that the obtained solution can be successfully implemented.

According to this decision support orientation of the aforementioned definition of financial modeling, its role involves all the phases of a decision support process beginning from designing and generating decision alternatives to making the most appropriate decision and implementing it. Specifically, the first phase (design and generation of alternatives) is very closely related to another form of financial modeling: financial engineering. Finnerty (3) and Mulvey, Rosenbaum, and Shetty (4) define financial engineering as "the design, development and implementation of innovative financial instruments and processes and the formulation of creative solutions to problems in finance."

The combination of financial modeling and financial engineering provides a wide set of operations research tools, including simulation, optimization, decision support systems (DSSs), expert systems, neural networks, and stochastic processes for effective financial decision making, taking advantage of the basic concepts and notions that financial theory provides in order to support well-defined specific financial decision problems.

This article focuses on the contribution of knowledge-based DSSs (KBDSSs) in financial modeling. KBDSS technology integrates the traditional (DSS) framework with expert systems (ESs) to provide enhanced decision support capabilities which are essential for real-time financial decision making. The contribution of KBDSSs to financial modeling is examined from the database and model base management point of view, the user interface point of view, and of course from the overall system's capabilities in supporting the financial decision-making point of view.

The next section provides a brief description of DSS and ES technologies (as KBDSSs originate from these two approaches), outlining their basic features and limitations. The following section illustrates how the integration of DSSs and ESs in the KBDSS framework can be achieved, as well as the expected benefits in financial modeling of such an integration. The two subsequent sections present the FINCLAS (FINancial CLASsification) DSS (5) and the FINEVA (FINancial EVAluation) KBDSS (6, 7), respectively, depicting how DSS and KBDSS technologies contribute in the modeling and analysis of corporate performance and viability, one of the most essential decision problems in financial management. The final section discusses the basic conclusions and findings of this research and outlines some possible future perspectives.

Decision Support Systems and Expert Systems

Among the tools used in financial modeling and financial engineering, DSSs and ESs constitute two essential approaches in supporting financial decision making. Both DSSs and ESs provide the means for implementing sophisticated decision support methodologies to make decisions in real time and take advantage of the increasing processing power of modern computers.

The concept of DSSs was introduced from a theoretical point of view in the late 1960s. Klein and Methlie (8) define a DSS as a computer information system that provides information in a specific problem domain using analytical decision models as well as techniques and access to databases in order to effectively support a decision maker in making decisions in complex and ill-structured problems. The basic goal of a

DSS is thus to provide the necessary information to the decision maker in order to help him get a better understanding of the decision environment and the alternatives he faces.

DSSs have been developed in several fields of financial management, including financial planning (9–12), financial analysis (13–15), portfolio management (16–18), and banking (19–21). The criticism of DSS development has been focused mainly on the assumptions underlying the structure and the operation of a DSS; overlooking these assumptions, either by the developer who does not make them clear to the user or by the user who does not pay attention to them, may lead to improper use of the system and to misinterpretation of the obtained results (8, 22).

Except for the DSS approach, ESs constitute a significant contribution from the field of artificial intelligence to financial modeling and financial decision making. The aim of ESs' development in the field of financial management is to represent and exploit the knowledge of experts in financial, credit, or investment analysis in a computerized system that will be able to draw conclusions and provide decision makers with recommendations on a specific financial problem at hand. An ES can thus be defined as a computer program that represents the knowledge and inference procedures of an expert to solve complicated problems, providing possible solutions or recommendations (8). The main characteristic and basic goal of an ES is its ability to simulate the human logic and reasoning, to draw conclusions, and to provide the corresponding explanations in an easily understandable form.

ESs have been criticized, however, mainly because of two significant limitations: (1) it is often very difficult to elicit precise knowledge from expert analysts and to represent it in an appropriate manner in the knowledge base of an ES, and (2) ESs' flexibility is limited, since they employ shallow knowledge (knowledge that is suitable only in specific and narrowly defined problem domains), because once this knowledge has been incorporated in the knowledge base it is very difficult to update.

In the international literature, several studies have been conducted during the last decade that investigate possible connections and relationships among DSSs and ESs. Ford (23) examined the similarities and differences between DSSs and ESs from the objectives and intents points of view, the operational point of view, the user point of view, and the development methodology point of view. According to the author, as far as the objectives and intents are concerned, although the fundamental goal of DSSs and ESs is basically the same (the improvement of the quality of decisions), their underlying philosophies and objectives differ. Concerning the operational point of view, DSSs allow the user to confront a decision problem in a personal manner, providing the ability to manipulate data and models in different ways. On the other hand, ESs provide little flexibility in the way the decision problem is analyzed. As far as the users are concerned, Ford argues that DSSs are primarily applied in the business or organizational fields, while ESs are typically associated with scientific research. The users of DSSs are involved in the development of the system, while the users of ESs do not participate in the development process. Finally, according to the development methodology, both DSSs and ESs are designed through an iterative or prototyping approach.

Doukidis (24) carried out a survey on sixty-seven ESs to investigate whether or not they employed DSS concepts. The survey was based on a questionnaire model composed of a list of key concepts of DSSs, such as their role, their design features, their components, and phases of the decision they support. The results of this survey show that three fundamental issues of DSSs are employed in ESs: semistructured task, support, and effectiveness. The main differences concern the boundary of the problem space and the way that the problem is solved. Henderson (*25*) investigated the existence of synergy between DSS and ES research. He concluded that in many respects, the similarities between these areas appear to dominate the differences. Finally, a critical review of DSSs and ESs can be found in the studies of Klein and Methlie (*8*) and Zopounidis, Doumpos, and Matsatsinis (*26*).

Knowledge-Based Decision Support Systems

According to the brief description of DSSs and ESs in the previous section, it is clear that DSSs are commonly used to perform a quantitative analysis of the decision problem under consideration (in this case the term quantitative is used to describe the mathematical formulation of the problem), while ESs are mainly oriented in employing a qualitative form of reasoning to address decision problems. Financial decisions are usually too complex and ill-structured, however, so that their modeling requires a qualitative approach to understand both the problem under consideration and its characteristics and basic features, as well as a mathematical formulation to describe the problem and obtain "optimal" or generally "satisfying" solutions.

To address this twofold nature of financial decisions and in the light of the ongoing research in both DSSs and ESs, financial and operational researchers as well as computer scientists have exploited the combination of DSSs and ESs in the framework of an integrated computerized system. The term knowledge-based decision support system has been consecrated and is being used to describe this new type of system that integrates the database and model-based management capabilities of DSSs with the inference and explanations abilities of ESs.

INTEGRATING DSSs WITH ESs

The integration of DSSs with ES technology can be achieved in two ways: either by incorporating several ESs in the different modules of DSS (database, model base, user interface), or by considering an ES and a DSS as two distinct but complementary parts of an integrated KBDSS.

In the former case, the DSS is the key component in the KBDSS framework, while the role of the ESs is rather supportive. More specifically, the ESs interact with the several modules of the DSSs, helping the decision maker (financial/credit analyst, investor, portfolio manager, etc.) to use the database and model base management capabilities as effectively and appropriately as possible. In addition, the ESs facilitate the development of user-friendly interfaces.

On the contrary, in the second approach for integrating DSSs and ESs, the structure of the KBDSS is considered as the combination of two major modules: an ES module and a DSS module. Both of these parts are used separately to support the financial modeling process, taking advantage of the specific characteristics and capabilities that each one can provide. Nevertheless, besides this separate use of the DSS and the ES, there can be a link between them, enabling the transfer of the obtained results among the two modules; the results obtained through an inference procedure carried out by the ES can be used as inputs for further analysis by the DSS component and vice versa.

BENEFITS OF INTEGRATING DSSs AND ESs IN THE KBDSS FRAMEWORK

Both DSSs and ESs have already been applied with relative success in the last three decades to the study and modeling of financial decision problems. Consequently, it would be of major interest to examine the possible advantages and benefits that are expected to come from their integration in the context of an integrated KBDSS. This has been an issue that has attracted the interest of researchers in the fields of DSSs and ESs.

Turban and Watkins (27) provide an excellent comprehensive discussion of this issue. More specifically, the authors discuss the benefits of integrating ESs and DSSs in terms of their possible contribution in database management, model base management, and user interface as well as in the overall capabilities of the resulting KBDSS. In particular, as far as the database and the database management system (DBMS) are concerned, DSSs provide database capabilities to ESs, while on the other hand ESs improve the construction, operation, and the overall capabilities of the DBMS, as well as the accessibility to large databases. Concerning the model base and the model base management system (MBMS), DSSs provide an initial problem structuring through standard models and computations, and also provide data to models, as well as storage of models developed by the decision makers in the model base. The use of ESs improves the model base management by supporting the generation of alternatives, the selection of the appropriate models according to the available data, and the structuring of the problem analysis process. Furthermore, ESs contribute to the interpretation of the results of the models, provide guidance to decision makers through the basic assumptions underlying the application of these models, and improve the sensitivity analysis and trial-error processes. The contribution of DSSs in the design of user-friendly interfaces mainly focuses on the incorporation of the appropriate presentation means, which match the requirements of the decision maker. On the other hand, ESs provide explanations concerning the use of the system, communication with the decision maker using natural language, interactivity in the problem-solving process, and tutoring capabilities. Finally, concerning the overall system capabilities, DSSs help the decision maker to get experience in data collection as well as in the implementation of several sophisticated decision models, and they also incorporate the preferences and decision policy of the decision maker in the decision-making process. ESs using the knowledge and experience of experts can provide intelligent advice as well as explanations concerning their estimations and conclusions.

On the basis of these contributions of DSSs and ESs in the development of integrated KBDSSs, one could distinguish the new possibilities, perspectives, and contribution of KBDSSs' development and implementation in the improvement of the decision-making process, especially in the field of financial modeling, in the following three main aspects:

- *Understanding the operation and the results of the system:* incorporating a knowledge base in a DSS can help the decision makers to understand the results of the mathematical models. The knowledge base provides the necessary explanations concerning the reasoning process of the system, its basic assumptions, and its operation. The methodology used by the system can thus be clearly presented to the decision makers, helping them to learn the decision analysis process of the problem under consideration. At the same time the interpretation of the results is achieved, avoiding their misunderstanding and misinterpretation. The quantitative results are transformed into qualitative explanations, which are easiest to understand and are often of greater significance to the decision makers.

  Specifically, in the field of financial management the significance of the decisions taken necessitates their full justification. For instance, in the credit-granting problem, the credit analyst should be able to argue upon the rejection of a loan application to an applicant, while on the other hand he or she should be able to justify the granting or rejection of a credit to the top managers of the bank or the credit institution. Although a mathematical model could be used to derive a credit-granting decision, the credit analyst can hardly use the score of a credit application obtained through a credit-scoring system to justify the acceptance or rejection of the application either to the applicant or to his or her senior officers. The justification must be based upon the special characteristics of the applicant (weaknesses or strengths on each evaluation criterion) and the way that these characteristics affect the final decision. A knowledge base incorporating the expertise of credit-granting experts, as well as knowledge on the mathematical models that are used, can provide a qualitative interpretation of the quantitative results and support the credit analyst in implementing the final decision.

- *The objectiveness and the completeness of the results is ensured:* the combination of the ES's results with those derived from mathematical models and analytical techniques increases the objectiveness of the final results. The subjective results of the ES (which depend on the expert's knowledge) are not final estimations of the system. Except for the expert's knowledge represented in the ES's results, the decision maker is also provided with the results derived from mathematical models from the fields of multicriteria analysis, multivariate statistical analysis, and mathematical programming. The results of this combination correspond not only to the expert's opinion, but also to the preferences and the policy of the decision maker.

  For instance, consider the portfolio selection problem, in which the objective of the investor is initially to identify the stocks, bonds, or mutual funds that constitute the best investment opportunities; then, taking into consideration his or her risk aversion policy as well as the available amount of money that he or she is willing to invest, the objective is to determine the "optimal" or more generally the "most satisfying" portfolio. An ES incorporating the knowledge of expert portfolio managers can be used to examine the current economic and stock exchange condition as well as the financial and stock market behavior of the stocks, bonds, and mutual funds and provide an evaluation of the available investment opportunities. An ES has difficulty analyzing all the special characteristics, behavior, and preferences of an investor, however. On the other hand, a sophisticated mathematical model can consider these key factors in portfolio selection and can be used to determine the efficient set of portfolios (considering the alternatives that have been identified in the previous stage as the most appropriate investment opportunities) and to select from this set the portfolio that meets the preferences of the investor and the constraints that he or she poses.

- *The structuring of the proper decision analysis is achieved:* the usefulness and the suitability of the decision analysis techniques often vary, depending on the available data of the examined decision problem. According to the existing data, the use of a certain analysis or a mathematical model may be unnecessary or even inappropriate, and consequently the decision maker could be led to incorrect estimations and conclusions. The knowledge concerning the problem domain represented in a knowledge base can be used to face such problems, recommending the decision analysis process and the appropriate analytical models that correspond to the available data. The structuring of the decision analysis process is thus achieved, ensuring the effectiveness, the applicability, and the validity of the decision analysis models and techniques.

A common problem of this type that is often overlooked in real-world financial applications involves the application of multivariate statistical methods that are based on specific statistical assumptions. For instance, applying linear discriminant analysis to predict business failure when qualitative variables should be considered violates the assumption that the variables follow a multivariate normal distribution. In this case a quadratic discriminant analysis would be more appropriate to use. Similarly, when the equal variance-covariance matrices assumption is violated, a logit or probit analysis should be applied instead of discriminant analysis (linear or quadratic). Using a knowledge base and depending on the specific type of data considered in financial decision problems such as business failure, recommendations can be provided on the methods and models that should be used to reach a decision. Furthermore, the ES can be used as a data-mining tool to analyze the characteristics of the alternatives that are considered (firms, investment projects, countries, loan applications, etc.) to determine their specific features, and even to identify possible outliers that are common in finance (as much as 10% of financial data may consist of outliers; 28) and that should be studied in more detail by the analyst.

Recently, several KBDSSs have been proposed in the modeling of financial decision problems: the ISPMS (intelligent stock portfolio management system) system (29), the PMIDSS (portfolio management intelligent decision support system) system (30), and the investment portfolio selection decision support system (31) for portfolio selection and management; the LASS (lending analysis support system) system (32), the CGX system (33), and the CREDEX (CREDit EXpert) system (34, 35) for credit-granting problems; the FINEVA system (6,7) and the KABAL (kabal is the Norwegian word for patience) system (36) for financial analysis; and the INVEX (investment advisory expert system) system (37) and the Cash Manager system (38) for capital investments.

The following two sections illustrate two systems for modeling financial decision problems regarding the assessment of corporate performance and viability. The first one, namely the FINCLAS system (5), is based on the DSS context. Its aim is to exploit the capabilities of the preference disaggregation approach of multicriteria analysis (39, 40) in order to provide support in the study of financial classification problems involving the assessment of corporate performance and viability. On the other hand, the second system, namely the FINEVA system (6, 7), is based on the KBDSS approach. The system combines an ES, with a multivariate statistical analysis method (principal components analysis) and with a multicriteria decision aid method (MCDA) to provide integrated estimations regarding the evaluation of corporate performance.

The FINCLAS System

The FINCLAS system is the outcome of an attempt to integrate powerful methodologies from the preference disaggregation approach of MCDA with DSS technology

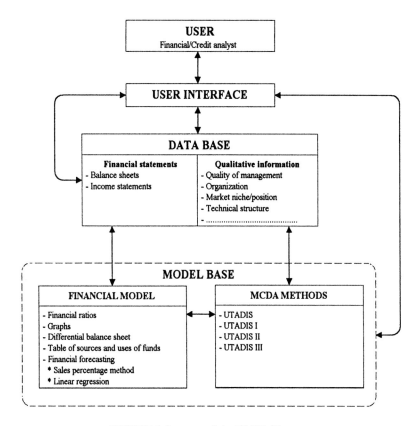

FIGURE 1. *Structure of the FINCLAS system.*

in order to provide financial/credit analysts with a user-friendly but powerful tool to study financial classification decision problems efficiently in real time.

The structure of the system is similar to the general structure of a DSS as proposed by Sprague and Carlson (*41*). The basic modules of the system include the database, the model base (financial and multicriteria model base), and the user interface (Fig. 1). There is a complete interaction and integration of these modules. The database management as well as the model base management are closely related to the friendly window-based user interface of the system, which enables the financial/credit analyst to easily access and handle the data of the firms and to exploit the financial modeling tools as well as the MCDA methodologies that are incorporated in the model base.

DATABASE

To perform a detailed, in-depth analysis of corporate performance and viability, two types of information are required: financial data and nonfinancial data regarding key factors for the operation of the firm, such as its management and organization, its technical structure, its market niche/position, and the market trend. This information is included in the database of the FINCLAS system.

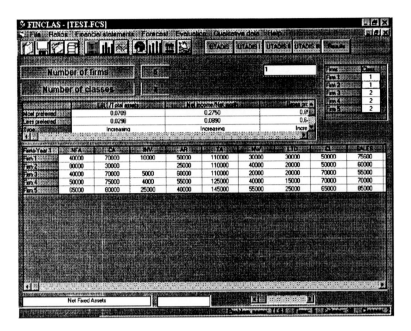

FIGURE 2. *Basic screen of the system (database).*

The financial data of firms are drawn from their financial statements (i.e., the balance sheet and the income statement) for a five-year period, which is commonly considered a pertinent time period from which to derive reliable estimations for the evolution of the basic financial characteristics of a firm. The financial data are further used by the financial model base of the system for the calculation of several financial ratios (e.g., profitability ratios, solvency and liquidity ratios, and managerial performance ratios), which are used in evaluation criteria for the classification of the firms. No specialized knowledge is needed to insert and handle the financial data of the firms in the database of the system. The system, using a user-friendly spreadsheet type of communication (Fig. 2), enables the financial/credit analyst to easily perform the basic database management activities, such as editing, storage, and retrieval of data.

In addition to the financial data of the firms, qualitative information is also included in the database of the FINCLAS system. This information involves the quality of management, the technical structure of the firm, its market position, its organization, the special know-how that the firm possesses concerning its production methods, the market trend, and so forth. These variables affect both the long-term and short-term operations of the firm, and they can be of even greater significance than the financial characteristics of the firm for the evaluation of corporate performance and viability. A different module of the database of the system is used to input such information to the system.

FINANCIAL MODEL BASE

The financial model base module of the FINCLAS system provides the financial/credit analyst with an arsenal of well-known modeling tools, including advanced graphical illustrations of the evolution of the financial ratios of the firms for the time period under consideration, the structure of the balance sheet and the income statement, statistical information regarding the special characteristics of each class of firms (mean, variance, etc.), the table of sources and uses of funds, and financial forecasting methods, such as the sales percentage method and linear regression. These tools are necessary in order to perform an initial descriptive financial analysis of the firms.

Graphical Illustrations

The financial model base of the FINCLAS system includes thirty financial ratios, which enable the financial/credit analyst to perform an extensive analysis of the financial characteristics of the firms concerning their financing, investment, dividend, and credit policies. Following the methodology proposed by Courtis (42), these ratios are categorized in three major groups: (1) profitability ratios, (2) solvency ratios (including liquidity), and (3) managerial performance ratios. Based on the financial data of the firms, the financial ratios are computed for a five-year period. (A shorter period can also be considered in case of a lack of data.)

The financial model base of the system provides a variety of graphical illustrations of the evolution of financial ratios as well as of the structure of the balance sheet and the income statement. This type of descriptive analysis is commonly used by financial/credit analysts as a preliminary, elementary but useful examination of the financial characteristics of firms in order to derive an overall view of their financial situations.

The Table of Sources and Uses of Funds

The table of sources and uses of funds constitutes a tool for the dynamic analysis of the inflows and outflows of the firm and their uses that affect its financial position in order to examine the investment and financing policy of a firm. Any decrease in assets or increase in total liabilities and stockholders' equity constitutes a source of funds, while any increase in assets or decrease in total liabilities and stockholders' equity constitutes a use of funds. The construction of the table of sources and uses of funds is achieved based on the changes in the accounts of the balance sheet for two successive years and using some additional information (e.g., purchases and sales of fixed assets, depreciation policy, and possible increase in capital stock by incorporation of retained earnings; Fig. 3).

Financial Forecasting Methods

The sales percentage method and linear regression are two simple financial forecasting methods commonly used in corporate finance. The aim of the sales percentage

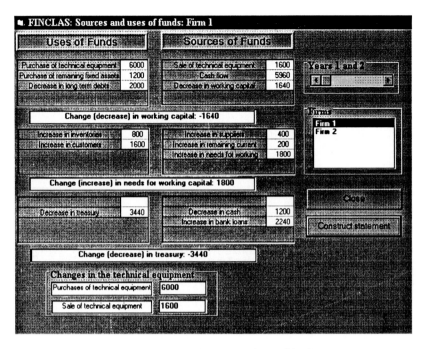

FIGURE 3. *Table of sources and uses of funds.*

method is to forecast the external financing required for a given increase in sales, as well as the percentage of the increase in sales that should be financed by external funds, according to the changes of the accounts of the balance sheet with regard to the increase in sales (Fig. 4). On the other hand, the linear regression method can be used to forecast the accounts of the balance sheet with regard to sales.

PREFERENCE DISAGGREGATION SORTING METHODS

Although all the financial modeling techniques that are incorporated in the financial model base of the FINCLAS system can provide useful information on the basic financial characteristics and policy of a firm, more sophisticated tools are needed to support financial/credit analysts in making a reliable estimation of corporate performance and viability. For this reason, an arsenal of MCDA methods are also included in the model base of the system. These methods originated from the preference disaggregation approach, which refers to the analysis (disaggregation) of the global preferences of the decision maker to deduce the relative importance of the evaluation criteria and develop the corresponding preference model as consistently as possible with the global preferences of the decision maker. This is achieved through ordinal regression techniques based mainly on linear programming formulations.

More specifically, the model base of the FINCLAS system incorporates the UTADIS method (UTilités Additives DIScriminantes; *43–46*) and three of its vari-

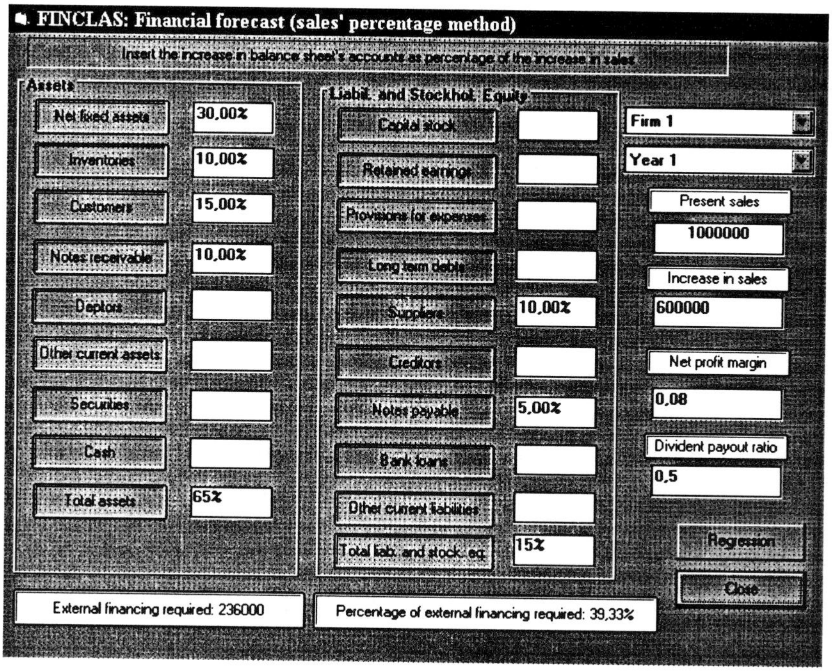

FIGURE 4. *Sales percentage method.*

ants, referred as UTADIS I, UTADIS II, and UTADIS III (*47, 48*). The UTADIS method, coming from the family of UTA methods (*44, 49*), is an ordinal regression method, based on the preference disaggregation approach of MCDA.

Given a predefined classification of the alternatives (i.e., firms) in classes, the objective of the UTADIS method is to estimate an additive utility function and the utility thresholds that classify the alternatives in their original classes with the minimum misclassification error. The estimation of both the additive utility function and the utility thresholds is accomplished through linear programming (LP) techniques.

$$\text{Minimize } F = \sum_{a \in C_1} \sigma^+(a) + \ldots + \sum_{a \in C_k} [\sigma^+(a) + \sigma^-(a)] + \ldots + \sum_{a \in C_q} \sigma^-(a)$$

s.t.

$$\sum_{i=1}^{m} u_i[g_i(a)] - u_1 + \sigma^+(a) \geq 0 \qquad \forall a \in C_1$$

$$\left. \begin{array}{l} \displaystyle\sum_{i=1}^{m} u_i[g_i(a)] - u_{k-1} - \sigma^-(a) \leq -\delta \\[2ex] \displaystyle\sum_{i=1}^{m} u_i[g_i(a)] - u_k + \sigma^+(a) \geq 0 \end{array} \right\} \quad \forall a \in C_k$$

$$\sum_{i=1}^{m} u_i[g_i(a)] - u_{q-1} - \sigma^-(a) \le -\delta \qquad \forall a \in C_q$$

$$\sum_{i=1}^{m} \sum_{j=1}^{a_i-1} w_{ij} = 1$$

$$u_{k-1} - u_k \ge s \qquad k = 2, 3, \dots, q-1$$

$$w_{ij} \ge 0, \sigma^+(a) \ge 0, \sigma^-(a) \ge 0$$

where $C_1, C_2, \dots, C_q$ are the q ordered predefined classes (C_1 the best, C_q the worst), $u_1, u_2, \dots, u_{q-1}$ are the corresponding utility thresholds that distinguish the classes (i.e., the utility threshold u_k distinguishes the classes C_k and C_{k+1}, $\forall k \le q-1$), σ^+ and σ^- are two misclassification error functions, s is a threshold used to ensure that $u_{k-1} > u_k$ ($s > 0$), and δ is a threshold used to ensure that $u[g(a)] < u_{k-1}$, $\forall a \in C_k$, $2 \le k \le q - 1$ ($\delta > 0$). a_i is the number of subintervals $[g_i^j, g_i^{j+1}]$ into which the range of values of criterion g_i is divided, and w_{ij} is the difference $u_i(g_i^{j+1}) - u_i(g_i^j)$ of the marginal utilities between two successive values g_i^j and g_i^{j+1} of criterion i ($w_{ij} \ge 0$).

Using the UTADIS method, the minimization of the total misclassification error is achieved in terms of distances of the misclassified alternatives from the utility thresholds using the two error functions $\sigma^+(a)$ and $\sigma^-(a)$. This objective may lead to placing some correctly classified alternatives very close to the utility thresholds, resulting in a poor generalizing (predicting) ability of the model. On the contrary, the UTADIS I method aims at minimizing the total misclassification error and at the same time maximizing the distances of the global utilities of the alternatives from the utility thresholds.

Both methods, UTADIS and UTADIS I, minimize the number of misclassified alternatives in an indirect manner through minimizing the magnitude of the misclassification errors. A more direct approach would be to minimize the number of the misclassified alternatives using the UTADIS II method. In this case the LP model of the UTADIS method is transformed into a mixed integer one using two Boolean variables, $M^+(a)$ and $M^-(a) \in \{0,1\}$, to indicate the misclassification of the firms. If an alternative is correctly classified then $M^+(a) = 0$ and $M^-(a) = 0$; otherwise, if $M^+(a) = 1$ or $M^-(a) = 1$ the alternative is misclassified. Consequently, the objective is to minimize the sum of $M^+(a)$ and $M^-(a)$. Finally, UTADIS III combines the objective functions of UTADIS I and II. Its aim is therefore to minimize the number of classifications and at the same time maximize the distances of the correctly classified alternatives from the utility thresholds.

In addition to the classification of the firms, through the UTADIS method and any of its variants the financial/credit analyst can determine the competitive level between firms of the same class (i.e., which are the best and the worst) according to their global utilities. Figure 5 illustrates the presentation of the classification results obtained through the preference disaggregation methods in the FINCLAS system. The original and the estimated class are presented, as well as the global utilities of the firms, the utility thresholds that distinguish the classes, the weights of the evaluation criteria, the total number of misclassifications, and the accuracy rate. The developed additive

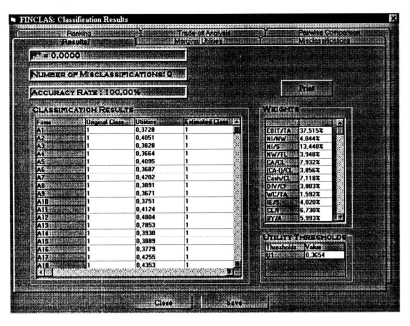

FIGURE 5. *Presentation of the classification results.*

utility model can be stored so that it can be used to evaluate new firms that are inserted in the database of the system (extrapolation).

The FINCLAS system has already been applied in the prediction of business failure (5), the assessment of credit risk (47), the prediction of company acquisition (50), and the appraisal of bank branches' performance (50), providing in any case very encouraging results both in terms of discriminating and predictive ability.

The FINEVA System

The FINEVA (6, 7) system is a multicriteria KBDSS for the assessment of corporate performance and viability. The basic characteristic of the FINEVA system is the combination of an ES with a multivariate statistical method (principal components analysis) and a multicriteria method to estimate the corporate performance and viability of firms. The basic parts of the FINEVA system and the way they interact are described in Fig. 6.

THE DATABASE

The database includes all the financial information necessary for the computation of financial ratios. This information can be drawn from balance sheets and income statements of the examined firms. A number of consecutive basic financial statements could also be included in the database to help the decision maker form important

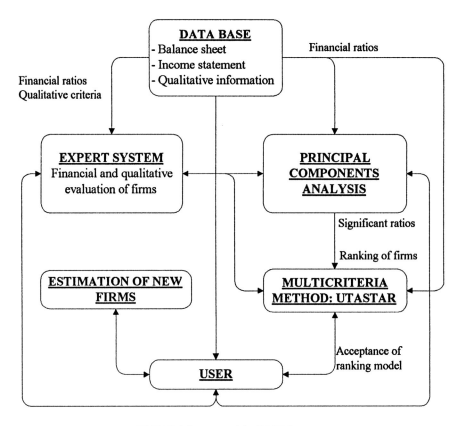

FIGURE 6. *Structure of the FINEVA system.*

trends for some classes of items on the balance sheet and income statement. In addition to the financial information necessary for the estimation of the financial status of a firm, some qualitative information is also significant, and therefore it is also included in the database of the system. Figure 7 illustrates the user interface of the system during the database management process.

The system takes advantage of the Microsoft's Windows 3.1/95 environment. A spreadsheet-type of communication (similar to the FINCLAS system) based on several menus and buttons (tools) is used to facilitate the efficient use of database management as well as of the overall system capabilities.

THE EXPERT SYSTEM

The ES part offers an initial evaluation and segmentation of the firms based on the examination of some financial ratios and qualitative criteria. The firms are categorized as those whose financial status is very satisfactory, satisfactory, medium, and not satisfactory.

The knowledge that is used by the ES was drawn from the international literature as

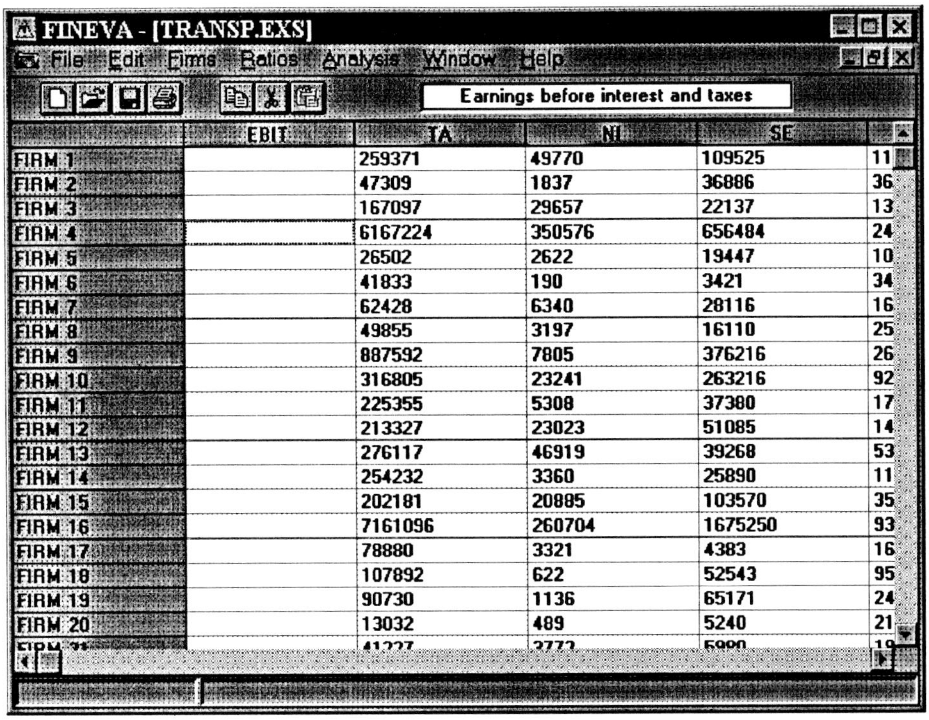

	EBIT	TA	NI	SE	
FIRM 1		259371	49770	109525	11
FIRM 2		47309	1837	36886	36
FIRM 3		167097	29657	22137	13
FIRM 4		6167224	350576	656484	24
FIRM 5		26502	2622	19447	10
FIRM 6		41833	190	3421	34
FIRM 7		62428	6340	28116	16
FIRM 8		49855	3197	16110	25
FIRM 9		887592	7805	376216	26
FIRM 10		316805	23241	263216	92
FIRM 11		225355	5308	37380	17
FIRM 12		213327	23023	51085	14
FIRM 13		276117	46919	39268	53
FIRM 14		254232	3360	25890	11
FIRM 15		202181	20885	103570	35
FIRM 16		7161096	260704	1675250	93
FIRM 17		78880	3321	4383	16
FIRM 18		107892	622	52543	95
FIRM 19		90730	1136	65171	24
FIRM 20		13032	489	5240	21

FIGURE 7. *Database of the FINEVA system.*

well as from experts in financial analysis, from academia, and from banking, through a series of meetings. The knowledge acquired is represented in the knowledge base through the production rules of the form: IF *conditions* THEN *conclusion* (*51*). The conditions part of a production rule may include one simple condition or a number of simple conditions combined with the logical operators AND, OR, and NOT. If all the conditions are fulfilled, then the rule is verified and the actions in the conclusion part of the rule are carried out.

Based on experts' experience in the field of financial analysis, limits concerning the possible values of each ratio and qualitative criterion have been set. Each financial ratio and qualitative criterion can be characterized as not satisfactory, medium, satisfactory, very satisfactory, or perfect, according to the corresponding limits posed.

Two examples of rules that the knowledge base includes are presented below. The first rule concerns the profitability of total assets and stockholder's equity, and the second rule concerns the estimation of a firm based on qualitative criteria.

if	financial profitability = very satisfactory	and
	industrial profitability = not satisfactory	or
	industrial profitability = medium	
then	profitability of total assets and stockholders' equity = satisfactory.	

if   managers' work experience = medium   and
        firm's market niche/position = medium   and
        firm's technical structure = satisfactory   and
        firm's organization = satisfactory   and
        firm's special competitive advantages = medium   and
        market trend = satisfactory

then   qualitative evaluation = satisfactory.

The inference engine of the ES utilizes both the backward and the forward chaining methods (8, 22). The combination of both forward and backward chaining provides the capability of confronting problems derived by incomplete information. The forward chaining method is very useful in cases in which the inference process should be controlled and guided to specific sets of rules in the knowledge base. On the other hand the backward chaining method is quite efficient in cases in which some hypotheses should be examined. The forward chaining method is thus used to guide the inference process to a set of rules, and the backward chaining method is applied within this set to derive a conclusion. This inference methodology is well suited to human logic and decision making. Moreover, through the inference engine the ES part of the FINEVA system provides explanations concerning the reasoning that was employed to reach a specific conclusion/estimation.

Figure 8 illustrates the communication between the ES part and the user (financial/credit analyst) during the estimation procedure of firms' performance and viability. The ES poses questions to the user, together with the necessary explanations concerning all possible answers. In the case of Fig. 8, the ES did not find any information in the database concerning the special competitive advantages of the examined firm. It thus poses the corresponding question to the decision maker. There are five possible answers: not satisfactory, medium, satisfactory, very satisfactory, and unknown. For each of these answers the corresponding explanations are provided in order to help the decision maker understand the modeling of the criterion. In this specific example, the ES explains that the special competitive advantages of a firm are not satisfactory when the firm does not possess any expertise for its production methods, the special competitive advantages of a firm are medium when the firm possesses a small amount of expertise for its production methods, and so on.

THE PRINCIPAL COMPONENTS ANALYSIS

Principal components analysis is included to assist the user in selecting the significant financial ratios. The principal components analysis is a factor method of descriptive character. In the case of corporate assessment, the principal components analysis shows the financial ratios that are the most important and that best describe the financial behavior of firms. The principal components analysis can also be used to classify firms in relevant categories, meaning that firms belonging to the same group have similar behavior and characteristics.

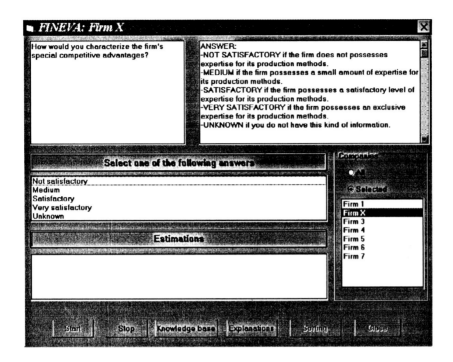

FIGURE 8. *The communication between the ES and the user during the estimation procedure.*

THE MULTICRITERIA METHOD

The FINEVA system also incorporates a multicriteria method in order to improve the system's capabilities in the evaluation of firms. The criteria used by this method are both financial ratios and qualitative variables that are chosen by the user (decision maker). The multicriteria method used by the system is called UTASTAR (52), an improved variant of the UTA method. Unlike the UTADIS method and its variants which are incorporated in the FINCLAS system, the UTASTAR method is oriented in the study of ranking problems. Consequently, instead of performing comparisons between the global utilities of the alternatives and the utility thresholds, in the UTASTAR method pairwise comparisons between the alternatives (firms) are performed in order to develop a ranking additive utility model to reproduce a predefined preordering (ranking) of the alternatives as consistently as possible.

More specifically, in the case of the evaluation of corporate performance, once the decision maker has expressed his judgment in the form of a ranking of the firms according to classes of risk, the system, by means of the ordinal regression method UTASTAR, optimally estimates the multicriteria additive utility functions (similarly to the UTADIS method), which are as consistent as possible with the decision maker's ranking. The preordering of firms required by the UTASTAR method is provided by the decision maker (sometimes with the help of the ES's results). Through the

UTASTAR method, the financial/credit analyst can determine a personal estimation model, which can be used as basic knowledge in the ES part (as a production rule based on the ranking or segmentation model) for the evaluation of new firms that are inserted in the database of the system. Figure 9 illustrates the presentation of the results obtained through the UTASTAR method in the FINEVA system. The results are presented both in a graphical form (ordinal regression curve) as well as in a table. Furthermore, several buttons can be used to store the developed additive utility model, to extrapolate it in new firms that are inserted in the system's database, to perform a trade-off analysis to resolve possible inconsistencies between the model and the preferences of the financial/credit analyst, and so forth.

The FINEVA system, using the multicriteria method UTASTAR, can also provide a segmentation (sorting) of firms into three predefined classes. In this case, the decision maker can propose two fictitious firms with their multicriteria evaluations in order to discriminate the set of firms (reference firms or reference profiles). These reference profiles are easy to determine on the basis of both the past experience of the decision maker and the repetitive character of financial decisions related to the assessment of corporate performance and viability, thus for a given firm (a) there are three possibilities.

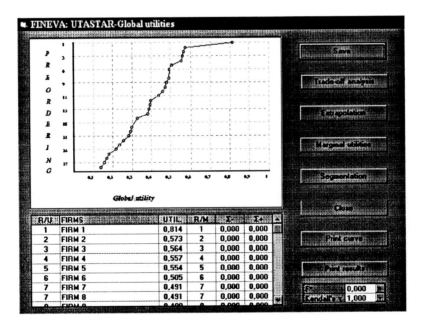

FIGURE 9. *Presentation of the results obtained through the UTASTAR method.*

$$u[g(a)] \geq u_1 \quad \Rightarrow a \in A_1 \quad \text{(acceptable)}$$

$$u_2 \leq u[g(a)] < u_1 \Rightarrow a \in A_2 \quad \text{(uncertain)}$$

$$u[g(a)] < u_2 \quad \Rightarrow a \in A_3 \quad \text{(unacceptable)}$$

where $u[g(a)]$ is the global utility of the firm (a), u_1 and u_2 are the global utilities of the two reference profiles called utility thresholds, all calculated by the UTASTAR method. The utility threshold u_1 distinguishes the firms among those that can be characterized as dynamic (acceptable) from those that need further study (uncertain). The utility threshold u_2 distinguishes the firms that need further study (uncertain) from those that can be characterized as bankrupt (unacceptable), then, by using the UTASTAR method, the system classifies the firms into these three classes.

The FINEVA system has been applied in the assessment of business failure risk of a sample of Greek industrial firms (7) as well as in the evaluation of the corporate performance of Greek transportation firms (53).

Concluding Remarks and Perspectives

The modeling of financial decision problems generally involves a complex process regarding both the qualitative description of the problem under consideration using the basic concepts and notions of financial theory as well as the development and implementation of mathematical formulations to achieve problem structuring and solution. On the other hand, since financial decisions are essential on a daily basis for banks, credit institutions, firms, investors, and stockbrokers, a powerful and efficient tool is required to derive real-time decisions.

This is the issue on which the major contribution of KBDSSs can be located. KBDSSs take advantage of the increasing capabilities provided by information technology and computer science to integrate the mathematical modeling and database management capabilities that characterize the DSS framework with the inference procedures and explanations capabilities of ESs. This integration provides new, enriched capabilities in financial modeling, and facilitates the use of the system by professionals who are not always familiar with the necessary mathematical tools to address financial decisions in an efficient and sophisticated manner.

This article examined how the integration of ESs and DSSs can be achieved in the KBDSS framework, and analyzed the main benefits and contributions of this integration in financial modeling. The FINCLAS and the FINEVA systems, which have been described, are two representative examples of how DSSs on the one hand and KBDSSs on the other can be used to improve financial modeling in order to support financial decisions in the field of corporate risk assessment.

As new technological advances are achieved in several fields of operations research such as multicriteria decision making, artificial intelligence, fuzzy sets, and optimization, embedding them in the existing framework of KBDSSs could considerably increase the effectiveness of the provided decision support.

REFERENCES

1. C. F. Lee, *Financial Analysis and Planning: Theory and Application,* Addison-Wesley, Reading, MA, 1985.

2. J. Spronk and W. Hallerbach, "Financial Modelling: Where to Go? With an Illustration for Portfolio Management." *Eur. J. Op. Res.,* **99**, 113–125 (1997).

3. J. D. Finnerty, "Financial Engineering in Corporate Finance: An Overview." *Finan. Mgt.,* **17**, 14–33 (1988).

4. J. M. Mulvey, D. P. Rosenbaum, and B. Shetty, "Strategic Financial Risk Management and Operations Research." *Eur. J. Op. Res.,* **97**, 1–16 (1997).

5. C. Zopounidis and M. Doumpos, "Developing a Multicriteria Decision Support System for Financial Classification Problems: The FINCLAS System." *Optimiz. Meth. Software,* **8**, 277–304 (1998).

6. C. Zopounidis, N. F. Matsatsinis, and M. Doumpos, "Developing a Multicriteria Knowledge-Based Decision Support System for the Assessment of Corporate Performance and Viability: The FINEVA System." *Fuzzy Ec. Rev.,* **1**, 2:35–53 (1996).

7. C. Zopounidis, M. Doumpos, and N. F. Matsatsinis, "Application of the FINEVA Multicriteria Knowledge-Based Decision Support System to the Assessment of Corporate Failure Risk." *Founda. Computing Dec. Sci.,* **21**, 4:233–251 (1996).

8. M. Klein and L. B. Methlie, *Knowledge Based Decision Support Systems with Applications in Business,* 2nd ed., Wiley, Chichester, Great Britain, 1995.

9. H. B. Eom, S. M. Lee, C. A. Snyder, and F. N. Ford, "A Multiple Criteria Decision Support System for Global Financial Planning." *J. MIS,* **4**(3), 94–113 (1987–1988).

10. R. L. Hayen, "Applying Decision Support Systems to Small Business Financial Planning." *J. Small Bus. Mgt.,* 35–46 (July 1982).

11. J. Jenkins, "Computer Based Financial Planning." *Omega,* **1**(5), 539–550 (1973).

12. R. H. Sprague, Jr., "Systems Support for a Financial Planning Model." *Mgt. Account.,* **53**, 29–34 (1972).

13. B. Mareschal and J. P. Brans, "BANKADVISER: An Industrial Evaluation System." *Eur. J. Op. Res.,* **54**, 318–324 (1991).

14. Y. Siskos, C. Zopounidis, and A. Pouliezos, "An Integrated DSS for Financing Firms by an Industrial Development Bank in Greece." *Decis. Sup. Syst.,* **12**, 151–168 (1994).

15. C. Zopounidis, A. Pouliezos, and D. Yannacopoulos, "Designing a DSS for the Assessment of Company Performance and Viability." *Computer Sci. Ec. Mgt.,* **5**, 41–56 (1992).

16. T. P. Gerrity, Jr., "Design of Man-Machine Decision Systems: An Application to Portfolio Management." *Sloan Mgt. Rev.,* **12**, 59–75 (1971).

17. M. G. Singh and R. Cook, "PRICE-STRAT: A Decision Support System for Determining Building Society and Bank Interest Rate Mixes." *Internat. J. Bank Mktg.,* **4**, 52–66 (1986).

18. C. Zopounidis, M. Godefroid, and C. Hurson, "Designing a Multicriteria Decision Support System for Portfolio Selection and Management," in *Advances in Stochastic Modelling and Data Analysis,* J. Janssen, C. H. Skiadas, and C. Zopounidis, eds. Kluwer Academic Publishers, Dordrecht, The Netherlands, 1995, pp. 261–292.

19. D. Langen, "An (Interactive) Decision Support System for Bank Asset Liability Management." *Decis. Sup. Syst.,* **5**, 389-401 (1989).

20. B. Mareschal and D. Mertens, "BANKS: A Multicriteria, PROMETHEE-based Decision Support System for the Evaluation of the International Banking Sector." *Revue des Systèmes de Décision,* **1**(2), 175–189 (1992).

21. R. H. Sprague Jr. and H. J. Watson, "A Decision Support System for Banks." *Omega,* **4**(6), 657–671 (1976).

22. E. Turban, *Decision Support and Expert Systems: Management Support Systems,* 3rd ed., Macmillan, New York, 1993.

23. F. N. Ford, "Decision Support Systems and Expert Systems: A Comparison." *Inform. Mgt.,* **8**, 21–26 (1985).

24. G. I. Doukidis, "Decision Support System Concepts in Expert Systems: An Empirical Study." *Decis. Sup. Syst.,* **4**, 345–354 (1988).

25. J. C. Henderson, "Finding Synergy Between Decision Support Systems and Expert Systems Research." *Decis. Sci.,* **18**, 333–349 (1987).

26. C. Zopounidis, M. Doumpos, and N. F. Matsatsinis, "On the Use of Knowledge-Based Decision Support Systems in Financial Management: A Survey." *Decis. Sup. Syst.,* **20**, 259–277 (1997).

27. E. Turban and P. R. Watkins, "Integrating Expert Systems and Decision Support Systems." *MIS Q.,* 121–136 (June 1986).

28. A. P. Duarte Silve and A. Stam, "Second Order Mathematical Programming Formulations for Discriminant Analysis." *Eur. J. Op. Res.,* **72**, 4–22 (1994).

29. J. K. Lee, H. S. Kim, and S. C. Chu, "Intelligent Stock Portfolio Management System." *Exp. Syst.,* **6**(2), 74–85 (1989).

30. J. B. Lee and E. A. Stohr, "Representing Knowledge for Portfolio Management Decision Making," working paper 101, Center for Research on Information Systems, New York University, Sept. 1985.

31. B. Shane, M. Fry, and R. Toro, "The Design of an Investment Portfolio Selection Decision Support System Using Two Expert Systems and a Consulting System." *J. MIS,* **3**(4), 79-92 (1987).

32. P. Duchessi and S. Belardo, "Lending Analysis Support System (LASS): An Application of a Knowledge-Based System to Support Commercial Loan Analysis." *IEEE Trans. Syst. Man Cyber.,* **17**(4), 608–616 (1987).

33. V. Srinivasan and B. Ruparel, "CGX: An Expert Support System for Credit Granting." *Eur. J. Op. Res.,* **45**, 293–308 (1990).

34. S. Pinson, "Credit Risk Assessment and Meta-Judgement." *Theory Dec.,* **27**, 117–133 (1989).

35. S. Pinson, "A Multi-Expert Architecture for Credit Risk Assessment: The CREDEX System," in *Expert Systems in Finance,* D. E. O'Leary and P. R. Watkins, eds. Elsevier Science Publishers, 1992, Amsterdam, The Netherlands, pp. 37–64.

36. G. Hartvigsen, "KABAL: A Knowledge-Based System for Financial Analysis in Banking." *Exp. Syst. Inform. Mgt.,* **3**(3), 213–231 (1990).

37. S. Vranes, M. Stanojevic, V. Stevanovic, and M. Lucin, "INVEX: Investment Advisory Expert System." *Exp. Syst.,* **13**(2), 105–119 (1996).

38. R. D. McBride, D. E. O'Leary, and G. R. Widmeyer, "A Knowledge-Based System for Cash Management with Management Science Expertise." *Annals Op. Res.,* **21**, 301–316 (1989).

39. C. Zopounidis, "Multicriteria Decision Aid in Financial Management," in *Plenaries and Tutorials of EURO XV-INFORMS XXXIV Joint International Meeting,* J. Barcelo, ed. Universitat Politècnica de Catalunya, Barcelona, 1997, pp. 7–31.

40. P. M. Pardalos, Y. Siskos, and C. Zopounidis, *Advances in Multicriteria Analysis,* Kluwer Academic Publishers, Dordrecht, The Netherlands, 1995.

41. R. H. Sprague, Jr. and E. D. Carlson, *Building Effective Decision Support Systems,* Prentice-Hall, Englewood Cliffs, NJ, 1982.

42. J. K. Courtis, "Modelling a Financial Ratios Categoric Framework." *J. Bus. Fin. Acc.,* **5**(4), 371–387 (1978).

43. J. M. Devaud, G. Groussaud, and E. Jacquet-Lagrèze, *UTADIS: Une Méthode de Construction de Fonctions d'Utilité Additives Rendant Compte de Jugements Globaux,* European Working Group on Multicriteria Decision Aid, Bochum, Germany, 1980.

44. E. Jacquet-Lagrèze and Y. Siskos, "Assessing a Set of Additive Utility Functions for Multicriteria Decision Making: The UTA Method." *Eur. J. Op. Res.,* **10**, 151–164 (1982).

45. E. Jacquet-Lagrèze, "An Application of the UTA Discriminant Model for the Evaluation of R&D Projects," in *Advances in Multicriteria Analysis,* P. M. Pardalos, Y. Siskos, and C. Zopounidis, eds. Kluwer Academic Publishers, Dordrecht, The Netherlands, 1995, pp. 203–211.

46. C. Zopounidis and M. Doumpos, "Preference Disaggregation Methodology in Segmentation Problems: The Case of Financial Distress," in *New Operational Approaches for Financial Modelling,* C. Zopounidis, ed. Physica-Verlag, Berlin-Heidelberg, 1997, pp. 417–439.

47. M. Doumpos and C. Zopounidis, "The Use of the Preference Disaggregation Analysis in the Assessment of Financial Risks," in *Managing in Uncertainty: Proceedings of VI International Conference AEDEM,* C. Zopounidis and J. M. Garcia Vázquez, eds. AEDEM Editions, Vigo, Spain, 1997, pp. 87–98.

48. C. Zopounidis and M. Doumpos, "A Multicriteria Decision Aid Methodology for the Assessment of Country Risk," in *Managing in Uncertainty: Proceedings of VI International Conference AEDEM,* C. Zopounidis and J. M. Garcia Vázquez, eds. AEDEM Editions, Vigo, Spain, 1997, pp. 223–236.
49. D. K. Despotis, D. Yannacopoulos, and C. Zopounidis, "A Review of the UTA Multicriteria Method and Some Improvements." *Founda. Computing Dec. Sci.,* **15**(2), 63–76 (1990).
50. C. Zopounidis and M. Doumpos, "A Multicriteria Sorting Methodology for Financial Classification Problems." in Abstracts and Papers of the 47th Meeting of the EURO Working Group "Multicriteria Aid for Decisions," Vol II, C. Zopounidis and I. Papoidimitriou, eds., Editions of the Technical University of Crete, Chamia, Greece, 1998, pp. 41–68.
51. N. F. Matsatsinis, M. Doumpos, and C. Zopounidis, "Knowledge Acquisition and Represention for Expert Systems in the Field of Financial Analysis." *Exp. Syst. Appl.,* **12**(2), 247–262 (1997).
52. Y. Siskos and D. Yannacopoulos, "UTASTAR: An Ordinal Regression Method for Building Additive Value Functions." *Investigação Operacional,* **5**(1), 39–53 (1995).
53. M. Doumpos, C. Zopounidis, and S. Hecker, "Multicriteria Evaluation of Transportation Firms in Greece," in *Transportation Systems,* M. Papageorgiou and A. Pouliezos, eds. Technical University of Crete, Chania, 1997, pp. 169–174.

BIBLIOGRAPHY

Barr, A. and Feigenbaum, E. *The Handbook of Artificial Intelligence,* vol. I, Morgan Kaufmann, Los Altos, CA, 1981.
Klein, M. and Methlie, L. B. *Knowledge Based Decision Support Systems with Applications in Business,* 2nd ed., Wiley, Chichester, Great Britain, 1995.
Sprague, R. H. Jr. and Carlson, E. D. *Building Effective Decision Support Systems,* Prentice-Hall, Englewood Cliffs, NJ, 1982.
Puppe, F. *Systematic Introduction to Expert Systems: Knowledge Representations and Problem-Solving Methods,* Springer-Verlag, New York, 1993.
Turban, E. *Decision Support and Expert Systems: Management Support Systems,* 3rd ed., Macmillan, New York, 1993.
Zopounidis, C. *New Operational Approaches for Financial Modelling,* Physica-Verlag, Berlin-Heidelberg, 1997.

CONSTANTIN ZOPOUNIDIS

USING DESIGN TO PROVIDE INTELLIGENT HELP IN INFORMATION PROCESSING SYSTEMS

As information processing systems (IPS) become more prevalent in the workplace there is an ever-expanding community of users that need to be instructed in their use. This requirement may be met by trainers and, to a lesser extent, by manuals (possibly presented online), however, the first solution is expensive, and the second limited in its objectives. The goal of the work described in this article is therefore to provide a methodology for the construction of integrated help systems that are capable of providing the quality of support of trainers but are as cheap and accessible as manuals.

This goal places extra constraints on the design and construction of the IPS, which must now be capable of taking account of the user's goals and previous experience if it is to be able to tune help adaptively to the context of use. Previous help systems have encountered problems integrating these requirements within a working application. The work described in this article addresses these by noting that the designer's description of an application contains much information that is useful in explaining its workings. It will show how extending the designer's description of the IPS (with a language that details how changes within the application occur) can allow for the construction of applications that are self-explicating. To this end an effects language is defined that connects the designer's description with the implemented functionality of the application, hence the two processes of design and construction are linked, and the act of building the application produces a system that a computer-based instructor can immediately use. In this article an extended design methodology will be described and it will be shown how to approach contributes to a system capable of supplying intelligent help.

Introduction

Many people now make use of computer applications to carry out tasks associated with their work, using the computer (or IPS) as a tool to achieve some specific goal. This can and does introduce problems since it places certain requirements on the users. How should they relate and represent their tasks to the IPS, and what exactly can the software achieve (i.e., what is the range of its functionality)? These difficulties mean that much time and money is spent on training people in the use of the particular IPS needed to carry out their assignments—time and money that could be saved if the application itself could teach the user while he or she was using the system for real.

The goal, then, for builders of instructional systems (variously known as intelligent tutoring systems (ITS) or intelligent help systems), is to construct systems that are able to coach a user in the intricacies of an application, offering help and advice as and when required. This goal places many extra constraints on the design of the IPS if it is to assist in delivering such help. It must have some knowledge of its own workings (a domain model) to understand the working context of the user. It must have some knowledge of the user (a user model) to be able to recognize that user's needs (and intentions), and it must have some knowledge of help giving (an instructor module) to decide on a suitable response to the user. In addition the IPS needs a communication manager to present information to users and to allow them to ask questions. This communication might be graphical or text-based, in the form of a dialogue or a straight piece of exposition. This article will outline the requirements of such a help system and will show the process of designing the application that might be used to construct the domain model. First we look briefly at the component parts of a help system and at the requirements that they need to meet.

Architecture of a Help System

Figure 1 gives one view of how a help system might be structured, showing its components and their relationships. Broadly speaking the instructor component has

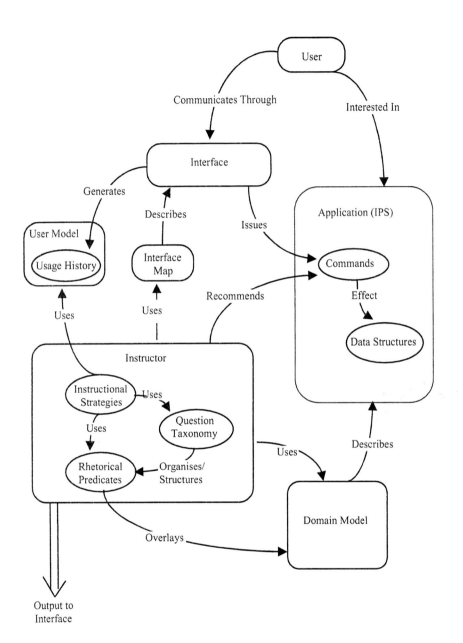

FIGURE 1. *Help system overview.* (Reprinted from C. Mallen, "Designing Intelligent Help for IPS." *Internat. J. Human–Computer Stud.,* **45**, 349–377, by permission of the publisher, Academic Press Limited, London.)

the general purpose of using the domain model to recommend commands to the user and to provide explanations of the behavior of the IPS. To this end the instructor has an instructional strategy subcomponent that employs knowledge about questions (the question taxonomy subcomponent), rhetorical predicates (the rhetorical predicate component, which accesses the domain model and returns information couched in terms that are familiar to the user, e.g. cause-consequence relations; Ref. *1*), and the user (through the user model) to provide suitable recommendations. These recommendations will include information about the application gained through the domain model, which supplies the understanding about the application that will form the content for any explanation the instructor may want to generate. The application itself consists of the data structures that contain the information that relates to the user's world, and that the user will want to access, and the commands that manipulate these. These commands will be issued via the interface through which the user communicates with the application.

The four components of the help system (domain model, user model, instructor module, and communication manager) must allow the system to

- Answer questions from the user that take account of its current workings and the state of the system. There have been many studies into categorizing the important questions required for help and explanation. (See, e.g., Refs. *3–5*.) Important categories include enablement ("How do I ... "), elaborate ("Tell me about ... "), and evaluation ("What happened ... ") questions.
- Provide operational descriptions and explanation (possibly with some conceptual or organizational overlay), but in ways that take account of the user's knowledge.

To effectively meet these requirements the help system should

- Recognize user plans. How does the help system recognize the task the user is doing and suggest actions?
- Tailor answers to the particular experience and knowledge of the user.
- Tailor answers to the user's current context.
- Change its answer to repeated questions. The answer to a question should be adjusted if the question has been asked previously. Repeated questions normally occur because the user wants a shorthand reminder or because the system is in a different state from when the original question was asked.
- Deal with issues of efficient usage (e.g., recommend placing repeated actions with a single action).
- Give advice on undoing actions (e.g., reversing, if possible, the results of a recently taken but unwanted, action).

Several computer-based help systems have been built to tackle the problems raised by each of these requirements, with different systems investigating how particular components can influence instructional and help-giving interactions. Some are described in the next section.

Examples of Help Systems

Previous help systems for IPS include UNIX Consultant (UC; *6*), So and Travis (*7*), Eurohelp (*8, 9*), and E-Help (*10*). UC and the So and Travis's system were both aimed at helping users of the Unix operating system, Eurohelp concentrated on an E-mail system, while E-Help supported a text editor. Each of these systems suffered limitations in the help they could provide. In E-Help, for example, a (user) task space was employed to recognize the inputs of the user as part of a domain task. This information enabled the system to suggest better (or alternative) tasks to the user. As the representation had no other detailed knowledge of the domain, however, it could offer only this useful but limited support.

In contrast, UC, a system concerned particularly with allowing communication in natural language, had no (user) task representation but did contain a detailed working model of the domain. Note that UC also contained a user model component, KNOME (*11*). This built a model of what the user knew by inference from a record of system usage. The model was used to classify the user's expertise and then to tailor responses to user questions. As there was no model for inferring a user's task or intention, however, the help system was limited to answering direct questions about the functionality of UNIX. So and Travis sought to improve this by using a five-level representation of the UNIX domain that extends from a description of the operating system objects through the command syntax up to the semantics of UNIX. Currently the syntactic levels are used to provide advice by parsing a user's input and correcting the syntax of fairly complicated sequences of commands. It is intended that this syntactic knowledge be used in conjunction with the semantic knowledge to provide more support at the user task level than is available with, for example, UC.

The Eurohelp system contained both a detailed working model (simulation) of the domain and a (user) task space related to operating in the domain. Its major drawback, however, was that it could not relate changes in the state of the domain to user tasks because it didn't have explicit knowledge of cause-effect relations that could closely link the two. This type of relation is needed to enable the domain state changes made by the user's commands to be linked to the domain state changes intended by the tasks (in the task space), which in turn relate to the goals of the user. This limitation in Eurohelp was caused in part by creating a generic functional description of the application that did not allow the specification of the main effects (or purpose) of the command and thus made no concessions to the way functions may be used in different contexts. In addition, this lack of knowledge of effect limited its ability to support the user in other important ways; for example, it was unable to relate user actions to changes in the domain, and so could not answer satisfactorily "What happened?" evaluation questions.

To address these problems requires to a greater or lesser extent an understanding of the domain that includes an ability to reason about the effects of actions taken in the domain. Building a domain model that meets these requirements is a difficult problem. For example, Neomycin (*12*) was constructed to extend the domain model of Mycin. This was to enable Mycin to generate explanations in a form suitable for human onlookers. Although Mycin contained a good working model of the domain that allowed it to diagnose (very effectively), it supplied inadequate explanations of its reasoning because it didn't provide the right sort of knowledge structures. Neomycin addressed this problem by introducing a new conceptualisation (or "epistemic map") of the domain. For this map Clancey argued it was necessary to make explicit the structural and strategic knowledge (the design knowledge) that was implicit in Mycin's domain model (essentially by "decompiling" the implicit strategic knowledge). This article will outline a methodology that is to provide just such an epistemic map for IPS. The methodology addresses in particular the general problem of connecting the elements of the working domain model model with an instructor's (more task-based) view of the world. It seeks to avoid the problems mentioned above by keeping the designer's description of the IPS (the "integrated" approach suggested in the Eurohelp* project report; Ref. 8, p. 345) and extending it with a language that details how change occurs (an effects language). Another approach is to design the system in such a way that it includes the knowledge of the users in the design stage (as opposed to knowledge about the user). (See, for example, Ref. 13, which outlines an approach whereby users become an important part of the design process.)

The important issue of how the generated help is to be presented and communicated to a user is not discussed in depth in this article. (Here the focus is on generating the content.) As is shown in Fig. 1, a full help system would have to make use of instructional knowledge in conjunction with a user model (for gauging a user's experience and intentions) to effectively help the user learn (in the sense of coming to know how this particular system is operated and behaves) about the domain. This requires knowledge about the user and his or her environment, and an implementation of theories of instruction and communication. All these are difficult problems that have been addressed by many researchers. (See, for example, Ref. 14 on learning theories; Refs. 15–17 on user modeling; and Refs. 18 and 19 on dialogue and communication.)

Presenting information to the user is the concern of effective interface design. A complete IPS normally consists of both an interface and an application, and both have an important bearing on the use of the IPS. Both should be guided by principles that help their design and construction. For the interface these are principles of presentation and principles of communication, and for the application these are principles of organization and principles of design. This article is particularly interested in the principles used to design and organize the underlying application, the argument being that by using these principles the help system will be capable of supplying better help than alternatives (with the same interface). There is an argument, however, that posits it is possible to have a completely transparent interface (in the sense of revealing an application's state and functionality) that for each user obviates the need for help. Interfaces can be designed to clearly reveal the functionality of the underlying application for most users, and indeed can be designed to adapt themselves to individual users' working patterns, (20). They have difficulty in revealing sequences of

---

*The system produced by the framework described in this article will be compared against the Eurohelp system, as this was the result of one of the most complete studies undertaken to investigate and develop online help. It was considered state of the art in 1990, and in the opinion of many has not been superseded since.

Help System Requirements	Definition	Domain Model Knowledge Sources
1. Static domain description	Ability to describe entities in a domain.	Design Description
2. Dynamic domain description	Ability to describe the way a domain changes.	Functional Description
3. Knowledge of Tasks	Knowledge of the way a domain is structured that relates to a users tasks when operating in that domain.	Design Description
4. Knowledge of Goals	Knowledge that the user may want to change the domain in a particular way, and a knowledge of how that change may be accomplished. Uses planning ability.	Design Description
5. Knowledge of Effects	Details of the particular way that an action causes a change in the domain. Relates the dynamic domain description and the knowledge of goals and tasks.	Functional Description
6. Ability to Communicate with User	Use of rhetorical predicates in answer frames managed by an instructor.	Instructor

FIGURE 2. *Some help system requirements.* (Reprinted from C. Mallen, "Designing Intelligent Help for IPS." *Internat. J. Human–Computer Stud.,* **45**, 349–377, by permission of the publisher, Academic Press Limited, London.)

actions, however. How can an interface analyze the current context and a user's past actions and reveal the next step to be taken (or worse, a set of alternative next steps with different consequences) without meeting the sorts of requirements laid out above? Even if the interface actions themselves can be revealed and demonstrated (*21, 22*) how are the consequences of the action to be revealed (short of actually taking the action, thereby changing the application state and allowing the interface to reveal the new state)? There is still a need for some underlying domain knowledge with which to reason about sequences of actions, and there is a need for an instructor to decide how to present this information.

This article is about whether and how the design description of a domain can be used to meet requirements of a help system and if this methodology has advantages over alternative techniques. (Similar approaches are being used to construct task models for computer-based agents; see, e.g., Ref. *23*.) These requirements are summarized in Fig. 2 and can be compared against the Wenger (*24*) requirements for an ITS and the Wasson and Akselsen (*25*) requirements for online assistance.

Using Design to Construct the Domain Model

Figure 2 shows the requirements a domain model needs to meet if it is to represent the application and thereby model (and reason about) its behavior. How is this domain model of the application to be constructed? Where should it come from? There are two broad approaches to building the domain model: (1) it can be constructed after the application has been built (retrofitted), or (2) it can be built as the application is constructed. The first route (retrofitting) was taken, for example, by Eurohelp (8), UC (6), and So and Travis (7). There are some problems for this route, particularly for large real-world applications. These include difficulties with building a representation that accurately models the behavior of the system, and difficulties in associating the effects of actions within the domain with the purpose of taking those actions (especially if an action's purpose depends on the context of its use).

To try and avoid these problems it might be more sensible to construct the domain model as the application is constructed (the "integrated" approach concluded by the Eurohelp project). If this route is taken, then the domain modeler can either (1) build the help representation in parallel with the application building, although this will probably improve the design, it suffers from some of the problems of (1) above; or (2) make the domain model "come out" of the design process itself. This has the advantage that the model produced will mirror the application. If it doesn't, then the application builder has strayed from the design. In addition, as the design process has to be gone through it seems a nice benefit (if only in terms of economy of time) for the domain model to be produced as part of the same process.*

If the design route is chosen, then the designer may create a new design methodology that also meets the help requirements, in which case it needs to be shown that this design methodology does allow the production of realistic applications. Alternatively they may use an existing methodology and see if it can already meet the help requirements. This has the advantage that it is already known that the methodology can build real systems. If it can be shown that the chosen design methodology can also address the particular requirements of help systems (which need to focus on how the system may be operated), then success will be achieved.

THE DESIGN PROCESS

The problem for any domain modeling language is maintaining the link between the dynamic behaviors of the domain and the descriptive language required for a ready understanding by the learner. The design process of an IPS is important because most of the concepts required by a help system are explicitly modeled during the design phase. If this information could be retained through the implementation phase then an IPS would be produced that is to some extent self-explanatory. Indeed, if the terminology used by designers is compared with the structures required for explana-

---

*It would be interesting to prove (or otherwise) the truth of the following conjecture. It is *necessary* for the domain model to come out of the design, otherwise there will always be discrepancies between the way chosen to model the system (and its behaviors) and the system itself. This must be considered an open question, however.

tion we can see some considerable overlap in language and concepts. For example, the Jackson structured design methodology talks about actions, world entities, goals, processes, and purposes. (See Ref. *26*.) This terminology can be compared against the rhetorical predicates used by Maybury (*27*) in his TEXPLAN system. He describes such predicates as "purpose" (function of entity or goal of action) and "event" (an accident, action, or process) as being key components in explanations. The domain model must therefore be susceptible to providing a description in these terms.

So the design methodologies, in their analyses, tend to describe the domain in the same terms that someone explaining the domain might use. This is not completely surprising; after all, a designer is called in to construct a tool to help some group of people achieve a task, and to build this tool successfully he or she must talk to the potential users in the terms we as humans use to describe them. As Gero (*28*, p. 28) says the "metagoal of design is to transform requirements, generally termed functions, which embody the expectations of the purposes of the resulting artefact, into design descriptions."

Traditionally, then, the designer departs with the description (or specification) and returns with a completed tool. If the solution to the problem is innovative or the tool is required to do a complex task, the likelihood is that the designer will have to explain the operation of the device and describe how it relates to the task in hand. If the tool is complicated and has much functionality (e.g., a computer application) the act of training may take some time, hence the desire for self-explicating systems. The problem arises because the act of constructing the tool from the design description (the process of implementation) loses the language of the specification (which supplies, e.g., the purpose of the tool) by allowing it to become implicit in the components that make up the tool. If this knowledge of purpose, which is in the design description, could be retained in some way, then we would have a tool able to explain itself, at least to some degree.

Computer applications exacerbate the problem because they reveal very little of their structure or intended use on first acquaintance. This is partly due to the fact that most consist of commands to manipulate data structures, both of which have lost a direct relation to the task the user is carrying out, hence computer applications benefit enormously from any "self-explanation". The goal, then, is to try and bridge the gap from the design to the tool, to retain the design information that is, to use a computer metamphor, "compiled out" during the implementation process. Fortunately, because computer applications are IPS, they lend themselves to solutions that require the maintenance of information. For example, they allow additional components and representational layers to be added to the system without complicating or changing the initial application. These layers can then be used to describe the application (or tool) and give lessons in its use.

Figure 3 shows a conceptual overview of the process of designing, constructing, and describing an IPS. What might be called the classic design process starts with the designer being requested to provide a system that allows some user population to carry out specified jobs. The designer starts by undertaking a user requirements analysis that reveals the entities and tasks called for in the domain and from which a conceptual model is constructed. A design methodology is then used to take this conceptual model and produce a more formal description (or specification) of the

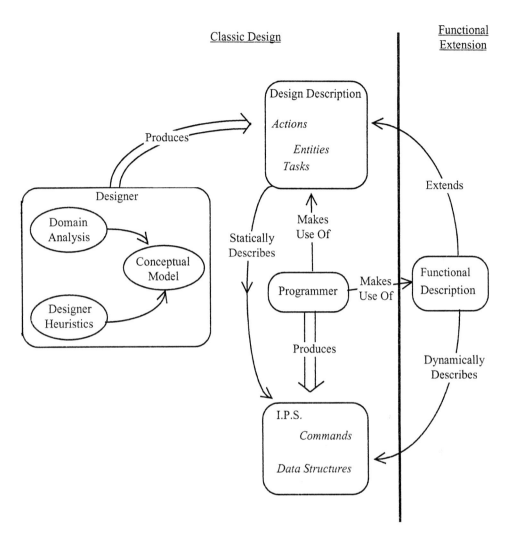

FIGURE 3. *The design process.* (Reprinted from C. Mallen, "Designing Intelligent Help for IPS." *Internat. J. Human–Computer Stud.,* **45**, 349–377, by permission of the publisher, Academic Press Limited, London.)

domain. This design description is then given to a programmer who produces code to implement an IPS that contains objects that may be manipulated in a way that mirrors the original requirements of the user population.

This user population will now be expected to translate its understanding of the domain into the language of the implemented system. This is, of course, the point at which a help system is required, to support the user in what is essentially a learning task (in the sense of coming to know how this particular system is operated and behaves), and one of the main problems for the help system is relating the functionality (of the implemented system) to the original user requirements. It is the job of the domain model component of the help system to link these two, but further complications arise because of the uncertainty introduced by allowing the programmer to translate the design description, which essentially provides a static description of the domain, into some code that must behave dynamically. The role of the functional description is to act as a bridge between the design description's static model and the implemented system's dynamic behavior, and so to plug this "knowledge gap" that is introduced by the programmer. This is why the functional description is so important to the help system; it significantly extends the help system's knowledge of the application and therefore the quality of support that may be given to the user.

In summary, a requirement for the domain model of a help system is that it should include both a static description of the objects or entities that exist in a domain and a description of the dynamic behavior that allow the state of a domain to change. This requires that the help system be able to plan a sequence of actions and understand the consequences of these actions, which in turn requires that it have some notion of a goal (or desired state of the application) and of effects (in the sense of an action causing an effect that changes the domain state) and hence some understanding of the ways in which a domain operates. It is precisely this sort of knowledge that is available from the design process.

CHOOSING A DESIGN METHODOLOGY

For producing the design description (the static application representation) of an application, it is necessary to chose a methodology that carries out the user requirement analysis and turns this into a domain specification that can be employed by a programmer to create an IPS. There are many software design methodologies that can do this; for example, OOAD (29) or Yourdon (30). In Ref. 2, the one chosen to demonstrate the ideas put forward here was Jackson system development (JSD), a popular and representative data-modeling methodology (31). This approach (data modeling) seems well-suited to supplying the structures required to describe systems in terms useful to a help system. In particular, the focus on entity analysis (used by JSD–SSADM, Ref. 32)—and OOAD) forces the domain of interest to be modeled in a way that makes explicit the structures necessary for its static description, and the way these structures interact supplies some of the dynamic information. Other, process-oriented design methodologies (e.g., that of Yourdon and Constantine, Ref. 30) were discounted because they did not explicitly supply this information (information that is necessary to meet the requirements of a help system).

For producing the functional description that captures more dynamic behavior, however, it is necessary to extend the Jackson design description with an effects language, and this is outlined below in an example taken from the design of an E-mail system. The design was used to implement an E-mail application, and the quality of the help it provided was evaluated in a small pilot study. (See Ref. 2 for further details.)

AN EXAMPLE OF THE DESIGN AND BUILD PROCESS USING JSD

The JSD methodology specifies the design process as three stages, or levels, at which the "level of abstraction is a gradient from physical machine detail to logical designs to conceptual models of the problem" (*33*, p. 6). The three steps are as follows:

1. The modeling stage—a description is made of the real-world problem, and important actions within the system are identified. This is followed by an analysis of the major structures within the system, called entities.
2. The network stage—the system is developed as a series of subsystems that communicate. The input and output between these subsystems is defined.
3. The implementation stage—the system is reduced to a set of concurrent communicating processes that can be implemented on a computer.

As already mentioned, describing an implemented system requires the establishment of a link between the physical machine detail, stage (3), and the designer's conceptual view of the system, stage (1). This bridge must allow a representation of the first stage to "parse" the third stage. In other words, an explainer must have a representation of the model analysis stage, and be able to directly relate it to the implemented system.

The first stage requires the domain to be analyzed in terms of entities and actions, and in order for sequenced process structure diagrams to be constructed. Entities are the objects that make up a domain. They can be both dynamic and static, and are defined by their actions. A dynamic entity uses actions to change other entities in the domain, while static entities suffer the effects of actions, but do not instigate changes themselves (very much like a field in a database; *33*, p. 17). Actions are thus the building blocks of the JSD model and entities represent groups of time-ordered actions known as process models. Entity and action are both hard to define further and require heuristics and common sense (i.e., designer experience) for their specification; however, the model process is the most stable part of the system and relates the basic entities to the organization of that which is being modeled. An example structure diagram is shown in Fig. 4 (taken from the design for an E-mail application).

The structure diagram shown reveals the procedure for a user (an entity in the IPS domain) who wishes to read a message stored in a folder (a common task when using E-mail). The process <Change Folder to Select and Read Message> may be used as many times as necessary (hence the interation), but each time the user instigates the procedure it is expected that he or she will go through the complete sequence of the two processes <Move-to-Folder> and <Read-Mail>. Having achieved <Move-to-Folder>, a process not shown in more detail here, the user entity should select and read a message from the mail retrieved. The structure diagram shows two actions <Select Message> and <Inspect Message>. Note that the actions are not further defined at this stage, and to extend the model requires the introduction of a "functional" level.

To maintain the relationship between the model and its implementation it is therefore necessary to introduce the functional level, the level below system actions,

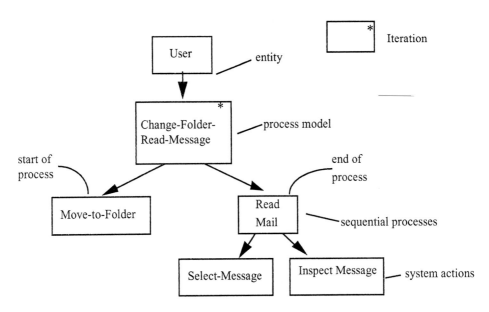

FIGURE 4. *JSD structure diagram.*

which connects directly to the underlying code. The functional description provides an important link between the designer's view of the application (as described by the structure diagrams) and the implemented code. It allows operational knowledge about the application (knowledge of commands) to be related to organizational information (knowledge about structure diagrams). This is useful because a third party, the user of the application, needs to acquire both types of knowledge to be able to operate in the world, (i.e., they need to form a model of the domain within which they relate commands to tasks and goals). In the terms so far used, a user task would equate to a structure diagram, a goal would be an effect or set of effects, and a command would be a command. The JSD methodology does not provide for this functional level so it is necessary to create an extra representation schema to describe effects, which in turn can be grouped together to form functional descriptions. This effect representation must give a clear description of the sorts of changes that can occur and it must give a complete representation of all possible changes. There are really only five types of changes; the (1) *creator* and (2) *destroyer* of individual entities in the world, and three effects on the attributes of an entity, (3) *setter* of the value, (4) *deleter* from the value, and (5) *adder* to the value of the attribute. There are two other effect types necessary, *inspector* and *message sender*, neither of which changes the state of the world (i.e., they don't change attribute values on any entity). The first, inspector, is used to access attribute values and so is required by users to gather information within a domain (e.g., to look at their mail messages). The second, message sender, allows for more complicated process connections between model processes. These two effects approximately equate, respectively, to the state vector and data stream connections used by the JSD methodology.

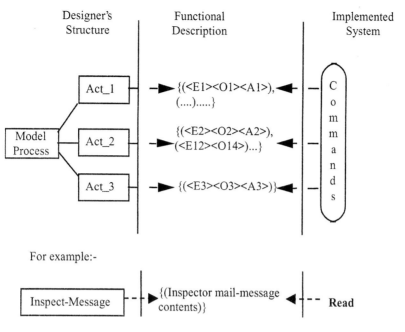

FIGURE 5. *Relationship of functional description to command design.* (Reprinted from C. Mallen, "Designing Intelligent Help for IPS." *Internat. J. Human–Computer Stud.,* **45**, 349–377, by permission of the publisher, Academic Press Limited, London.)

The first two effects, creator and destroyer, can be represented as a couplet of the form (<effect type> <entity>), while the last five, setter to message sender, are represented by triplets of the form (<effect type> <entity> <attribute>). A set of these couplets and triplets associated with a system action is known as the functional description of the system action. Figure 5 shows how the functional description relates the commands in the application with the system diagrams produced by the designer.

Figure 5 shows the three representation schema necessary to fully describe an IPS, the JSD description, the implementation code, and a "functional hierarchy". The relationships between the three are as follows: (1) the JSD description gives the design analysis of the domain, which leads to (2) the implementation code, while (3) the "functional" level bridges the "semantic gap" between the two. Essentially the functional level provides a language for describing how the system actions can affect entities. As the implemented system can also be described in these terms, a link is created between the designer's view of the system and the implementation itself. It is this link that can be exploited by a help system to meet some of the requirements of online help.

Does Design Meet the Requirements?

The previous sections have shown how the design description can be related to an application. How does this enable a help system to better meet the requirements outlined at the beginning of this article?

- Issues of plan recognition involve mapping user's work onto a task space. One of the advantages of using the JSD design methodology is that it is based on identifying tasks and producing the sequences of actions required to complete these. These sequences of actions are grouped together by structure diagrams. This allows the usage model's (i.e., the user's) record of commands to be compared against the structure diagrams of the design description to interpret the user's actions as part of some task. In addition, the effects language can be used to allow the help system to look for tasks (through the structure diagrams) that produce the same effects by invoking different commands and that might be more efficient. The structure diagrams, as part of the design, bring this organization to the system's functionality and provide a link between effects and tasks that is missing from, for example, UC and Eurohelp.
- Tailoring answers to particular users. This should be dealt with by an instructor component using the usage model, but it should be noted that the structure diagrams can be used to organize the usage model.
- Tailoring answers to a user's current context. This can be a problem for systems that retrofit a model of the domain. They have to ensure that the system state and the model state are in step, and that actions in the model accurately reflect the consequences of actions in the domain. In practice this is very difficult. Here, in the designer model, the actual domain state and the recent user actions are inspected. The design description (through the effects language) can then be used both to analyze what has just happened and to predict what will happen if a certain action is taken. The actions can also be recognized as being part of a task.
- Answering repeated questions (i.e., is the answer to a question adjusted if it has been asked previously.). Repeated questions normally occur because the user wants a shorthand reminder or because the system is in a different state from when the original question was asked. Again this should be dealt with by an instructor component using a record of the user's questions, but in the latter case the designer model helps by providing a task-based context for the application's commands.
- Issues of efficiency (e.g., replacing repeated actions with a single action). In Eurohelp this was looked on as an opportunity for supplying active help, for telling the user something new, or for reminding the user of some functionality he or she had already used (by inspection of the usage model). In the approach described here the instructor can look for repeated actions in the user model and then check the structure diagrams for a single task that will produce the same repeated effect.
- Undoing actions. This issue is not dealt with effectively as there are problems with deciding what the reverse of an effect is (or indeed as task). In some cases, however, it may be possible to produce a task that returns the user to the state he or she was in before taking the wrong action.

Figure 6 shows an example of the sort of help that may be given to the user. It is taken from the E-mail system that was designed and implemented using the methodology described in this article. (For details on its construction and the results of a pilot study see Ref. *2.*)

In summary, the design description is particularly good for task/plan recognition and for allowing the instructor to combine both the user (usage) model and the current application state when answering questions. By binding the design methodology and the effect language together a help system is able to deal with problems the user is having with the dynamic behavior of the IPS. This is an area that has proved difficult for previous help systems.

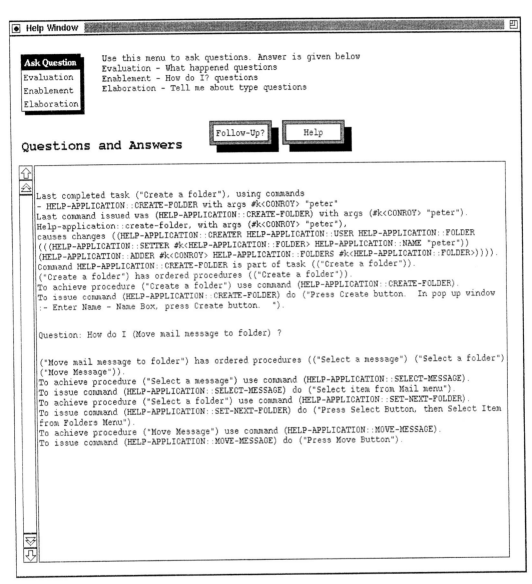

FIGURE 6. *Screen shot of help provided by E-mail application.*

Some Limitations of the Design Description

This work lays out an approach to constructing IPS that are able to support users in their application of computer software. The goal has been to improve on the help provided by previous systems. It is now worth considering the limitations on the range of help able to be supplied by the system. The first issue to consider is whether or not there are questions a user might want to ask of the help system that are not supported by using the design description.

The help provided by the design description allows instruction to be given to the user on actions that may be taken or on events that have just occurred, and as such the answers need to be sensitive to the context in which the user's question is asked (i.e., the current state of the application together with a recent history of commands issued, and possibly of questions asked by the user). The design description does not cater to general questions (e.g., "Tell me about the mail system"), and those about the purpose and management of the application and its entities (e.g., questions such as "Why should I use folders?" or "When should I save a message to a file?"). These types of questions which, for their answers, refer to a constant metalevel function and purpose (and as such are independent of the current state of the application) might be best answered either by using prestored online text (to describe what might be called the general management of the application), or by a prestored tutorial. (In fact, Eurohelp adopted this latter method.) To generate answers to these questions would require knowledge about both the semantics of the entities in the application (their "purpose") and how the information represented by these entities influences the user's behavior, issues with which this work has not dealt.

Another issue that should be addressed is that of the types of users able to benefit from the help provided. It should be made clear that the intention of the work described here was not to provide comprehensive help that could accommodate all users, whatever their experience, and allow them to immediately understand and use the system; rather the help is intended to support those who have at least a limited ability in application use (informed, perhaps, by an introductory tutorial), and to enable them to employ its functionality more fully and effectively. It is meant to address those areas that prestored online help systems cannot deal with; for example by making use of the current state of the application in replying to "What happened..." and "How do I..." questions (as described in the earlier example). Further, these answers are tailored in a limited way to the user. Because the system has no detailed user model and no capability to recognize misconceptions, however, the answers may tend to force the user to the same view of the application as the designer who produced the task space. A more sophisticated system might try to recognize patterns or sequences in the user's actions and try to adapt its task space to include and designate these behavior clusters (e.g., by using a mechanism for recombining elements of existing tasks; See e.g., the work on adaptive systems; Ref. *34*).

Summary

This article has outlined the need for and requirements of intelligent help to provide support with the use of IPS. It has looked particularly at the domain model required by a help system and the difficulties of integrating this within a working application. The possibility of using a design methodology and an effects language to supply the domain model has been put forward. The main advantage of the approach is that the principled design and construction of the IPS leads efficiently to systems that can provide instruction when used in conjunction with the other components of the help system. Indeed, an avenue for exploration that suggests itself is the use of the effects language and the help system as a design support environment for the actual construction of IPS.

There is, however, some way to go before intelligent help systems are fully realized and commonplace, with much important work being done on communication (*18*) and instructional strategies (*35*) as well as the representation of appropriate knowledge about the domain (*36*).

REFERENCES

1. R. Pilkington, *Intelligent Help: Communicating with Knowledge-Based Systems*, Paul Chapman, 1992.
2. C. L. Mallen, "Designing Intelligent Help for Information Processing Systems." *Internat. J. Human–Computer Stud.*, **45**, 349–377, 1996.
3. C. Paris, "Generation and Explanation: Building an Explanation Facility for the Explainable Expert System Framework," in *Natural Language Generation in Artificial Intelligence and Computational Linguistics,* C. Paris, W. Swartout, and W. Mann, eds. Kluwer Academic Publishers, 1991, pp. 49–82.
4. R. Pilkington, "Question-Answering for Intelligent On-Line Help: The Process of Intelligent Responding." *Cog. Sci.*, **16**, 455–491 (1992).
5. K. Lang, A. Graesser, S. Dumais, and D. Kilman, "Question Asking in Human–Computer Interfaces," in *Questions and Information Systems,* T. Lauer, E. Peacock, A. Graesser, eds. Lawrence Erlbaum, London, 1992, pp. 131–166.
6. R. Wilensky, D. Chin, M. Luria, J. Martin, J. Mayfield, and D. Wu, "The Berkeley UNIX Consultant Project." *Computa. Linguis.*, **14**, 35–84 (1988).
7. B. So and L. Travis, *A Step Toward an Intelligent UNIX Help System: Knowledge Representation of UNIX Utilities,* research report #CS-TR-94-1230, University of Wisconsin–Madison, 1994.
8. J. Breuker, ed., *Eurohelp: Developing Intelligent Help Systems,* EC Amsterdam, 1990.
9. R. Winkels, *Explorations in Intelligent Tutoring and Help,* IOS Press, Amsterdam, 1992.
10. R. Ohyama and Y. Yamamoto, "A Methodology to Build Active help Systems," *Proceedings of JCSE 93, 1993.*
11. D. Chin, "KNOME: Modeling What the User Knows in UC," in *User Models in Dialogue Systems,* A. Kobsa and W. Wahlster, eds. Springer–Verlag, 1989, pp. 74–107.
12. W. J. Clancey, "The Epistemology of a Rule-Based Expert System." *AI,* **20**, 215–251 (1983).
13. L. Erskine, D. Carter-Tod, and J. Burton, "Dialogical Techniques for the Design of Web Sites." *Internat. J. Human–Computer Stud.,* **47**, 169–196 (1996).
14. S. Ohlsson, "Artificial Instruction: A Method for Relating Learning Theory to Instructional Design," in *Adaptive Learning Environments,* M. Jones and P. Winne, eds. Springer–Verlag, 1990, pp. 55–84.
15. R. Burton, "Diagnosing Bugs in a Simple Procedural Skill," in *Intelligent Tutoring Systems,* D. Sleeman and J. S. Brown, eds. Academic Press, 1892, pp. 157–184.
16. J. Martin and K. van Lehn, "OLAE: Progress Towards a Multi-activity, Bayesian Student Modeller," *Proceedings of AI-ED 93,* 1993, pp. 410–417.
17. A. Paiva, J. Self, and J. R. Hartley, "On the Dynamics of Learner Models," *ECAI-94: European Conference on Artificial Intelligence,* 1994, pp. 178–182.
18. J. D. Moore, *Participating in Explanatory Dialogues,* MIT Press, London, 1995.
19. A. Cawsey, "Planning Interactive Explanations." *Internat. J. Man-Machine Stud.,* **38**, 169–200 (1993).
20. T. Kuhme, *Adaptive Action Prompting—A Complementary Aid To Support Task-Oriented Interaction in Explorative User Interfaces,* tech. rep. GIT-GVU-93-19, Georgia Institute of Technology, 1993.
21. R. Moriyon, P. Szekely, and R. Neches, "Automatic Generation of Help from Interface Design Models," *Proceedings of Human Factors in Computing Systems,* CHI 94, ACM Press, 1994.
22. R. Frank and J. Foley, "Model-based User Interface Design by Example and by Interview," *Proceedings of the ACM Symposium on User Interface Software and Technology,* ACM Press, 1993, pp. 129–137.
23. C. Rich and C. Sidner, "COOLAGEN: When Agents Collaborate with People," in *Readings in Agents,* M. Huhns and M. Singh, eds. Morgan Kaufmann, San Francisco, 1997, pp. 117–124.

24. E. Wenger, *Artificial Intelligence and Tutoring Systems,* Morgan Kaufmann, Los Altos, 1986, pp. 330–340.
25. B. Wasson and S. Akselsen, "An Overview of On-Line Assistance: From On-Line Documentation to Intelligent Help and Training." *Knowl. Egr. Rev.,* **7**, 289–322 (1992).
26. M. Jackson, *System Development,* Prentice–Hall, 1983.
27. M. T. Maybury, "Communicative Acts for Explanation Generation." *Internat. J. Man–Machine Stud.,* **37**, 135–172 (1992).
28. J. S. Gero, "Design Prototypes: A Knowledge Representation Schema for Design." *AI Mag.,* **11**, 26–36 (1990).
29. K. Rubin and A. Goldberg, "Object Behaviour Analysis." *Commun. ACM,* **35**, 48–62 (1992).
30. E. Yourdon and L. Constantine, *Structured Design,* Prentice–Hall, 1979.
31. P. Harmon and C. Hall, *Intelligent Software Systems Development,* Wiley, 1993, pp. 303–307.
32. M. Goodland and C. Slater, *SSADM: A Practical Approach,* McGraw–Hill, 1995.
33. A. Sutcliffe, *Jackson System Development,* Prentice–Hall, 1988.
34. S. Tyler, J. Schlossberg, R. Gargan, L. Cook, and J. Sullivan, "An Intelligent Interface Architecture for Adaptive Interaction," in *Intelligent User Interfaces,* J. Sullivan and S. Tyler, eds. ACM Press, 1991, pp. 85–110.
35. I. Fernandez-Castro, A. Diaz-Ilarraza, and F. Verdejo, "Architectural and Planning Issues in Intelligent Tutoring Systems." *J. AI Ed.,* **4**, 357–395 (1993).
36. M. Benaroch, "Roles of Design Knowledge in Knowledge-Based Systems." *Internat. J. Human–Computer Stud.,* **44**, 689–722 (1996).

BIBLIOGRAPHY

Pilkington, R. *Intelligent Help: Communicating with Knowledge-Based Systems,* Paul Chapman, 1992.
Lauer, T., Peacock, E., and Graesser, A., eds. *Questions and Information Systems,* Lawrence Erlbaum, London, 1992.
Breuker, J., ed. *Eurohelp: Developing Intelligent Help Systems,* EC Amsterdam, 1990.
Moore, J. D. *Participating in Explanatory Dialogues,* MIT Press, London, 1995.
Wenger, E. *Artificial Intelligence and Tutoring Systems,* Morgan Kaufmann, Los Altos, 1986.
Sutcliffe, A. *Jackson System Development,* Prentice–Hall, 1988.

CONROY MALLEN

VISUAL DISPLAY QUALITY

Introduction

If you ask anyone if he or she would like to trade the display he or she currently uses for the one used previously, you will certainly get *no* for an answer. Why? Because the quality of the present display is higher. It has a better resolution, color capabilities, and a larger screen area; it looks brighter, sharper, and more stable; it can display variable pitch fonts; and so forth. In other words, the visual characteristics and the flexibility have improved.

This article is about the visual characteristics of computer displays and the way in which these affect the quality of the human–visual display interaction. This article would probably never have been written if the visual quality of displays was without problems. Unfortunately, just as with other aspects of human–computer interaction the visual aspects have to be designed very carefully, otherwise the user will suffer.

The structure of the article is as follows. First an outline if given of the nature and consequences of suboptimal adaptation of the technical artefact to the capacities and peculiarities of its human user. Next an attempt is made to arrive at a definition of visual display quality (VDQ); the design effort and innovations that have resulted from VDQ problems are discussed briefly. This is followed by an overview and short evaluation of the three main research approaches to VDQ. The main parameters that affect the visual quality are discussed next. This is done in clusters of factors that strongly interact with each other. Where necessary, special attention is given to flat panel display (FPD) technology. In the final section, the presented material is integrated and some general conclusions are drawn.

DISPLAY TECHNOLOGY

Due to rapid developments in the area of hardware and software, the computer's interface has been adapted substantially to the world of humans, therefore, even the layman can interact directly with the machine. It is predominantly through the technological developments of visual display units (VDUs) that direct user–computer interaction has become the rule rather than the exception. The physical display characteristics (e.g., the resolution and speed of the hardware) of VDUs have improved dramatically over the last fifteen years. The early personal computer (PC) displays were capable of displaying 320*200 points; a modern display can handle 1600*1200 points. The standard is 1024*768. Instead of fixed (5*7 dot) characters, software characters can be displayed, and proportional fonts are becoming popular. Furthermore, the traditional cathode ray tube (CRT) technology has lost ground to FPD technologies, such as the liquid crystal. Finally, the introduction of multicolor displays, apart from adding a great deal of appeal to the display, has dramatically increased the versatility of the medium.

The CRT technology has been challenged by a number of FPD technologies, which has resulted in a surge of improvements for both technologies and an increase in user choice. The size, power consumption, and therefore heat dissipation of the CRT make it unsuitable for laptops and notebook computers. Although energy and space can be saved by introducing FPDs, the CRT still is the main display technology because of its large screen area, high luminous efficiency, superior color gamut, and reliability.

A first important choice for the display purchaser is that between color and monochrome. Many of today's applications are designed for use on a multicolor display because, for example, color is used for structuring information. These applications are often more difficult to use on a monochrome display. Certainly, color is an important asset of display quality, but in all current technologies corresponds which a loss in resolution and luminous efficiency, as well as higher cost.

Currently the most popular and most promising FPD technology is the liquid crystal display (LCD). Its low voltage requirement and low power consumption make it well suited for battery-operated computers, although at present the large and higher-quality FPDs still consume too much energy for this application. Liquid crystal is not a light-emitting material, and therefore an LCD depends on ambient light or a separate light source (a backlight) for image formation. This formation is achieved through control of the amount of reflection or transmission of light.

LCDs can be made using a number of technologies, which may show one or more of the following defects: slow response speeds, changing luminances—even inversion—as a function of the viewing angle, and/or no grey scale capabilities. The most promising technology is the thin film transistor (TFT) LCD, with good performance in terms of speed, color gamut, and grey scale capability. This, however, is costly, difficult to produce for large sizes, and has a relatively high power consumption.

Electroluminescent displays have the advantage of being self-luminous, offering the prospect of extremely thin and lightweight displays. The major problems are color gamut, power consumption, and grey scale (1).

DISPLAY WORK

As a result of technological developments, a new class of work appeared—display work. Just like technology, display work has undergone enormous changes. In the beginning, display work was conducted in specialized departments where monotonic and highly specialized tasks with a short work cycle (predominantly data entry) were performed by workers with limited education. The specialization of both workers and tasks has largely disappeared. Work with display units is encountered in all levels of organizations, and there is a large diversity of tasks carried out with displays. In current office environments, the ratio of displays to workers often approximates 1. As more and more tasks can be performed efficiently with a computer the amount of display work grows. This results in an increase of the duration and frequency of display work per worker. Enduring display work (e.g., longer than two hours a day on the average) is now common practice for millions of workers. If the trend of office flexibilization gains ground, it has the potential to change the organization of work fundamentally. This will further increase the amount and versatility of display work (e.g., for communication tasks).

Display work has always been associated with a number of health complaints and health hazards, especially on the work floor. MacMorrow (2) mentions the following categories: adverse pregnancy outcomes, eye strain and visual fatigue, migraine headaches, photosensitive epilepsy, muscle pain, aches, and strains, skin rashes, and stress. These problems have received much interest from the research community. In one bibliography (3) only a few studies pertaining to eye strain, visual fatigue, and visual discomfort dating before 1976 are reported; 133 such studies were conducted in the period from 1976 to 1980. In a few years time the number of studies thus increased dramatically. Just as with investigations of other problems related to display work, this trend has not changed fundamentally since 1980.

A review (4) devoted to human factors research on displays revealed that 34 percent of the studies were devoted to visual fatigue, 26 percent to the display itself (font and display design), and a further 11 percent to illumination and reflections. More recently five large international WWDU (work with display units) conferences (5–9) prove that the problems are still alive, with a large number of contributions regarding visual fatigue and closely related topics such as reflections.

Although most problems were at first attributed to the display, research has shown that the design of the workplace and the contents and organization of display work are also strongly related to a number of problems. These arise when automation is considered a mere technological problem, neglecting the issues of work organization and job design. With respect to visual problems, the situation is far from clear. The low accessibility of the technological aspects of displays [for practicing ergonomists and work(place) designers] often leads to an attitude in which the (display) technology is more or less taken for granted. Because the display forms the basis of the visual interaction process between worker and machine, this means that important opportunities for better design remain unused.

Visual Display Quality

AN ERGONOMICS APPROACH

Visual display quality must be regarded not merely as the result of the technical specifications of the display but as an important aspect of a human-display combination as a functional system, performing its functions in a physical, psychological, and task-related context.

The discussion of display-related visual problems is in fact a discussion of the health and productivity of the worker. This is demonstrated by the model given in Fig. 1. The essence of this model is that it considers the human to be a processor of "stressing factors." The processing capacity may vary or change considerably over individuals and time. One source for the decline of the processing capacity can be traced to stress symptoms and stress consequences. The stress symptoms in the model refer to temporary effects of processing the stressing factors, such as an increased pulse rate, longer reaction times, visual fatigue, or decreased depth of reasoning. The symptoms arise from the physical and/or mental load on the worker and have consequences for

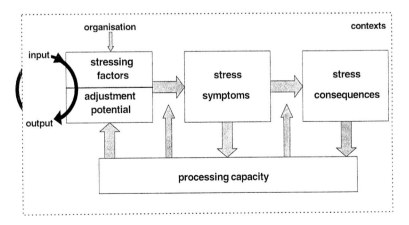

FIGURE 1. *Model of work stress. Source: adapted from Ref. 10; based on Ref. 11.*

the processing capacity and mode, which may change due to (unwanted) symptoms. An example is the buildup of visual fatigue during prolonged display work (*12, 13*). Recovery from the symptoms begins when the load is no longer applied. The time required for full recovery may vary considerably, but recovery should occur fast enough in order to prevent cumulative effects that are not or are hardly reversible (i.e., stress consequences). Repetitive strain injuries (*14*) developed by data-entry workers and mouse users are examples of stress consequences. A visual equivalent is not currently known; there is no evidence that the visual system may actually be damaged by viewing a display.

Probably the most important characteristic of well-designed (display) work is that the processing capacity of the worker and the load imposed on the worker are in balance. In order to increase the processing capacity and thus the productivity of the worker, the latter should be provided with adjustment potential. Adjustment potential refers to all methods to moderate the load to bring the stressing factors within the limits of worker capacity (e.g., the contrast and brightness controls on a display). Well-designed work minimizes the occurrence of unwanted stress symptoms and prevents unwanted stress consequences. With respect to VDQ, there are two ways of achieving this. First, the characteristics of the display should match the human visual information-processing characteristics. This amounts to minimizing the load imposed on the user by the display. Second, the user should be given the adjustment potential that is needed to customize the visual aspects of the display to the task requirements, the characteristics of the task, and the environment, as well as individual characteristics.

An electronic display is a device that transforms an electric signal in an image. The quality of the displayed image is therefore determined by the quality of the display and the quality of the video signal. Until the 1980s the display and video signal generator were generally integrated into one box, called the video display terminal (VDT). Mainly through the rise of PC and workstation technology in the 1980s, the display and signal generator have become separated both logically and physically. The signal generator is now called the graphics card and has moved close to the computer's Central Processing Unit (CPU) for optimal processing speed. Typically a graphics card offers the user several to many trade-off combinations of temporal, spatial, and color resolution in order to satisfy the image requirements for different applications. Modern displays have multisynchronizing capabilities to handle the different resulting image frequencies.

In order to provide a clear picture of how the quality of the images that are displayed is determined, we must regard a hierarchy of factors. The display is the most prominent factor; it sets the limits to the image quality that can be attained. It constitutes the physical interface with the user and normally provides the user with some adjustment potential (e.g., in the form of adjustable display brightness and contrast). The degree to which the capabilities of the display are actually used depends heavily on the graphics card/driver combination that is applied. Again, this combination offers adjustment potential; usually it can be configured. Modern applications and environments, however (e.g., Windows), also exert a large influence on the displayed images. This includes soft fonts and color usage. Although standard settings in this respect are often present, user-friendly applications offer the user a great deal of freedom in the customization (sometimes so complex that users are afraid to try anything else). At the highest level, the environment exerts an influence on the actual image quality. Important aspects of the environment are the lighting and workplace layout.

If the visual quality of displays is specified in terms of perceptually relevant characteristics of the resulting images (instead of, e.g., hardware terms), the factors on all the above-mentioned levels are included.

VDQ Definition

Although much research into displays has concentrated on visual aspects, there is no accepted definition of VDQ. On the contrary, a wide variety of (explicit or implicit) operational definitions is encountered.

The quality of display-generated images can be assessed in a number of ways, depending on the target of the study, the consequent operationalization of "quality," and the assumptions one is willing to make about the human observer. The term *image quality*, which is commonly used to denote the visual quality of display-generated images, covers only part of the factors involved in VDQ. Even this term is not used unambiguously. Snyder (*15*) states that image quality has been used generally in two contexts: that of physical measurements of the image itself and that of perceived or measured quality from the human observer (i.e., behavioral measurements). Roufs and Bouma (*16*) came to the same type of distinction.

From an ergonomical viewpoint, VDQ pertains to the consequences for visual information processing and the degree of adjustment to the task requirements of software- and hardware-generated (sequences of) images in an operational environment. The measurement and specification of VDQ should therefore be user-centered. From the basic ergonomical rule that technology should be adapted to the user and not vice versa in the first place, it follows that the link with technology must not be lost in order to generate applicable design knowledge. Some current measurement approaches do not satisfy these two requirements.

The inclusion of the interactions with the task and the environment in the definition of VDQ would preclude a preventive use of VDQ knowledge were it not that both the task and the environment can be accounted for either by modeling or by providing operational limits.

VDQ AND DESIGN

The introduction of computers and displays in the workplace changes the demands on the physical and organizational aspects of work design. VDQ considerations have stimulated research and design in the three broad areas discussed below.

Display Design

Much research and development has concentrated on VDQ deficiencies in CRTs. Prominent are the topics of resolution, flicker, and reflection. The development of new display technologies introduced new topics, such as the response speed of the display, display element (DEL) shape and separation, viewing angle, and brightness.

The shape and layout of display elements on FPDs has been studied on several occasions and has resulted in the development of methods to stack color elements and of nonorthogonal display element rasters. The size of the gaps between FPD DELs has decreased, so much higher fill factors (percentage of active area) are attainable. Much effort has been put into the development of high-contrast and high-brightness LCDs. Techniques have been developed to solve the notorious LCD viewing-angle problem. (See the subsection "LCD Aspects.") The color gamut of the youngest generation of TFT LCDs approaches that of a color CRT. Significant drops in the production costs of LCDs due to improvements in the production process are expected to have a positive influence on the retail price in the near future.

With respect to CRTs, screen resolution and size have increased, among other things, to accommodate a large number of text lines per screen and characters per line, while maintaining an acceptable viewing distance and symbol size. Temporal resolution has increased from 50 Hz to about 70 to 100 Hz in modern displays in order to eliminate visible flicker. Filters, coatings, and other techniques have been developed to cope with reflections, as well as to reduce radiation. Attempts were undertaken to improve the color gamut of CRTs (e.g., by applying extra coatings with inactive colored material).

Workplace Design

Both the displays and the input devices used with computers obliterated the traditional office furniture concepts. With respect to VDQ, the lighting of the workplace is probably the most critical factor, although viewing distance and position of the display are also important in the design of the workplace. First, specialized display workplaces (e.g., for data entry) were developed. Later, as display work increased throughout the organizations, display work had to be integrated with the more traditional functions. Since the 1980s a small revolution has taken place in the design of office furniture and lighting. In order to create enough space for the keyboard and to maintain an acceptable viewing distance, the depth of desks was increased in order to accommodate the CRT. In order to adjust display height to the prescribed vertical viewing angle, fixed and height-adjustable plateaus and flexible display arms were developed, as well as desks in which this function was integrated. Because the physical size and weight of displays steadily increased from small 14-in. black-and-white to bulgy 21-in. full-color monitors weighing over 30 kilograms, the search for design solutions in furniture has become a continuous process. The diversity of tasks carried out with a display also increased. Some new application areas brought along new requirements. For Computer Aided Design (CAD) applications, special furniture has been developed that allows both sitting and standing work. In order to cope with the larger (color) monitors, new workplace layout concepts were introduced in which corner desk elements (which are extra deep) function as display workplaces. Not only the office but also its furniture has become more flexible. A modern line of furniture consists of system elements in all sorts of shapes. This allows the workplace to be adapted to tasks, users, and hardware.

Increasing quality and decreasing costs of FPDs will inevitably lead to a situation in which for many display tasks the CRT is the less attractive technology. This development will not leave the desktop unchanged, because FPDs have a much smaller "footprint," and do not have to be placed vertically in front of the user. The usually recommended CRT working posture requires a horizontal viewing angle to the middle or the top of the screen. Posturally, however, there is no objection to a more downward gaze angle—even up to about 50 degrees (17–19). This is sufficient to allow placement of the FPD directly on the desk. In a flexible office, where the same workplace is used by different users and where a single worker uses different types of workplaces for different types of tasks, workplace design and furniture design may have to be reconsidered.

Daylight and display work are difficult to combine. Direct sunlight creates high-contrast shadows in the room and on the desktop and may wash out displayed images. Furthermore, bright window areas are often in the direct field of view of the worker and thus act as a disability glare source or create large contrasts with the display or task. Finally, the walls and objects in the room become an indirect reflection source when lit by the bright sun. Because sensing daylight as well as the outside view are psychologically important, completely darkening the office is not a good idea. Besides, daylight is free; electricity for artificial lighting is not. The control of daylight is therefore a "topic" in workplace design. Both inside and outside control systems, often consisting of vertical or horizontal blinds, are in common use and may or may not be equipped with light sensors for automatic operation. A perfect control of daylight is almost impossible; therefore, the office or workplace also has to be adapted to the specific daylight situation of the room. The two most important considerations here are that no daylight falls directly on the monitor and that there is no window directly behind the monitor so that the worker can be blinded.

Artificial lighting became a widespread problem when computer displays penetrated the ordinary work environments. Reflection, display surround contrast problems, and glare caused by high lamp luminosities within the direct visual field have been tackled in a number of ways. The low illumination level approach was a very "direct" response to the problems of display surround contrast and reflection, but low illumination levels introduce problems with nondisplay-related tasks and have adverse psychological effects. Individual workplace lighting is expensive, leads to "light anarchy" on the work floor, and requires insight by the workers into how to solve lighting problems. In landscaped offices, individually lit workplaces lead to inhomogeneous luminance distributions, and each lamp is a potential source of glare for neighbors.

Based on a more thorough analysis of the problems, a new type of luminary for fluorescent tubes was developed: the "dark light," a luminary in which the tube (and thus the high-luminosity glare source) was shielded from direct view and in which the light was directed (or better–reflected) into the room by aluminum mirror optics. The mirror optics made it possible to direct the light straight down. Because no light is directed at a large angle from vertical and there is (almost) no luminosity at the luminary, direct local reflections are reduced drastically and much less light falls on the vertical screen surface, reducing the level of diffuse reflection. Unfortunately, a room lit this way looks "dead." It is not possible to tell where the light comes from or which luminary is on or off. People do not feel well in such an environment. Nowadays, mirror optics are applied in a less extreme fashion, allowing for the better spread of light, maintaining some level of luminosity at the luminary, and creating a balanced atmosphere. In order to restore the ecological truth that all light comes from above, luminaries have been developed that combine mirror optics with the more conventional translucent diffusor lighting (with limited luminosity). These solutions nowadays are acceptable because the image quality of modern displays has improved. When FPDs with a low reflection factor are used instead of CRTs the strict control of light becomes less important. If such displays are used more or less horizontally, like paper, the problem of direct glare also diminishes because of the downward gazing angle.

Software Design

In software design, the VDQ depends on the use of the capabilities of the graphics card and monitor in order to facilitate efficient information transfer. This aspect of software design relies heavily on the available knowledge concerning human perception.

Much research has been done in the field of color perception, so that the functional use of color (i.e., task support through selective color usage) comes within the reach of the designer. The same is true with respect to gray scale requirements.

Another aspect concerns the design of fonts. Important design dimensions have been identified and related to legibility. Combined with a drastic improvement in the resolution capability of the hardware over the last decade, designers are able to create fonts with good "inherent" legibility. Software fonts may be attractive for lots of reasons, but there are some risks involved. The software generally does not guard or warn the user against characters that are too small or character strokes that are too thin.

Finally, most quality software can handle the (resolution and color) flexibility that graphics cards have to offer.

RESEARCH APPROACHES TO VDQ

Engineering Approach

The engineer tries to capture human factors in formulas and thresholds. In display design, this means adopting a model of human visual perception and extracting limits and recommendations for the relevant design parameters. There are several hazards in this approach; human visual perception is extremely complex and a subject of ongoing research, and therefore any model has to be a simplification, disregarding many important aspects of image quality. Furthermore, the models are based primarily on threshold circumstances, which cannot always be extrapolated to the suprathreshold conditions of the average display in use. The relevance of visual parameters generally is not included in the models. (A good example of the engineering approach to VDQ and a large collection of engineers' display quality measures can be found in Ref. *20*.)

In the field of digital image coding, processing, and transmission, many measures are used to compare the resulting images with the originals. These pixel error metrics are usually not supported by human factors research, and their value as image quality measures is limited to their abstract domain.

"Medical" and Psychophysiological Approach

Numerous studies are reported in which display work or image quality is studied in relation to visual complaints and visual fatigue. In fact, Helander et al. (4) found that the most frequently encountered measures in the empirical work reviewed were the visual measures of vergence, accommodation, and acuity, followed by self-reported visual strain. (See also "Subjective Approach" below.) Oculomotor measures, including eye movement recordings, prevail in laboratory investigations. Ophthalmological measures and self-reports are predominantly used in field studies. The number of studies in this category specifically investigating the visual quality of displayed images is minor to the number of studies related to workplace and environmental factors or to job characteristics.

Chapanis (21) summarized the evidence for visual effects of VDU work as follows:

> Numerous studies have repeatedly found more complaints about visual discomfort, dysfunction and visual fatigue among VDT users...Some field and laboratory studies have also demonstrated changes in some visual functions when working with a VDT. Others have not. Whenever changes have been demonstrated, however, they have all been minor and the condition has reverted to normal after a period of rest.

Indeed, there is no evidence that interaction with a VDU could actually damage the visual system (i.e., lead to visual stress consequences). This does not automatically imply that stress symptoms will be minor, however. Unfortunately, problems with the sensitivity of the present type of measure have been reported (22, 23), and in a review of research on health aspects of VDT work (24), it is concluded that many physiological measures lack consistency and strength in their relation with VDT work and sometimes show a discrepancy with subjective symptoms. Because the effects of visual quality deficiencies are not of a gross physical nature, it is not surprising that physiological measures are insensitive.

Miyao et al. (25) compared a high-resolution display with a low-resolution display by measuring eye movement, blink rate, and task performance. The authors concluded that "visual fatigue...could not be satisfactorily measured." For the readability of sufficiently large characters, no significant difference was found between high- and low-resolution display. In another study, Collins et al. (26) found the steady-state accommodation response (which follows a very short transient adaptation phase) to be relatively accurate and stable across a wide range of screen conditions in short-term VDT viewing. Responses were not very sensitive to variations in color, contrast, and screen polarity. In a field study, Woo et al. (27) compared measurements of the visual function of two groups of workers (VDT and non-VDT) by acuity, contrast sensitivity, refraction, accommodation, phoria and some other measures. The results indicated that there were (only) subtle changes in some aspects of vision for both VDT and non-VDT workers. Results such as these indicate that the measurement or evaluation of

VDQ through stress symptoms is problematic. Rey and Bousquet (*28*) claim that the disparity of results concerning visual strain in VDT operators originates from the complexity of pathways linking VDT work to symptoms of visual discomfort or disability. This claim seems reasonable, as stress symptoms are not directly and uniquely caused by a single stressing factor. In fact, multiple factors, including individual processing capacity and adjustment potential, contribute to the process of stress symptom development.

The conclusion from the above discussion is that we are dealing with gross measures of inadequate adaptation between worker and display, therefore, finding symptoms is indicative of maladaptation, and adequate measures should be taken. In general, improving the adaptation of the worker to the VDU by optical correction of visual anomalies gives some relief from stress symptoms (*29*), but this should be considered a first step only.

Behavioral Approach

Outcome Measures. Another approach to VDQ research and display work investigations is to focus on task performance. The idea behind this approach is that there exists a positive relation between the worker–display adaptation and the quality or quantity of task performance. There are two important sources of variation that may affect the nature and strength of the relation between VDQ and task performance. The first is interindividual and intraindividual variation in capacity and the effort that is allocated to the (experimental) task. In general, if task requirements increase, more effort will be put into task performance, therefore, error rates or performance speeds will remain fairly constant over a range of conditions. This not only has a negative effect on the sensitivity of outcome measures but it may also provide a distorted picture of VDQ effects (*30*). Using threshold tasks, by definition requiring 100 percent effort, is no solution because there is no guarantee that the same processes are involved in suprathreshold task performance.

The second source pertains to the nature of the task. Many performance tasks, especially tasks used in an experimental setting, require very specific information processing or motor behaviors. Tasks such as locating target characters in text or verifying number strings may therefore produce outcomes that are not representative of real-world tasks. Furthermore, the (relatively) short duration of performance tasks in most investigations precludes the buildup of stress symptoms as in real-life situations.

Much performance research has concentrated on reading from displays (e.g., attempting to explain the differences between reading from paper and VDU). In a review of this research, Mills and Weldon (*31*) concluded that more research is needed because many investigations concentrated on legibility instead of readability and because text attributes and display characteristics were studied in isolation. They also discussed the possibility that certain measures lack sensitivity. Their conclusion typically pertains to the above-mentioned problem sources. Tinker (*32*) already concluded that the effects of individual font and text attributes were small. It seems that in general performance tasks are just not sensitive enough for these individual effects to show up. This may explain why Gould and Grischkowsky (*33*) found no differences in reading speed and accuracy for VDU font sizes over the wide range of

16 to 34.5 minutes of arc. On the basis of a number of experiments, Gould et al. (*34, 35*) concluded that the quality of text on a VDU is determined by the combined effect of several attributes. Dillon (*36*) reached the same conclusion on the basis of an extensive review of the literature.

Subjective Approach. The main methods used in the subjective approach are ratings and psychophysical scaling. The "subjective" part of this approach is that the users or experimental subjects act as their own measurement instrument. Generally the measurement scale is prescribed by the researcher, but the user quantifies the sensation, perception, or opinion on this scale. Because we are dealing with visual human–display interaction, one obvious advantage of subjective measurement methods over others is that direct estimations of VDQ aspects can be obtained that include the effects of information processing by the human observer. The psychological evaluation of sensations or perceptions is an integral part of this processing, which is regarded as a drawback of the approach by some but an advantage by others. Both direct (rating of contrast, brightness, etc.) or indirect measures (rating of eye trouble, headache, etc.) of VDQ may be obtained. For purposes of design, direct and specific measures should be preferred.

A frequently used psychophysical method is the matching technique. In VDQ research this technique is used, for example, for the prediction of the visibility of flicker (*37*). Just as in paired comparisons, in which subjects give a comparative judgment of two simultaneously or serially presented stimuli, this technique works even when differences between stimuli are small. A disadvantage is that both techniques can only be applied in an experimental setup.

In order to obtain detailed evaluations of VDQ aspects, the display evaluation scale (DES) was developed (*38, 10*). In a number of experiments, this rating scale was shown to be more sensitive than outcome measures (*39–41*). With the DES, it was shown that several parameters in the luminance domain and font parameters have a U-shaped relation with visual quality and can thus be optimized (*10*). The DES was successfully applied in the investigation of FPD contrast, of brightness perception, of the contribution of color contrast to legibility, and of text attributes.

Psychophysical and psychometric techniques can be used not only to evaluate VDQ but also to investigate and model human perception. (See any Handbook on human perception.)

Other applications of subjective measurements are found in the collection of (dis)comfort data, (visual) fatigue, and health complaints. This is usually done by means of rating scales or multiple-choice items. A common drawback is the non-specific results of the measurements because they are only indirectly related to VDQ aspects, but in experimental situations it may be possible to relate the obtained scores to specific conditions.

Position of the ISO 9241 Standard

The International Organization For Standardization (ISO) standardization process regarding visual displays has not been completed as of this date; several subjects are still worked on. Of the intended seventeen parts, only the numbers 1 (general introduction), 2 (guidance on task requirements), 3 (visual display requirements), 10 (dialogue principles), and 14 (menu dialogues) have been published (*42*). Three parts are of specific interest here: part 3, the final drafts for part 7 (reflections), and part 8 (displayed colors). Parts 5 and 6, which are in draft stage, give the requirements for workstation layout and environment, respectively. A separate standard (13406-2) will be devoted to visual display requirements of FPDs.

The guidelines found in parts 3, 7, and 8, as well as in the FPD standard, are based on research findings, predominantly coinciding with the engineering approach and the behavioral (outcome measure) approach. Part 3, which is the basic part for visual aspects, is based on a somewhat outdated terminal concept of visual displays. Modern displays, however, are much more flexible than traditional terminals. This immediately raises the question of what configuration (or how many) to test for compliance to the standard. The standard itself does not give any hint in this respect. In practice, manufacturers will be inclined to select one—probably the best—configuration for compliance testing. Unfortunately, users may actually use other graphics cards, resolutions, and so forth. Currently part 3 is under the periodical review stage, but Koizumi (*42*) states that "the speed of recent technological innovation seems to be much faster than that of now advancing and now retreating technical programme of the international standardisation."

The standard compliance test of part 3 of the standard is typically an engineer's test. It consists of taking measurements of physical characteristics of the display, for which limits (mostly underlimits) are specified. Some of the typical shortcomings of the "engineering approach" apply to this test. An alternative compliance test is also specified, but its validity as a compliance route is restricted to (non-CRT) displays that cannot be evaluated by the measurement test. The user test requires that a number of subjects perform a difficult task on a reference display and on the test display. In addition, the test display is judged on comfort, relative to the reference display. The test display fails the test if either the performance or comfort of the test display (or both) is statistically worse than of the reference. Apart from the problem of finding a suitable reference display, the originally proposed alternative test had a number of shortcomings (e.g., for reasons mentioned in the subsection "Behavioral Approach"), and several improvements have been suggested (*43, 44*). The subject is still worked on (e.g., *45, 46*) for mainly two reasons. First, it is difficult to design an efficient test that makes up a valid and reliable measure of the topics covered by the twenty-five physical measures specified in the primary compliance route, as well as to convince all voting members of the quality of such a test. Second, it is felt that much is at stake. By omitting the user (performance) test the user would disappear beyond the horizon, which is difficult to accept in an ergonomics standard.

Aspects of Visual Display Quality

BRIGHTNESS, POLARITY, REFLECTIONS, AND FLICKER

Brightness and Screen Polarity

The brightness of a display is the perceptual correlate of its luminance, which includes reflected luminance. It is not quite clear how different parts of the display (object or ground) contribute to the perceived brightness (*47, 48*), although there is evidence that brightness in text screens is determined (predominantly) by the brightest part and not by the largest area, which is the background (*41*). If the brightness is increased, the contrast sensitivity of the visual system is also increased (*49*). The optimal brightness for a display depends on the brightness of the surroundings, the contrast that is needed on the display, the presence and severity of reflections (see the subsection "Reflections" below), and the effects on image sharpness. It is generally accepted that a brightness contrast between display and surroundings decreases visual comfort and performance (*50*), however, for contrast ratios up to 1:20 this relationship is not very critical (*51*). In order to minimize the contrast between display and surround, a positive screen polarity (dark characters on a bright background) is often recommended. This recommendation, however, is based on the notion that brightness is determined by the largest area, therefore it is probably best to make the choice for positive or negative (bright characters on a dark background) polarity contingent on the relative severity of reflections and flicker or the discriminability of colors, which is better in negative polarity.

In order to achieve a high contrast between information and background, large luminance differences are needed. As the lower luminance on the display increases, the higher luminance should be increased in order to maintain sufficient contrast. Due to the reflection of ambient light and internal reflections of the glass layers of the display the lower luminance can never reach zero, and in practice is often 5 cd/m² or more. A practical upper limit for the brightness of CRTs is the point at which image sharpness is reduced because the tails of the bell-shaped luminance point spread overlap neighboring pixels and thus increase their luminance. Optimum brightness estimations, obtained under 150 lux horizontal ambient light and 0,8 cd/m² diffuse reflection (*10*) ranged from about 20 to 40 cd/m² for luminance modulations (see the subsection "Contrast") of .9 and .2, respectively. The ISO standard requires that a display is capable of achieving a luminance of at least 35 cd/m². As more reflections are present, a higher luminance level of the brightest area is required to maintain an acceptable contrast.

Reflections

Some portion of the light incident on the screen surface will be returned by the glass and phosphor layers of the display. The amount of reflection is dependent on the amount of incident light and the reflection characteristics of the display. Reflected light adds to the luminance output of the screen, therefore, it raises the brightness while it lowers the contrast, by having a stronger effect on the dark area of the display than on the area of higher luminosity. Depending on the characteristics of the surface layers, a CRT reflects from about 3 to 30 percent of the incident light (*50*). Stewart (*52*) mentions upper limits of about 27 percent for the phosphor layer and an additional 4 percent for the glass layer. A modern, high-quality CRT does not have to reflect more than 3 to 4 percent. For comparison, a high-quality TFT screen may reflect only 1 percent.

Reflection affects the performance and comfort of working with displays and is among the most important problems in the relation between human and display (with flicker and sharpness). Because reflections add a constant value to the luminance output of the display, the contrast between foreground and background of the image is reduced. This can deteriorate the visibility of the image and may even wash out (part of) the image completely. When reflections are present black is no longer black, but grey. Further, the inhomogeneous luminance resulting from local reflections may have an adverse effect on fast visual adaptation processes (*51, 48*) and thereby lower visibility. Even color perception can be affected by reflections (*53*), depending on the spectral composition of the reflected light. Stewart (*52*) indicated that strong reflections from the surface glass layer can lead to incorrect focusing (on the mirror image instead of the phosphor layer). In a survey among 905 VDT users Schleifer et al. (*54*) found that screen reflections were noticed by 55 percent of the respondents. Forty percent of these indicated that reflections led to some visibility loss and 15 percent assessed the loss of visibility as "medium" or "high."

In order to diminish the effects of screen illumination, several approaches can be taken. The ambient illumination and workplace layout can be carefully designed in order to avoid illumination of the screen. Filters or glass surface treatments (etching or coating) can be applied, but these often reduce image quality rather than improve it (*55*), for example, by reducing contrast, brightness, and/or image sharpness. The screen surface can also be shielded from illumination without affecting image quality by means of a hood resembling the lenshood on a camera. Finally, reflections can be diminished by choosing for a positive polarity with a high background luminance. Because the background area is much larger than the foreground area, this reduces the relative contribution of reflections to the luminance output of the display. This latter solution, however, may introduce or increase the problem of visible flicker.

Flicker

Flicker is a temporal variation in brightness that is inherent to refreshed display systems such as the CRT. If rise and decay times of the phosphors and the raster frequency are out of balance (too low a refresh rate to maintain a stable phosphor luminance), flicker may become apparent. On ordinary CRTs, flicker may be observed by flicker-sensitive observers for raster frequencies up to about 90 Hz (*56*). At 80 Hz about 5 percent of users detect flicker; at 70 Hz, this is about 10 percent (*57*). Sensitivity to flicker increases with increasing luminance and area. In most cases, flicker goes unnoticed in the small character area even if the luminance is relatively high. In a large background area, flicker is noticed even at moderate luminance and may become quite disturbing at a higher luminance. Perceived flicker can therefore be eliminated by selecting a negative screen polarity. Visibility of flicker also depends on the position of the display in visual field (*58*). Flicker sensitivity is higher in the visual periphery and may become a strong distracter in the corners of one's visual field when looking at other parts of the desktop. The best solution for flicker is to use very high raster frequencies. This requires very high bandwidths of the electronic circuitry. High frequency displays, capable of a 100 Hz refresh rate, are becoming more widespread nowadays, but driving these displays to their limits may decrease image sharpness because of inaccuracies of the electron beam. Another option that has been in common use is to reduce flicker by refreshing the screen in an interlaced fashion, each refresh cycle writing only half of the display lines (even and odd). This doubles the vertical scan frequency without increasing bandwidth. Unfortunately, interlace refresh introduces a number of special visual interferences that are perhaps even less acceptable than flicker (59).

Invisible Flicker. High temporal frequencies that are above the flicker fusion threshold (i.e., not visible during eye fixations) can exert a negative influence on the visual behavior and are suspected to induce visual fatigue. High temporal frequencies have been shown to perturb eye movements during reading. Two explanations for this effect have been offered. The first explanation is that flicker disturbs the inhibitory processes that mask retinal smear during saccades (60–63). Due to the imperfect masking, the saccade length tends to shorten and as a consequence the eyes land in the wrong position in the text. This often leads to an increase in the amount of small corrective saccades that follow initial fixation. The second explanation is that the sparseness of temporal sampling of the image introduces raster frequency-dependent waiting times before information processing can start after fixation (64).

Whereas Boschman and Roufs (65) did not find performance and saccade length differences in a target search task and a reading task on 50 and 100 Hz television, Thomson and Saunders (66) found a relation between TV watching and sensitivity to high frequencies. More specifically, they found scan direction-dependent differences in flicker sensitivity when eye movements were allowed. The mean of this "rolling flicker threshold frequency" was about 10 Hz higher than without eye movements. Furthermore, the sensitivity to vertical scan directions from top to bottom (as in normal TV and VDT) was lower than for other scan directions. This effect was stronger as subjects spent more hours a day viewing TV or raster-scanned VDTs. A possible explanation for this effect is direction-sensitive temporal frequency adaptation. The topic of high-frequency light modulation is also relevant in office lighting. The light of fluorescent tubes used with magnetic ballasts shows a deep modulation with a frequency of 100 (Europe) or 120 (United States) Hz. In a study by Veitch and McColl (67) the visual performance scores of university students were lower in the 120 Hz magnetic ballast lighting condition than in the electronic ballast (20–60 kHz) condition. Wenneberg et al. (68) found differences in comfort judgment and Electro Encephalogram (EEG) recordings related to nonvisible high and low light modulation between subjects who claimed to be hypersensitive to electricity and a control group without symptoms. In the first group, the effects of modulation were significantly stronger. Most hypersensitive subjects report that the problems started when they were exposed to VDTs or, to a lesser extent, to fluorescent tube lighting. The authors suggest that hypersensitivity to electricity might in fact be sensitivity to flickering light.

CONTRAST, SHARPNESS, AND RESOLUTION

Contrast

The importance of contrast as a factor in VDQ is obvious: without contrast, objects or characters cannot be distinguished from their background. In formulas, contrast is always defined as a relation of the foreground and background luminance. The ratio of the luminances is commonly rather inaptly called "contrast ratio," or C_R. As

Weber's law is applicable for a large part of the range of luminances in visual perception, sometimes log C_R is used. The infinite range of C_R sometimes poses problems, therefore another definition of contrast (C_M, the "luminance modulation" or "Michaelson's contrast") is becoming more common. It is defined as the ratio of the difference and the sum of the luminances, and has an absolute range from 0 (no contrast) to 1 (maximum contrast). The two contrast measures can be converted easily.

$$C_m = \frac{C_R - 1}{C_R + 1} \qquad C_R = \frac{1 + C_m}{1 - C_m}$$

The ISO standard requires a minimum contrast of 3:1 or $C_m = 0.5$. Under normal conditions, however, higher contrasts are preferred. Although the standard provides only an underlimit for contrast, contrast optima have been identified (*10*). With a relatively low illumination of 150 lux on the desktop, for display luminances between 10 and 100 cd/m², the calculated optimal C_m varied between 0.9 and 0.5, respectively.

The problem in the determination of contrast lies in the size of the screen area used for the measurement of the luminances. The standards (e.g., Ref. *69*) prescribe the measurement of peak luminances in very small areas (one-eighth of the width of a pixel). For most color displays, the luminance peaks of the three base colors are well separated and the ISO protocol is not applicable. It clearly disagrees with the integrating structures in human perception, which was also demonstrated for subjective contrast evaluations in simulations of monochrome flat panel displays (*70*). Spenkelink and Besuijen (*70*) found contrast ratings and measurements with 1° areas highly correlated. For most displays, a luminance-measuring area of 1° can therefore be recommended. This method might, however, be less suitable for contrast measurements on CRTs with thin characters.

In practical situations, ambient light sources are the most common decremental factor to contrast. Glare diminishes the contrast sensitivity, and specular and diffuse reflections diminish the actual contrast by adding a constant (locally) to foreground and background luminance. Coatings on the screen surface or mountable filters can lower the effect of reflections on contrast. This comes at the price of a reduction of brightness for density filters or a reduction of sharpness for etching type filters.

Sharpness

Sharpness, also named focus quality or acuity, is very closely related to contrast. One could in fact argue that sharpness is the contrast of the high spatial frequencies. Low contrasts go together with less sharp images, but if the higher frequencies cannot be displayed, high contrasts do not yield sharper images. Sharpness is influenced by the point spread function (PSF) of the dots on the display, the matching of the pixel frequencies of the graphics card to the dot pitch of the display for CRTs, and the convergence of the colors for color CRTs. (See the subsection "Color and Color Convergence" below.) A good measure for sharpness is the maximum brightness gradient of an image, which Lourens et al. (*71*) found to correlate well with subjective ratings.

Resolution

Resolution is one of the most frequent terms used to describe display quality; it is either defined as the maximum number of visible horizontal (and vertical) lines or the smallest discernable detail on the display. There are also several definitions of visibility and discernability, resulting in numerous definitions of resolution. (See Ref. *20*.)

The term resolution is also used to describe the capabilities of graphics cards; this resolution, however, can only be seen on a display with the right combination of size, dot pitch, and refresh rate. In practice there is often a mismatch between graphics card resolution and display dot pitch. Take, for example, the combination of 1280×1024 graphics card resolution mode and a 15-in. display with a 0.25-mm dot pitch. In theory, a 15-in. (380-mm) diagonal display has a 12-in. (304-mm) width and a 9-in. (228-mm) height, but the actual active visible area is always smaller, its diagonal usually not exceeding 14 in. (355 mm), so the number of dots will always be smaller than $304/0.25 = 1216$ in the width and $228/0.25 = 912$ in the height of the display. Furthermore, the pixels on the display are not square because displays have a 4×3 aspect ratio and the graphics card resolution mode delivers a 5×4. These mismatches can lead to a loss of small detail in the image and aliasing effects, like Moiré patterns in dithered colors or grey levels. The resolution that counts can only be seen on the display.

Flat panel displays are designed for a fixed resolution and refresh rate. They provide a one-on-one mapping of the pixels on the graphics card to the DELS on the display.

MTF

The description of the spatial spectral transmission of a display by a modulation transfer function (MTF) provides a more general approach to the spatial frequency aspect of VDQ. Whereas resolution only describes the highest visible frequency, MTF techniques involve matching the spatial frequency spectrum of the display system to the contrast sensitivity function (CSF), which is the contrast sensitivity of the human eye as a function of the spatial frequency. For this purpose, the contrast threshold function (CTF), the inverse of the CSF, is set out against the MTF. The frequencies for which the MTF curve is lower than the CTF curve cannot be seen on the display. The frequency at which the curves cross is called the limiting resolution. Figure 2 demonstrates the concept of the MTF. The exact shape and location of the detection threshold curve is specific for the system under consideration.

The quality of the display can then be specified in several integral difference measures (*15*), such as MTF area (MTFA; *72*), square root integral (SQR; *73*), and the sum of just noticeable differences (JNDs; *74*).

Many aspects of visual perception, however, are not accounted for in the CSF. Sensitivity depends on the brightness of the stimulus and the surround, the color, and the presence of other frequencies in the stimulus. There are even conditions for which the sensitivity of the eye is far greater: the hyperacuity phenomena (e.g., Vernier acuity: a roughly tenfold increase in spatial sensitivity for the detection of small shifts in straight lines).

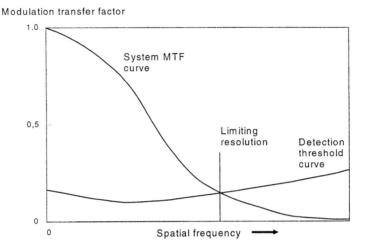

FIGURE 2. *The MTF concept.*

COLOR AND COLOR CONVERGENCE

Color

Color can serve three fundamentally different functions. In some display tasks, color is the actual work object, and the most important consideration is the accuracy of color reproduction. Color may also be used to support cognitive functions such as alerting and classification. In this case, color is used as a coding dimension. Finally, on the level of information reception, color is sometimes applied in order to facilitate object discrimination or legibility.

All visible colors can be produced as a light mixture of the three primary colors— red, green, and blue. This principle is applied in color displays; the CRT has display elements composed of a red, green, and blue phosphor. The three primaries can be thought of as the corner points of a triangle within which all the possible colors fall. The same principle has led to the construction of color spaces in which all natural colors can be specified by two coordinates. The two dimensions of these color spaces coincide with the perceptually relevant opponent color pairs red-green and blue-yellow. In the Commission Internationale de L'Eclairage (CIE) 1976 uniform chromaticity-scale diagram (75) the x axis, denoted by u′, corresponds to the green-red dimension and the y axis, denoted by v′, corresponds to the blue-yellow dimension.

Color for Contrast. The use of color as a contrast enhancer should be advised against; the addition of color contrast was found to increase subjective ratings of contrast, but had no positive effect (or even a deteriorating effect) on legibility ratings (76, 77). Perhaps color contrast should be interpreted as an uncomfortable form of contrast. In the forthcoming ISO standard (part 8) the use of extreme colors for contrast is somewhat conservatively restricted as follows. For bright characters on a dark background spectrally extreme colors, defined as any display color for which $v' < 0.2$ (extreme blue) or $u' > 0.4$ (extreme red), must not be used. In positive polarity, the combination of extreme blue characters with an extreme red background is not allowed. Furthermore, extreme colors that produce depth effects may not be used for continuously viewing or reading.

Color Coding. Much research has been done regarding the optimal color set and number of colors for coding (*78–80*). Color can be a very strong coding dimension and may improve task performance, but is only effective if some basic rules and facts are taken into account.

First of all the use of color must be functional and provide task support (e.g., by making important information visually stand out or by grouping like items through identical colors), but there is more. Many colors are associated with psychological attributes (such as warm or cold, soft or hard), which should not be violated. The connotation of some colors is strongly conditioned, such as red for danger and green for safe. The connotation of colors varies to some extent from culture to culture (both white and black are colors associated with death). Standardization in specific environments (such as yellow for oil in the process industry) may also contribute to the development of fixed connotations. Further, the perceived color not only depends on the spectral content of the stimulus, but also on the neighboring colors, the ambient light, and the observer. About 8 percent of the male population has deficient red-green color vision. Other types of color blindness or color weakness exist, but do not have such a high prevalence. The density of color receptors in the eye falls off with eccentricity. As a result, the color of small objects can only be seen in the center of one's visual field. Furthermore, the visual system is relatively insensitive for blue because there are relatively few blue-sensitive cones in the eye (about 5% of the total), therefore, the forthcoming part 8 of the ISO standard requires that extreme blue images subtend at least 2°.

For design purposes many sources (e.g., *81, 82*) indicate that no more than four or five colors should be used simultaneously and no more than about seven to eleven total (for an entire sequence of displays) if colors have to be identified. ISO 9241-8 advises to use no more than six colors and allows no more than eleven colors to be used. For the ordering of items by color it is often suggested that the spectral order (red-orange-yellow-green-blue-indigo-violet) be used (e.g., *80*). In all cases, care should be taken that the difference between colors is large enough to prevent confusion and if necessary to warrant absolute identification.

Color as a Work Object. The variety of display systems—displays and graphics cards—on the market makes the implementation of portable color coding applications virtually impossible. This problem is even greater for applications in which color is the actual work object. No two display systems are the same, even, with the same types of display and graphics card. There will always be differences in the specifications of some components, and these specifications will change with the aging of the system. Feedback from a color-measuring device is essential for the accurate reproduction of colors on a display (*83*). Because the color gamut of the display is rather limited some natural colors cannot be specified on the display.

Color Convergence

One of the most difficult aspects in the control of color CRT images is the convergence of the three primary colors in all areas of the display screen. A white line on a color CRT is composed of red, green, and blue lines superimposed; if there is any spatial error in this process, the line will have colors on the side, separate colored lines may even be visible. Correction of misconvergence in one area of the screen usually invokes a new misconvergence in another area; in practice, all displays reveal misconvergence on some side of the screen at closer inspection. Misconvergence is measured as the largest distance between lines of primary colors that should be converged; special lenses with scaling can be used for inspection. The subjective quality of a color display reduces significantly as misconvergence increases above 0.2 mm (*84*), or 20 percent of stroke width (*85*).

SYMBOLIC INFORMATION

Because graphical presentations constitute an almost unexplored area, we shall restrict the discussion of symbolic information to the presentation of text and reading. Reading consists of two types of processes: visual processes concerned with information intake, and cognitive processes pertaining to the interpretation of information (e.g., Ref. *86*). In the present context, VDQ relates to "legibility in context"; that is, legibility parameters such as font size or shape, line width, or spacing as factors in the reading process (which is of a cognitive nature). We shall discuss the most relevant parameters in turn.

In order to obtain a good character set, the individual characters should be easily recognized. The chance that characters are confused should be minimized (i.e., the differences between characters should be sufficiently large). This can only be achieved if a large enough character matrix is used. If a character is built up of 7*9 DELs there is not as much freedom in the design of a character set as with large matrices (e.g., because small details cannot be applied). The largest matrix size that can be used depends on the resolution of the display and the number of characters per line and number of lines that need to be displayed. Because of the limited resolution, television is not very suitable for text presentation and much effort has been put into the design of an acceptable character for teletext presentation (*87*). Furthermore, from the visual quality point of view, there are interactions between character matrix and display. The DEL aspect ratio, for instance, influences the shape of the displayed characters; the DEL size determines the displayed size. The display technology, screen polarity, luminance, contrast, and colors affect the visual quality of the characters (e.g., the effective stroke width is strongly influenced by display polarity and luminance). Although software fonts offer the user a great deal of flexibility, some applications by default deliver thin characters that fall short of legibility. The reason that characters may be displayed with strokes that are too thin lies in the discreteness of the display; the stroke width is rounded to the nearest pixel. The actual stroke width thus depends on the enlargement (zoom factor) with which the text is displayed.

Although the display standard prescribes a minimum viewing distance of 40 cm, there is good evidence that people prefer a viewing distance that is longer than the 40 to 50 cm that is often assumed. This probably is related to the increased vergence effort at short viewing distances (*88*). Jaschinsky-Kruza (*89*) found a mean optimal distance of 65 cm and reports a mean of 74 cm and a range of 51 to 99 cm (*90*).

Estimates of optimal character size (generally expressed as the visual angle spanned by the height of an uppercase *H*) show large variations. For printed text, Tinker (*32*) found an optimum of 9 to 10 point, which is about 16 to 18 minutes of arc. For video display characters, Jaschinsky-Kruza (*89*) found a mean optimal size of 22 minutes of arc, whereas Muter and Maurutto (*91*) report an optimum size of about 30 minutes of arc. The actual optimum (*10*) depends on other aspects of image quality, and in addition, on the viewing distance. Under conditions of good image quality and a viewing distance of 80 cm, an optimum character height of about 20 minutes of arc was found (*10*). The standard requires a minimum size of 16 minutes of arc and mentions an optimum of 20 to 22 minutes of arc. A simple rule of thumb is that the characters should preferably measure 1/170–150 of the viewing distance.

Duchnicky and Kolers (*92*) determined reading rates for different line widths, character widths, and number of displayed lines. The reading rates had a positive relation with line width. Gould and Grischkowsky (*33*) did not find performance differences except for extreme line widths, and they found a broad optimum of 16 to 36.4 degrees of arc. Tinker produced a range of 10 to 38 picas, which at a viewing distance of 50 cm would be about 6 to 18 degrees. In a paired comparison and a rating experiment, an interaction between line width and line spacing was obtained (*10*). The optimal line width increased with leading.

In reading, the eyes have to move horizontally over the lines of text, and at the end of a line a jump has to be made to the beginning of the next lower line. Line spacing facilitates these processes. Tullis (*93*) reviewed the literature on formatting text on displays. The (sparse) studies of line spacing he reviewed found either increasing or decreasing performance with increasing line spacing. Tullis suggests that different studies had conditions sampled from different parts of an inverted U-shaped function that actually relates line spacing in alphanumeric displays with performance. In Ref. *10* leading (line spacing expressed as the amount of white space between descenders and the ascenders of the next lower line) was investigated in relation to character height. The U-shaped function suggested by Tullis was reproduced. The optimum leading depended somewhat on character height (which also adds to the vertical distance between lines) and was in the range of 10 to 15 minutes of arc for characters between 10 and 30 minutes of arc. The positive relation between leading and line width was already mentioned.

LCD ASPECTS

Rise and Decay Time

The time needed to get a pixel from 10 to 90 percent of maximum contrast is called rise time or turn-on-time. The time needed to get a pixel from 90 to 10 percent of maximum contrast is called decay or turn-off time. In some types of LCDs, especially supertwisted nematic, these times are long. During a change of screen content on these displays, old and new information will be visible at the same time, making, for example, the reading of text while scrolling impossible. In a draft for the ISO FPD ergonomic requirements (ISO CD 13406-2) quality classes are defined for the image formation time, the sum of turn-on and turn-off times. For image formation times higher than 55 msec, applications using scrolling, animation, and pointing devices detectably lose contrast; above 10 msec, motion artifacts can be distracting. Motion artifacts are undetectable with image formation times below 3 msec, given high enough refresh rates.

Angle of View

With certain types of LCDs, colors can be shifted or contrast can even be inverted if the display is viewed from a different angle. This is caused by a switching state-dependent tilt of the crystals. A display should be legible from any angle up to at least 40° from the normal to the surface of the display (*69*). A number of techniques have been developed that improve the viewing angle. A preventive but still expensive technique is "in-plane switching," which prevents tilting of the liquid crystals as they are switched. A corrective but less expensive technique is the addition of a nonlinear compensating film to the top layer of the display.

Other Aspects

There are a number of other defects typical to LCDs, which cannot easily be placed in any of the categories above, but have one thing in common: they should not be visible. These defects include pixel faults, a picture element that lacks the possibility to demonstrate the range of luminance or color that the average pixel has. Another problem is the appearance of trailing lines in the background of objects with sharp contrasting borders.

Concluding Remarks

The CRT is and always has been *the* electronic display medium. Nevertheless, it must be concluded that a number of characteristics that are inherent to the CRT technology conflict with the demands of the human visual system. The PSF of CRT phosphors and the temporal refreshing characteristics are two examples that clearly demonstrate this. It is therefore not surprising that new technologies that do not have these characteristics, such as the liquid crystal, form a potential threat to the hegemony of the CRT. Although these new technologies have their own VDQ (and other) problems, these might very well be easier to solve. The development of the LCD technology is a good example. Improvements in the quality of LCDs succeeded each other rapidly. This trend seems to continue. Other technologies, such as the electroluminescence, plasma, and field emission, also rapidly develop.

Although VDQ has improved continuously for the last one or two decades the need for further improvement is still there. As long as display users can be discriminated from nonusers with respect to visual complaints and fatigue, there is work to be done.

A multidisciplinary approach to VDQ, requiring a better integration of the different research approaches, is needed in order to deal effectively with the psychological, behavioral, and engineering and design issues. The fact that a separate ergonomic standard for FPDs is forthcoming, in addition to the standard for CRTs, indicates that the standards stand too close to the technology, and too far away from human visual perception. Perception does not make a distinction between technologies! The outcome measure approach remains under pressure because of the experienced difficulties in formulating a valid and sensitive performance task for an alternative compliance route. The subjective approach is mature enough to show that it can fill the gap. To summarize, the picture of VDQ that emerges from research and practical experience is quite complex when considered in detail, but it has a few important dimensions. First, VDQ must be considered in the application environment. The relation with the physical environment in practical terms is the most difficult dimension of VDQ to design. Second, VDQ aspects can be separated into two classes: the aspects that should be avoided (e.g., flicker, reflections, misconvergence, viewing angle restrictions) or optimized (e.g., brightness, contrast, sharpness, character and text formatting characteristics, rise and decay times). Third, many aspects interact with each other (e.g., brightness-contrast-sharpness) and thus should not be designed or customized individually. Finally, the display hardware and software should exhibit the capacity to achieve a high VDQ for a range of environmental circumstances, and fine-tuning should take place in operational circumstances, therefore, tools and guidelines to assist in this customization should be developed.

REFERENCES

1. A. C. Lowe, "Display Requirements for Computer Workstations of the Future." *Proc. Eurodisplay '93*, 89–92 (1993).

2. N. MacMorrow, "Ergonomic Aspects of Computer Use," in *Encyclopedia of Microcomputers*, vol. 6, A. Kent, and J. G. Williams, eds. Dekker, New York, 1990, pp. 325–341.

3. R. A. Matula, "Effects of Visual Display Units on the Eyes: A Bibliography (1972–1980)." *Human Factors*, **23**(5), 581–586 (1981).

4. M. G. Helander, P. A. Billingsley, and J. M. Schurick, "An Evaluation of Human Factors Research on Visual Display Terminals in the Workplace," in *Human Factors Review: 1984*, F. A. Muckler, et al., eds. Human Factors Society, Santa Monica, CA, 1984.

5. G. Knave, and P. G. Widebäck, eds., "Work with Display Units 86," selected papers from the International Scientific Conference on Work with Display Units, Stockholm, May 12–15, 1986.

6. L. Berlinguet and D. Berthelette, eds., "Work with Display Units 89," selected papers from the International Scientific Conference on Work with Display Units, Montreal, Sept. 11–14, 1989.

7. H. Luczkak, A. E. Cakir, and G. Cakir, "Work with Display Units: WWDU 1992," abstract book, Third International Conference on Work with Display Units, Berlin, Sept. 1–4, 1992.

8. A. Grieco and G. Molteni, et al., eds., *WWDU '94*, vols. 1–3, University of Milan, Oct. 2–5, 1994.

9. H. Miyamoto, S. Saito, et al., eds., *Proceedings of WWDU '97*, Tokyo, Nov. 3–5, 1997.

10. G. P. J. Spenkelink, "Visual Display Units: The Perception of Image Quality," Ph.D. thesis, University of Twente, Enschede, Netherlands, 1994.

11. F. J. H. van Dijk, M. van Dormolen, M. A. J. Kompier, T. F. Meijman, "Herwaardering model belasting-belastbaarheid." *Tijdschrift voor Sociale Gezondheidszorg*, **68**, 3–10 (1990).

12. R. R. Mourant, R. Lakshmanan, et al., "Visual Fatigue and Cathode Ray Tube Display Terminals." *Human Factors*, **23**(5), 529–540 (1981).

13. R. A. Tyrrell and H. W. Leibowitz, "The Relation of Vergence Effort to Reports of Visual Fatigue Following Prolonged Near Work." *Human Factors*, **32**(3), 341–357 (1990).

14. J. B. Coe, "Posture as a factor in Repetitive Strain Injuries: The Technological Epidemic," E.S.A.N.Z. 21st Annual Conference, Sydney, 1984, pp. 119–123.

15. H. L. Snyder, "Image Quality: Measures and Visual Performance," in *Flat Panel Displays and CRT's*, L. E. Tannas, ed. VNR, New York, 1985.

16. J. A. J. Roufs and H. Bouma, "Towards Linking Perception Research and Image Quality." *Proceedings of the SID*, **21**(3), 247–270 (1980).

17. D. R. Ankrum, "A Challenge to Eye-Level, Perpendicular to Gaze Monitor Placement." *Proceedings of the 13th Triennial Congress of the International Ergonomics Association*, **5**, 35–37 (1997).

18. K. I. Fostervold and I. Lie, "The Ecological Viewpoint." *Proceedings of WWDU '97*, Tokyo, 1997, pp. 147–148.

19. I. Lie and K. I. Fostervold, "VDT Work with Different Gaze Inclinations," in *Work with Display Units 94*, A. Grieco, B. Molteni, et al., eds. Elsevier Science, Amsterdam, 1995, pp. 137–142.

20. S. Sherr, *Electronic Displays*, 2nd ed., Wiley, New York, 1993.

21. A. Chapanis, "Human Factors in Computer Systems," in *Encyclopedia of Microcomputers*, vol. 8, A. Kent and J. G. Williams, eds. Dekker, New York, 1991, pp. 305–324.

22. J. P. de Groot and A. Kamphuis, "Eyestrain in VDU Users: Physical Correlates and Long Term Effects." *Human Factors*, **25**(4), 409–423 (1983).

23. L. R. Hedman and V. Briem, "Short-Term Changes in Eyestrain of VDU Users as a Function of Age." *Human Factors*, **26**(3), 357–370 (1984).

24. K. Nishiyama, "Ergonomic Aspects of the Health and Safety of VDT Work in Japan: A Review." *Ergonomics*, **33**(6), 659–685 (1990).

25. M. Miyao, S. S. Hacisalihzade, et al., "Effects of VDT Resolution on Visual Fatigue and Readability: An Eye Movement Approach." *Ergonomics*, **32**(6), 603–614 (1989).

26. M. Collins, B. Davis, and A. Goode, "Steady-State Accommodation Response and VDT Screen Conditions." *Applied Ergon.*, **25**(5), 334–338 (1994).

27. G. C. Woo, G. Strong, E. Irving, and B. Ing, "Are There Subtle Changes in Vision After Use of VDTs?" in *Work with Display Units 86*, B. Knave and P. G. Widebäck, eds. North Holland, Amsterdam, 1987, pp. 490–501.

28. P. Rey and A. Bousquet, "Visual Strain of VDT Operators: The Right and the Wrong," in *Work with Computers: Organizational, Management, Stress and Health Aspects*, M. J. Smith and G. Salvendy, eds. Elsevier Science Publishers B.V., Amsterdam, 1989, pp. 308–315.

29. I. Lie and R. Watten, "VDT Work, Oculomotor Strain and Subjective Complaints," in *Work with Display Units '92*, Berlin, Sept. 1–4, 1992.

30. D. Gopher and R. Braune, "On the Psychophysics of Workload: Why Bother with Subjective measures?" *Human Factors*, **26**, 519–532 (1984).

31. C. B. Mills and L. J. Weldon, "Reading Text from Computer Screens." *ACM Comp. Surv.*, **19**(4), 329–358 (1987).

32. M. A. Tinker, *Legibility of Print*, Iowa State University Press, Ames, 1963.

33. J. D. Gould and N. Grischkowsky, "Does Visual Angle of a Line of Characters Affect Reading Speed?" *Human Factors*, **28**, 165–173 (1986).

34. J. D. Gould, L. Alfaro, V. Barnes, R. Finn, and N. Grischkowsky, "Reading Is Slower from CRT displays than from Paper: Attempts to Isolate a Single-Variable Explanation." *Human Factors*, **29**(3), 269–299 (1987).

35. J. D. Gould, L. Alfaro, R. Finn, B. Haupt, and A. Minuto, "Reading from CRT Displays Can Be as Fast as Reading from Paper." *Human Factors*, **29**, 497–517 (1987).

36. A. Dillon, "Reading from Paper Versus Screens: A Critical Review of the Empirical Literature." *Ergonomics*, **35**(10), 1297–1326 (1992).

37. B. E. Rogowitz, "Flicker Matching: A Technique for Measuring the Perceived Flicker on a VDT." *SID 83 Digest*, 172–173 (1983).

38. G. P. J. Spenkelink, K. Besuijen, and J. Brok, "An Instrument for the Measurement of the Visual Quality of Displays." *Behav. Inform. Tech.*, **12**(4), 249–260 (1993).

39. G. P. J. Spenkelink, "An Experiment on Actual Displays and Simulator: Validation of Methods and Simulator," report of the Esprit project OS1593 on behalf of the EC, University of Twente, Enschede, Netherlands, 1989.

40.   G. P. J. Spenkelink, "A Validation Study of the High End Simulator," report of the Esprit project OS 1593 on behalf of the EC, University of Twente, Enschede, Netherlands, 1990.

41.   G. P. J. Spenkelink and K. Besuijen, "Brightness: Highest Luminance or Background Luminance?" in A. Grieco, G. Molteni, et al., eds. *Work with Display Units '94*, selected papers, North-Holland, Amsterdam, 1995, pp. 311–316.

42.   N. Koizumi, "ISO 9241 Series: Past, Present and Future," *Proceedings of WWDU '97*, Tokyo, 1997, pp. 151–152.

43.   O. Ostberg, H. Shahnavaz, and R. Stenberg, "Legibility Testing of Visual Display Screens." *Behav. Inform. Tech.*, **8**(2), 145–153 (1989).

44.   D. Travis, T. F. M. Stewart, and C. Mackay, "Evaluation of Image Quality." *Displays*, **3**, 139–146 (1992).

45.   J. Besuijen and G. P. J. Spenkelink, "User Tests for ISO 9241-3," *Proceedings of WWDU '97*, Tokyo, 1997, pp. 103–104.

46.   D. Travis and T. Stewart, "Statistical Methods for Testing the Visual Quality of Displays." *Displays*, **18**, 29–36 (1997).

47.   B. A. Rupp and S. E. Taylor, "Retinal Adaptation to Non-Uniform Fields: Average Luminance or Symbol Luminance?" *Behav. Inform. Tech.*, **5**(4), 375–379 (1986).

48.   D. L. Lassiter and E. J. Rinalducci, "The Effects of Transient Adaptation in Simulated VDT Operations." *SID Digest*, 153–156 (1986).

49.   L. A. Olzak and J. P. Thomas, in *Handbook of Perception and Human Performance*, K. R. Boff et al., eds. Wiley, New York, 1986.

50.   S. Kokoschka, "Visibility Aspects of VDUs in Terms of Contrast and Luminance." *Behav. Inform. Tech.*, **5**(4), 309–333 (1986).

51.   U. Pawlak, "Ergonomic Aspects of Image Polarity." *Behav. Inform. Tech.*, **5**(4), 335–348 (1986).

52.   T. F. M. Stewart, "Eyestrain and Visual Display Units: A Review." *Displays*, 25–32 (April 1979).

53.   W. Xu and Z. Zhu, "The Effects of Ambient Illumination and Target Luminance on Colour Coding in a CRT Display." *Ergonomics*, **33**(7), 933–944 (1990).

54.   L. M. Schleifer, S. L. Sauter, and R. J. Smith, "Ergonomic Predictors of Visual Complaints in VDT Data Entry Work." *Behav. Inform. Tech.*, **9**(4), 273–282 (1990).

55.   H. L. Snyder, "Lighting, Glare Measurement and Legibility of VDTs," in *Ergonomics and Health in Modern Offices*, E. Grandjean, ed. Taylor & Francis, London, 1984, pp. 295–304.

56.   D. Bauer, M. Bonacker, and C. R. Cavonius, "Frame Repetition Rate for Flicker-free Viewing of Bright VDU Screens." *Displays*, **1**, 31–33 (1983).

57.   C. Sigel, "CRT Refresh Rate and Perceived Flicker." *SID 89 Digest*, 300–302 (1989).

58.   J. L. Brown, "Flicker and Intermittent Stimulation," in *Vision and Visual Perception*, C. H. Graham, ed. Wiley, New York, 1965.

59.   D. Bauer, "Is Interlace Refresh a Practical Method for Reducing VDU Flicker?" *Displays*, 33–36 (Jan. 1984).

60.   W. Becker, G. Kieffer, and R. Jurgens, "Sensory Stimuli Can Interrupt or Perturb Saccades in Mid-Flight," in *Fourth European Conference on Eye Movements*, G. Luer and U. Lass, eds. Academic, New York, 1987, pp. 103–105.

61.   C. Neary and A. J. Wilkins, "Effects of Phosphor Persistence on Perception and the Control of Eye Movements." *Perception*, **18**, 257–264 (1989).

62.   A. Kennedy, "Eye Movement Control and Visual Display Units," in *Visual Processes in Reading and Reading Disabilities*, D. M. Willows et al., eds. Lawrence Erlbaum, Hillsdale, NJ, 1993, pp. 215–236.

63.   A. Kennedy and W. S. Murray, "'Flicker' on VDU Screens." *Nature*, **365**, 213 (1993).

64.   B. Bridgeman and M. Montegut, "Faster Flicker Rate Increases Reading Speed on CRTs." *Proceedings of SPIE*, **1913**, 134–145 (1993).

65.   M. C. Boschman and J. A. Roufs, "Reading and Screen Flicker." *Nature*, **372**, 137 (1994).

66.   W. D. Thomson and J. Saunders, "The Perception of Flicker on Raster-Scanned Displays." *Human Factors*, **39**(1), 48–66 (1997).

67.   J. A. Veitch and S. L. McColl, "Modulation of Fluorescent Light: Flicker Rate and Light Source Effects on Visual Performance and Visual Comfort." *Lighting Res. Techn.*, **27**(4), 243–256 (1995).

68. A. Wenneberg, P. Nylen, and R. Wibom, "Flickering Light—A Possible Cause for 'hypersensitivity to electricity,'" *Proceedings of WWDU '97*, Tokyo, 1997, pp. 207–208.

69. *ISO/DIS 9241-3, Visual Display Terminals Used for Office Tasks—Ergonomic Requirements, Part 3: Visual Display Requirements*, ISO, 1992.

70. G. P. J. Spenkelink and K. Besuijen, "The Perception and Measurement of Contrast: The Influence of Gaps Between Display Elements." *Behav. Inform. Tech.*, **13**(5), 320–327 (1994).

71. J. G. Lourens, T. C. du Toit, and J. B. du Toit, "Assessing the Focus Quality of Television Pictures," in *Human Vision, Visual Processing and Digital Display*, SPIE vol. 1077, 1989, pp. 35–41.

72. W. N. Charman and A. Olin, "Tutorial: Image Quality Criteria for Aerial Camera Systems." *Photog. Sci. Egr.*, **9**, 385–397 (1965).

73. P. G. J. Barten, "The SQRI Method: A New Method for the Evaluation of Visible Resolution on a Display." *Proc. SID*, **28**(3), 253–262 (1987).

74. C. R. Carlson and R. W. Cohen, "Visibility of Displayed Information: Image Descriptors for Displays," technical report ONR-CR213-120-4F, Office of Naval Research, Arlington, VA, 1978.

75. CIE, *Colorimetry*, 2nd ed., CIE 15.2, 1986.

76. G. P. J. Spenkelink and K. Besuijen, "Colour Contrast and Luminance Contrast in Text Displays." *SID 94 Digest*, 502–505 (1994).

77. G. P. J. Spenkelink and J. Besuijen, "Chromaticity Contrast, Luminance Contrast, and Legibility of Text." *J. SID*, **4**(3), 135–144 (1996).

78. K. L. Kelly, "Twenty-two Colors of Maximum Contrast." *Colour Egr.*, **3**, 26–27 (1965).

79. R. C. Carter and E. C. Carter, *Applied Opt.*, **21**(16), 2936-2939 (1982).

80. A. Marcus, *Graphic Design for Electronic Documents and User Interfaces*, ACM, New York, 1992.

81. M. W. Landsdale and T. C. Ormerod, *Understanding Interfaces: A Handbook of Understanding Human–Computer Dialogue*, Academic Press, 1994.

82. B. Schneiderman, *Designing the User Interface: Strategies for Effective Human–Computer Interaction*, Addison–Wesley, 1992.

83. H. Widdel and D. L. Post, eds. *Colour in Electronic Displays*, Plenum, New York, 1992.

84. P. J. Robertson and M. R. Jones, "Subjective Reactions to Misconvergence on a Colour Display." *Displays Tech. Appl.*, **5**, 165–169 (1984).

85. N. P. Milner, J. L. Knowles, and S. P. Lovett, "Ergonomic Investigation of Misconvergence on Colour Visual Display Terminals." *Displays*, **10**, 81–92 (1989).

86. H. Bouma, "Visual Reading Processes and the Quality of Text Displays," in *Ergonomic Aspects of Visual Display Terminals*, E. Grandjean and E. Vigliani, eds. Taylor & Francis, London, 1980, pp. 101–114.

87. F. L. van Nes, "A New Teletext Character Set With Enhanced Legibility," *IEEE Trans. Electron. Dev.*, **33**, 1222–1225 (1986).

88. H. Heuer, G. Hollendiek, et al., "Die Ruhelage der Augen und ihr Einfluss auf Beobachtungsabstand und visuelle Ermüdung bei Bildschirmarbeit." *Zeitschrift für Experimentelle und Angewandte Psychologie*, **36**, 538–566 (1989).

89. W. Jaschinsky–Kruza, "On the Preferred Viewing Distances to Screen and Document at VDU Workplaces." *Ergonomics*, **33**(8), 1055–1063 (1990).

90. W. Jaschinsky–Kruza, "Eyestrain in VDU Users: Viewing Distance and the Resting Position of Ocular Muscles." *Human Factors*, **33**(1), 69–83 (1991).

91. P. Muter and P. Maurutto, "Reading and Skimming from Computer Screens and Books: The Paperless Office Revisited?" *Behav. Inform. Tech.*, **10**(4), 257–266 (1991).

92. R. L. Duchnicky and P. A. Kolers, "Readability of Text Scrolled on Visual Display Terminals as a Function of Window Size." *Human Factors*, **25**, 683–692 (1983).

93. T. S. Tullis, "The Formatting of Alphanumeric Displays: A Review and Analysis." *Human Factors*, **25**(6), 657–682 (1983).

ANNOTATED BIBLIOGRAPHY

Dillon, A., "Reading from Paper Versus Screens: A Critical Review of the Empirical Literature." *Ergonomics*, **35**(10), 1297–1326 (1992). An extensive overview of literature about reading from displays.

Olzak, L. A. and Thomas, J. P., in *Seeing Spatial Patterns Handbook of Perception and Human Performance*,

K. R. Boff et al., eds. Wiley, New York, 1986. Information about the basic sensory processes, as well as about higher processes involved in perception.

Sherr, S., *Electronic Displays*, 2nd ed., Wiley New York, 1993. Gives an insight into the engineering approach to VDQ and the technological aspects of several display types.

Snyder, H. L., "Image Quality: Measures and Visual Performance," in *Flat Panel Displays and CRT's*, L. E. Tannas, ed. VNR, New York, 1985. An overview of image quality research.

Tinker, M. A., *Legibility of Print*, Iowa State University Press, Ames, 1963. Although not recent, is probably still the best source of experimental data about effects of text parameters on legibility.

Widdel, H. and Post, D. L., eds., *Color in Electronic Displays*, Plenum Press, New York, 1992. Provides an overview of all aspects concerning color display and perception.

GERD P. J. SPENKELINK
KO BESUIJEN